LEARNING
Computer Literacy with
Microsoft® Office 2003

Paul Wray

PEARSON

Prentice
Hall
DDC

Vice President and Publisher: Natalie E. Anderson
Executive Acquisitions Editor: Jodi McPherson
Executive Editor: Jennifer Frew
Manufacturing Buyer: Natacha St. Hill Moore
Technical Editor: Jan Snyder
Cover Designer: Amy Capuano
Composition: Shu Chen
Associate Director, Multimedia Production: Karen Goldsmith
Manager, Print Production: Christy Mahon
Printer/Binder: Quebecor World Book Services/Dubuque
Cover Printer: Phoenix Color Corporation

Credits and acknowledgements borrowed from other sources and reproduced, with permission, in this textbook are as follows:

> Microsoft, Windows, PowerPoint, Outlook, FrontPage, Visual Basic, MSN, The Microsoft Network, and/or other Microsoft products referenced herein are either trademarks or registered trademarks of Microsoft Corporation in the U.S.A. and other countries. This book is not sponsored or endorsed by or affiliated with Microsoft Corporation.

Copyright © 2004 by Pearson Education, Inc., Upper Saddle River, New Jersey, 07458. All rights reserved. Printed in the United States of America. This publication is protected by Copyright and permission should by obtained from the publisher prior to any prohibited reproduction, storage in a retrieval system, or transmission in any form or by any means, electronic, mechanical, photocopying, recording, or likewise. For information regarding permission(s), write to the Rights and Permissions Department.

10 9 8 7 6 5 4 3 2 1
ISBN 0-13-147673-4

Contents

Contents

Introduction

About this Book

This book is designed to help you become computer literate as you learn to use features of Microsoft® Windows XP and Microsoft Office 2003.

Lesson 1 **introduces computers** and summarizes their components, types, and the workers who make their livings directly in the computer industry.

Lesson 2 shows you how to use some of the features of **Windows XP**. It introduces the desktop, My Computer, and Windows Explorer. It includes exercises to help you learn to locate files and programs.

Lessons 3 through 8 cover the basics of Microsoft Office 2003 and important features of the following four applications:

- **Microsoft Office Word 2003**, a word processing program, used for creating and editing documents and for **desktop publishing**.

- **Microsoft Office Excel 2003**, a spreadsheet program, used for analyses and graphing of numerical data.

- **Microsoft Office PowerPoint 2003**, a presentations program, used for creating sales and other presentations that can be shown via computer or given using overhead transparencies.

- **Microsoft Office Access 2003**, a database program, used for organizing and sorting information.

Lesson 9 introduces **computer communications**, including local area networks and the Internet.

Lesson 10 deals with **personal computer care**, giving simple instructions for keeping your machine running efficiently. This lesson includes information about backup, hard disk management, and general care and use instructions.

Appendix A presents a brief **history of computers**.

How to Use this Book

Most exercises contains two main parts:

- **NOTES** explain the application and its features. These notes contain **Try It!** activities that lead

you step-by-step through the feature being presented. You should perform the steps described in each Try It! activity.

- **EXERCISE DIRECTIONS** give step-by-step instructions for using the software to perform a function or create a particular document.

Menu Items and Keyboard Shortcuts

Throughout this book, you will see directions like the following:

Click File, Open (Alt+F, O).

The words refer to menu options on the window. Alt+F, O indicates a keyboard shortcut. It means to hold down the Alt key and press the F key then press the O key.

You will also see references to keyboard shortcuts like the following:

Ctrl+F6

This notation means to hold down the Ctrl key and press the F6 key.

Data and Solution Files

The **data files** on the accompanying CD-ROM are provided so that you can concentrate on the tasks essential to the exercise's objective rather than on typing or data entry. Data files are preceded in the text by a CD-ROM symbol ☯ to indicate that a data file can be used.

For some exercises, you can use files you created in earlier exercises. Directions use a keyboard symbol ⌨ to indicate files created in previous exercises.

When a keyboard and diskette appear within the same direction, you may use either the file you created or the data file.

For example, a typical direction might read:
    Open ⌨**Firstdoc**, or open ☯**02Firstdoc** from the data files.

About the CD-ROM

Copy Data Files

You can copy data files to a hard drive.

1. Open Windows Explorer. (Right-click on the **Start** button ![start] and click **Explore**.)

2. Be sure that the CD is in your CD-ROM drive. Select the CD-ROM drive letter from the All Folders pane of the Explorer window.

3. Click to select the **Datafiles** folder in the Contents of (CD-ROM drive letter) pane of the Explorer window.

4. Drag the folder onto the letter of the drive to which you wish to copy the data files (usually **C:**) in the All Folders pane of the Explorer Window.

Access Data Files: The data files for Access are read-only. Read the instructions at the beginning of Lesson 8, Exercise 2 to learn how to remove the read-only attribute. In addition, it is a good idea to work on a copy of the Access data files so that the hard drive retains the original files copied from the CD-ROM.

Directory of Data Files on CD

Lesson 1: Introduction to Computers

Learn about Computers and Computer Careers

- What is a Computer?
- Personal Computer Hardware
- Peripherals
- Bits and Bytes
- Computer Speed and MHz and GHz
- Software
- Computer Types
- Computer Workers

Introduction to Computers

Learn about Computers and Computer Careers
■ What is a Computer? ■ Personal Computer Hardware ■ Peripherals ■ Bits and Bytes
■ Computer Speed and MHz and GHz ■ Software ■ Computer Types ■ Computer Workers

NOTES

What is a Computer?

- A computer is a machine that receives **input** (data), performs **processing**, and produces **output** (information).

- Uses of the computer can be viewed as variations of input–processing–output. This is as true of complex tasks, like computer simulations of weather events, as it is of common ones, like typing a letter. Some examples of input–processing–output are given in the following table.

- If the input contains errors, the output will contain errors. Sometimes computers break down. But most "computer errors" result from human errors—bad data or bad programming.

Input: Data entered into a computer.

Processing: Actions that computer programs perform on the input.

Output: Results of processing.

INPUT	PROCESSING	OUTPUT
Text typed on the keyboard	Formatting and preparation for printing by word processing program	Letter, book report, memo, story
Text typed on the keyboard and pictures inserted from disk drive or diskette	Text formatting, picture placement, sizing, and scaling in desktop publishing program	Newsletter, advertisement, flyer
Text and numbers typed on the keyboard	Calculations performed in spreadsheet program	Banking record, budget, grade book
Text and numbers typed on the keyboard	Formatting into tables, sorting, searching, selection of data in database program	Address book, membership list, product sales report, employee information
Temperatures, wind velocities and direction, air pressure readings, frontal boundaries, humidity readings, jet stream location and speed	Calculations based on meteorological research and assumptions and comparisons with a database of weather patterns	Weather forecast

⌨ Try It!

- Think of examples of input–processing–output from your own experience that you might add to the table.

Personal Computer Hardware

- **Hardware** refers to all the pieces of physical equipment that make up a computer system. The computer hardware you are most familiar with is probably the **personal computer** or **PC**.

2

Personal Computer Hardware

3.5" diskette
(floppy)

CD-ROM, DVD
or Writable CD/DVD

Hard drive

Diskette (floppy) drive

CD-ROM, CD/RW,
DVD, or DVD/RW

Motherboard

Expansion
slots/cards

Speakers

Mouse

Laser Printer

Monitor

Keyboard

Power Supply Fan

- A PC includes several pieces of hardware or *devices*:

  - The **power supply** is a device (not shown in the illustration) that distributes electricity to the various components of the system. The electrical cord runs from the power supply to an electrical outlet. The power supply also includes a fan that cools the internal components.

  - The **motherboard** is the largest circuit board inside your personal computer. It contains millions of electronic circuit elements on chips of silicon. These chips store programmed instructions in active memory (see RAM on the next page). They also execute the instructions stored in other chips. The motherboard has expansion sockets or slots (known as the bus, see the next page). These slots permit installation of additional circuit boards.

  - On the motherboard are some special **ROM** (<u>R</u>ead-<u>O</u>nly <u>M</u>emory) chips that contain the **BIOS** (<u>B</u>asic <u>I</u>nput/<u>O</u>utput <u>S</u>ystem). The BIOS is the component that checks your computer's components and causes the operating system to start.

  - To work properly, the BIOS needs to know the configuration of your computer's hardware. This hardware information is stored in the **CMOS** (<u>C</u>omplementary <u>M</u>etal <u>O</u>xide <u>S</u>emiconductor)—a chip

CMOS Setup

If you've ever noticed the message *Press F1 (or some other key) for setup* when you start your computer, you have seen the keystroke that lets you change the CMOS settings for your computer.

For more information about BIOS and CMOS, see such Web sites as http://burks.bton.ac.uk/bur ks/pcinfo/hardware/bios_s g/bios_sg.htm and http://www.sysopt.com/ bios.html

3

whose configuration is controlled by a setup program. The CMOS includes information about the following components:

- ◆ System date and time
- ◆ Mouse
- ◆ Keyboard
- ◆ Hard drive (number of drives and their sizes)
- ◆ Floppy disk drive(s)
- ◆ CD-ROM drive

- The settings are permanently saved in a 64-byte piece of CMOS. The CMOS power is supplied by a small battery, so its contents are not lost when the PC is turned off.

- The **CPU (<u>C</u>entral <u>P</u>rocessing <u>U</u>nit)** is a chip, located on the motherboard, which performs mathematical calculations and logic functions (determining if one value is greater than another, and so on). The CPU is often referred to as the brain of the computer because it administers the functions of the other components. When users say their machine has a Pentium 4 processor, they are talking about the CPU chip.

Expansion Card

- The **bus** is the main communication path, or series of paths, on the motherboard that connects the system's components with the CPU. The bus also connects external components through **expansion slots**. These slots can contain plug-in **cards** that let the computer communicate with other devices, such as monitors and printers.

- **RAM (<u>R</u>andom <u>A</u>ccess <u>M</u>emory)**, special chips connected to the CPU, is the area where programs and data reside while in use. When you start an application (Office Word, for example), the computer places the program into RAM. If you then open a document, it also loads the document into RAM.

Memory Modules

  - ◆ When you save a document, the CPU copies the document from RAM to permanent storage. When you close a document, the CPU frees up the memory that was occupied by the document. When you close a program, memory is also freed up.

  - ◆ RAM holds data only so long as it has electricity. If the machine is turned off or loses power, information in RAM is lost. That's why any changes not saved before the machine is turned off cannot be retrieved.

  - ◆ In modern PCs, RAM capacity is measured in megabytes. (See the section "Bits and Bytes" on page 6 for a definition of bits and bytes.) In general, the more RAM your computer has, the better it is able to run programs that require processing power.

Peripheral
Device that is not part of the central computing machinery.

Peripherals

- A **peripheral** is a device connected to the computer through the bus. Many essential components of a PC system are peripherals, including monitors, keyboards, and disk drives. Printers and scanners are also peripherals.

- Some peripherals, because of their small size or delicate nature, are mounted directly inside the computer case. Video boards, inboard modems, and sound cards are devices inside the computer that depend on the bus.

- Peripherals are often divided into two categories—**input** devices and **output** devices. Some peripherals serve as both input and output devices, so the categories are not exclusive. Some common peripherals and their functions are described below.

  - The **monitor** is an output device that displays input and the results of processing. Most monitors on PCs use a <u>c</u>athode <u>r</u>ay <u>t</u>ube (CRT) similar to that used in television sets. (In fact, some computers can use TV sets as monitors.) Laptop computers more often use <u>l</u>iquid <u>c</u>rystal <u>d</u>isplay (LCD) technology in their monitors.

  - The **mouse** is an input device that you use to control a pointer that displays on the monitor. A wide variety of mouse pointing devices exists. Some are moved over a surface and may be wireless; some let you use your thumb or fingers to roll a ball that moves the pointer; others, especially on laptop computers, work when you drag your finger across a small screen called a *touch pad.*

    Regardless of the mouse type, when the pointer is located at the spot where you want the software to respond, you click the left button once (**click**), the right button (**right-click**), or the left button twice rapidly (**double-click**). Wheel mice, such as the Microsoft IntelliMouse, include a wheel between the two buttons. The wheel can be used for scrolling and zooming in Microsoft Office 2003.

    The mouse pointer changes appearance to indicate that the system is working. These appearance changes are described in later exercises.

  - The **keyboard** is an input device with alphabetic, numeric, and function keys in a standardized layout. (Some keyboards change the location of certain keys and include keys that other keyboards do not have.) The special keys (such as the **F**unction, **Ctrl** (control), and **Alt** keys) are used alone or in combinations to cause programs to perform actions.

  - Most computers contain a **hard disk** (or **hard drive**) and a **diskette drive**. You may also have another kind of removable storage drive such as an Iomega® Zip® drive with disks that store 100 Megabytes and more. Diskettes and Zip disks can be removed and carried from one computer to another; hard disks are installed inside the computer and are not considered portable.

    Disk drives are identified by letter. The typical personal computer has a diskette drive identified as A:. It probably also has a hard drive known as C:.

    Hard disks and diskettes and their drives serve as both input and output devices.

    - When output such as a letter is stored (saved) on a hard disk or diskette, the disk is an output device.
    - When you retrieve data from a disk, it serves as an input device.

  - **CD-ROM** (<u>C</u>ompact <u>D</u>isk-<u>R</u>ead-<u>O</u>nly <u>M</u>emory) and **DVD** (<u>D</u>igital <u>V</u>ideo <u>D</u>isc or <u>D</u>igital <u>V</u>ersatile <u>D</u>isc) disks are input devices. Without special equipment, you cannot save data to a CD-ROM, but you can retrieve information from one if you have a CD-ROM drive on your computer. Many recent personal computers come with a **CD writer**, a CD-ROM device that lets you record on a CD-R or CD-RW disc.

LCD Monitor and Laptop

IntelliMouse

Saving Your Work
Remember that no work on the computer is stored permanently unless it is saved from the computer's RAM (memory where the work is performed) to a diskette or hard drive.

Examples of Storage Devices

Iomega Zip Disk

External Iomega Zip Drive

Hard Disk

- **Modems** and other telecommunication hardware (when used with the appropriate software) serve as sources of both input and output. Telecommunication gives you access to the world outside your personal computer—to such services as America Online (AOL) and that vast network of computers known as the **Internet** or **World Wide Web**. A modem may be installed inside the computer case (an internal modem) or the modem may be connected through a communications port (external modem).

- **Printers**, next to monitors and disk drives, are the most common output devices. A wide variety of printer types is available:

  - **Laser** printers use copier-like technology to spread patterns of toner and affix it to paper using heat.
  - **Ink Jet** and **Bubble Jet** printers spray ink onto paper to produce the output.
  - **Plotters** use a needle to draw on paper; they are frequently used by engineers and architects to produce schematic drawings.
  - **Dot-matrix** printers use a pattern of steel pins in a moving print head to imprint dots through a ribbon onto paper. They generally can print graphic images.
  - **Impact** printers push images of letters and symbols (cast in metal or plastic) through a ribbon onto the paper. These are usually the slowest and oldest of the printer types and generally cannot print graphic images. Some of these printers are called "daisy wheel" printers because the printing element looked like a flower with its petals containing the characters to be printed.

- **Scanners**, which let you create files from pictures, drawings, or text, are input devices.

- **Voice input** devices (microphones) are becoming more common as hardware and software makers improve their efficiency.

Laser Printer

More on Printers
The following Web site contains a brief description of the operation of "daisy wheel," dot matrix, ink jet, and laser printers.

http://www.repairfaq.org/REPAIR/F_printfaq.html

Bits and Bytes

- Your personal computer operates through a vast number of on/off switches called **binary digits** or **bits** (bit is short for **B**inary dig**IT**). All the reception of input, processing, and output are accomplished by bits that are either turned on or turned off.

- Bits are grouped together into **bytes**, a string of 8 bits that can be translated by the computer into a letter or an action. For example, when you press the capital letter A on the keyboard, a signal from the keyboard passes to the computer and gets translated into a string of 8 bits that are represented like this: 01000001. Each 0 represents a switch that is turned off and a 1 represents a switch that is turned on.

- A byte is the most common measurement of storage in the digital computer.

Size	Number of Bytes
Kilobyte	1,024 (8,192 bits)
	1 thousand bytes
Megabyte	1,024,000
	1 million bytes

Size	Number of Bytes
Gigabyte	1,024,000,000 1 billion bytes
Terabyte	1,024,000,000,000 1 trillion bytes

Computer Speed and MHz and GHz

- The speed of your personal computer is measured in megahertz (MHz) or gigahertz (GHz). A Hertz is a single oscillation (up-and-down movement) per second of an electromagnetic wave. When coupled with the prefix *mega*, it refers to millions of wave oscillations per second; when used with the prefix *giga,* it refers to billions of wave oscillations per second.

- In the computer, the activity of the CPU microchip is coordinated by a clock that is part of the chip. Thus, a 400 MHz chip has a clock that receives electricity and switches on and off 400 million times per second. It is twice as fast as a chip that has a 200 MHz clock. Similarly, a 1.2 GHz chip is three times as fast as a chip with a 400 MHz clock.

- The clock speed of your computer describes how quickly computations are performed in RAM. A personal computer's overall speed and efficiency, however, depend not only on the speed of the CPU but also on the following:

  - *Size of RAM.* If RAM is too small for the kind of processing being performed, the system may place some of the data or program on the hard drive temporarily while processing other data. If your machine is slow, watch the light that indicates that the hard drive is in use. If it lights up and goes out frequently while your program is processing, your computer may not have enough RAM. Most recent computers come with 256 or more MB of RAM, but a computer that is primarily for games or computer-aided design may profit from more RAM.

  - *Speed and capacity of the hard disk.* If the hard disk does not take advantage of the latest technology or is filled nearly to capacity, the computer's efficiency will be impaired.

  - *Speed of the bus.* If the CPU operates at 400 MHz and the bus at 50 MHz, the bus slows the computer down when the CPU is communicating with cards in the bus slots. More recent bus speeds, however, reach from 133 to 1,000 MHz and more.

Software

- **Software** refers to the instructions that allow a computer to run and act on the data that is input. Software is usually divided into two types: operating system software and application software. Software and **programs** mean the same thing.

- **Operating system software** includes instructions that allow a computer to run. BIOS startup involves checking for equipment attached to the computer, such as the keyboard, to ensure that it is working and can communicate with the computer's operating system. Operating system startup completes the **boot-up** (computer startup) process and prepares the computer's components and environment for actual use. Unix, Linux, Mac OS, Windows 2000, and Windows[XP] are examples of operating systems.

- **Application software** includes programs that allow you to make the computer do what you want—write a letter, browse the Internet, draw a picture, create a computer program.

- Application software depends on the operating system. It uses operating-system-specific instructions to tell the operating system to do something. Because application software interacts with the operating system in this way, applications designed for one operating system (Windows, for example) cannot run on a different operating system (Unix or Mac OS, for example).

- Most of this book focuses on the use of application software—specifically four of the applications that make up the Microsoft Office 2003 suite of applications.

Computer Types

- The computer with which you are most familiar, and the one with which you will probably have the most direct contact throughout your life, is the personal computer. But you will have indirect contact with other, larger computers.

- If you make a career in science, higher mathematics, advanced computing, or military or industrial research, you may use a **supercomputer**. Supercomputers are the fastest problem solvers available. They work at extremely high speeds. Often, they process data in "parallel," breaking a complicated problem into smaller units, each of which is handled by a part of the computer, then combined to produce the final result. (Some recent "supercomputers" are made from a large number of personal computers linked together because each PC can function like a part of a large computer.)

- **Mainframes** are machines that many large companies use to manage the huge amounts of data required to keep their operations running. For example, your local telephone company gathers usage data from a large number of telephone users, calculates the charges, and produces telephone bills. For this huge undertaking, the company requires a machine that can handle a large database, process rapidly, and print quickly. While many personal computers manage several gigabytes (billions of bytes) of storage, mainframe computers control and process terabytes (trillions of bytes) of storage.

- Mainframes may still control as much as 90% of the data major businesses rely on for their critical applications, such as inventory, manufacturing, billing, and other accounting activities. For such applications, mainframes offer superior performance, reliability, and security, and they are usually easy to expand as the business grows.

- If you work at a telephone company, you may use a PC to gain access to the large amounts of information stored under the control of a mainframe. You may also use a "dumb" terminal (keyboard and monitor) directly connected by a network to the mainframe. The terminals are called "dumb" because, unlike PCs, they have no processing capabilities of their own but simply give users direct access to mainframe computing capacities.

- **Minicomputers**, first developed in the late 1960s and early 1970s, used to be distinguished from mainframe computers because they had smaller processing and storage management capabilities. The distinction has

Application

The term *application* comes from the idea that a group of programs work together to *apply* the abilities of the computer to a specific task, such as word processing or weather forecasting.

Source for Definitions

For more definitions of mainframes and minicomputers, see the following Web sites:

http://foldoc.doc.ic.ac.uk/foldoc

http://www.currents.net/resources/dictionary/dictionary.html

Mainframe Computer

broken down in recent years for two reasons (which have also contributed to the growth of the personal computer):

- Computer chips and storage capacities have increased rapidly, and small machines can now manage much more storage and process much more rapidly than earlier ones.

- Minicomputers are often linked in networks so companies (and universities, in particular) can use several networked minicomputers to perform the same tasks as one mainframe. Access to minicomputers, like access to mainframes, may be through dumb terminals or PCs.

- **Personal computers** come in a wide variety of styles and sizes. Some are designed for the **desktop**, with a cathode ray tube or LCD monitor separate from the rest of the computer.

- **Laptop** computers and **Personal Digital Assistants (PDAs)** grow lighter and sturdier with each new version. Laptops are compact with built-in liquid crystal display monitors that provide crisp displays. Most hand-held computers are used for a specific purpose, such as taking notes and sending/receiving messages. Their portability makes them ideal for salespeople and other business professionals who travel a great deal.

Personal Computers

Laptop Computer

PDAs

Computer Workers

- Computer chips, hard disks, diskette drives, CD-ROM and DVD drives, and all other computer components are designed by **electronics engineers**. They include hardware and software engineers. These professionals specialize in microcircuitry or imaging technology or hundreds of other areas involved with the design and manufacture of computing equipment.

- Supercomputers, mainframes, and minicomputers require specially trained personnel to keep them running efficiently. Most mainframe installations have a **systems programmer** who has studied the inner workings of the mainframe operating system and knows how to keep it working correctly.

- In addition, such installations may have a person in charge of managing disk storage, called a **DASD** (Direct Access Storage Device) manager. Just as you may accumulate a great deal of data that you no longer need on your personal computer, a mainframe installation may pile up data it should archive (file permanently elsewhere) and information needed only temporarily. The DASD manager sees to it that the installation gets the most efficient use of its storage capacity.

- Mainframe installations usually also have a staff of **application programmers** who ensure that the programs the organizations need are created, maintained, and improved. Such programmers work on fixing problems in programs, adding new features, and creating special programs to perform specific tasks. Application programmers are necessary because many of the programs that run on mainframes are not purchased from a software supplier.

- Companies like Microsoft, Corel, Adobe, MacroMedia, Sega, Nintendo, and other software vendors also employ application programmers. They use a variety of programming languages to create and enhance the companies' products.

- **Database administrators and developers** are people who specialize in designing and overseeing the maintenance of databases (see the introduction to Lesson 8).

- **Network administrators** are people who specialize in making sure that a company's local area network (see Lesson 9) operates efficiently. They need to be well-acquainted with the operation and maintenance of personal computers.

- **Help desk professionals** are people who are trained to provide help to users of applications. They work in the information processing department of large organizations and are called upon to install programs on PCs, answer questions about how to use programs, and help users recover from problems.

- Those who manage, support, and maintain computer installations are known as **information systems** personnel. Their specialties may be housed in a department called **MIS** (Management Information Systems) or **IT** (Information Technology), and the department head may be a corporate officer called the **CIO** (Chief Information Officer).

- **Web site designers and programmers** are those who decide what Web pages should look like and those who prepare the code that make Web pages perform properly. Sometimes Web page design and programming are done by the same person. In many cases, however, a graphics professional designs the look of a Web site, and a programmer makes sure that the Web site looks and works as designed.

- Web site programmers know how to use Web building tools like HTML (hypertext markup language) and Java and special-purpose programs like Microsoft FrontPage or Dreamweaver.

To illustrate input-processing-output, the following exercise asks you to start Windows' Calculator and perform some addition. Note that the illustrations in this section and throughout the Microsoft Office 2003 lessons are taken from Windows XP in the default Windows XP style.

In this book, "Click" means to press and release the left mouse button. "Double-click" means to press and release the left mouse button twice quickly. "Right-click" means to press and release the right mouse button.

EXERCISE DIRECTIONS

Start the Calculator

1. Move your mouse pointer to the Start button on the Windows desktop.

2. Click the Start button ![start] .

3. Move your mouse pointer up to Run ![Run...] and click the left mouse button.

   The Run dialog box appears.

Illustration A. Run Dialog Box

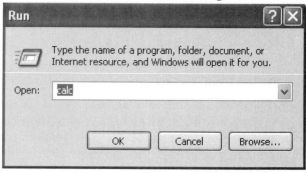

4. Type **calc**, and press the Enter key or click the OK button [OK].

The Calculator starts and displays as shown in Illustration B.

Illustration B. Calculator

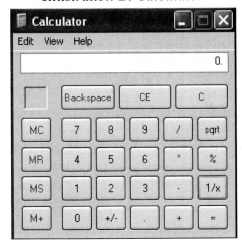

INPUT: Enter Data

In the following steps, you may enter data by:

- Clicking buttons on the Calculator window.
- Typing the data using the numbers near the top row of the keyboard.
- Typing the data using the number pad at the right of the keyboard if the Num Lock indicator is lit.

  To turn Num Lock on and off, press the Num Lock key on the number pad.) (Some keyboards, such as those on laptop computers, may not have a number pad.)

1. Click or type the number *50*.

   The number 50 appears in the Calculator's display.
2. Enter the + (plus sign).
3. Click or type the number *49*.

   The number 49 appears in the Calculator's display.

PROCESSING: Get Result

1. Press Enter, enter the = (equal sign), or enter the + (plus sign).

   The number 99 appears in the Calculator display.
2. Leave the number displayed; don't clear the display.

Additional Input-Processing-Output

1. Click the MS (memory save) button  on the calculator, or press Ctrl+M (hold down the Ctrl key and press M).

   The result is stored in the Calculator's memory, as indicated by the M in the upper left just below the display, as shown in Illustration C.

Illustration C. Stored Memory Indicator

M	Backspace
MC	7	8

2. Click the C (Clear) button or press the Esc key to clear the 99 from the display.
3. Click or type the number *37*.

   The number 37 appears in the Calculator's display.
4. Enter the + (plus sign).
5. Click or type the number *48*.

   The number 48 appears in the Calculator's display.
6. Enter the + (plus sign).

   The number 85 appears in the Calculator's display.
7. Click or type the number *59*.

   The number 59 appears in the Calculator's display.
8. Enter the + (plus sign).

   The number 144 appears in the Calculator's display.
9. Enter the + (plus sign).
10. Click the MR (memory recall) button [MR].

    The data stored in the calculator's memory by Memory Save is recalled for processing.
11. Click or type the = sign.

    The number 243 appears in the Calculator display, as shown in Illustration D.

OUTPUT: View Results

By following the directions, you have:

- Entered numbers from the keyboard for input.
- Requested the program to add those numbers (perform processing).
- Reviewed the output.

Illustration D. Final Result

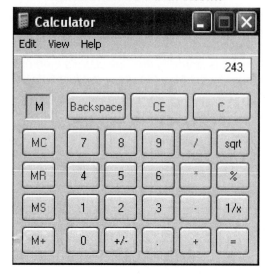

Clear and Close the Calculator

1. Click the MC (memory clear) button ⬚MC⬚ or press Ctrl+L to clear the Calculator's memory.

2. Click the C (clear button) ⬚C⬚ or press the Esc key to clear the display.

3. Click the Close button ❌ in the upper right of the Calculator, or press Alt+F4 to exit the calculator.

Your Computer

How many of the following peripherals are accessible to your computer? Note that they may be directly attached or accessible through a network connection.

- Keyboard
- Monitor
- CD-ROM or DVD player
- Diskette or other drive with removable disks to which you may save data
- Scanner
- Printer
- Mouse
- Sound system
- Printer
- Microphone for voice input

Computers and Careers

To learn more about careers in computing, use the library, Internet, or interviews with computer professionals and write a brief report about any of the following as a career:

- Applications programmer
- Systems programmer
- Computer operator
- Network administrator
- Web site developer
- Database administrator
- Database developer
- Help systems developer
- Technical writer

Look in the Help Wanted ads of the newspaper from a fairly large city. Look at classifications under Computers, Computing, and so on. Also try non-computer fields. List the number of different software applications mentioned in requirements for the jobs.

Do any of the positions mention specific hardware?

Lesson 2: Introduction to Windows

Exercise 1: Get Started with Windows

- ◆ Microsoft Windows
- ◆ The Desktop
- ◆ Desktop View and Mode of Operation
- ◆ Mouse Pointing Device
- ◆ Select an Object
- ◆ Open an Object
- ◆ Windows Mouse Pointer Shapes
- ◆ Important Keystrokes
- ◆ Shut Down Windows

Exercise 2: Learn Windows Basics

- ◆ Understand the My Computer Window
- ◆ Understand the Toolbar
- ◆ Use Menus
- ◆ Use Tips
- ◆ Use Property Sheets
- ◆ Use What's This?
- ◆ Use a Dialog Box

Exercise 3: Get Started with Windows Explorer

- ◆ About Windows Explorer
- ◆ Other Ways to Start Windows Explorer
- ◆ Switch from Window to Window
- ◆ Change the Look of Windows Explorer
- ◆ How Windows Organizes Permanent Storage
- ◆ Move Around in Windows Explorer

Exercise 4: Manage Files with Windows Explorer

- ◆ Select Multiple Objects
- ◆ Create and Name a Folder
- ◆ Refresh the Explorer Window
- ◆ Copy or Move Objects
- ◆ Send a Shortcut to the Desktop from Windows Explorer
- ◆ Rename an Object
- ◆ Delete and Restore Objects

Exercise 5: Work with the Desktop

- ◆ Change Desktop Appearance
- ◆ Create a Folder on the Desktop
- ◆ Send a Shortcut to the Desktop from the Programs Menu
- ◆ Use Other Options on Programs Menu Right-Click Menu
- ◆ Use Pin to Start Menu Option
- ◆ Use Other Start Menu Options
- ◆ Use the Start Menu

Exercise 1

Get Started with Windows

■ **Microsoft Windows** ■ **The Desktop** ■ **Desktop View and Mode of Operation**
■ **Mouse Pointing Device** ■ **Select an Object** ■ **Open an Object**
■ **Windows Mouse Pointer Shapes** ■ **Important Keystrokes** ■ **Shut Down Windows**

NOTES

Microsoft® Windows®

■ Microsoft Windows is the leading operating system software for personal computers. While a very few installations may still use MS- or PC-DOS® (Disk Operating System) and others work with Unix, Linux, or some other operating system, most businesses have adopted Windows. (Apple® installations use Mac® OS, the operating system for the Apple Macintosh®.)

■ Windows is a **GUI** (**Graphical User Interface**). This means that the work you do often depends on your ability to use a mouse and to click on icons, menus, options, and buttons. The GUI was first developed at a Xerox® think tank in California's well-known Silicon Valley in the early 1970s. It was then adapted by Steve Jobs and Steve Wozniak when they created the first Apple computers.

■ During the 1980s, Microsoft developed its Windows GUI to compete more directly with Apple and to offer a similar appearance and consistent usage from one application to another. When you work in Windows, you can take some things for granted regardless of the software program, as you will see as you work through the exercises in this lesson.

■ In 1999 Microsoft released Windows 2000, an upgrade to Windows NT, its operating system used primarily in network environments. In 2000, Microsoft released Windows Me (Millennium Edition), an upgrade to Windows 98. Windows Me was designed primarily for use in homes and small organizations.

■ In 2001, Microsoft introduced Windows XP, the successor to all these Windows versions. Like Windows 2000, it is based on Windows NT but is intended to be the Windows operating system for the future.

■ To give you access to the computer and what it contains—icons, files, applications, printers, and so on—the Windows GUI displays a window—a rectangular area that lets you view and use a specific computer feature.

The Desktop

■ When you start your machine, Windows displays the desktop. A sample desktop is shown on the next page. The desktop you see when you start your machine may look different. In a new Windows XP installation, for example, the desktop may contain no icons except the Recycle Bin. The illustration shows the author's Windows XP desktop, which has a number of icons that the author added to it.

Windows Versions
Windows 98, Windows 2000, Windows Me (Millennium Edition), and Windows XP are *versions* of the Microsoft Windows operating system.

This lesson describes Microsoft Wndows XP.

GUI
Acronym for Graphical User Interface (an acronym is a shortened form of a phrase).

Interface
The manner in which a computer system presents information to another computer or to a user.

■ Your desktop may include **icons** not shown in the illustration. For example, you may have icons that give you access to Microsoft Office 2003 functions. This row of icons is called the **Office Shortcut bar** and is described in Lesson 2. The elements in this illustration are described in the table that follows the illustration.

Icon

An icon is a graphic symbol that represents a program, application, or other computer feature.

Sample Windows XP Desktop

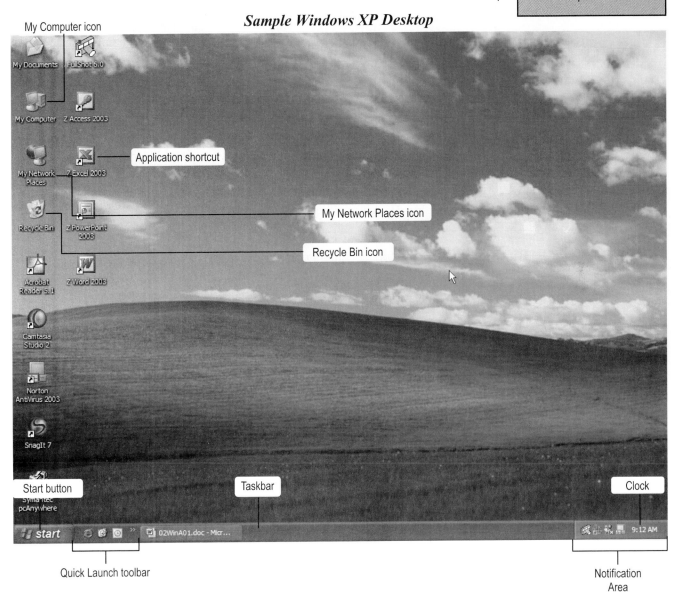

Icon/Object	Description
My Computer	**My Computer**. Gives you access to all the programs, documents, data files, floppy drives, and CD-ROM drives on your computer. The icon may be absent but can be added if desired.
Z Word 2003	**Application Shortcut**. Some applications automatically place an icon on the desktop to give you a quick way to start the application. These are called application shortcuts and are indicated by the curving arrow ⬈ on the icon. The icon illustrated here is for Microsoft Office Word 2003. The author has renamed the shortcut so that it displays at the end of the icons on the desktop in alphabetical order.

Icon/Object	Description
My Network Places	**My Network Places**. Lets you browse through the work stations, printers, drives, and folders on your network (a group of computers that share computing resources). If you are not logged in to a network, you can open this icon but will receive a message that the network cannot be found. The icon may be absent.
Recycle Bin	**Recycle Bin**. Stores the files you delete. Opening this icon allows you to see all files deleted since you last emptied the Recycle Bin. You can retrieve any files you may have deleted by mistake (if you have not yet emptied the Recycle Bin). You can also empty the Recycle Bin to free up space on your hard drive. (Deleted files are not actually removed from your computer until you empty the Recycle Bin.)
start	**Start button**. Opens the Start menu, from which you can access programs and open documents.
Quick Launch toolbar	**Quick Launch toolbar**, which contains the Show Desktop icon that lets you switch to the desktop quickly. The Quick Launch toolbar also usually has a button that starts your Internet browser and one for Windows Media Player, a popular Microsoft music and video player.
02WinA01.doc - Micr...	**Taskbar**. As you work with applications, application and document names appear on the taskbar. To switch to a different document or application, you can click its button on the taskbar.
(notification area icons)	**Notification area (system tray) application shortcuts**. Some applications place an icon in the area at the right end of the taskbar called the notification area or system tray. These icons often indicate programs that are already running; some provide a quick way to start the associated program.
8:15 PM	**Clock**. Shows the current time of day. Double-clicking it allows you to change the time, the date, or your time zone. The clock can set itself to the exact time.

Double-Click and Single-Click Modes of Operation

- Windows offers two basic modes of operation:

  - In **single-click** mode, you activate an icon on the desktop or open an item in a folder by a single click of the left mouse button. You select items by pointing to them.

  - In **double-click** mode, you open an icon on the desktop or open an item in a folder by a clicking the left mouse button twice rapidly, and you select items by pointing to them and clicking the left mouse button once.

- The instructions and illustrations in this book generally assume the double-click mode because it is the most often used and is the default in Windows XP discussed in this book. If your computer is in single-click mode and you are instructed to double-click an icon, you need to remember to single-click instead.

- **Is my system in single-click or double-click mode?** When **single-click** is on, the icons on the screen are underlined or display an underline when you point to them with the mouse. This underlining means that the objects can be activated (opened) with a single click of the left mouse button.

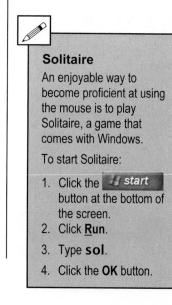

Solitaire

An enjoyable way to become proficient at using the mouse is to play Solitaire, a game that comes with Windows.

To start Solitaire:

1. Click the ⊞ start button at the bottom of the screen.
2. Click **Run**.
3. Type **sol**.
4. Click the **OK** button.

■ When **double-click** mode is on, the icons are not underlined even when you point to them. You can look at the upper-left corner of the screen to determine which style is on, as shown in the following illustration.

Single-Click

Double-Click

Mouse Pointing Device

■ The mouse is a device that controls a pointer on the computer monitor. Some mice slide across a surface to move the pointer on the screen; others have a ball that you roll with your thumb or fingers; others (usually on laptop computers) let you drag your finger across a touch pad. The pointer initially is an arrow . When the arrow points to an **object**, you can click a mouse button to request the operating system to act upon that object.

■ The mouse for Windows has at least two buttons. It may have three. The IntelliMouse has two buttons with a wheel between them. The wheel can be used to scroll quickly in most applications. The following terms are used to describe mouse actions.

- **Point**. Slide the mouse to move the pointer until it rests on an object.
- **Click**. Point at an object on the screen, press the left mouse button once, and release it.
- **Double-click**. Press and release the left mouse button rapidly two times.
- **Right-click**. Press and release the right mouse button. In most instances, a shortcut menu appears to let you select options appropriate to the object being clicked.
- **Click and drag** or **drag** an object. Point to an object, press the left mouse button and hold it down, and then move the mouse. The object moves as the mouse pointer moves. Releasing the left mouse button usually leaves the object in the new location.
- **Right-click and drag** an object. Point to an object, press the right mouse button and hold it down, and then move the mouse. The object moves as the mouse pointer moves. Releasing the right mouse button displays a menu of actions that can be taken on the object.
- **Draw a rectangle to select objects in a list**. Point to a blank area outside an object, click and hold down the left mouse button, and draw a rectangle around the object(s) you want to select. You may begin at any corner and draw the rectangle in any direction; you release the mouse button when the rectangle includes the objects you wish to select.

Object

This book refers to icons, buttons, folders, files, drives, programs and other elements displayed in windows as objects. When you request an action of Windows, you are requesting it to process (act upon) one of these objects.

Click and Drag Object

Point, click, and hold the left mouse button, and then drag the mouse to move the object.

- **Drag to select text**. Point to the letter with which you want the selection to begin. Hold down the mouse button and move the mouse pointer to select the text you want, and then release the mouse button. Once the text is selected, it is shaded, and you can treat the selected text as a unit for formatting, copying, cutting, or deleting.
- **Shift+Click**. Hold down the Shift key, point to an object, and click the left mouse button.
- **Ctrl+Click**. Point to an object, press and hold down the Ctrl key on the keyboard, then click the left mouse button.

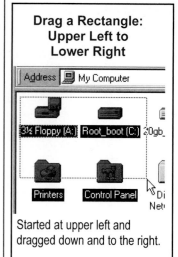

Drag a Rectangle: Upper Left to Lower Right

Started at upper left and dragged down and to the right.

Select an Object

- Windows uses the term **select** to refer to marking one or more objects that you wish to work with. You can tell an object is selected when it changes color, usually from lighter to darker. Sometimes users say such an object is highlighted, which is just another way of saying that the object is **selected**.

- If more than one object is selected, you can treat the selection as if it were a single object. The table below tells you how to select an object or group of objects in the two different modes of operation (styles).

To select ...	Double-click mode	Single-click mode
One object	Click the object.	Point to the object.
Adjacent objects	Draw a rectangle around the objects to be selected. **OR** 1. Click the first object you want to select; this action defines one corner of a rectangle. 2. **Shift+Click** the last object to be selected; this action defines the opposite diagonal corner of the rectangle.	Draw a rectangle around the objects to be selected. **OR** 1. Point to the first object you want to select; this action defines one corner of a rectangle. 2. Hold the Shift key and point to the last object to be selected; this action defines the opposite diagonal corner of the rectangle.
Non-adjacent objects	**Ctrl+Click** each object.	**Ctrl+Click** each object.

Open an Object

- When you want to work with the feature associated with an icon or process a file, you **open** the object by a single-click or a double-click. The following table lists the mouse and mouse/keyboard combined actions that let you open objects.

To open ...	Double-click mode (Classic style)	Single-click mode (Web style)
One object	Double-click the object. **OR** Select the object, and press Enter.	Click on the object. **OR** Point to the object and press the Enter key.
Multiple objects	Select the objects, and press the Enter key. *Note that on the desktop, only one of the objects will open. In other windows, all selected objects will open.*	Select the objects, and press the Enter key. *Note that on the desktop, only one of the objects will open. In most windows, all selected objects will open.*

Windows Mouse Pointer Shapes

- The mouse pointer changes shape depending on where you are in a window and what you are trying to do. Common mouse pointer shapes are described below. Other pointer shapes will be described as you encounter them in the applications.

Pointer	Description
	Normal select. Left-slanted arrow points to objects, such as icons, menu options, or toolbar buttons.
	Busy. The system is busy processing; no other action can be performed until this pointer disappears.
	Working in background. The system is busy processing, but you can perform other actions by pointing and clicking. **Background and Foreground:** When the system is processing in the **background**, you can perform other tasks. Printing from Word, for example, can run in the background, while you continue working. When the system is processing in the **foreground**, you cannot perform other tasks. Save, close, and exit are examples of functions that run in the foreground.
	Not available. The pointer is in an area of the window where nothing can be selected or activated.
Adjust, resize, move arrows.	
	Two-headed arrows let you drag the boundaries of objects. When you click and drag, the object expands or shrinks in the direction you drag the boundary.
	Column adjust. Two-headed arrow on vertical bar lets you change the width of a column. You can drag the boundary between two columns, or double-click (in most environments) to activate AutoFit, which adjusts the column to fit the longest entry.
	Horizontal resize. The horizontal version appears when the pointer rests on the middle of a left or right boundary; dragging it changes the proportions of the object.
	Vertical resize. The vertical version appears when the pointer rests on the middle of a top or bottom boundary; dragging it changes the proportions of the object.
	Diagonal Resize. One of the slanted versions appears when the pointer rests on a corner of the object; dragging it maintains the proportions of the object as you resize it.
	Move. In some applications, when you select a graphic and hold the left mouse button, this four-headed arrow appears and you can drag the object.
	Text select. I-beam shows where the insertion point will be positioned when you click the left mouse button. If you drag it, you select text. The insertion point (a blinking vertical bar) shows where the next key you press will take effect. For example, if you press the Backspace key, the insertion point moves left and deletes the character. The Delete key deletes the character to the right of the insertion point.
	Link select. The hand indicates that the text or icon pointed to is a link to another document or Web page.
	Line select. Right-slanted arrow lets you click to select text in word processing programs. It appears when you let the mouse pointer rest to the left of the text in an unmarked area of the screen called the **selection area**. You can drag the pointer to select multiple lines, or double-click to select a paragraph.

Important Keystrokes

Escape Key

- The **Esc** (Escape) key is used to cancel actions. For example, if you activate a menu option that you do not want to use, pressing the Esc key usually closes the menu or dialog box without any command being executed.

- **Ctrl+Esc** is a shortcut to activate the Start menu. It is the same as clicking the Start button ![start] or pressing the Windows key (see the next paragraph).

Windows Key

- The Windows key ![Windows key icon], located between the Ctrl and Alt keys on some keyboards, opens the Start menu. It is the same as Ctrl+Esc or clicking the Start button.

Application Key

- The Application key ![Application key icon], located between the Ctrl and Alt keys on some keyboards, opens a shortcut menu for the active object. For example, if you select My Computer on the desktop and press the Application key, the shortcut menu for My Computer opens. This action is the same as pointing to the object and right-clicking.

Alt+Tab or Alt+Esc

- Alt+Tab or Alt+Esc lets you switch from one open window to another. Alt+Tab displays a box with an icon for each window; Alt+Esc activates the window or selects the window's button on the taskbar if the window is minimized. When the taskbar button is selected, you can press the Enter key to restore the application.

Alt+F4

- Alt+F4 closes the current window. It is equivalent to clicking the Close button ![X] in the upper-right corner of the window.

Shut Down Windows

- To shut down Windows, click the Start button ![start] on the Windows taskbar and click on the Shut Down option as shown in the illustration on the next page. (The options on your Start menu may be different.)

- Note that the illustrations show some underlined characters. In some versions of Windows, the underlines may appear only when you point to the option or press the Alt key. Underlined characters indicate **shortcut keys**. Holding the Alt key and press the key for the underlined letter has the same effect as clicking the option.

Keystroke notation

When you see a keystroke such as **Alt+F4**, it means:

Press and hold down the **Alt** key, and then press the **F4** key.

This is the standard way to indicate keystroke combinations.

The notation **Alt+V, T** means press and hold down the **Alt** key and press the **V** key, then release both keys and press the **T** key.

Start Menu

- When you click Shut Down, the Shut Down Windows dialog box shown below appears and the desktop turns dim. Note that the dialog box may say "Turn Off Computer."

Shut Down Windows Dialog Box

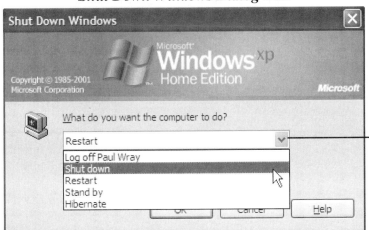

Click this drop-down arrow to display the list of options, select **Shut down**, then click the OK button or press the Enter key.

- The Shut Down Windows dialog box offers several options. (If you are working on a network, another option may appear to let you log in under a different ID.)

    - **Log off** *name*. Closes all programs and prepares the computer to be used by someone else. A new user enters his/her name and password to access Windows.

- **Shut down**. This option starts Windows' shutdown routine that may end with the message **It is now safe to turn off your computer** displayed in the middle of a dark screen. Most newer computers, however, turn off automatically without displaying this message.

- **Restart**. This option restarts your computer. If your computer has had problems, you may need to restart the computer to clean up memory and begin with a refreshed Windows environment.

- **Restart in MS-DOS mode** Restarts the computer in DOS mode. This mode is sometimes necessary for certain DOS programs and utility programs.

- **Stand by**. This option lets you leave your computer on and available for use without restarting but using less electricity than normal. If you lose power while in stand-by mode, any unsaved work is lost. Some newer keyboards have a "sleep" button that places Windows into stand-by mode. By default, Windows places your computer in stand-by mode when it has been idle for 20 minutes.

- **Hibernate**. Saves any options and settings you have changed and shuts down your computer so that when you start again, the settings are restored as they were when you shut down. (Select Help in the dialog box for more information.)

In this exercise, to help you become familiar with Windows, you will open and close some windows.

EXERCISE DIRECTIONS

Move the Recycle Bin and Arrange Icons

1. On the desktop, click the picture on the Recycle Bin and drag it to a different position on the desktop.
2. Right-click on an area of the desktop that does not have an icon.
3. Point to Arrange Icons By and click Name, as shown in Illustration A.

Illustration A. Arrange Icons by Name

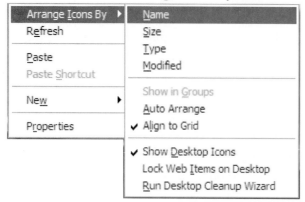

The Recycle Bin icon returns to it previous location.

Open and Close Objects

1. On the desktop, double-click (open) the Recycle Bin icon.
   The Recycle Bin window opens.
2. Click the Close button ☒ in the upper-right corner of the window.
   The Recycle Bin window closes.
3. Click the Start button **start**.
4. Move the mouse pointer to Help and Support ⊙ Help and Support and click.
   The Windows Help and Support Center opens.
5. Click the Close button ☒ in the upper-right corner of the window.
   The Windows Help and Support Center closes.

Shut Down Windows

1. Click the Start button **start**.
2. Click Shut Down or Turn Off Computer.
3. On the Shut Down Windows dialog box, select Shut Down.
4. Click the OK button ⎢ OK ⎥.

Exercise 2

Learn Windows Basics
■ Understand the My Computer Window ■ Understand the Toolbar ■ Use Menus
■ Use Tips ■ Use Property Sheets ■ Use What's This? ■ Use a Dialog Box

NOTES

Understand the My Computer Window

- To look at the components of your computer, you open the My Computer window.

💻 Try It!

1. Click the Start button 🟦 **start** .

2. Click the My Computer menu option 🟦 **My Computer** .

   The My Computer window is shown in the following illustration.

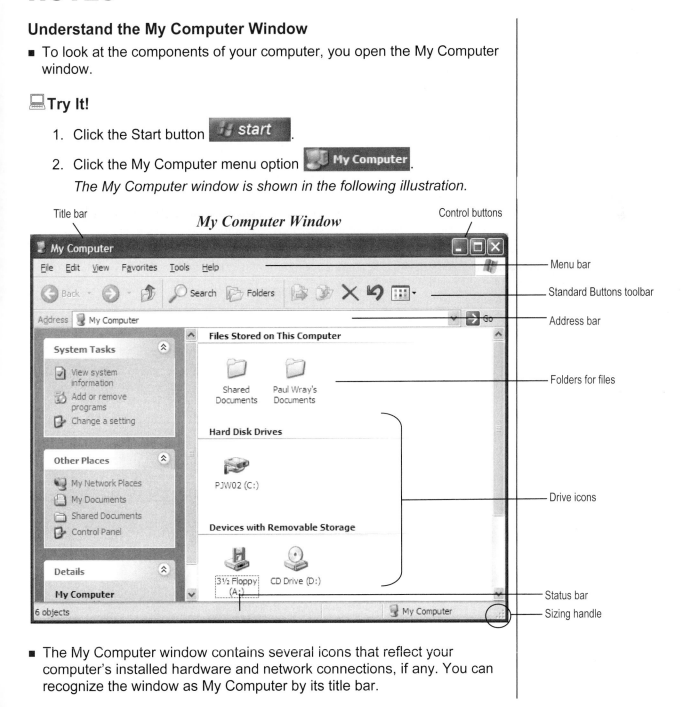

My Computer Window

- The My Computer window contains several icons that reflect your computer's installed hardware and network connections, if any. You can recognize the window as My Computer by its title bar.

- The My Computer window shows several important parts that are common to all Windows' windows. Each part is described in the table that follows.

Window Part	Description
Title bar	Identifies the contents of the window.
Control buttons	Allow you to control the size of the window and to close it.
Minimize ▬	Turns the window into a button on the Windows taskbar. The taskbar then displays the icon for the window and its name. When a window is minimized, you can return it to its previous position by clicking its button on the taskbar.
Maximize 🗖 **Restore** 🗗	Different versions of the same button. When clicked, the **Maximize** button causes the window to take up the entire monitor screen. The **Restore** button appears when a window is maximized. When you click it, the window returns to the size it was before it was maximized. Double-clicking the title bar is the same as clicking the Maximize or Restore button, whichever is currently displayed.
Close ✖	Closes the window. If the window is an application, you exit the application. Pressing Alt+F4 is the same as clicking the Close button.
Menu bar	Displays menu options. When you click on a word, a list of commands or options appears. These commands let you perform work with the objects (documents, icons) that appear in the window.
Toolbars	The **Standard Buttons** toolbar contains buttons that activate a shortcut to a command. For example, the **Up** button 🔼 lets you go up a level in the storage structure of your computer. (You'll learn more about the structure of storage later in this lesson.) Your buttons may have text labels. **Address bar**. Indicates which computer component is currently displayed. To display the toolbars, click the View menu, click Toolbars (Alt+V, T), and select the toolbar you wish to turn on. Be aware that menu bars and toolbars can be moved, expanded, shrunk, and turned on and off. The ways to manage the position and size of toolbars are generally outside the scope of this book; when moving or expanding is necessary, however, the book explains what you need to do.
Icons	Pictorial representations of computer objects. The My Computer window has icons for all the drives to which you currently have access. It may also show other objects such as shared folders and folders you use to manage your computer.
Status bar	Gives you important information about what the window contains and what work is being done. To display a status bar if it is not showing, click the View menu and then click Status Bar (Alt+V, B).
Sizing handle ◢	When a window is not maximized, to change its size: 1. Point to an edge or corner of the window until the pointer changes into a double-headed arrow ⤢ ↔ ↕. 2. Click and drag in either direction indicated by the arrow to enlarge or shrink the window. When the status bar is displayed and the window is not maximized, the window has a special sizing handle. You can click and drag the sizing handle in any direction.

Understand the Toolbar

- You can use the Standard Buttons toolbar in most windows to help you manage files. This section describes the default toolbar buttons. Your toolbar will not have all the options listed. If a button is not listed, it is not a default in your version of Windows.

💻**Try It!**

Display the Toolbar and Address Bar

1. With My Computer open, if the Standard toolbar is not displayed, click <u>V</u>iew, <u>T</u>oolbars, <u>S</u>tandard Buttons.
2. If the Address bar is not displayed, click <u>V</u>iew, <u>T</u>oolbars, <u>A</u>ddress Bar.
   The Address bar appears at the end of the toolbar when it is first activated.
3. Click the icon for your hard drive C:\.

Windows Standard Toolbar and Address Barr

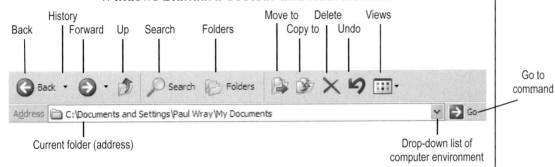

- The buttons of the toolbar and the elements of the Address bar are described in the following table. The buttons described are those that appear by default on the toolbars. Note that the Move to, Copy to, Delete, and Undo buttons may not appear on the toolbar.

Element	Description
Back, Forward	Click the Back button to return to a previous location. Click the Forward button to revisit a location after you've used the Back button.
	Both the Back and Forward buttons have History drop-down lists to let you choose a specific location that you've already visited.
Up	Available on windows that display folder contents; lets you move up one level in the folder organization.
Search	Opens Search as the left pane of the window so you can look for folders, files, text within a file, or information on the Internet if you have an Internet connection.
	Menu equivalent = <u>V</u>iew, <u>E</u>xplorer Bar, <u>S</u>earch (Alt+V, E, S)
	Keyboard shortcut = Ctrl+E
Folders	Opens Folders as the left pane so you can locate folders and files.
	Menu equivalent = <u>V</u>iew, <u>E</u>xplorer Bar, F<u>o</u>lders (Alt+V, E, O)
History	Opens History as the left pane so you can locate folders or files you have visited recently.
	Menu equivalent = <u>V</u>iew, <u>E</u>xplorer Bar, <u>H</u>istory (Alt+V, E, H)
	Keyboard shortcut = Ctrl+H
Cut	Removes a selected object and places it on the Clipboard, a special area of Windows memory. You can then paste the object into another place. This button is used throughout Windows and its menu equivalent and keyboard shortcut are always the same.
	Menu equivalent = <u>E</u>dit, Cu<u>t</u> (Alt+E, T)
	Keyboard shortcut = Ctrl+X
Copy	Places a copy of a selected object on the Clipboard. You can then paste the copy into another place.
	Menu equivalent = <u>E</u>dit, <u>C</u>opy (Alt+E, C)
	Keyboard shortcut = Ctrl+C

Element	Description
Copy to	Copies the object and opens a dialog box that lets you choose where to paste the object. **Menu equivalent** = Edit, Copy To Folder (Alt+E, F)
Paste	Pastes the contents of the Clipboard into the selected area. **Menu equivalent** = Edit, Paste (Alt+E, P) **Keyboard shortcut** = Ctrl+V
Move to	Opens a dialog box that lets you choose the folder to which you want to move the object. **Menu equivalent** = Edit, Move To Folder (Alt+E, V)
Undo	Reverses the most recent action. You can use this button to correct errors and to reverse actions that you did not want to perform. **Menu equivalent** = Edit, Undo (Alt+E, U) **Keyboard shortcut** = Ctrl+Z
Delete	Erases the object currently selected and places it in the Recycle Bin.
Properties	Displays the properties box for the selected object. It does not appear by default on toolbar. **Menu equivalent** = File, Properties (Alt+F, R) **Keyboard shortcut** = Right-click the object, select Properties from the shortcut menu.
Views	The Views button works the same as in My Computer. It changes the way the objects in the right pane are displayed. **Menu equivalent** = View, List (Alt+V, L) **Menu equivalent** = View, Details (Alt+V, D) **Menu equivalent** = View, Thumbnails (Alt+V, H) **Menu equivalent** = View, Tiles (Alt+V, S)
Address	Shows the name of the drive and folder currently open. Click the drop-down list arrow at the end of the address bar to display a list of the components of your computer. You can use this list to switch drives in Windows Explorer.

Use Menus

■ As illustrated by the My Computer window, menus appear at the top of most windows. Menus offer a list of commands from which you choose the one you want to execute. Sometimes the command is executed immediately. Sometimes the option displays a submenu. Sometimes the option displays a dialog box. The menu bar from My Computer is shown in the following illustrations.

My Computer Menu Bar

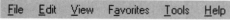

File   Edit   View   Favorites   Tools   Help

■ To activate a menu, either:

- Click the name of the menu you want to display.
  OR
- Press Alt+the underlined letter on the menu bar (Alt+F, for the File menu, for example). The underscores may not appear until you point at the option or press the Alt key.

Menus in Microsoft Office 2003

When you click a menu in a Microsoft Office 2003 application (such as Word), some available menu commands may not be visible. You can double-click the menu name to see all the options when the menu opens.

File Menu (My Computer)

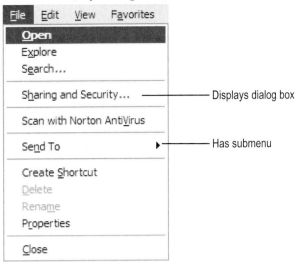

- Note that some commands appear in black letters while others are gray or dim. Options in black are available for selection; options in gray or dim letters are not available. Available options depend on the object (icon, folder, text, and so on) selected for processing.

- Commands followed by a small right arrow, as pointed out in the preceding illustration, offer submenus from which you choose a command. Other commands are followed by an ellipsis (…) to indicate that they activate a dialog box (see the next section for more on dialog boxes).

- To choose a menu option, slide the mouse to the option and click. If the option has a submenu, slide to the option, then slide to the desired command on the submenu, and then click. Instead, you can press the key of the underlined letter, for example O for Open.

- To close a menu, click anywhere outside the menu.

Try It!

Practice Using Menus

1. With the My Computer window open, click the View menu (Alt+V).

2. Click Status Bar (B).

   If the status bar was displayed, it disappears. If it was not displayed, it appears at the bottom of the window. A check mark indicates that an option is on and can be turned off by selecting the option.

3. Click View, List (Alt+V, L).

   The objects in the window appear in a list rather than as icons. A dot on a menu item indicates that it is currently the active option of several options.

4. Click View, Details (Alt+V, D).

   The objects are listed with additional information, including total size and free space for each drive.

5. Click View, Icons (Alt+V, N).

6. In the My Computer window, select the icon for your hard drive **(C:)**. The icons on the author's computers are shown in the following illustrations. The hand in the illustration indicates that the drives are shared across a local area network.

Hard Drive C: Icon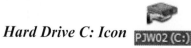

7. With the drive selected, click <u>F</u>ile, <u>O</u>pen to open the drive.

   A window opens showing the contents of the drive. Depending on your system settings, the C: drive window replaces the My Computer window, or it opens as a separate window.

   By default, in single-click mode, the drive window replaces the My Computer window.

8. Look at the taskbar.

   If the taskbar shows only the button for drive C:, the drive window replaced the My Computer window. If two buttons appear, the drive contents opened in a separate window.

Taskbar Button

9. If you have one button on the taskbar, click the Back button

   or the Up button on the Standard Buttons toolbar.

   If you have two buttons on the taskbar, click the Up button on the Standard Buttons toolbar.

   The My Computer window reappears.

Use Tips

- When you rest the mouse pointer on an object, Windows displays a tip that gives information about the object. The simplest form of tip appears when you point to a toolbar button and the name of the button appears as shown at the right.

- When you point to other objects, different kinds of information may appear. For example, when you point to a drive in the My Computer window, the drive free space and total size appear, as shown at the right.

Try It!

1. Point to and rest the mouse pointer on the Control Panel option <img> Control Panel under Other Places in the left side of the My Computer window.

   A tip appears giving information about the purpose of the Control Panel.

   Provides options for you to customize the appearance and functionality of your computer.

Use Property Sheets

- Windows' objects have **properties**—characteristics, settings, or options—that Windows displays to provide information or uses to determine how to manage an object. For example, a hard drive has a Total Size property

Toolbar Button with ScreenTip

Hard Drive Icon with ScreenTip

and a Free Space property that Windows can display in a ScreenTip or **property sheet** (a specially formatted window).

- Some property sheets only display information; others let you change settings to manage the appearance or behavior of an object.

Try It!

View Drive Properties

1. In the My Computer window, point to or select the icon for hard drive C:.

2. Right-click the icon to display a shortcut menu.

    OR

    If the hard drive is selected, click File (Alt+F) on the menu.

3. Click Properties (R).

    A property sheet similar to the one in the following illustration appears. If a property sheet contains a text field such as Label in the illustration, you can change data on the sheet. Some information on a property sheet is for display only; it cannot be changed through the property sheet

Property Sheet

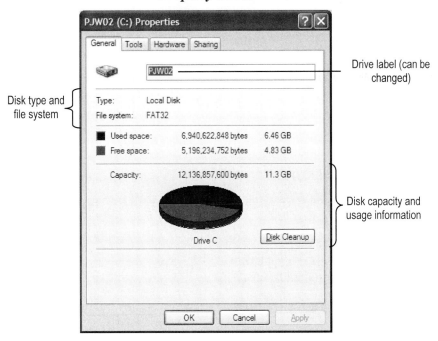

Disk type and file system

Drive label (can be changed)

Disk capacity and usage information

Use What's This?

- Another type of tip, called What's This?, is available in some contexts.

Try It!

1. Right-click on the Disk Cleanup button Disk Cleanup.

2. Click What's This? (W).

    Windows displays a ScreenTip that gives information about the button (or other object).

3. After reviewing the tip, click the Cancel button to close the property sheet and return to the My Computer window.

Disk Cleanup Button What's This? ScreenTip

> Click to specify disk cleanup options on the selected drive. You can use Disk Cleanup to free disk space by deleting temporary files and uninstalling programs.

Use a Dialog Box

- Windows uses a **dialog box** (a specially formatted window with some similarities to a property sheet) to request information from you that will control processing. You select options or type text to tell Windows or an application program the **parameters** you want to use for a particular command or set of commands.

🖥Try It!

1. Click Tools, Folder Options (Alt+T, O).

   Windows displays the Folder Options dialog box.

2. Look at the options displayed. The rest of this book assumes that the options are set as shown in the illustration.

3. Under Tasks, select Use Windows classic folders (I).

4. Under Browse folders, select Open each folder in the same window (M).

5. Under Click items as follows, select Double-click to open an item (single-click to select) (D).

6. Click the OK button ⬚ OK ⬚.

7. Click the Close button ❌ on the My Computer window.

8. Shut down Windows unless you are continuing with the Exercise Directions.

Folder Options Dialog Box

Parameter
A setting, value, or other specification that tells Windows or an application program the options you want to use when processing data.

In this exercise, you will practice opening and closing Windows.

EXERCISE DIRECTIONS

Minimize, Maximize, Restore, and Close

1. Open My Computer as you learned in the first Try It! activity in this exercise.
2. Click the Minimize button ▬.
   The My Computer window becomes a button on the Windows taskbar.
3. Click the My Computer button on the taskbar.
   The My Computer window returns to its former size and position.
4. Click the Maximize button ▢ on the Window's title bar.
   The My Computer window enlarges to fill the entire monitor screen.
5. Click the Restore button ▣ on the Window's title bar.
   The My Computer window returns to its former size and position.
6. Double-click the title bar.
   The My Computer window enlarges to fill the entire monitor screen.
7. Double-click the title bar again.
   The My Computer window returns to its former size and position.
   If a window is maximized, double-clicking the title bar is the same as clicking the Restore button. If a window is not maximized, double-clicking the title bar is the same as clicking the Maximize button.
8. Click the Close button ✖ in the upper-right corner of the window.
   The My Computer window closes.

Open the Recycle Bin

1. Open the Recycle Bin.

2. Maximize the window by double-clicking the title bar.
3. Restore the window by double-clicking the title bar.
4. Click the Minimize button ▬.
5. Click the Recycle Bin button on the taskbar to restore the window.
6. Make sure the window is not maximized, then click on the title bar and drag the window around the monitor screen.
   Any window that is not maximized can be moved in this way. You may find it useful to move a window around to be able to see elements on the desktop that the window hides.

Display Button Labels

1. With the Recycle Bin open, click View, Toolbars (Alt+V, T) on the menu bar.
2. Click Customize (C).
   Windows displays the Customize Toolbar dialog box.
3. Click in the Text options box, and select one of the following:
   - Show text labels to show a label under each button.
   - Selective text on right to use the default in which Windows displays text for some buttons.
   - No text labels to turn text labels off.

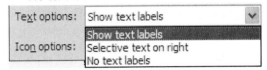

Note that these steps also work in the My Computer and My Network Places windows.

4. Click the Close button [Close] on the dialog box.
5. Click the Close button ✖.
   The Recycle Bin closes.

Open the Help Window

1. Click the Start button .
2. Move the mouse pointer to Help and Support (?) Help and Support or Help and click.
   The Windows Help feature opens.
3. Click the Close button ✖ in the upper-right corner of the window.
   The Windows Help window closes.
4. Shut down Windows.

Exercise 3

Get Started with Windows Explorer

■ About Windows Explorer ■ Other Ways to Start Windows Explorer
■ Switch from Window to Window ■ Change the Look of Windows Explorer
■ How Windows Organizes Permanent Storage ■ Move Around in Windows Explorer

NOTES

About Windows Explorer

- In addition to My Computer, Windows offers another way to look at what your computer contains—Windows Explorer. Windows Explorer is a window that lets you look through the drives and folders on your computer to find folders and files that you want to use.

- You can start Windows Explorer in a number of different ways. You will learn at least two of them in this exercise.

⌨ Try It!

1. Right-click the Start button 🪟 start .
2. Click Explore.

   Windows Explorer opens and displays the contents of the Start Menu folder, as shown in the illustration that follows.

Explorers
Windows Explorer is not Internet Explorer, Microsoft's Web browser. Windows Explorer lets you look at what's on your computer; Internet Explorer is designed for browsing the World Wide Web.

Windows Explorer

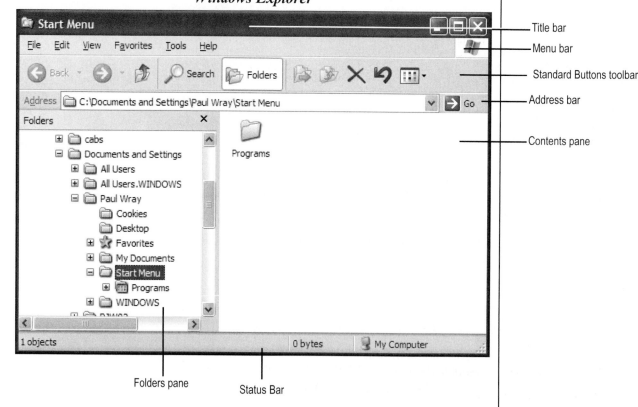

Title bar
Menu bar
Standard Buttons toolbar
Address bar
Contents pane
Folders pane
Status Bar

- The Windows Explorer window is divided into two parts called **panes**.
  - The left pane, Folders, shows the folders in the drive currently selected. It also lists the other drives on your computer, which you can see by scrolling up and down.
  - The right pane lists the folders and files in the object selected in the left pane.
- The following table describes the parts of the Windows Explorer window.

Window Part	Description
Title bar	Tells you which drive and folder you are currently exploring. The Start Menu's contents depend on the user who is logged in.
Menu bar	Offers menu options.
Toolbar	The Standard Buttons toolbar appears as on other windows. Additional buttons may appear if they have not been visible on other windows.
Address bar	The Address bar may not appear. It gives the detailed path to the folder selected in the left pane. You can turn it on and off through View, Toolbars, Address Bar (Alt+V, T, A).
Folders pane	Pane that lists all folders on your computer. Note the Close button ☒ in the upper right of the Folders pane. If you click this Close button, the Folders pane closes. To reopen it, click View, Explorer Bar, Folders (Alt+V, E, O).
Legend bar	In Details view, the legend bar at the top of the right pane displays a heading for each displayed column.
Right (Contents) pane	The right pane lists the objects in the folder currently selected in the Folders pane. The illustration on the previous page shows Icons view. You can switch views to Thumbnails, Tiles, List, or Details using the View menu or the Views button ⊞▾ on the toolbar.
Status bar	Gives information about the number and size of objects selected in the panes. If the Status bar is not displayed, click View, Status Bar (Alt+V, B).

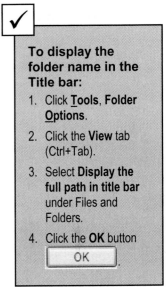

To display the folder name in the Title bar:

1. Click **Tools**, **Folder Options**.
2. Click the **View** tab (Ctrl+Tab).
3. Select **Display the full path in title bar** under Files and Folders.
4. Click the **OK** button

[OK]

Other Ways to Start Windows Explorer

- You can start Windows Explorer in a variety of ways.

Try It!

1. On the Quick Launch toolbar (usually at the left end of the Windows taskbar), click the Show Desktop icon 🖳.

   The Desktop appears and the Windows Explorer window minimizes.

2. Open My Computer (see Exercise 2).

3. Right-click on drive C:.

4. Click Explore.

   Windows Explorer opens in a new window with a display of the contents of drive C:.

5. In the left pane, select Documents and Settings (or any other folder).

6. Minimize the window (click the Minimize button 🗕).

7. In the My Computer window, click the Folders button 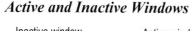, or click <u>V</u>iew, <u>E</u>xplorer Bar, F<u>o</u>lders (Alt+V, E, O) on the menu bar.

8. Click the identifier of drive C: in either the left or right pane.

   Note that you can open drive C: and then display the Folders option of the Explorer bar. You now have three windows open.

9. Minimize the window.

Switch from Window to Window

- At any time, only one window is **active**. The active window is the one in which you are currently working. You can tell which window is active because its title bar is in a dark color. The inactive window has a lighter color of title bar.

- In the following illustration, the active window is the Windows Explorer with Documents and Settings. The inactive window is the one showing drive C:. A portion of the desktop forms the background.

Active and Inactive Windows

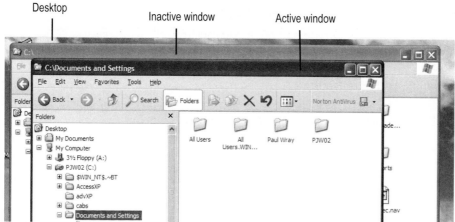

- Windows offers several ways to switch from one open window to another.

  - If a portion of an inactive window is showing, click on the displayed portion to activate it.

  - You can click on the button for the window on the taskbar.

Taskbar Buttons for My Computer and Two Windows Explorer Windows

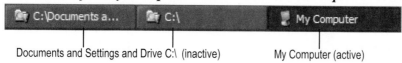

  - You can also switch from one open window to another by holding down the Alt key and pressing the Tab key. Each time you press Tab with Alt held down, Windows selects one of the open windows indicated by its icon. In the illustration on the next page, seven windows are open, so Alt+Tab cycles through all seven.

    When the icon for the window you want to activate is selected, release the Alt key. The window is activated.

Switch Between Open Windows

C:\Documents and Settings\Paul Wray\Start ...

🖥 Try It!

1. Click the taskbar button of each open window in turn.
2. Click the hidden (inactive window) if a portion of it is showing.
3. Click the taskbar button of an inactive window to activate it.
4. Use Alt+Tab to switch to an inactive window.
5. Close all open windows by clicking the Close button ☒ on each.

Change the Look of Windows Explorer

■ Windows offers a wide variety of tools and features for viewing drives, files, and folders through Windows Explorer. You can experiment with the options until you find the set of options that best suits the way you like to work.

🖥 Try It!

1. Open Windows Explorer using any of the ways described earlier in this exercise.

2. On the toolbar, click the Views button ⊞▾.

   Windows displays a list of view options. This is the same list that is available on the View menu.

View Options

   Thumbnails
   Tiles
   Icons
   ● List
   Details

3. Select List (L).

   The icons in the right pane change to a list of items.

Windows Explorer Right Pane List

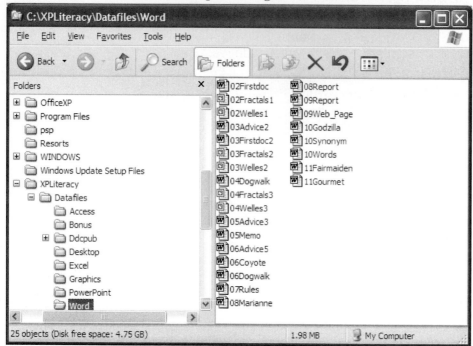

4. Click the Views button 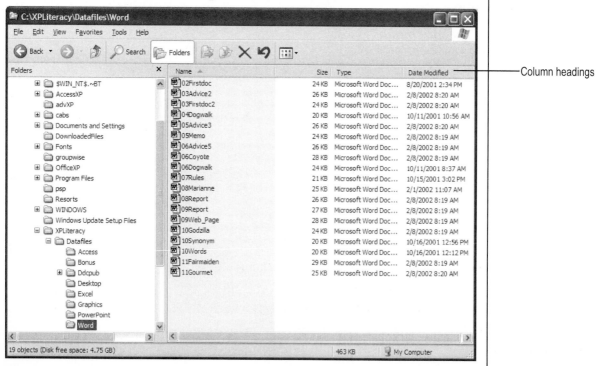 and select Details.

   The right pane shows a list of items with additional information, as shown in the following illustration.

   The column headings tell you the size of the file, its type, and the date it was modified.

5. Click the Close button ☒ to close Windows Explorer.

Windows Explorer in Details View

Column headings

How Windows Organizes Permanent Storage

- Windows organizes permanent storage by drive letter, folder name, and file name. In your computer, the highest level of organization is the Desktop. The Desktop contains My Computer, which contains drives. Drives contain folders. Folders contain other folders and files.

- When you look at the Explorer window, you see this organization in list form. The hierarchy is reflected by indentations.

Organization Reflected in Windows Explorer

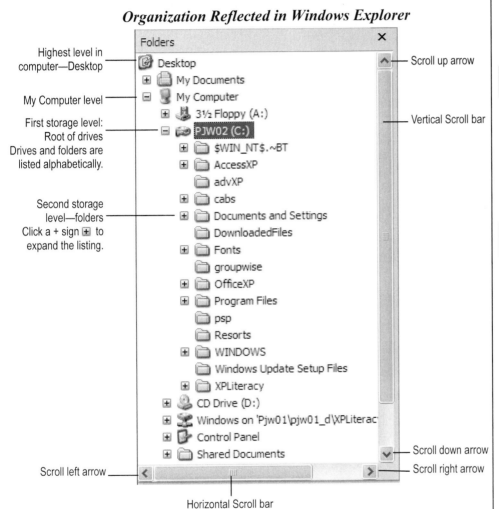

Highest level in computer—Desktop

My Computer level

First storage level: Root of drives Drives and folders are listed alphabetically.

Second storage level—folders Click a + sign ⊞ to expand the listing.

Scroll up arrow

Vertical Scroll bar

Scroll down arrow

Scroll right arrow

Scroll left arrow

Horizontal Scroll bar

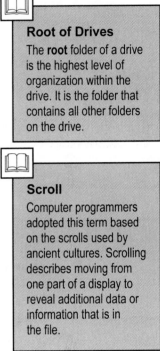

Root of Drives

The **root** folder of a drive is the highest level of organization within the drive. It is the folder that contains all other folders on the drive.

Scroll

Computer programmers adopted this term based on the scrolls used by ancient cultures. Scrolling describes moving from one part of a display to reveal additional data or information that is in the file.

Move Around in Windows Explorer

- Now that you know something of its organization, you can look through your computer using Windows Explorer.

🖥 Try It!

1. Open My Computer, right-click drive C:, and select E<u>x</u>plore.

2. Maximize Windows Explorer if it is not already maximized. (Double-click the title bar or click the Maximize button 🔲.)

3. Move your mouse pointer to the left pane, and click the Desktop.

   The right pane shows the contents of your desktop. You may have only the Recycle Bin icon.

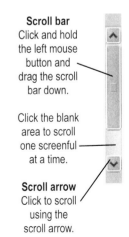

Scroll bar
Click and hold the left mouse button and drag the scroll bar down.

Click the blank area to scroll one screenful at a time.

Scroll arrow
Click to scroll using the scroll arrow.

4. Click the drive C: entry.

    The right pane shows the contents of drive C:.

5. Click the – sign (**collapse** button) ⊟ to the left of the drive C: entry.

    The collapse button ⊟ changes to a + sign (expand button) ⊞.

    The expand and collapse buttons let you display and hide the contents of objects in the left pane.

6. Click the expand button ⊞ to the left of the drive C: entry.

7. In the left pane, look for the Program Files folder ⊞ 📁 Program Files .

8. Click the expand button ⊞ for the Program Files folder.

    A list of folders appears underneath the Program Files folder. Your screen should look something like the one in the following illustration. The contents of your folder will be different. (So far, the right pane has not changed unless you accidentally clicked a folder.)

    ### Expanded Program Files Folder in Explorer's Left Pane

    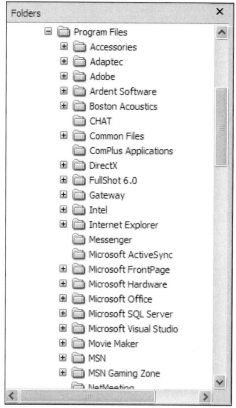

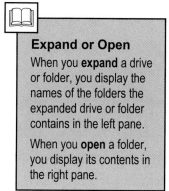

Expand or Open

When you **expand** a drive or folder, you display the names of the folders the expanded drive or folder contains in the left pane.

When you **open** a folder, you display its contents in the right pane.

9. Click the Program Files folder 📁 Program Files in the left pane to open it.

    The Program Files folder icon looks open ⊟ 📂 Program Files , and its contents are displayed in the right pane, as shown in the illustration on the next page. Windows may display a message indicating that the folder contains files critical to your system's operation. Click Show files if your operating system displays the message.

Windows Explorer with Windows Folder Open

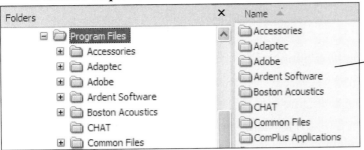

Portion of contents of Program Files folder

- In Windows Explorer, folders are indicated by the folder icon. For example, if you have Details view on, you may see the Common Files folder that looks like this:

- Files are indicated by other icons. If the file belongs to an application, such as Word, the Word icon appears to the left of the file name in Explorer's right pane.

■ The common way to refer to the location of a folder or file is called the **path**. For example, a Word file named **Firstdoc** stored in the My Documents folder is identified by the following path:

  C:\My Documents\Firstdoc.doc

C: identifies the drive, *My Documents* names the folder, and Firstdoc.doc is the file name. (The **file extension** does not have to be used, but is given here for completeness.) Any subfolders are included between backward slashes (backslashes); for example, in the path below, PaulData is a subfolder of My Documents:

  C:\My Documents\PaulData\2ndDoc.doc

Try It!

Locate a File

1. Make sure that the Program Files folder is open .

2. Move your mouse pointer to the right pane.

3. Switch to Details view if it is not already selected.

4. Locate the Microsoft Office folder in the right pane .

   If necessary, click on the scroll bar to the right of the pane, hold down the left mouse button, and drag down until you see the Microsoft Office folder.

   (If you cannot find the folder, the person who installed your Office programs did not use the default name for the installation folder. To complete this Try It! activity, you'll need to find the folder where Office was installed.)

5. Open the Microsoft Office folder.

   The Microsoft Office folder's contents are displayed. An alphabetical list of folders appears. Note that the list is usually alphabetical by folder name, then by file name.

Subfolder

Sometimes folders within other folders are called subfolders.

File extension

Three-character code that identifies the type of file. **.exe** identifies an application or program file. **.dll** identifies another type of program file. **.doc** indicates a Word document.

Single or Double-click?

If you are working in double-click mode, you single-click a folder listed in the left pane to open it, but double-click a folder in the right pane. (In single-click mode, a single click opens a folder.)

6. Open the Office11 folder  or 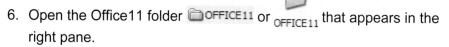 that appears in the right pane.

   An alphabetical list of folders and files appears.

7. Click the Views button ⊞▾ and select <u>D</u>etails.

8. Click on the scroll bar to the right of the right pane, hold down the left mouse button, and drag down until you see the Excel application file. (The .EXE extension may not appear on your screen.)

   <table>
   <tr><td>⊠ EXCEL.EXE</td><td>9,838 KB</td><td>Application</td></tr>
   </table>

9. Look at other files in the list.

   Each is identified by an icon as well as the file name. In Details view, the file type and date and time modified also appear. As you work with Explorer, you'll learn to recognize the icons for different types of files.

🖥 Try It!

Display File Extensions

If file extensions are already displayed skip this Try It! activity.

1. In Windows Explorer, click <u>T</u>ools, Folder <u>O</u>ptions, View tab.

   The Folder Options dialog box appears, as shown in the illustration on the next page.

2. Deselect (uncheck) the option *Hide file extensions for known file types.*

   Known *means that Windows can identify the application that uses the file type.*

3. Click the OK button [OK].

   The file extensions now appear with the file names in the right pane.

4. Click the Back button ◀ Back on the Standard Buttons toolbar, and then click it again.

5. Click the Forward button ▶ ▾.

   If you click the drop-down arrow on the Forward or Back button, you can select the window you want to display.

6. Click the Up button.

7. Click the Up button again. Review the contents of the right pane, and then continue to click the Up button until the right pane displays the contents of the Desktop. Review the contents of the right pane at each click.

8. Close Windows Explorer.

Explorer View, Folder Options Dialog Box

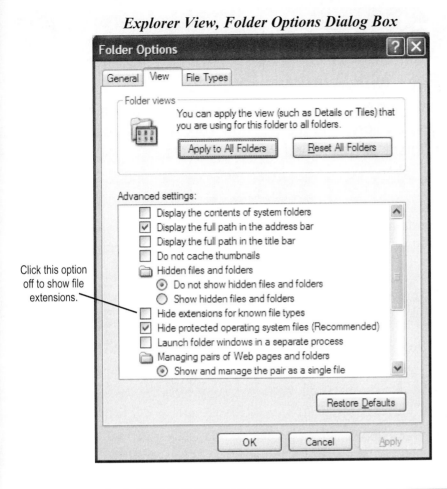

Click this option off to show file extensions.

In this exercise, you will practice moving around in Windows Explorer.

EXERCISE DIRECTIONS

Explore Folders

1. Start Windows Explorer (if it is not already open).
2. Maximize the Explorer window if necessary.
3. Locate the data files for this book.

   They may have been copied to your hard drive or network, or they are on the CD that comes with the book.

4. Click the Datafiles folder to display its contents in the right pane.
5. Open the Graphics folder in the right pane.
6. Click the Views button 🔡▾ and select Thumbnails.

   The image files in the right pane display as pictures.

   Thumbnails view is available in other windows as well.

7. Click the Up button ⬆ on the Standard Buttons toolbar.
8. Open the Word folder in the right pane.
9. Double-click the first file listed, 💿 **02Firstdoc**.

   Word 2003 starts and displays the file.

10. Click the upper, application Close button ❌ to close Word.

Exercise 4

Manage Files with Windows Explorer
■ Select Multiple Objects ■ Create and Name a Folder ■ Refresh the Explorer Window
■ Copy or Move Objects ■ Send a Shortcut to the Desktop from Windows Explorer
■ Rename an Object ■ Delete and Restore Objects

NOTES

■ Through Windows Explorer, you can perform a number of file and desktop management tasks. In this exercise, you will learn to:

  • Create and name a folder

  • Refresh the Explorer window

  • Create a shortcut

  • Copy or move objects

  • Rename an object

  • Delete and restore objects

Select Multiple Objects

■ In windows that display lists, including many application Open dialog boxes, you can select more than one object to be processed (copied, moved, deleted, or opened) at the same time.

Try It!

Select Adjacent Objects

1. Start Windows Explorer, locate the data files for this book, and open the Word folder.

2. Switch to Details view.

   You can use any view you wish, but the steps below are intended for Details or List view.

3. In the right pane, select the first object displayed.

4. Slide your mouse down about 10 objects.

5. Press the Shift key and click the object.

   All the objects from the first through the last object you clicked are selected.

6. Click anywhere outside the list to deselect the objects.

Try It!

Select Non-Adjacent Objects

1. Click the second object in the list.

2. Hold down the Ctrl key and click the sixth object in the list.

3. Hold down the Ctrl key and click the ninth and tenth objects in the list.

4. Click anywhere outside the list to deselect the objects.

Create and Name a Folder

- To create a folder, you select the drive or folder into which you want to place the new folder, and then use the menu to create the folder.

💻 Try It!

Create a New Folder at the Root Level of Drive C:

1. In Windows Explorer, open drive C: by clicking on its icon in the left pane.

2. Use the Views button  or <u>V</u>iew menu to switch to List view.

3. Click <u>F</u>ile, Ne<u>w</u>.
   The File New menu appears, as shown in the following illustrations.

File, New, Folder

<u>File</u>	Edit	<u>V</u>iew	F<u>a</u>vorites	<u>T</u>ools
Ne<u>w</u>	▶		📁 Folder	
Create <u>S</u>hortcut		🔲	Shortcut	
<u>D</u>elete		📦	Briefcase	

4. Click <u>F</u>older (F).
   Windows creates the folder and places it at the end of the displayed objects in the right pane, as shown at the right.

   Note that the name is surrounded by a rectangular box 📁 New Folder. *This box indicates that the object name can be edited. You are now ready to give the New Folder a name.*

5. Type **My 1st Folder** and press the Enter key.
   Because the text in the box was highlighted, what you type replaces the previous entry. You now have a new folder on drive C: called My 1st Folder.

New Folder

📄 SCANDISK
📄 SETUPXLG
📁 New Folder

New Folder appears at the bottom of the list.

Refresh the Explorer Window

- Note that the folder is still listed in the right pane after all the file names. You can display it in the list of folders by refreshing the view.

💻 Try It!

- Click <u>V</u>iew, <u>R</u>efresh.

  My 1st Folder is now listed among the folders in the correct alphabetical position. You may need to scroll up to find it. It will also appear in the left pane when the C: drive is expanded.

  Refreshing the Explorer window is necessary from time to time when you have been processing a lot of files and folders. Explorer reads the disk once when you open it, but may not retrieve information from the disk again unless the changes have been made through Explorer.

  For example, suppose you have Explorer open, then start Excel and create a new spreadsheet. If you return to Explorer, you may not see the new spreadsheet in its proper position in the right pane of the folder where you saved it until you refresh the display.

Copy or Move Objects

- Once you have created a folder, you probably want to put something into it. One way is to copy or move objects from another folder. The method outlined in the following Try It! activity can be used to copy or move an object from one folder to another even if the target folder is on another drive.

🖥 Try It!

Use Copy and Paste

1. In Windows Explorer, locate the Datafiles folder for this book. (The data files are on the CD that comes with the book if they have not been copied to a hard drive.)

2. Switch to Details or List view to be compatible with the illustrations in this section.

3. Open the Excel subfolder to display the Excel data files, and select the file ⊙**02Lunch**.

4. Do one of the following:

   - Press Ctrl+C.
   - Right-click ⊙**02Lunch** in the right pane, and select <u>C</u>opy.
   - Click <u>E</u>dit, <u>C</u>opy (Alt+E, C).

5. In the left pane of Windows Explorer, scroll until you locate My 1st Folder.

6. Open My 1st Folder. (The right pane should be empty.)

7. Do one of the following:

   - Press Ctrl+V.
   - Right-click My 1st Folder in the left pane, and select <u>P</u>aste.
   - Click <u>E</u>dit, <u>P</u>aste (Alt+E, P).

   The Windows Explorer window should be similar to the following illustration.

02Lunch Copied to My 1st Folder

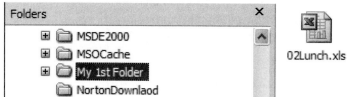

🖥 Try It!

Use Right-Click Drag and Drop

1. In the right pane, display the Excel data files again.

2. Select ⊙**02Select** through ⊙**03Students**.

3. In the left pane, scroll to My 1st Folder, but do not open it.

   Windows Explorer should look similar to the following illustration.

Excel Files Ready to be Copied to My 1st Folder

4. In the right pane, right-click on any of the selected files and hold down the right mouse button.

5. Drag the selected files to the left pane and position them so that My 1st Folder is selected.

Right-Click Drag to Copy Files

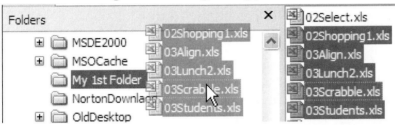

6. When My 1st Folder turns dark, release the right mouse button.

   Windows displays the shortcut menu, shown in the following illustration.

Right-Click Drag Copy/Move Menu

7. Select Copy Here (C).

   Move Here is the default (bold lettering) when you are moving from one folder to another within the same drive. If you are copying from your CD drive, the default will be Copy Here.

Use Left-Click Drag and Drop

- Note that you can click and drag using the left mouse button, but you must keep in mind the following.

  o When you left-click and drag from one folder to another within the same drive, you move the files.

  o When you left-click and drag from one drive to another, you copy the file.

  o If the file being dragged is an application file, such as Excel.exe, you create a shortcut to the file in the new folder or on the new drive.

  o You can always copy files with left-click and drag by holding down the Ctrl key when you click and drag.

🖥 Try It!

Use Toolbar

1. Display the Excel data files in the right pane.

2. Select the following files using the Ctrl key:
   - **04Scrabble3**
   - **07Scrabble4**
   - **08Scrabble7**
   - **09Scrabble4**

3. Click the Copy To button .

   To move an object, click the Move To button [   ].

   Windows displays the Copy Items or Move Items dialog box.

4. Find and select My 1st Folder as shown in the following illustration.

   Copy Items Dialog Box

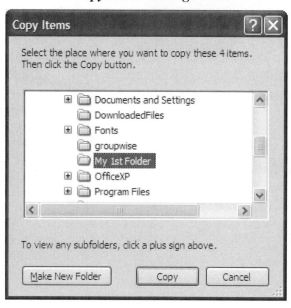

5. Click the Copy button [Copy].

   The files are copied into My 1st Folder.

Copying Progress Message

When the object you copy is a folder, the entire contents of the folder are copied. If the copy takes more than a few seconds, Windows displays a progress message box, indicating that the operation is taking place.

Copy/Move Progress Message Box

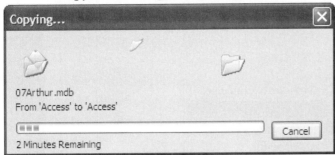

Send a Shortcut to the Desktop from Windows Explorer

- A shortcut is an icon that lets you open an application, folder, or file without going through the Start menu, My Computer, or Windows Explorer. You can drag a shortcut from where it is created and place it on the desktop or in another folder.

- Shortcuts are identified by a curving jump arrow that appears as part of the object's icon. For example, a shortcut to PowerPoint on the desktop might look like the one at the right.

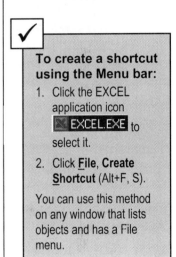

🖥Try It!

1. In Windows Explorer, locate the following folder:

   C:\Program Files\Microsoft Office\Office11

   This folder contains all the application files for the Microsoft Office components.

   Open the Program Files\Microsoft Office\Office Folder

2. Locate the EXCEL application file in the right pane. Use any view you wish. The illustration below shows the Excel application in List view.

   Excel Application File in List View

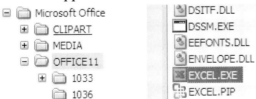

   Note that your file name may not show the .EXE extension.

3. Right-click on the icon to display a shortcut menu.

4. Point to Send To on the shortcut menu, and select Desktop (create shortcut), as shown in the following illustration.

To create a shortcut using the Menu bar:

1. Click the EXCEL application icon **EXCEL.EXE** to select it.

2. Click **File**, **Create Shortcut** (Alt+F, S).

You can use this method on any window that lists objects and has a File menu.

Send to Desktop (create shortcut)

Windows creates the shortcut and places it on the desktop with the name Shortcut to EXCEL. If a shortcut with the same name already exists, the name is Shortcut (2) to EXCEL.

You can create a shortcut to any object displayed in the Explorer window in this way. You can use this method in windows like My Computer, Control Panel, or any window that lists objects. You can also use this method on items on the Start menu.

5. To see the shortcut if it is not visible, click the Show Desktop button on the Quick Launch toolbar.

Rename an Object

- You can rename objects in the Explorer window, on the desktop, and in any window that displays a list of objects.

🖥 Try It!

1. Click the Show Desktop button on the taskbar to display the desktop.

2. Select the Shortcut to EXCEL icon, and press the F2 key.

   OR

   Point to the shortcut and right-click to display a shortcut menu, and click Rename or Rename.

   This action surrounds the shortcut name with a box, indicating that it is ready for editing, as shown at the right.

3. To replace the text, just begin typing.

   OR

   To edit the text, press the left or right arrow key to position the insertion point where you want to begin editing.

4. Make the entry read **Excel 2003**.

5. When you finish editing or typing, press the Enter key.
   The icon remains selected.

6. Click on any blank area of the screen to deselect the icon.

Delete and Restore Objects

- Just as it is easy to place shortcuts on the desktop, it is easy to remove them.

Delete a Shortcut

🖥️ **Try It!**

1. Click and drag the Excel 2003 shortcut across the desktop to the Recycle Bin icon.

2. When the Recycle Bin icon is selected, release the mouse button.

   Windows displays a message like the following:

   Confirm Delete Message

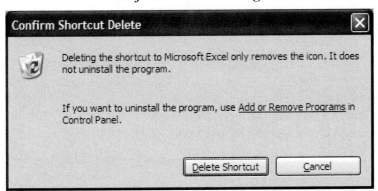

3. Click the Delete Shortcut button [Delete Shortcut] to confirm that you want to delete the shortcut.

4. Open the Recycle Bin.

5. Locate the shortcut you just deleted.

   It will be listed as Excel with a type of Shortcut.

6. Click the name and drag it to the desktop.

   The shortcut is restored.

7. Close the Recycle Bin.

8. Select the Excel shortcut again.

9. Press the Delete key.

   Windows displays the Confirm ... Delete message.

10. Click the Delete Shortcut button [Delete Shortcut] to confirm that you want to delete the shortcut.

    You can use either method to remove objects from the desktop. And you can restore objects to the desktop by dragging them from the Recycle Bin list to the desktop.

🖥️ **Try It!**

Delete Objects using Windows Explorer

1. In Windows Explorer, open My 1st Folder.

2. Select one file, and click the Delete button ✖ on the toolbar or press the Delete key.

3. Answer Yes to the Confirm File Delete message.

4. Display the desktop (click the Show Desktop button 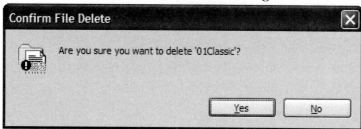).

5. Open the Recycle Bin.

6. Verify that the file you deleted is in the Recycle Bin.

   Objects deleted in this way are sent to the Recycle Bin.

7. Close the Recycle Bin window.

8. Switch back to My 1st Folder.

9. Select several files, right-click, and select <u>D</u>elete from the shortcut menu.

10. Answer <u>Y</u>es to the Confirm File Delete message.

11. In the left pane, select the C: drive.

12. Locate My 1st Folder in the right pane.

13. Click Delete button on the toolbar or press the Delete key.

14. Answer <u>Y</u>es to the Confirm File Delete message.

- Objects deleted from removable media such as diskettes are not sent to the Recycle Bin. Once deleted, they cannot be restored from the Recycle Bin. Windows indicates that a file is about to be deleted by using the word *delete* in the Confirm File Delete message.

Windows File Delete Message

Confirm File Delete

Are you sure you want to delete '01Classic'?

| <u>Y</u>es | | <u>N</u>o |

In this exercise, you will use Windows Explorer to work with objects.

EXERCISE DIRECTIONS

Create, Copy, and Rename a Folder

1. Open Windows Explorer.
2. Locate and open C: drive in the left pane.
3. Click File, New, Folder.

   The New Folder icon appears at the end of the list in the right pane.
4. Name the folder **My 2nd Folder**.
5. Select My 2nd Folder, and press Ctrl+C.
6. Press Ctrl+V.

   A new folder appears named Copy of My 2nd Folder.
7. Right-click Copy of My 2nd Folder, and click Rename.
8. Rename the folder **My 3rd Folder**.

Copy Files and Create a Shortcut

1. Using techniques you learned in the earlier part of this exercise, copy two files from the Word data files into the **My 2nd Folder**.
2. Right-click **My 2nd Folder**.
3. Point to Send To, and select Desktop (create shortcut).

   A shortcut to My 2nd Folder is placed on the desktop.
4. Open the shortcut to **My 2nd Folder** on the desktop.

   The shortcut opens the folder on the C: drive.
5. Close the My 2nd Folder window.

Copy a Folder to the Desktop and Delete

1. Locate **My 3rd Folder** on the desktop.
2. Copy the folder.
3. Display the desktop and paste the copy of My 3rd Folder on the desktop.
4. Drag the My 3rd Folder icon to the Recycle Bin.
5. Confirm the deletion.
6. In Windows Explorer, locate and select **My 3rd Folder** on the C: drive.
7. Click the Delete button ⊠ or press the Delete key.
8. Confirm the deletion.

Delete a Shortcut and Delete the Folder

1. On the desktop, select the shortcut to My 2nd Folder.
2. Drag it to the Recycle Bin.
3. Confirm the deletion.
4. Display My 2nd Folder in the right pane of Windows Explorer.
5. Delete the folder.
6. Confirm the deletion.
7. Close all open windows, and shut down Windows.

Exercise 5

Work with the Desktop

■ Change Desktop Appearance ■ Create a Folder on the Desktop
■ Send a Shortcut to the Desktop from the Programs Menu
■ Use Other Options on Programs Menu Right-Click Menu
■ Use Pin to Start Menu Option ■ Use Other Start Menu Options ■ Use the Start Menu

NOTES

Change Desktop Appearance

- If you have rights to do so, you can change the appearance of the Windows desktop to suit your style of working.

- If you share the machine in Windows XP or Windows 2000 and have to log in under a name that is unique to you, you can change the desktop without affecting its appearance for other users.

💻 Try It!

1. Right-click on an area of the desktop that has no icons.

2. Click Properties (R).

3. Click the Settings tab.

   Windows displays the Display Properties property sheet Settings tab, as shown in the following illustrations.

Display Properties, Settings Tab

Restrictions on Changing Desktop

Many installations where several users share the same machine—schools, for example—install security software that does not permit you to change the appearance of the desktop.

Programs such as Foolproof™ and Deep Freeze® are widely used in schools to prevent students from customizing the computer.

4. Under *Screen resolution*, click and drag the indicator to the left or right.

Set Screen Resolution

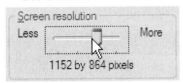

Moving the pointer to the left sets the monitor display to a lower resolution (fewer pixels or screen dots); to the right sets the display to a higher resolution if possible.

The appropriate resolution for any monitor depends on the size of the monitor, the quality of the graphics card installed in your computer, and your eyesight.

5. Click the Apply button [Apply] to review the effect of the settings before setting them.
   OR
   Click the OK button [OK] to accept the new settings.
   OR
   Click the Cancel button [Cancel] or press the Esc key to return to the desktop without changing the settings.

Create a Folder on the Desktop

- You can easily create a folder on the desktop.

🖳Try It!

1. Right-click on an area of the desktop where there are no icons.
2. Click New, Folder.
   The New Folder appears on the desktop ready to be renamed.
3. Name the folder **My 4th Folder**, and press the Enter key..
   You can drag objects from any window into this new folder.

Send a Shortcut to the Desktop from the Programs Menu

- In the last exercise, you sent a shortcut to the desktop from Windows Explorer. You can also send a shortcut to the desktop from the Start menu. Since many applications place an entry on the Start menu, you may find it helpful to create desktop shortcuts for applications you use often.

🖳Try It!

1. Click the Start button [start] .
2. Click All Programs [All Programs ▶] (P).
3. Point to Microsoft Office.
4. Point to Microsoft Office PowerPoint 2003.
5. Right-click to display a shortcut menu.

6. Point to Send To (N), and click Desktop (create shortcut)

Windows sends a shortcut for PowerPoint to the desktop.

Send PowerPoint Shortcut to the Desktop

Use Other Options on Programs Menu Right-Click Menu

- As you can see, the shortcut menu that appears when you right-click a Programs menu item offers a number of options that you may wish to take advantage of.

Windows Programs Menu Shortcut Menu

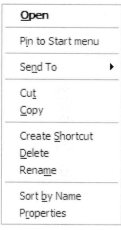

Option	Description
Open	Opens the object. If the object is an application, the application starts.
Pin to Start menu	**Windows XP only**: Places the object on the Start menu. It remains on the Start menu until you deselect this option for it. Thus, the item is *pinned* to the Start menu.
Send To	Sends a copy of, or shortcut to, the object to the place you select. Possible destinations include the Desktop, Mail Recipient, My Documents, or a disk drive with removable disk.
Cut, Copy	Lets you move or copy the item to another location.
Create Shortcut	Creates a shortcut to the object in the current location.
Delete	Sends the selected item to the Recycle Bin.
Rename	Lets you rename the item.
Sort by Name	Sorts the items on the Programs menu alphabetically. When you install new programs on your computer, they are usually added to the bottom of the Programs menu. You can use this option to sort the items alphabetically again.
Properties	Displays a property sheet for the item.

Use Pin to Start Menu Option

- If you wish such programs as Word or Excel always to appear on the Windows XP Start menu, you can use the Pin to Start menu option of the Programs menu right-click menu.

🖳Try It!

1. Click the Start button ![start] .
2. Click All Programs ![All Programs] (P).
3. Point to Microsoft Office.
4. Point to Microsoft Office Word 2003 and right-click to display the shortcut menu.
5. Select Pin to Start menu (I).

   Word will always appear on the Start menu. (You will not have to click All Programs to start Word.)

Use Other Start Menu Options

- The default Windows XP desktop does not contain My Computer, My Documents, and other icons that earlier versions placed there by default. You can easily show them on the desktop, however.

🖳Try It!

1. Click the Start button ![start] .
2. Point to My Documents, and right-click to display the shortcut menu.
3. Select Show on Desktop.

Windows XP Show on Desktop Option

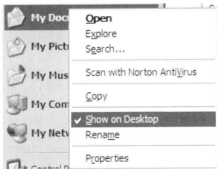

The icon for My Documents appears on the desktop. The option remains on the Start menu as well.

You can use this option for My Pictures, My Music, My Computer, and My Network Places.

Desktop Items

You can also choose which items to display on the desktop using the following steps.

1. Right-click a blank area of the desktop.
2. Click **Properties** on the shortcut menu.
3. Click the Desktop tab.
4. Click the **Customize Desktop** button

   [Customize Desktop...]

5. On the General tab, select the Desktop icons you wish to display.

Use the Start Menu

- You can use the Start menu in all the ways described so far in this lesson. You can also use the Start menu to start programs, open files, or create new Microsoft Office files. In the following Try It! activity, you will start Word, and open and locate a file from the data files for this book.

💻Try It!

1. Click the Start button **start**.

2. Point to and click Microsoft Office Word 2003.

   Word opens and displays a new, blank document.

3. Click File, Open on the menu bar to display the Open dialog box.

   The Open dialog box usually opens your My Documents folder.

4. Click the drop-down arrow on the Look in box just under the title bar and select the C: drive, as shown in the following illustration.

   The illustration shows that the drop-down list operates very much like the left pane of Windows Explorer.

Open Dialog Box

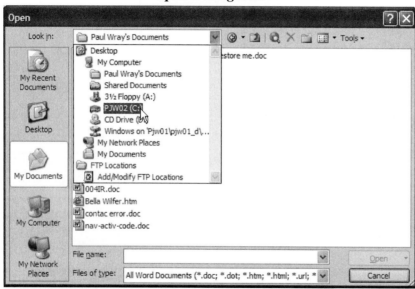

5. Click the drop-down arrow on the Look in box again and locate the Datafiles folder for this book.

6. Open the Word folder in the Datafiles folder.

7. Double-click the ⊘**05Memo** file to open the file or select the file name and click the Open button ⌊ Open ⌋.

   You can use this same general procedure in Open, Save As, and Insert dialog boxes to locate folders and files that you want to work with in any application.

8. Click File, Exit, or click the upper Close button ☒ on the Word window to close the file and exit Word.

Open the 05Memo Data File

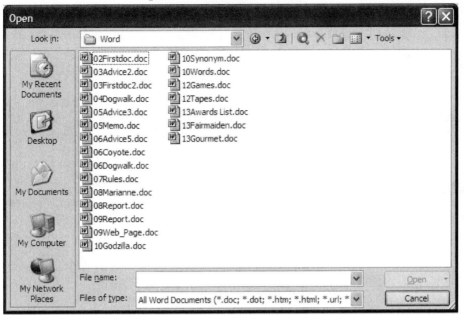

In this exercise, you will create a new folder and a new shortcut; copy a folder to the desktop; move a shortcut to the desktop; and delete objects from the desktop and from the Explorer window.

EXERCISE DIRECTIONS

Create a Folder on the Desktop

1. Right-click a blank area of the desktop (not on an icon).
2. Click New, Folder.
3. Name the folder **My 5th Folder**.

Copy and Rename a Folder

1. Select My 5th Folder.
2. Press Ctrl+C.
3. Press Ctrl+V.
4. Rename the copy **My 6th Folder**.

Delete a Folder

1. Locate **My 5th Folder** on the desktop.
2. Drag it to the Recycle Bin to delete it.
3. Confirm the deletion message.
4. Locate **My 6th Folder** on the desktop.
5. Drag it to the Recycle Bin to delete it.
6. Confirm the deletion message.
7. Locate any other folder you created on the desktop and delete it.

Send a Shortcut to the Desktop

1. Using the Start menu, Programs menu, shortcut menu, send a shortcut for Microsoft Office Access 2003 to the desktop.
2. Display the desktop and right-click a blank area.
3. On the shortcut menu, select Arrange Icons By Name.

Open a PowerPoint File

1. Using the Start menu, Programs menu, start Microsoft Office PowerPoint 2003.
2. Click File, Open, and locate the data files for PowerPoint.
3. Open the file ☺ **02Welles**.
4. Close the file and exit PowerPoint.

Lesson 3: Learn Microsoft Office 2003 Basics

Learn Microsoft Office 2003 Basics I

- ♦ About Microsoft Office 2003
- ♦ Create/Open an Office Document
- ♦ Insertion Point Movement
- ♦ Understand Menus
- ♦ Use Toolbars
- ♦ Set Toolbars on Two Rows and Always Show Full Menus
- ♦ Zoom Option
- ♦ Close Programs and Documents

Learn Microsoft Office 2003 Basics II

- ♦ Use In-Document Options Button
- ♦ Use the Task Pane
- ♦ Use Help

Learn Microsoft Office 2003 Basics I

■ About Microsoft Office 2003 ■ Create/Open an Office Document
■ Insertion Point Movement ■ Understand Menus ■ Use Toolbars
■ Set Toolbars on Two Rows and Always Show Full Menus
■ Zoom Option ■ Close Programs and Documents

NOTES

About Microsoft Office 2003

■ Microsoft Office 2003 is an integrated set of applications that can be used alone or together to create documents, spreadsheets, databases, presentations, and keep track of schedules and contacts. Microsoft Office 2003 Professional includes the following applications:

- Microsoft Office Word 2003 for word processing

- Microsoft Office Excel 2003 for spreadsheets

- Microsoft Office Access 2003 for databases

- Microsoft Office PowerPoint 2003 for presentations

- Microsoft Office Outlook 2003 for scheduling and contacts (Outlook is not covered in detail in this book.)

Create/Open an Office Document

■ Microsoft Office 2003 in Windows offers a variety of ways to start an Office application.

Start menu

The Start menu lets you:

- Click a recently used application displayed in the left pane of the menu.

- Click the icon of an Office application that you have pinned to the Start Menu.

- Open one of the applications by pointing to All Programs, locating the application's icon, and clicking it.

- Start a new Office document by pointing to All Programs, locating the New Office Document command (usually at the top of the menu), and clicking it.

- Open an existing Office document by pointing to All Programs, locating the Open Office Document command (usually near the top of the menu), and clicking it.

- Double-click the desktop shortcut for the application.

Other Microsoft Office 2003 Editions
Microsoft Office 2003 comes in many flavors. For a full description of the varieties available, see http://www.microsoft.com/office/editions/prodinfo/faq.mspx.

Windows Explorer

In Windows Explorer, you can:

- Double-click the name of a document you want to open. The appropriate application starts and the document opens.

- Double-click the name of the program in the Microsoft Office\Office folder.

Try It!

Create a document using the Start, All Programs menu:

1. Click the Start button **start**, point to All Programs, click **New Office Document**.

   Office displays a dialog box similar to the following. Note that you will have fewer options available.

New Office Document Dialog Box

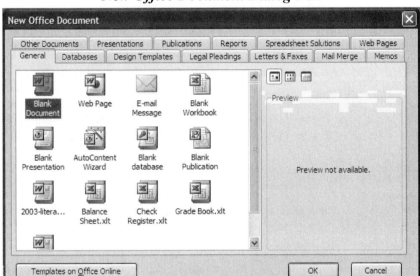

2. Double-click the document type you want to create.

   - Blank Document, Web Page, or E-mail message (Microsoft Office Word 2003). E-mail message also starts Outlook 2003.
   - Blank Workbook (Microsoft Office Excel 2003).
   - Blank Presentation or AutoContent Wizard (Microsoft Office PowerPoint 2003).
   - Blank database (Microsoft Office Access 2003).

   Office starts the application and creates the new document.

3. For this Try It! Activity, choose Blank Workbook.

Try It!

Open an existing document using the Start, All Programs menu:

1. Find out where the data files for this book are located.

   If you, your teacher, or a network administrator has not copied the files to your hard drive or a network drive, the data files will be on the CD-ROM that comes with the book.

2. Click the Start button .

3. Click the All Programs button `All Programs` ▶.

4. Click **Open Office Document**.

5. Click the Look in drop-down list and select the drive and folder that contain the data files.

6. Double-click the Datafiles folder to open it.

7. Double-click the Word folder to open it.

8. Double-click the file ⊙ **02Firstdoc**.

   Office Word starts and opens the document.

   All Windows Open dialog boxes have a similar appearance and work the same way. If the document you want is not displayed in the display/workspace, change drives and folders until you find the document you want.

Open Office Document Dialog Box

Insertion Point Movement

- You can move the insertion point (a blinking vertical line |) by pointing with the mouse and clicking to position the insertion point at the mouse pointer.

- You can also move the insertion point by using the arrow, Home, End, Page Up, and Page Down keys on the keyboard. The arrow keys are located to the right of the standard keyboard layout and are repeated on the number pad keys. To use the insertion point movement keys on the number pad, Num Lock must be off. The insertion point movement keys are shown in the illustration that follows.

Application-specific Shortcut Keys

For a complete list of shortcut keys for a specific Microsoft Office application, use the Help menu of the application. Type shortcut keys in the search box and press Enter to find the list of keys.

Insertion Point Movement Keys (Windows Keyboard)

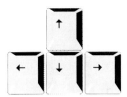

- Each key may be pressed by itself or combined with the **Ctrl** key and/or **Shift** key.

- **Ctrl+** one of these keys increases insertion point movement. For example, in Office Word the **up arrow** moves the insertion point up one line; **Ctrl+up arrow** moves the insertion point up one paragraph.

- **Shift+** one of these keys selects text as well as moves the insertion point. For example, **Shift+up arrow** selects up one line from the current insertion point position. **Ctrl+Shift+up arrow** selects to the beginning of the current paragraph from the current insertion point position.

- When held down, these keys repeat the action described.

Try It!

1. In the open Word document (**02Firstdoc**), press and hold down the right arrow key, and watch how the insertion point moves.
2. Press and hold down the left arrow key.
3. Press and hold down the down arrow, then the up arrow key.
4. Press Ctrl+right arrow key and watch how the insertion point moves.
5. Press Ctrl+left arrow.
6. Press Shift+up arrow, then press the down arrow by itself to end selection.
7. Press Ctrl+Shift+right arrow to select one word at a time.
8. Press the left arrow key by itself to end selection.

Understand Menus

- When you activate a Microsoft Office 2003 menu, some of its options may not display immediately. You can cause all the options on a menu to display by doing any of the following:

  - Double-click the menu name.

  - Click the option arrows at the bottom of the menu .

  - Linger on the menu name or option arrows without clicking.

- The following illustration shows the Word Format menu as it first appears and with all options showing.

✓

Ctrl+ and Shift+

Ctrl+up arrow means to hold down the Ctrl key and press the up arrow key. This is the standard way of indicating key combinations.

Shift+up arrow means to hold down the Shift key and press the up arrow key.

Word Format Menu

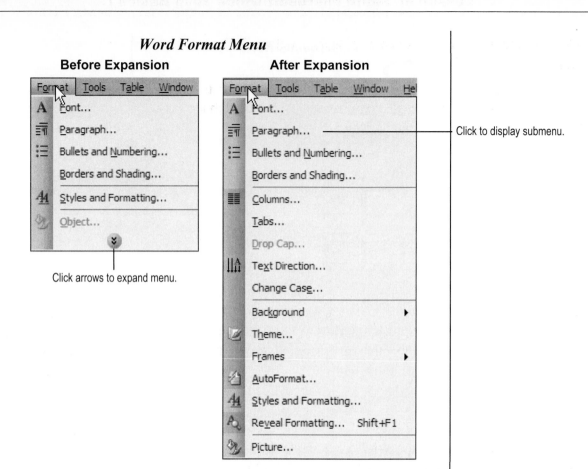

Before Expansion

After Expansion

Click to display submenu.

Click arrows to expand menu.

💻 Try It!

1. In the open Word document (**02Firstdoc**), click the <u>T</u>ools menu.
2. If it does not expand automatically, double-click the menu name to show all the options.
3. Click <u>W</u>ord Count.
4. Review the statistics that appear.
5. Click the Close button [Close]

Use Toolbars

- In Microsoft Office 2003, the Standard and Formatting toolbars appear on the same line on the application window, as shown in the following illustration.

Standard and Formatting Toolbars on One Line

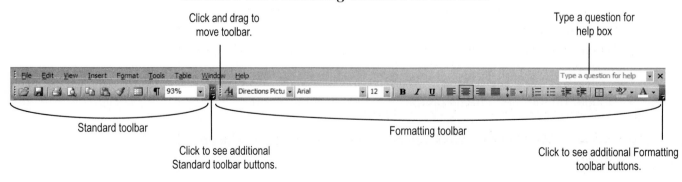

Click and drag to move toolbar.

Type a question for help box

Standard toolbar

Formatting toolbar

Click to see additional Standard toolbar buttons.

Click to see additional Formatting toolbar buttons.

- To see additional buttons for a toolbar, click the Toolbar Options button 🞂.

- You can also drag one of the toolbars to a second line. If your toolbars are already on two lines, you can drag the lower one up to put both toolbars on the same line.

💻 Try It!

1. Point to the handle ⋮ that separates the toolbars.

   The mouse pointer turns into a four-headed arrow ✛.

2. Click and drag the toolbar to a new position, as shown in the following illustration.

Drag Formatting Toolbar to New Line

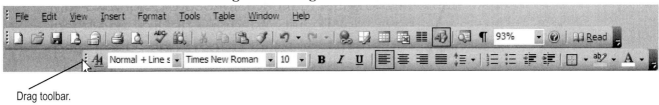

Drag toolbar.

Set Toolbars on Two Rows and Always Show Full Menus

- The illustrations in this book show the Formatting toolbar on a separate line below the Standard toolbar. You can move either toolbar to the second line, but illustrations in this book usually place the Formatting toolbar on the second line, as shown in the following illustration.

Standard and Formatting Toolbars on Separate Lines

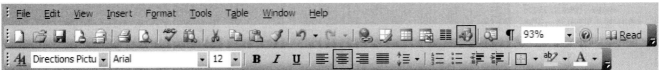

- In each Microsoft Office application (except Access), you can choose to show the toolbars on two rows and display menus that are always expanded. It is suggested that you set your toolbars and menus as outlined in the following Try It! activity.

💻 Try It!

1. Continuing to use Word, click Tools, Customize (Alt+T, C).

2. Click the Options tab (Alt+O) to display the dialog box shown in the following illustration.

3. Select Show Standard and Formatting toolbars on two rows (S). (This option is not available in Access 2003.)

4. Select Always show full menus (N).

5. Click the Close button [Close] (Enter).

6. Click the upper-most Close button ✖ on the window to close the application.

Customize Dialog Box

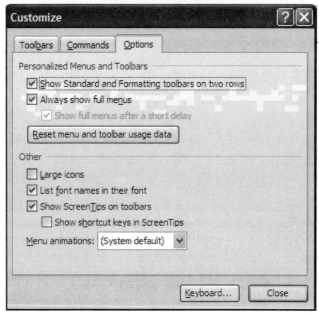

Zoom Option

- The Zoom option lets you enlarge and shrink the size of the characters displayed in a document. To activate the zoom option, do one of the following:

  - Click <u>V</u>iew, <u>Z</u>oom on the application's menu bar to display the Zoom dialog box, as shown in the illustrations on the next page. As you can see, different applications offer different zoom options.

  - In Word, the Zoom dialog box has a slightly different appearance when <u>V</u>iew, <u>P</u>rint layout has been selected before selecting <u>V</u>iew, <u>Z</u>oom.

Zoom Dialog Boxes

Excel

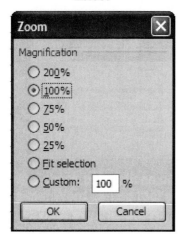

Word (Normal view)

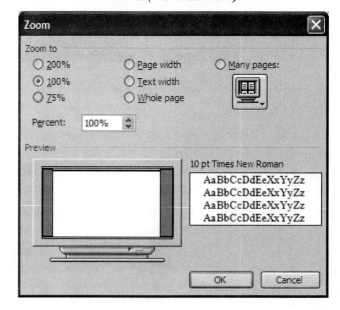

- Click the Zoom drop-down box on the Standard toolbar, as shown below.

Zoom Drop-Down Boxes

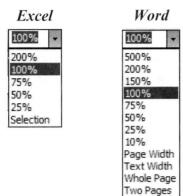

- If you have the **IntelliMouse** or another mouse that has a wheel between the two mouse buttons, hold down the Ctrl key and turn the wheel forward to zoom in (enlarge) or turn it backward to zoom out (shrink).

Close Programs and Documents

- In Microsoft Office 2003 applications, you can have several documents open simultaneously. You can close a document without closing the application.

- To make this possible, Microsoft Office 2003 application windows have two sets of control buttons (Minimize, Maximize/Restore, and Close). The top set operates on the application window; the bottom set operates on the current document as shown in the illustration that follows.

Application and Document Control Buttons

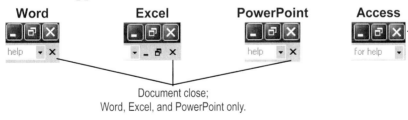

Document close;
Word, Excel, and PowerPoint only.

- To close a document and leave the application open, click on the lower Close Window button ☒ .
- To close an application, click on the upper Close button ☒.
- In **Word**, if you have more than one document open, the upper Close button ☒ closes only the current document. If only one document is open, the upper Close button closes the application.

- **Excel** is the only application that allows you to minimize, restore/maximize individual documents.

- **Access** has no lower Close button because it allows only one open database at a time. (More than one copy of Access may be open at the same time, but each instance of Access can open only one database at a time.)

IntelliMouse

✓

Close Documents and Programs
Alt+F4 closes the currently active window throughout the Windows operating system.

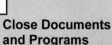

Application control; all applications have them.

- In addition, for Word, Excel, and PowerPoint documents, each open document has a separate button on the taskbar. If you have two Word documents open at the same time, each is identified by a button on the taskbar. In Access, each open object has a separate button on the taskbar.

- You can switch between open documents or objects by clicking their taskbar buttons. In the illustration, three Word documents are open. To activate one of them, you must click the button to display a shortcut menu of the open documents. In addition, one PowerPoint presentation and one Excel workbook are open.

Document Buttons on Windows Taskbar

3 Open Word documents (one is active window)   PowerPoint presentation   Excel workbook

In this exercise, you will practice opening and closing Microsoft Office 2003 applications.

EXERCISE DIRECTIONS

Open Office Word

1. Start Word using the Start menu, All Programs option.
2. Note the title bar, menu bar, and toolbars.
3. Look at the task pane at the right side of the window. You'll learn more about the task pane in Lesson 4. (If the task pane is not displayed, click View, Task Pane on the menu bar.)
4. Click Tools, Customize to open the Customize dialog box.
5. If necessary, change the options so that the toolbars display on two rows and full menus display.
6. Look at the status bar at the bottom of the window. Note the grayed-out buttons (REC, TRK, EXT, and OVR).
7. Right-click in the document window.
   Note the formatting and other options that appear.
8. Click anywhere in the document to close the shortcut menu.

Type in Word and Use Zoom

1. Type the following:

   To type a few words in Word is not hard. It is not a task that takes much time when you get to it.
2. Click on the Zoom drop-down box and select 200%.

3. Note the increased size of the letters.
4. Change the Zoom to Page Width.
5. Change the Zoom to 75%.
6. Close and exit Word by clicking on the application Close button.

Open and Close Office Excel

1. Start Excel using the Start menu, All Programs option.
2. Note the title bar, menu bar, toolbars, and the task pane.
3. Right-click on any cell in the grid.
   Note the options that appear on the shortcut menu.
4. In the Type a question for help box, type **text color** and press the Enter key.
   Note that the option Change formatting of text *probably contains the information you want.*
5. Click *Change formatting of text*, review the topics displayed, and click *Change the text color*.
6. Read the procedure, then close the Help window.
7. Close the open document by clicking on the lower of the two Close buttons—the Close Window button.
8. Close and exit Excel by clicking on the application Close button.

■ Use In-Document Options Button ■ Use the Task Pane ■ Use Help

NOTES

Use In-Document Options Button

- As you work in a Microsoft Office 2003 document, you may see a small blue box ▭ or a button such as 🔲 appear under a word or cell. When you point to the button, a drop-down arrow appears 🔲 ▾.

- When you click the button or the drop-down arrow, a drop-down list of options appears, as shown in the illustrations that follow.

- Use these options as task shortcuts.

In-Document Options Buttons

Word AutoCorrect Options

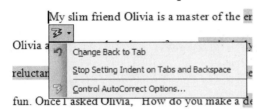

Excel AutoFill Options

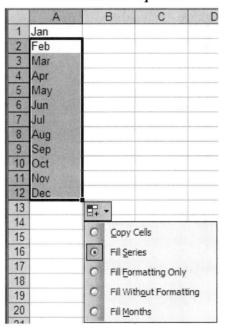

Use the Task Pane

- Each Microsoft Office 2003 application includes a task pane that appears along the right side of the application window, as shown in the following illustration of the PowerPoint window.

- When an application first opens, the task pane offers a quick way to initiate actions. In the following illustration, note that options for getting started and a list of recently opened presentations are shown.

Task pane

Microsoft Office PowerPoint Window with Task Pane

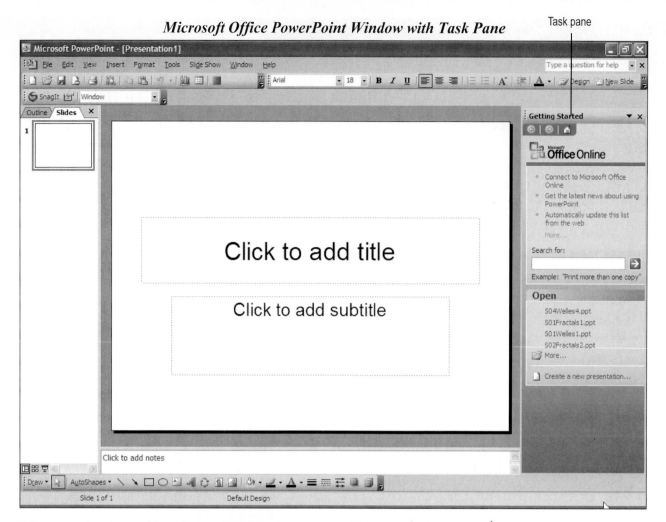

- When you begin working, the task pane changes to offer actions that are appropriate to the work you are doing. For example, if you click **Create a new presentation**, the task pane appears as shown in the following illustration.

New Presentation Task Pane

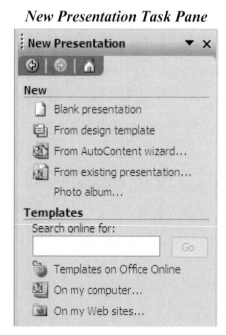

- If you click **From design template** on the New Presentation task pane, the task pane appears as in the following illustration.

Slide Design Task Pane

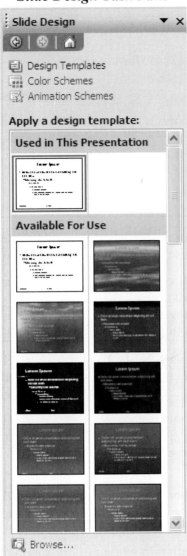

- Note that the options are categorized and that a scroll bar gives access to additional options. In this case, the categories show templates used in the current presentation and templates available for use.

- A click of the Browse button Browse... displays a dialog box so you can search for other templates.

Try It!

1. Start PowerPoint.
2. In the Getting Started task pane, click *Create a new presentation*.
3. In the New Presentation task pane, click *From design template* under *New*.

Design Template

A PowerPoint design template is a pre-defined layout and color scheme that you can use as the basis for a presentation.

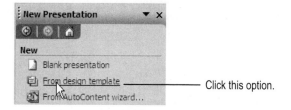

——————— Click this option.

The task pane displays images of design templates for presentations.

4. Point to the images under *Available For Use*.

5. Let the mouse pointer rest on the left image in the second row to display the ScreenTip *Ocean.pot* as shown in the following illustration, then click to select it.

Select Ocean .pot

The large slide to the left of the task pane displays the background defined by the Ocean design template.

6. Leave the PowerPoint presentation open.

Try It!

Show/Hide the Task Pane

You can show or hide the task pane.

- If the task pane is open, click its Close button ✕, or click <u>V</u>iew, Tas<u>k</u> Pane (Alt+V, K) to hide it.

- If the task pane is hidden, click <u>V</u>iew, Tas<u>k</u> Pane (Alt+V, K) to show it.

Use Help

- Microsoft Office 2003 applications offer several ways to initiate the Help function.

  - Type a question in the Type a question for help box.

  - Press the F1 key.

  - Click the Help button 🔘 on the Standard toolbar.

    NOTE: If you have a constant connection to the Internet, your Office application may search for help on the Microsoft Web site.

Use Type A Question For Help Box

- The Type a question for help box is a rectangular field at the far right end of the menu bar. The following illustration shows the Type a question for help box with the ScreenTip displayed.

Type A Question For Help Box with ScreenTip

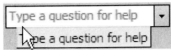

- If the Type a question for help box does not appear, you can cause it to display by completing the following Try It! activity. You can follow the same steps to turn off the display of the Type a question for help box.

Try It!

Show/Hide Type A Question For Help Box

1. Click View, Toolbars (Alt+V, T).
2. Select Customize (C) to display the Customize dialog box.
3. With the dialog box open, point to the Type a question for help box, and right-click.

   The application displays an option box as shown in the following illustration.

Show/Hide Type A Question For Help Box

Click to turn on or off.

4. To turn off the Type a question for help box, click to remove the check mark next to Show Ask a Question Box. To turn on the Type a question for help box, make sure the check mark is displayed.
5. Click the Close button [Close] on the Customize dialog box.
6. Exit PowerPoint without saving the open presentation.

Type a Question in the Type A Question For Help Box

You can activate help by typing a question in the Type a question for help box in the upper right of the application window.

After typing your question, press the Enter key. The Microsoft Office application starts a search for help on the question.

- If you have constant Internet access, the application searches for help on the Microsoft Web site.

- If you do not have constant Internet access, the application searches for help in the files installed with the Microsoft Office application.

- Even if you have a constant Internet connection, you can search for help in the files by choosing the Offline Help option at the bottom of the Search Results pane. See the next Try It! activity for how to do this.

🖳Try It!

1. Start Excel.

2. In the Type a question for help box, type **enter data**, as shown in the following illustration.

Type A Question For Help Box

3. Press the Enter key.

   If you have a live Internet connection, Excel searches for help on the Microsoft Web site.

   If you do not have a life Internet connection, Excel searches for help in the files installed with the application.

4. To search offline (not on the Web site) even if you have a live internet connection, click the option at the bottom of the Search Results Pane and select Offline Help.

5. Click the arrow button to activate the offline search, as shown in the following illustration.

   The left side shows the selection of the option; the right side shows the completed selection.

Search Offline for Help

Click to search offline.

The Illustration on the left shows the Search Results pane from the Microsoft Web site. The illustration on the right shows the Search Results pane from a search of the Office files.

Search Results Pane
Online Search Results   *Offline Search Results*

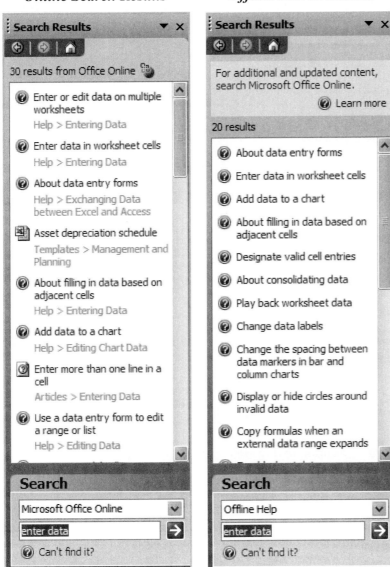

6. In the Search Results pane, click *Enter data in worksheet cells*.

   The Excel Help window opens, as shown in the following illustration. Your Help window may differ from the one illustrated, which has been expanded to make it easier to read.

Excel Help Window

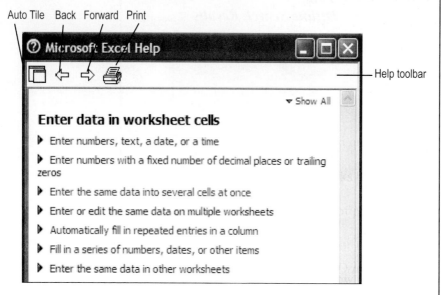

The buttons on this window are explained in the following table.

Button	Description
Auto Tile	Changes the display so that the Search Results pane, the Excel window, and the Help window display.
Back	Click this button to return to the previous topic.
Forward	Click this button after using the Back button to return to a topic you've viewed before.
Print	Click to send the currently displayed topic to the printer.

7. Click the arrow to the left of *Enter numbers, text, a date or a time.*

   A procedure appears, as shown in the following illustration.

Help Procedure

Enter data in worksheet cells

▼ Enter numbers, text, a date, or a time

1. Click the cell where you want to enter data.
2. Type the data and press ENTER or TAB.

   Numbers and text in a list

   1. Enter data in a cell in the first column, and then press TAB to move to the next cell.
   2. At the end of the row, press ENTER to move to the beginning of the next row.
   3. If the cell at the beginning of the next row doesn't become active, click **Options** on the **Tools** menu, and then click the **Edit** tab. Under **Settings**, select the **Move selection after Enter** check box, and then click **Down** in the **Direction** box.

   Dates   Use a slash or a hyphen to separate the parts of a date; for example, type **9/5/2002** or **5-Sep-2002**. To enter today's date, press CTRL+; (semicolon).

   Times   To enter a time based on the 12-hour clock, type a space and then **a** or **p** after the time; for example, **9:00 p.** Otherwise, Microsoft Excel enters the time as AM. To enter the current time, press CTRL+SHIFT+: (colon).

8. Click the Close button ☒ on the Help pane.

The Help pane closes, and the Excel window expands.

9. Close Excel without saving the document by clicking on the

application Close button ▾ _ 🗗 ✕ .

Application Close button

Office Assistant

■ By default, Microsoft Office 2003 applications do not activate the Office Assistant. Therefore, this text does not describe its use. You can control whether the Office Assistant displays by completing the following steps.

1. Click the Help menu.

2. Click **Show the Office Assistant** or **Hide the Office Assistant**.

In this exercise, you will open and close Microsoft Office 2003 applications and use Help.

EXERCISE DIRECTIONS

Open PowerPoint

1. Start PowerPoint using any method you prefer.
2. Note the title bar, menu bar, and toolbars.
3. Look at the task pane at the right side of the window.
4. Click Tools, Customize to open the Customize dialog box.
5. Change the options so that the toolbars display on two rows and full menus display.
6. Look at the status bar at the bottom of the window. Note Slide number, template name (Default Design), and language.
7. Note also the buttons at the lower left of the window. Linger on the buttons to display the ScreenTip for each one—Normal View, Slide Sorter View, and Slide Show from current slide (Shift+F5).
8. Click in the box—called a placeholder—that says *Click to add title.*
9. Type your name, then click anywhere outside the box.
10. Close the PowerPoint application without saving the presentation.

Use Help in Word

1. Open Word.
2. In the Type a question for help box in the upper right of the window, type: **text color**

Illustration A

3. Press the Enter key.
4. Click the option that reads *Change the color of text.*
5. Briefly review the procedure.
6. Click the blue word *toolbar* in the procedure to open the explanation of how to display a toolbar.
7. After reviewing the explanation, click on the blue *toolbar* again to close the explanation.

   ✓ *You can also click the Show All option* ▾ Show All *in the upper right of the Help pane to display all explanations in a help topic.*

   ✓ *You can then click the Hide All option* ✕ Hide All *to close the explanations.*

8. Click the Close button ☒ to close the Help window.
9. Close the open document by clicking on the lower of the two Close buttons.
10. Click the No button ❘ No ❘ when asked if you want to save the changes to the document.
11. Close and exit Word by clicking on the application Close button.

Open and Close Access

1. Start Access using the method you prefer.
2. Click the New button on the taskbar.
3. Note the options in the New File task pane.
4. Click *Blank database* under *New*.
   The File New Database dialog box opens, asking you to name and save the new database.
   Access requires that you name and save any new database that you create.
5. Click the Cancel button at the bottom of the dialog box.
6. Exit Access by clicking the application Close button.

Lesson 4: Microsoft Office Word 2003

Exercise 1: Become Familiar with Microsoft Office Word 2003
- The Word Window
- Features of Word's Window
- The Menu Bar
- Create a New Document Using the Task Pane
- Save an Unnamed Document
- Save As

Exercise 2: Use Word's Standard Toolbar
- The Standard Toolbar
- Create a New Document Using the Toolbar
- Open a Document
- Save
- The Date Function
- Print Preview
- Print
- What is a Paragraph?
- Proofreader's Mark for Paragraph

Exercise 3: Format Paragraphs and Text
- The Formatting Toolbar
- Align Paragraphs
- Fonts and Font Names
- Change Font
- Change Font Size
- Use Bold, Italic, Underline

Exercise 4: Use Proofing Tools
- AutoCorrect
- AutoFormat As You Type
- Automatic Spell Checking
- Spell Check
- Automatic Grammar Checking
- Grammar Check

Exercise 5: Use Editing Tools
- Default Tab Stops
- Insert and Overtype Modes
- Undo
- Redo
- Proofreader's Marks for Bold and Italic

Exercise 6: Enhance the Text
- Highlight
- Change Text Color
- Use Other Text Enhancements
- Use Symbols

Exercise 7: Use Bullets and Numbers; Cut, Copy, and Paste
- Introduction to Bullets and Numbering
- Bullets
- Numbering
- Cut, Copy, and Paste

Exercise 8: Format Paragraphs
- Change Line Spacing
- Control Spacing between Paragraphs
- Create Indented Paragraphs
- Use Format Painter
- Use the New Line Key

Exercise 9: Manage Multi-page Documents
- Insert Page Breaks
- Use Headers and Footers
- Use Page Setup
- Set Margins

Exercise 10: Find and Replace Text
- Use the Thesaurus
- Find and Replace Text

Exercise 11: Create Tables
- Introduction to Tables
- Create a Table
- Move within a Table
- Enter Text in a Table
- Use the Tables and Borders Toolbar

Exercise 12: Format Tables
- Insert and Delete Columns and Rows
- Adjust Column Widths
- Position a Table Horizontally
- Add Shading to a Cell
- Use Table AutoFormat

Exercise 13:
- Challenge Exercises

Exercise 1

Become Familiar with Microsoft Office Word 2003
■ The Word Window ■ Features of Word's Window
■ The Menu Bar ■ Create a New Document Using the Task Pane
■ Save an Unnamed Document ■ Save As

NOTES

The Word Window

■ When you start Word, the Word window opens. The following illustration shows important features of the window. Your window may differ from the one shown.

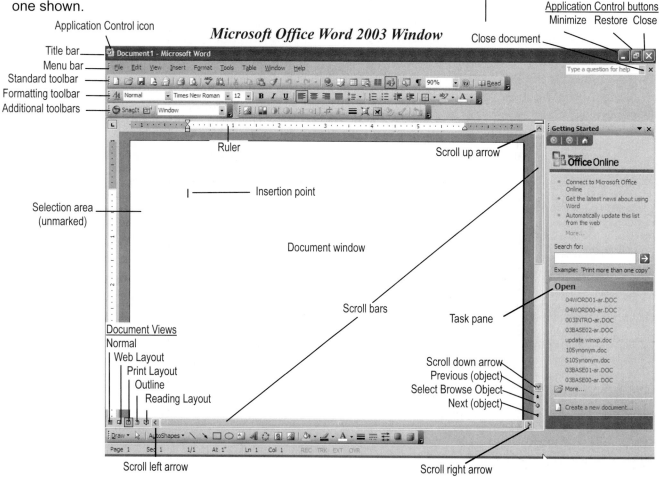

Microsoft Office Word 2003 Window

Features of Word's Window

■ Many of the items on the Word window are already familiar to you. Those already described in Lesson 2 are not included here.

Window Item	Description
📄 **Application Control icon**	Displays the Application Control menu. The active commands on this menu are the same as the Application Control buttons at the right side of the window.

Window Item	Description
Toolbars	By default, Word displays two toolbars. Other toolbars are available if you click <u>V</u>iew, <u>T</u>oolbars (Alt+V, T).
Ruler	Lets you view and set paragraph indents, tab stops, page margins, table column widths, and page column widths. If the ruler is not displayed, click <u>V</u>iew, Ru<u>l</u>er (Alt+V, L).
Selection area	Unmarked area along the left side of the document window. When you move the mouse pointer into this area, it turns into a right-pointing arrow. When you click while pointing with this arrow, you select the line, paragraph, or object to the right.
View buttons	Display the document in one of several views. **Normal** view is best for typing, editing, and formatting text quickly. **Web Layout** view shows the document as it would appear on a Web page. Text appears larger and wraps to fit the window—not the way it will actually print. **Print Layout** view is used when you want to position graphics on a page, edit headers and footers, and adjust page margins. It is also used for working with page columns and drawing objects. **Outline** view lets you build an outline using Word's built-in heading styles. You can then build a document based on the outline in Normal or Print Layout view and switch back to Outline view to see its structure. **Reading Layout** view displays two pages of a document side-by-side in the Word window.

Move Toolbars
The toolbars initially appear on the same line on the window. You can drag the Formatting toolbar to a separate line, as described in the Basics lesson.

The Menu Bar

<u>F</u>ile <u>E</u>dit <u>V</u>iew <u>I</u>nsert F<u>o</u>rmat <u>T</u>ools T<u>a</u>ble <u>W</u>indow <u>H</u>elp

To use shortcut keys to display a menu, hold down the Alt key and press the underlined letter to open the menu. For example, to open the File menu, press Alt+F.

Menu	Contains commands for:
<u>F</u>ile	Creation, retrieval, layout, storage, and printing of files.
<u>E</u>dit	Rearranging document contents, undoing and repeating actions, and finding and replacing text and objects.
<u>V</u>iew	Choosing the way in which a document is displayed, and working with headers and footers.
<u>I</u>nsert	Inserting objects and files in documents.
F<u>o</u>rmat	Changing the appearance of text and documents.
<u>T</u>ools	Checking spelling and grammar, performing mail merge, running macros, and customizing documents.
T<u>a</u>ble	Creating and formatting tables and sorting data.
<u>W</u>indow	Displaying currently open documents.
<u>H</u>elp	Getting explanations of Word's components, commands, and options.

Create a New Document Using the Task Pane

- When Word starts, a new document is ready for you to begin typing. The title bar usually displays *Document1*. The next new document created during a **session** is called *Document2*. Each succeeding new document gets the next higher number.

Try It!

1. Start Word.

   Word creates a new blank document when it starts. Normally, you begin working in the new document that Word creates on starting. In this activity, however, you are going to create another new document.

2. Click File, New on the menu bar.
   The task pane appears if it is not already displayed.

3. In the New Document task pane, under *New*, click *Blank document*.
   OR
   Under *New from template*, click *Normal.dot*, which is the name of Word's **default template**.
   This action creates a second document (probably with the name Document2 *in the title bar) using Word* **default** *margins, font, font size, and paragraph format.*

- **Important Note:** Look at the Windows taskbar. The taskbar now has buttons representing Word documents, as shown below:

Word Taskbar Buttons

- The original new document is on the left in the illustration. The new document just created is on the right. It is active as indicated by the button's appearance. You can switch between the two documents by clicking the taskbar button of the one that is not active. When you have more documents open than can comfortably fit on the taskbar, the system displays a single button that indicates how many documents are open:

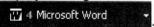

- You can also switch from one document to another by clicking Window and the document name or by pressing Ctrl+F6.

Save an Unnamed Document

- Although Word displays something like *Document2* on the title bar, the document is not named and stored permanently until you save it.

Try It!

1. Display either blank document.

2. Type your name and address in the document. Press Enter after each line.

3. Click File, Save As (Alt+F, A).
   OR
   Click File, Save (Alt+F, S).

Session

A session begins when you start an application and ends when you exit the application.

Template

A template is a document that defines the basic structure of a Word document. A template provides the pattern for a document.

The default template is *Normal.dot*. Unless you change them, the defaults are as follows:

- Top and bottom margins at 1".

- Left and right margins at 1.25".

- Paragraph is single-spaced.

- Font is Times New Roman, 12 point, regular.

The template also contains a variety of other information that defines the appearance and structure of a document.

For more about templates, enter **template** in the Type a question for help box, and select About templates from the list of options.

82

OR

Click the Save button .

When you choose Save As or Save for an unnamed document, the Save As dialog box appears, as shown below.

Save As Dialog Box

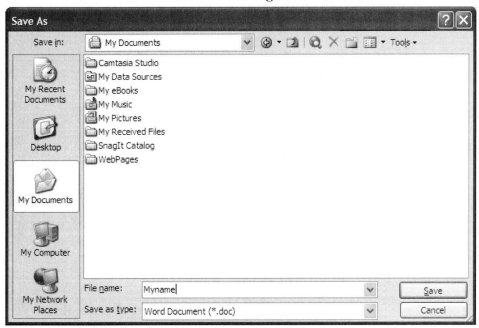

4. Click the drop-down arrow ▾ at the right of the Save in box and select the drive and folder into which you want to save the document.

5. Click in the File name box and type **Myname**.
   You can type over or delete the name that Word suggests.

6. Click the Save button , or press Enter.
   Word saves the document in the folder you specify with the name **Myname**.

Save As

- When you want to save an existing document under another name, use the following procedure.

🖳 **Try It!**

1. Add your phone number as the last line in the document.

2. Click File, Save As (Alt+F, A).
   The Save As dialog box appears.

3. Select the drive and folder into which you want to save the document.

4. Click in the File name box and type **Myname2**.
   You can type over or delete the name that Word suggests.

5. Click the Save button , or press Enter.
   Word saves the document in the folder you specify with the name Myname2.

Default

A default value is a parameter used by the software unless you change it. Word sets default margins, font, font size, and paragraph formats so that you can begin working without worrying about those settings.

Word also sets My Documents as the default folder for saving files you create. If you want to save a file elsewhere, you have to navigate to the folder and save it else.

Close Buttons

Word, unlike the other Microsoft Office applications, displays two Close buttons.

When more than one Word document is open, click on either Close button on the window to close the document. The other open documents will remain open.

6. Close the document.

   Note that the other blank document remains open.

7. If you are continuing with the Exercise Directions, leave the blank document open.

   OR

   If you are not continuing with the Exercise Directions:

   a. Click the document Close Window button to close the blank document.

   b. Click the application Close button to exit Word.

In this exercise, you will type three paragraphs and watch how the Word window changes. Pay special attention to the status bar at the bottom of the window. You will also correct typing errors and save the document.

EXERCISE DIRECTIONS

Create and Save a Document

1. Create a new Word document.
2. Click File, Save As.
3. In the Save in box, select the drive and folder where you want the document to be stored.
4. Type **Firstdoc** in the File name box.
5. Press Enter or click Save.

   The file is saved as Firstdoc.

   From now on, the Exercise Directions will simply tell you to save the document and what name to give it. You'll have to remember to complete the dialog box as necessary. Refer to the directions on page 82.

Simple Typing

1. Beginning at the first available line in the document window, type the text shown in Illustration A.

   If you make a mistake while typing, don't worry about correcting it until you have typed the entire document. Ignore any red or green wavy lines that appear.

   Word's AutoCorrect feature may correct some typing errors automatically. AutoCorrect is described in Exercise 4 of this lesson.

2. Press Enter twice at the end of each paragraph to create a blank line between paragraphs.
3. Press Ctrl+S or click File, Save, to save the document.

   No dialog box appears. The document is saved with its current name.

Correct Errors

1. Read through what you typed and check for errors.
2. To correct errors, point with the mouse to the word you need to change and click once.
   This action places the insertion point (blinking vertical line) in the incorrect word.
3. Once in the word, use one or more of the following actions to correct it:
   - Position the insertion point next to the error using the mouse pointer or the left and right arrow keys.
   - Type the correction.
   - Press the Delete key to erase a letter to the right of the insertion point.
   OR
   - Press the Backspace key to erase a letter to the left of the insertion point.
4. Save the document.
5. Close the document, and exit Word.

Illustration A

You can use menus to do much of your work in Office Word 2003. You can open a menu by clicking on the menu name (File) or by holding down the Alt key and pressing the underlined letter on the menu.

You can select an item on a menu by pressing the underlined letter of the item. For example, a shortcut to display the Save As dialog box is Alt+F, A. (Hold down the Alt key while you press the F key, then release it and press the A key.)

As you type and edit, sneak a peek at the status bar. Its information changes as you type. It tells you where the insertion point is in the document. It gives the page and section numbers. It also tells you how far down from the top of the paper (At 2.9") you are, the line number of the page, and the column number of the insertion point.

Exercise 2

Use Word's Standard Toolbar

■ The Standard Toolbar ■ Create a New Document Using the Toolbar
■ Open a Document ■ Save ■ The Date Function ■ Print Preview
■ Print ■ What is a Paragraph? ■ Proofreader's Mark for Paragraph

Standard Toolbar

New Open Save Print Print Preview

NOTES

The Standard Toolbar

■ The Standard toolbar, shown above, has buttons for creating, opening, saving, and printing documents. It also has buttons for checking spelling, cutting, copying, pasting, and undoing and redoing typing and commands. Toolbar buttons are described as you use them in the exercises in this lesson. The toolbar, shown above, has a button for creating e-mail documents and for searching for documents on your computer or network.

Create a New Document Using the Toolbar

■ To create a new document using the Standard toolbar, click the New

button ☐. Word creates a blank document using the defaults. It does not display the New dialog box. Clicking the New button is the same as:

- Pressing Ctrl+N.

OR

- Clicking File, New, (Alt+F, N).

OR

- Clicking *Blank Document* in the task pane.

Open a Document

■ You can open a document using the Standard toolbar or the menu.

🖵Try It!

1. Start Word.

   Click the Open button 📂, press Ctrl+O, or click File, Open (Alt+F, O). *Word displays the Open dialog box, shown on the next page.*

2. Open 🖫**Firstdoc** from your files, or open ⊙**02Firstdoc** from the data files. (Select the file name and click the Open

   button [Open ▼], or double-click the file name.)

3. Save the document as **Firstdoc2**, but leave it open.

■ **Note:** When you start Word and open a document, Word closes the new document it created on starting unless you have changed the new document. That's why when you open **Firstdoc** only one document appears on the Windows taskbar.

Open Dialog Box

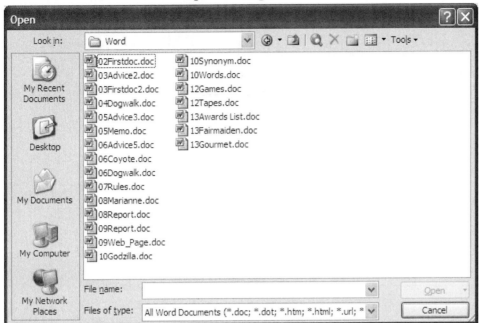

Save

■ If a document has been saved once, it has a name. If you make changes to the document, you need to save it again. Save your work often. Any changes that have not been saved may be lost if your computer suffers a power failure or the Microsoft Office application stops responding.

🖥️ Try It!

Change the Document

1. Place the insertion point at the top of **Firstdoc2**.

2. Press the Enter key twice.

3. Press the up arrow key twice to move the insertion point back to the top of the document.

4. Type **Use Menus**.

5. Click the Save button , press Ctrl+S, or click File, Save (Alt+F, S) to save the changes.

AutoRecover

Microsoft Office 2003 includes a feature that helps you recover lost data automatically.

If an Office program runs into a problem and freezes (stops responding), you can often close the program in a controlled way using the Windows Close Programs or Windows Security feature.

When you re-open the Office application, a Document Recovery task pane appears that lists the files recovered when you shut down the Microsoft Office application.

You can then choose the document(s) you want to recover if any.

Note that such recovery is not always possible so you still must save your work regularly.

The Date Function

- Word offers you an easy way to insert the current date into a document. The Date function is particularly useful in letters and memos.

⌨ Try It!

1. Place the insertion point at the top of **Firstdoc2**.

2. Press the Enter key twice.

3. Press the up arrow key twice or Ctrl+Home to move the insertion point back to the top of the document.

4. Click Insert, Date and Time to display the dialog box shown in the illustration below.

Date and Time Dialog Box

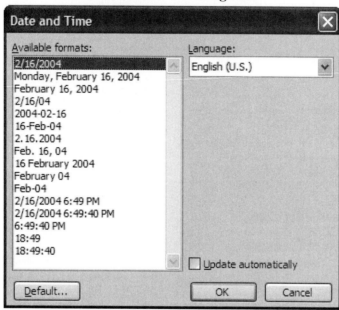

5. Double-click the date format selected in the illustration, or select it and click the OK button .

   Note the option at the bottom of the dialog box, Update automatically. If you select this option, the inserted date changes automatically when you open the document on another day.

   When you see the phrase Today's Date in the exercise illustrations in this book, insert the current date without selecting the Update automatically option.

6. Save **Firstdoc2**, but leave the document open.

Print Preview

- To see a document as it will appear when printed, use Print Preview. The document appears in the Print Preview window, as shown in the illustration on the next page. Your screen size and appearance may differ from the illustration.

Update automatically

For most of your letters, memos, and reports, it is a good idea **not** to update the date automatically. Often, you want to retain the original date of the document as a permanent record.

Print Preview

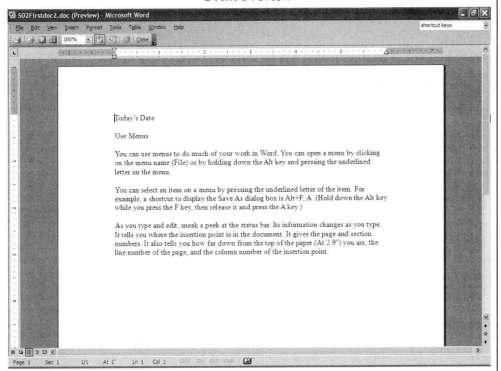

💻Try It!

1. Click the Print Preview button 🔍, or click <u>F</u>ile, Print Pre<u>v</u>iew (Alt+F, V).

    Note the menu bar and toolbar that appear in the Print Preview window.

Print Preview Toolbar

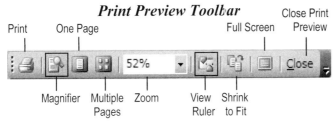

2. Move the pointer to the document window and click.

    When the pointer reaches the document, it changes to a magnifying glass. When you click the document, the preview enlarges to 100%.

3. Click the document again.

    The preview reduces to a smaller percentage. You can also use the Zoom drop-down list to enlarge and reduce your view of the document.

4. Click the document again to return to 100% magnification.

5. Click the Magnifier button 🔍 to turn it off.

    When you move the pointer back to the document, it changes to an I-beam, indicating that you can edit the document in Print Preview.

6. Click on the word *select* in the second paragraph.

    You are now in edit mode.

7. Click the Magnifier button 🔍 again to turn it back on and end edit mode.

8. Click the One Page button 🗔.

   The view shows the entire page.

9. To close the Print Preview window and return to the main Word window, click the Close button `Close`, or press the Esc key.

Print

- When you are satisfied with the document's appearance, you are ready to print it.

💻 Try It!

1. Click the Print button 🖨.

   This action sends the current document or selection directly to the printer. It does not display the Print dialog box.

   OR

   Press Ctrl+P, and click the OK button `OK` or press Enter.

   OR

   Click File, Print (Alt+F, P), and click the OK button `OK` or press Enter.

2. Close **Firstdoc2**, and exit Word.

What is a Paragraph?

- Word does not format text line-by-line. Instead, it formats each paragraph as a unit. Word defines a paragraph as the text between the place you press Enter and the place you press it again. If you want a blank line, you press the Enter key twice, creating a blank paragraph that also happens to be a blank line. The illustration below shows three paragraphs.

This·is·a·paragraph·of·one·line.¶
¶
The·preceding·paragraph·has·no·text,·while·this·one·has·more·than·
one·line.·The·paragraph·is·the·major·unit·of·formatting·in·Word.·
Each·time·you·press·the·Enter·key,·you·are·creating·a·paragraph·
whether·you·have·no·text·in·it,·one·word,·several·words,·or·several·
lines.¶

Proofreader's Mark for Paragraph

- The proofreader's mark for paragraph is the ⁋ symbol. When you see this symbol, insert a paragraph (press the Enter key).

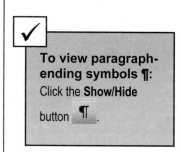

✓

To view paragraph-ending symbols ¶:
Click the **Show/Hide** button ¶.

In this exercise, you will create and format some notes of advice about using a word processor.

EXERCISE DIRECTIONS

Create a Document

1. Start Word to create a new document and type the text shown in Illustration A. Start at the first available line in the document window.

   The illustration uses one space after a period at the end of a sentence.

   Don't worry if your lines end at different words from those shown in the illustration.

2. Save the document as **Advice2**.
3. Correct any errors you find.

4. Use the Date function to replace *Today's Date* on the first line of the new document with the current date.
5. Press Enter where the proofreader's mark for a new paragraph appears.

   If you make a mistake, don't worry about correcting it until you have typed the entire document.

6. Print Preview the document.
7. Print the document.
8. Save the document.
9. Close the document, and exit Word.

Illustration A

Today's Date ⁊⁊ Learn what you need to know to finish the job at hand. As you take on more difficult assignments, you can expand your knowledge. ⁊⁊ For example, to use Microsoft Office Word to create documents, you need only to start Microsoft Office Word, type, press Enter to end paragraphs and create blank lines, save, and print what you've created. ⁊⁊ If you can handle these, you can create a wide variety of documents. You can write full-block letters, single-spaced stories, acceptable memos, class notes, and e-mail messages. ⁊

Exercise 3

Format Paragraphs and Text
■ The Formatting Toolbar ■ Align Paragraphs ■ Fonts and Font Names
■ Change Font ■ Change Font Size ■ Use Bold, Italic, Underline

Formatting Toolbar

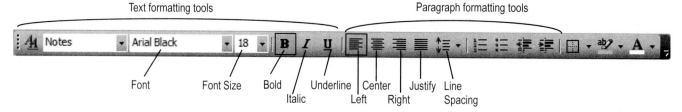

Text formatting tools   Paragraph formatting tools

Font   Font Size   Bold   Underline   Center   Justify   Line
                              Italic   Left   Right   Spacing

NOTES

The Formatting Toolbar

■ Using the buttons on the Formatting toolbar, you can apply the most commonly used formats to text and paragraphs. **Text** formatting controls the look of the letters, numbers, and symbols in a document. **Paragraph** formatting controls the position and spacing of the lines.

Align Paragraphs

■ The Formatting toolbar offers four paragraph alignment options, as shown in the illustration that follows.

Align Left	*Center*
A left-aligned paragraph begins at the left and wraps unevenly on the right.	A centered paragraph has lines that are evenly divided on each side of the midpoint. Shorter lines look like this.
Align Right	*Justify*
In a right-aligned paragraph, text begins at the right margin and wraps unevenly at the left margin.	In a justified paragraph, the text begins at the left but wraps evenly at the right margin. Word adds space to each line to make all lines, except the last, end at the same place.

💻**Try It!**

1. Open ⌨**Firstdoc2** from your files, or open 💿**03Firstdoc2** from the data files.

2. Save the document as **Firstdoc3**.

3. Place your insertion point in the second full paragraph, the one that starts *You can select….*

4. Click the Center button ▤, or press Ctrl+E.
   The paragraph is centered.

5. Click the Align Right button ▤, or press Ctrl+R.
   The paragraph is right-aligned.

6. Click the Justify button ▤, or press Ctrl+J.
   The paragraph is justified.

7. Click the Align Left button ▤, or press Ctrl+L.
   The paragraph is left-aligned.

8. Leave **Firstdoc3** open.

Fonts and Font Names

- The term **font**, also called typeface, refers to the look of characters.

Serif and Sans Serif Fonts

- **Alphanumeric** fonts traditionally used for the body of documents are divided into two general groups, serif and sans serif.

Alphanumeric
Consisting of letters, numbers, and punctuation marks.

Serif Face Times New Roman	Sans Serif Face Arial
Times New Roman characters have serifs—little curlicues on the character. Some people feel that serifs help guide and focus the eye when you read printed matter.	Arial characters have no serifs. Most people find that when they read material online, it is easier to read sans serif rather than serif typefaces.

Decorative and Script Fonts

- Two other alphanumeric font types, decorative and script, are used widely for emphasis and capturing the reader's attention.

Decorative Face Braggadocio	Script Face Brush Script MT
Braggadocio may be used for flyers and attention-getting headings.	Brush Script, in small doses, is useful for emphasis and gaining a reader's attention.

Symbol Font

- A fifth font type consists of symbols.

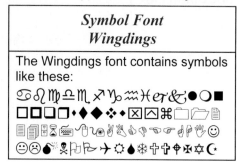

Change Font

■ By default, Word uses Times New Roman, a serif font. In this exercise, you'll use Times New Roman and Arial, a sans serif font that also comes with Windows.

💻 Try It!

1. Select the first three words of the first full paragraph in **Firstdoc3**.

2. Click the Font drop-down list arrow 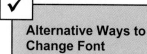 ── Click drop-down arrow.

   The drop-down list of fonts appears as shown in the following illustration.

   Font Drop-Down List

3. Select Arial.

   The text changes from Times New Roman to Arial.

4. Leave **Firstdoc3** open.

✓

Alternative Ways to Change Font
Press **Ctrl+D**.

OR

Click **Format**, **Font**, **Font** (Alt+O, F, Alt+F).

These two actions display the Font dialog box. You can change the font using the dialog box.

OR

Press **Ctrl+Shift+F**.

This selects the font name box on the Formatting toolbar. You can then use the cursor down—and up—arrow key to select a different font, and then press Enter.

Change Font Size

- By default, Word uses a font size of 12 points.

Try It!

1. Select the first three words of the second full paragraph of **Firstdoc3** if they are not already selected.

2. Click the Font Size drop-down list arrow 12 ▾.
   The font size drop-down list appears as shown in the following illustration.

Font Size Drop-Down List

3. Change the font size to 14 points.
   The first three words are larger than the rest of the paragraph.

4. Leave **Firstdoc3** open.

Use Bold, Italic, Underline

- **Bold**, *italic*, and underline are used for emphasis. Follow a simple rule for using these embellishments: emphasize sparingly. These techniques are used for headings, for book titles, and to draw attention to an important point. When overdone, they detract from the appearance of your work.

Try It!

1. Select the first word of the first full paragraph of **Firstdoc3**.

2. Click the Bold button **B**, or press Ctrl+B.
   Bold increases the width, height, and darkness of characters.

3. Select the second word of the first full paragraph of **Firstdoc3**.

4. Click the Italic button *I*, or press Ctrl+I.
   Italic slants the text to the right.

5. Select the third word of the first full paragraph of **Firstdoc3**.

6. Click the Underline button <u>U</u>, or press Ctrl+U.
   Underline draws a single line under the characters.

7. Save and close **Firstdoc3**, and exit Word unless you are continuing with the Exercise Directions.

- The Font dialog box offers a number of other options for embellishing text. These will be described as you have occasion to use them in the exercises in this book.

Point

A point is a printer's measure equal to 1/72 of an inch.

The **point size** of a font is the height of its tallest character.

In this exercise, you will use paragraph and text formatting to change the appearance of the document you created in the previous exercise.

EXERCISE DIRECTIONS

Change Paragraph Formats

1. Open 🖮 **Advice2** from your files, or open 💿 **03Advice2** from the data files. It is shown in Illustration A.
2. Click <u>F</u>ile, Save <u>A</u>s and save the document as **Advice3**.
3. Replace *Today's date* with the current date.
4. Place the insertion point in the date.
5. Click the Align Right button ▤ to align the date at the right margin.
6. Press the End key to move the insertion point to the end of the line.
7. Press the Enter key twice.
8. Type the following title: **Advice to New Users**
9. Click the Center button ▤ to center the title.
10. Save the document.

Change Paragraph Formats

1. Click <u>E</u>dit, Select A<u>ll</u>, or press Ctrl+A.
2. Click on the Font Size drop-down list arrow [14 ▾].
3. Change the font size to 14 point.
4. Click on the Font drop-down list arrow [Arial ▾]
5. Change the Font to Arial.
6. Select the centered title (*Advice to New Users*).
7. Change the font size to 24 point.
8. Make the text of the heading bold and italic.
9. Save the document.

Save and Print the Document

1. Print Preview the document.
2. Print the document.
3. Compare your results to Illustration B.
4. Close the document, and exit Word.

Illustration A. Advice2

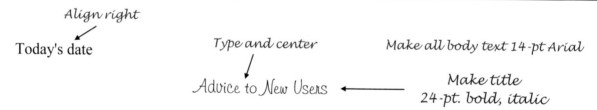

Align right

Today's date

Type and center

Make all body text 14-pt Arial

Advice to New Users ←

Make title
24-pt. bold, italic

Learn what you need to know to finish the job at hand. As you take on more difficult assignments, you can expand your knowledge.

For example, to use Microsoft Office Word to create documents, you need only to start Microsoft Office Word, type, press Enter to end paragraphs and create blank lines, then save and print what you've created.

If you can handle these, you can create a wide variety of documents. You can write full-block letters, single-spaced stories, acceptable memos, class notes, and e-mail messages.

Illustration B. Desired Result (Advice3)

Today's Date

Advice to New Users

Learn what you need to know to finish the job at hand. As you take on more difficult assignments, you can expand your knowledge.

For example, to use Microsoft Office Word to create documents, you need only to start Microsoft Office Word, type, press Enter to end paragraphs and create blank lines, then save and print what you've created.

If you can handle these, you can create a wide variety of documents. You can write full-block letters, single-spaced stories, class notes, acceptable memos, and e-mail messages.

Exercise 4

Use Proofing Tools

■ AutoCorrect ■ AutoFormat As You Type ■ Automatic Spelling Check
■ Spelling Check ■ Automatic Grammar Checking ■ Grammar Check

NOTES

AutoCorrect

- The AutoCorrect feature automatically corrects a number of common typing mistakes. For example, if you type *teh* or *hte*, Word changes it to *the* as soon as you press the spacebar. Click <u>T</u>ools, <u>A</u>utoCorrect to display the AutoCorrect dialog box shown below.

Save AutoCorrect Entries

AutoCorrect entries are saved with the Normal template (the one Word uses to create blank documents).

To save the Normal template and the entries you add to AutoCorrect, hold down the Shift key and click **<u>F</u>ile, Save All**.

Word saves all open documents and templates. If an open document has not been saved, the Save As dialog box appears so you can name it.

AutoCorrect Dialog Box, AutoCorrect Tab

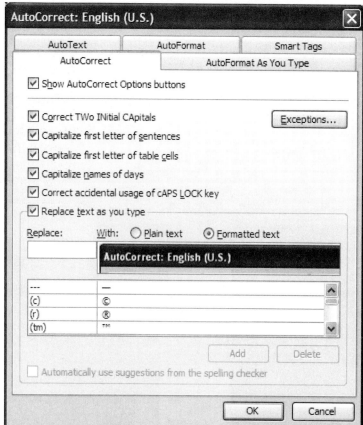

- Note the check box options on the dialog box. These indicate common errors that Word can correct automatically.

  - **Correct TWo INitial CApitals** changes the second letter of a word to lowercase if you accidentally type two capital letters at the beginning.

  - **Capitalize first letter of <u>s</u>entences** changes the first letter of a sentence to a capital letter if you forget to capitalize it yourself.

- **Capitalize first letter of table cells** changes the first letter of an entry in a table cell.

- **Capitalize names of days** changes the first letter of a day of the week to a capital letter.

- **Correct accidental usage of cAPS LOCK key** changes all characters to their proper case (upper or lower).

- **Replace text as you type** tells Word to replace selected text with what you type on the keyboard.

- The **Replace... With** feature lets you customize AutoCorrect to your typing habits.

- Common symbols can be created through the AutoCorrect feature. For example, to insert a copyright © symbol, you can type (c). Word changes the entry to the symbol.

- Sometimes you may wish to override an automatic correction. For example, you might want to type *(c)* rather than the copyright symbol. To do so, press Ctrl+Z immediately after typing the entry that gets corrected. Word undoes the correction and retains what you typed.

- Many commonly misspelled words are already included in Word's AutoCorrect feature. Review the sentences below. The first set was created using Ctrl+Z to retain the errors. The second set was created by letting Word automatically correct the error.

Add to AutoCorrect
1. In the **Replace** box, type the word incorrectly.
2. In the **With** box, type the word correctly.

Words Not in AutoCorrect
If you misspell a word in a way that is not in the AutoCorrect **Replace With** table, Word cannot correct it automatically. For example, Word does not correct *troubelshoot*.

Common Errors Word Can Correct

He is an independant spirit.
Have you read the Declaration of Independance?
Is there a wrod you often mispell?

He is an independent spirit.
Have you read the Declaration of Independence?
Is there a word you often misspell?

Repeated Words

- Word detects repeated words and marks them as spelling errors. The word *the*, for example, often gets repeated when you are revising something you have written. Word underlines the second occurrence of the word to remind you to correct it.

AutoFormat As You Type

- The second tab on the AutoCorrect dialog box controls several other automatic text format features of Word. Those that are most important are in the Replace as you type section of the dialog box:

  - **"Straight quotes" with "smart quotes"** tells Word to use typesetting quotation marks when you type either the single or double quotation marks. Smart quotes are curled (" " '), like typeset quotation marks. If you want to use the symbol for inches, however, you need the straight quotation marks, for example 6' 3". Use Alt+Backspace or Ctrl+Z to return to the straight marks.

- **Ordinals (1st) with superscript** formats ordinal numbers (1st, 2nd, and so on).

- **Fractions (1/2) with fraction character (½)** changes certain fractions to a single character; ¼ and ¾ change, but 1/3 and 1/8 do not.

- **Hyphens (--) with dash (—).** Word automatically converts certain hyphens into one of the following characters:

  - **en dash (–),** approximately the width of an **n**. To create an en dash, type space-hyphen-space or space-hyphen-hyphen-space and the next word, for example **Jones - the** becomes **Jones – the**.

  - **em dash (—),** approximately the width of an **M**. To create an em dash, type hyphen-hyphen and the next word, for example **Jones--the** becomes **Jones—the**.

- ***Bold* and _italic_ with real formatting** lets you type *text* to format the text as bold, and _text_ to format the text as italic. For example:

  Automatic Spelling Check = **Automatic Spelling Check**
  Automatic Spelling Check = *Automatic Spelling Check*
  *Automatic Spelling Check* = ***Automatic Spelling Check***

- **Internet and network paths with hyperlinks** causes Word to format Internet addresses as hyperlinks. For example:

  www.phschool.com = <u>www.phschool.com</u>
  http://www.phschool.com = <u>http://www.phschool.com</u>

  Text is automatically underlined and colored blue to indicate a hyperlink. When you click the text, Word attempts to open your Internet browser and link you to the Internet address.

Automatic Spelling Check

- Word automatically checks for spelling errors as you type. When it detects an error that it cannot correct automatically, it underlines the word with a wavy red line, as shown in the illustration that follows.

Spelling Errors

My barother was an only child.
Sue loves ice creem.
Fred Malkin was marriede to Maria.

- The wavy underline (shown here in gray) indicates that Word does not recognize the spelling. You need to look at each word underlined in red to determine if it is correct. *Malkin*, in the previous illustration, is spelled correctly. The other underlined words need to be corrected.

Automatic Spell Checking

If misspelled words are not underlined in your Word document, you may need to turn on the automatic spell check feature.

1. Click **Tool, Options**.
2. Click the **Spelling & Grammar** tab.
3. Select the option **Check spelling as you type**.
4. Click **OK**.

💻 Try It!

1. Start Word and open a new document.

2. Type the following lines exactly as shown:

    My barother was an only child.

    Sue loves ice creem.

    Fred Malkin was marriede to Maria.

3. Place your mouse pointer on *barother*.
    It should be underscored by a red wavy line.

4. Right-click.
    Word displays a shortcut menu that gives possible corrections, as shown in the illustration that follows.

Spelling Check Shortcut Menu

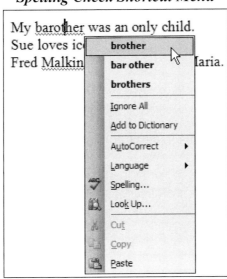

5. Click the correct word.
    If the correct word does not appear, click anywhere outside the menu and edit the word to correct the error.

6. Right-click on the word *creem*.
    Note the AutoCorrect option on this shortcut menu.

7. Click this option and the correct word, as shown on the following page.
    When you click the correct word, Word changes the word in the document and adds the entry in the AutoCorrect Replace...With table.

8. Right-click on the name *Malkin*.

9. Select Ignore All from the shortcut menu.
    Word will now ignore the word wherever it appears in the document.

10. Leave the document open.

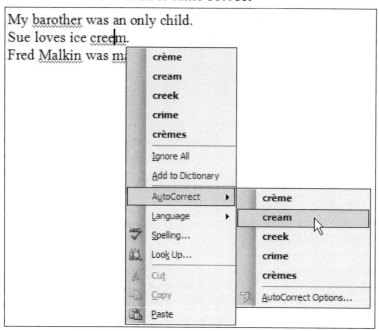
Add to AutoCorrect

Spelling Check

- It is always a good idea to run a separate spelling check on a completed document. Word detects some errors with a separate spelling check that you may not notice with an automatic spelling check; in addition, it is faster than right-clicking on every misspelled word.

Try It!

1. Click the Spelling and Grammar button 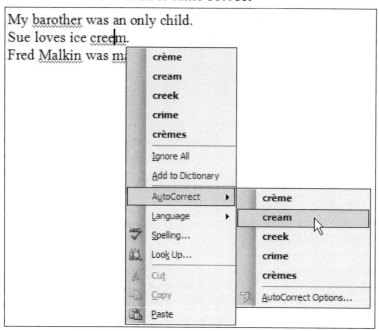 on the Standard toolbar, or press the F7 key.

   OR

   Click Tools, Spelling and Grammar (Alt+T, S).

   When Word encounters an error, it displays the Spelling and Grammar dialog box, as shown in the illustration on the following page.

2. Click the Change button | Change | to replace the word in red with the selected word in the Suggestions box.

3. Click OK.

4. Leave the document open.

- The command buttons on the Spelling dialog box are described below.

   - | Ignore Once | bypasses the word without changing it.

   - | Ignore All | bypasses the word every time it occurs in the document. This is useful if you have used a name several times in a document.

Spelling and Grammar Dialog Box

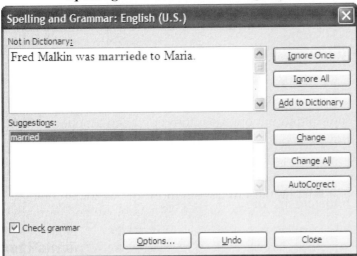

In the Not in Dictionary: box, Word displays the offending word in red. In the Suggestions box, it displays a list of possible corrections.

- **Add to Dictionary** adds the word with your spelling to its dictionary. The next time it encounters the word, it accepts the spelling. Use this option, for example, if Word always marks your name as incorrectly spelled.

- **Change** Before clicking this command, select the correct word in the Suggestions box. Word changes the word in red to the word you selected.

- **Change All** Before clicking this command, select the correct word in the Suggestions box. Word changes the word in red to the suggested word and automatically changes all other occurrences of the error throughout the document.

- **AutoCorrect** Before clicking this command, select the correct word in the Suggestions box. Word changes the word in red to the selected suggestion and adds the correction to the AutoCorrect.

■ If you start the spelling check in the middle of a document, Word checks the entire document and returns to the point where you started.

Automatic Grammar Checking

■ Word automatically checks for grammatical errors as you type. When it detects an error, it underlines the offending word or phrase with a green wavy line (gray in the illustration below), as shown in the illustration that follows.

Grammar Error

He don't have no right to do that.

Note that Word marks the double-negative, but it does not underline the subject–verb agreement error. (The correct verb is doesn't.)

Resume and Undo Edit

You may see two other buttons during a spell check operation:

The **Resume** button appears if you click in the document to edit while spell check is in progress. The dialog box remains displayed. When you click the button, the spell check continues.

The **Undo Edit** may appear when you start spell check or after you have made an edit in the **Not in Dictionary:** box while spell check is in progress. Click the button to resume spell checking.

Automatic Grammar Checking

If grammatical errors are not underlined in your Word document, you may need to turn on the automatic grammar check feature.

1. Click **Tool**, **Options**.

2. Click the **Spelling & Grammar** tab.

3. Select the option **Check grammar as you type** in the lower part of the dialog box.

4. Click **OK**.

🖥️ Try It!

1. Press Enter after the word *Maria*.
2. Type the following line, exactly as shown.
   He don't have no right to do that.
3. Press the Enter key.
4. Place your mouse pointer (I-bar I) on the underlined word.
5. Right-click.

   Word displays a shortcut menu that gives possible corrections, as shown in the illustration that follows. The pointer changes to a selection arrow ⬉.

Grammar Check Shortcut Menu

6. Click the correct word (*any*).

   Note that the subject-verb agreement error (He don't) is now marked.
7. Leave the document open.

Grammar Check

- Grammar checking is another useful tool. Word detects more errors in grammar when you run a separate grammar check than it does with the automatic grammar check feature.

🖥️ Try It!

- To run a grammar check, you may need to set the grammar check option so that Word includes the grammar check when you run a spelling check.

  1. Click Tools, Options (Alt+T, O).
  2. Click the Spelling & Grammar tab on the Options dialog box, as shown in the illustration on the following page.

     Note the options in the Grammar section of the dialog box.
  3. Click Check grammar with spelling to run a grammar check at the same time as a spelling check.
  4. Click the OK button [OK].

Options Dialog Box: Spelling & Grammar Tab

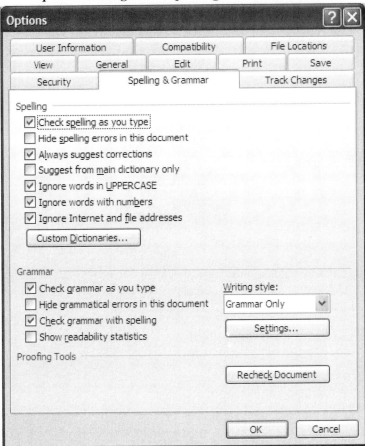

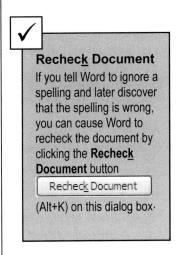

Recheck Document

If you tell Word to ignore a spelling and later discover that the spelling is wrong, you can cause Word to recheck the document by clicking the **Recheck Document** button

Recheck Document

(Alt+K) on this dialog box·

Try It!

1. Move the insertion point to the beginning of the document.

2. Click the Spelling and Grammar button , or press the F7 key.

   When Word encounters an error, it displays the Spelling and Grammar dialog box, as shown in the illustration on the following page.

   The possible error is in green (dark in the illustration) and the Suggestions box contains the correction.

Grammar Check Example

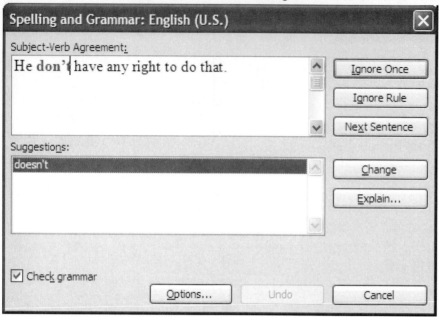

3. To see an explanation of the error, click the Explain button
    [Explain...].

    The Office Assistant displays an explanation of the possible grammatical error, as shown in the following illustration.

Office Assistant Explanation of Grammatical Error

Subject-Verb Agreement

The verb of a sentence must agree with the subject in number and in person.

• Instead of: What <u>was</u> Stephen and Laura like as schoolchildren?
• Consider: What were Stephen and Laura like as schoolchildren?

• Instead of: Tom <u>watch</u> the snowy egret stab at the fish.
• Consider: Tom watches the snowy egret stab at the fish.

4. Click the Change button [Change] to correct the error.
5. Click OK.
6. Close the document without saving it.
7. Exit Word unless you are continuing with the Exercise Directions.

> *In this exercise, you will take advantage of AutoCorrect, run a spelling check, and grammar check to improve your documents.*

EXERCISE DIRECTIONS

Use AutoCorrect

1. Create a new Word document and type the text in Illustration A exactly as shown below.

   You'll discover that Word automatically fixes all the errors in the sample.

   If Word does not automatically correct your typing, you may have inadvertently typed the text in a way that prevents automatic correction. You can right-click the misspelled word to correct it.

Illustration A: AutoCorrect Practice

> I like broccolli.
> Teh right spirit makes all the difference.
> Try something nwe evrey day.
> I could of been a contender.
> Their is no reason to wait.
> It is better to give than to recieve.

2. Save the document as **AutoCorrect**.
3. Close the document, but leave Word open.

Use Spell and Grammar Check

1. Open 💿 **04Dogwalk** from the data files.
2. Save the document as **Dogwalk**.
3. Press F7 to spell and grammar check the document.

   You can right-click the misspelled words, but it may be quicker to press the F7 key and go through all the errors at once.

   When you press F7, Word performs its spelling and grammar check at the same time.

4. Click the Underline button [Undo] if it appears when *seter* is highlighted the first time.

   The spelling check runs after you click the button.

5. Select the Change All button [Change All] the first time *seter* shows up.

   Word automatically corrects each occurrence of seter as it goes through the document.

6. Make all other necessary corrections and click OK when the check is complete.
7. If your system did not perform the grammar check, follow the steps on page 104 to turn on the grammar check option.
8. Compare your final result with the result in Illustration B on the next page.
9. Save the document, but leave it open.

Print Preview and Print

1. Print Preview the document.
2. Print one copy.
3. Save the document, but leave it open.

Proofread Your Printout

1. Proofread your document carefully. Some errors cannot be caught by spelling check or grammar check.
2. Did you find them? Did you find others?

   Spelling check and grammar check are no substitute for careful proofreading. They will not find hug when you mean huge; they will not find feat when feet is the correct word; nor will they find form when from is what you want.

3. Correct the errors by typing the correct words.
4. Save the document.
5. Reprint the document.
6. Close the document and exit Word.

Twice a day I take my Irish setter for a walk. He pulls so hard on his leash that sometimes I feel that he is the master and I am the dog.

When we walk down a steep hill, his legs start going so quickly that I'm afraid he'll pull my feat right off the ground. But if I say, "Slow down, boy!" he just picks up speed, and we go sailing down the block. Yesterday, that hug setter almost pulled me into a patch of poison oak. If my setter doesn't slow down soon, I'll have to find a different way to walk him.

I have just thought of something that I can do. Form now on, I'll wear my roller blades. Then he can go as fast as an Irish setter likes, and I'll go flying with him (unless he runs across the grass).

Exercise 5

Use Editing Tools
■ Default Tab Stops ■ Insert and Overtype Modes ■ Undo ■ Redo
■ Proofreader's Marks for Bold and Italic

NOTES

Default Tab Stops

- By default, Word sets a tab stop every ½ inch (0.5"). To indent the first line of a paragraph, you can press the Tab key once and Word indents the line 0.5".

- Tabs are useful for indenting lines and for aligning items in lists such as the headings of a memorandum. In this exercise, you will use the default tab stops. In a later exercise, you will practice setting some tab stops.

- The tab appears as a right arrow → when the Show/Hide button ¶ is on, as shown below.

Show/Hide ¶

Select this button to display formatting characters such as the paragraph mark, tab, space, and line break.

Tools, Options, View tab

In the Options dialog box, View tab, you can turn on some nonprinting characters to display even when the Show/Hide button is not clicked.

Show/Hide On
Formatting Characters Displayed

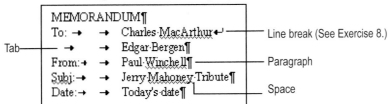

Insert and Overtype Modes

- By default, Word starts in **Insert mode**. Characters you type appear at the insertion point and existing text moves to the right.

- In **Overtype mode**, Word replaces existing text one character at a time. Each keystroke replaces a character—including any tabs and new line characters—until you reach the end of the paragraph. At the end of the paragraph, your new text appears as if inserted.

- To start Overtype mode, press the Insert key or double-click the grayed-out OVR button on the status bar. The OVR button label turns dark when Overtype mode is on, as shown in the illustration that follows.

Overtype Mode On

- If the Insert key does not initiate Overtype mode, double-click the OVR button.

- To turn Overtype mode off, press the Insert key or double-click the OVR button.

Undo

- Most Windows-based applications offer an **Undo** feature. In Word, Undo lets you remove the effects of as many as 300 actions. As you type and format paragraphs and text, Word stores the actions in its undo **buffer** or **stack**.

> **Buffer (stack)**
> A buffer is an area in memory that a program uses to store data temporarily. Actions are stored in the undo buffer and can be used to reverse actions until you exit Word.

🖥 Try It!

Undo One Action

1. Open 📠**Advice3** from your files, or open 💿 **05Advice3** from the data files.
2. Insert the current date in place of the date or *Today's Date*.
3. Save the file as **Advice5**.
4. Select the date. (Just place the insertion point anywhere in the date.)
5. Click the Align Left button ≣.
   The date is left-aligned.
6. Click the Undo button ↺.
   OR
   Press Ctrl+Z.
   The date is once again right-aligned.

🖥 Try It!

Undo Several Actions

1. Select the title.
2. Click the Bold button **B**.
3. Select the first full paragraph.
4. Press the Delete key.
5. Place the insertion point in the new first paragraph.
6. Click the Center button ≣.
7. Click the drop-down list arrow of the Undo button ↺▾.
   A list of recent actions appears.

Undo Drop-Down List

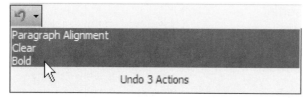

8. Point to Bold and click to reverse the formatting you just performed.
   The document returns to its previous state. You can undo the first action or a group of recent actions.
9. Leave the document open.

Redo

- After you have undone some actions, you can redo them by clicking the Redo button ⟳ ▾ or its drop-down list arrow. The Redo function works like the Undo function except that it reinstates the actions you reversed.

🖳 Try It!

1. Click the drop-down list arrow of the Redo button ⟳ ▾ .

   A list of recently undone actions appears.

Redo Drop-Down List

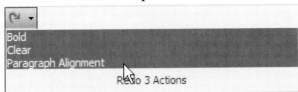

2. Click the Paragraph Alignment option.
   The edits you just undid are restored.
3. Close the document without saving it. Exit Word unless you are continuing with the Exercise Directions.

Proofreader's Marks for Bold and Italic

- The proofreader's mark for bold is a wavy underline: ﹏﹏﹏﹏

- The proofreader's mark for italic is: (a capella)——— *ital*

In this exercise, you will format text and paragraphs, type in Overtype mode, and use the Undo and Redo features.

EXERCISE DIRECTIONS

Open and Save a Memorandum

1. Open 💿 **05Memo** from the data files to display the data document.
2. Turn on Show/Hide by clicking the Show/Hide button ¶ .
3. Save the document as **Memoclub**.

Format the Heading and Address

1. Center the title paragraph—*MEMORANDUM*.
2. Make the title text Arial, 24-point bold, underlined.
3. Position the insertion point to the left of the word *To:*.
4. Press the Enter key twice.

   If you press Enter twice after MEMORANDUM, you may end up with more space than necessary between the title and the addressee of the memo.

5. Replace each space after each colon with a tab.
   a. Press the Insert key to enter Overtype mode.
   b. Position the insertion point immediately after the colon.
   c. Press the Tab key twice.
   d. Press the Insert key to return to Insert mode.
   e. Delete one of the tabs after the word *Subject:* to align the address entries.

6. Save the document.
7. Make the following entries bold: *To:, From:, Subject:* and *Date:*.
8. Insert a blank paragraph between the entries.
9. Insert two blank paragraphs after the *Date:* line.
10. Save the document.

Format the Body

1. Insert a blank line between the body paragraphs.
2. Make the following words and phrases bold:
   - *Holiday Bash* (paragraph 1)
   - *December 17* (paragraph 1)
   - *Shooby Doop Wah Dah* (paragraph 3)
3. Italicize the following phrases:
   - *Earth Angel* (paragraph 1)
   - *Teenager in Love* (paragraph 1)
   - *There's a Moon Out Tonight* (paragraph 1)
   - *a capella* (paragraph 2)
4. Make the following phrase bold, italic 16 points.
   Long Live Doo-Wop! (paragraph 4)
5. Center the *Long live Doo-Wop!* paragraph, and then undo the paragraph alignment.
6. Save the document.

Spell and Grammar Check, Print Preview, Print

1. Spell and grammar check the document.
2. Save the document.
3. Print Preview the document.
4. Print one copy.
5. Proofread your printout, make any necessary corrections, save the document, and print it again.
6. Compare your results with Illustration B.
7. Close the document, and exit Word.

Illustration A. 05Memo

Bold   — Center and set to Arial, 24-pt. bold, underlined.

MEMORANDUM
¶¶ To: All members of the Doo-Wop Golden Oldies Club ¶
From: Ms. Lettis Singalong ¶
Subject: Name That Group Contest ¶
Date: Today's date ¶¶
Our Holiday Bash takes place on December 17. At that time, we will be holding our third annual Golden Oldies Club Contest. This year's contest is called Name that Group. If you plan to enter, study up on the groups who made famous such immortal tunes as Earth Angel, Teenager in Love, and There's a Moon Out Tonight to name just three. ¶
Come prepared to name the group, sing a line or two, and laugh as we enjoy ourselves remembering the greats of Doo-Wop. We look forward to hearing the winners raise their voices in gleeful a capella harmony! ¶
Dinner starts promptly at seven and the contest begins at 8:30. Our favorite group, Shooby DoopWah Dah, will entertain while we eat. ¶
Long live Doo-wop!

ital

Illustration B. Desired Result

MEMORANDUM

To: All members of the Doo-Wop Golden Oldies Club

From: Ms. Lettis Singalong

Subject: Name That Group Contest

Date: Today's Date

Our **Holiday Bash** takes place on **December 17**. At that time, we will be holding our third annual Golden Oldies Club Contest. This year's contest is called Name that Group. If you plan to enter, study up on the groups who made famous such immortal tunes as *Earth Angel*, *Teenager in Love*, and *There's a Moon Out Tonight* to name just three.

Come prepared to name the group, sing a line or two, and laugh as we enjoy ourselves remembering the greats of Doo-Wop. We look forward to hearing the winners raise their voices in gleeful *a capella* harmony!

Dinner starts promptly at seven and the contest begins at 8:30. Our favorite group, **Shooby DoopWah Dah**, will entertain while we eat.

Long live Doo-Wop!

Exercise 6

Enhance the Text
■ Highlight ■ Change Text Color
■ Use Other Text Enhancements ■ Use Symbols

NOTES

Highlight

■ Another way to call attention to text is to highlight it. Word lets you highlight text in color, with the default color as yellow, which prints as a light gray on most black-and-white printers.

💻 Try It!

1. Open 🖵 **Dogwalk**, or open 💿 **06Dogwalk** from the data files.
2. Save the document as **Dogwalk6**.
3. Select the word *leash* in the first paragraph.
4. Click the Highlight button 🔲 on the Formatting toolbar.

💻 Try It!

To Highlight Several Words

1. Click the Highlight button 🔲 to turn on Highlight mode.
   The mouse pointer becomes 🖊 (an I-beam with a highlighter pen).
2. Locate the words *Irish setter* in the first paragraph.
3. Hold the left mouse button and drag the pointer to select the words.
   The text is highlighted and the pointer remains ready for more highlighting.
4. Highlight the words *huge setter* in the second paragraph.
5. Click the Highlight button 🔲 or press Esc to turn off Highlight mode.

💻 Try It!

Change Highlight Color

1. Click the drop-down arrow next to the Highlight button .
2. Click the color you want to use as the highlighting color.
3. Highlight the words *poison oak* and *my setter* in the second paragraph.
4. Print Preview and print the document.
5. Save and close the document, but leave Word open.

> ✏️
> **Highlight Color**
> Choose a light color—yellow, turquoise, light green, or light gray—for the highlight color. If you choose a dark color, the text may not be visible when you print on a black-and-white printer.

Change Text Color

■ Color also draws attention to text. By default, Word prints text in black. Its default alternative color on the Font Color button is red, which prints as dark gray or black on most black-and-white printers.

Try It!

1. Open **Advice5**, or open ⊙ **06Advice5** from the data files.
2. Save the document as **Advice6**.
3. Select the title.
4. Click the Font Color button **A** on the Formatting toolbar.

Try It!

Change Color for Color Button

1. Go to the bottom of the document, and press the Enter key once.
2. Click the drop-down arrow next to the Font Color button **A** ▾.
3. Click the color you want to use as the text color.
4. Type **I can learn word processing.** in the new color.
5. Save the document, but leave it open.

Use Other Text Enhancements

■ Word also offers other enhancements that can be used to call attention to text. The four *font effects* shown in the illustration below are best used in headlines and attention-getting spots in flyers and announcements.

Text Enhancements (Font Effects)

Try It!

1. Select the title in **Advice6**.
2. Click Fo̲rmat, F̲ont to display the Font dialog box, as shown in the illustration on the next page.
3. Click Shado̲w, and click the OK button [OK].

   You can review the effect in the Preview area of the dialog box. Clicking OK lets you see the effect in relation to the rest of the text.

4. Click anywhere outside the title and review the result.
5. Select the title again.

   The four font enhancements are in the center of the Effects section.

6. Display the Font dialog box again and choose O̲utline and click OK.

   Outline and Shadow can be used together.

7. Click anywhere outside the title and review the result.

✎

Use Color Sparingly

Use color sparingly as a means of emphasizing text.

Font Dialog Box

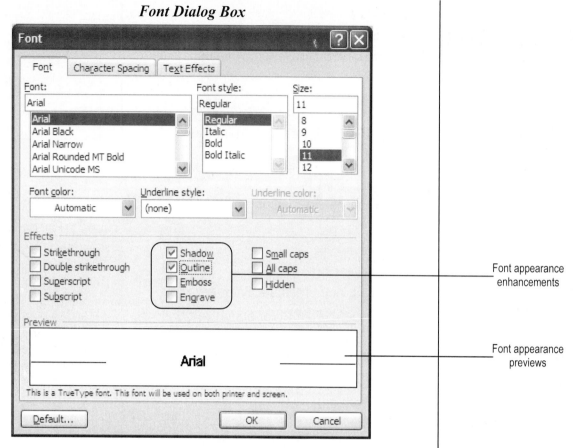

Font appearance enhancements

Font appearance previews

8. Apply the other two font appearance effects by following steps 6 and 7.

   Note that Emboss and Engrave cannot be used at the same time as Outline or Shadow.

9. Save the document, but leave it open.

Use Symbols

- Symbols are useful for calling attention to text and decorating your document. The Wingdings font that comes with Windows contains a number of symbols that you may wish to use.

💻 Try It!

1. Place the insertion point to the left of the title in **Advice6**, press the spacebar twice, and move the insertion point to the left of the spaces.

2. Click Insert, Symbol (Alt+I, S) to display the Symbol dialog box, as shown in the illustration on the following page.

3. Click the Font drop-down list and select Wingdings in the list of available symbol fonts, if it is not already displayed.

4. Find the finger that points to the right ☞ (third row, seventh from the left).

   You may have to scroll up to locate the top rows of symbols. If the symbol appears in Recently used symbols, you can double-click it to insert it in the text.

Symbol Dialog Box

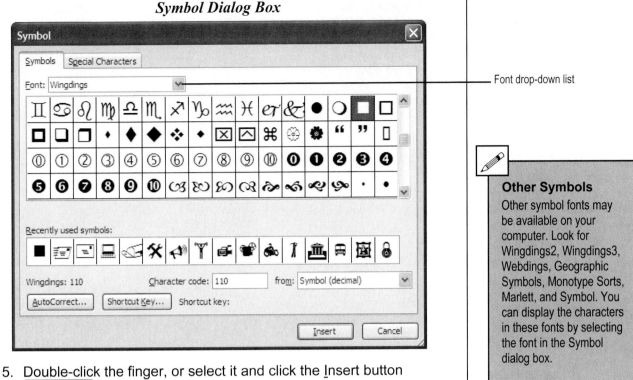

Font drop-down list

Other Symbols
Other symbol fonts may be available on your computer. Look for Wingdings2, Wingdings3, Webdings, Geographic Symbols, Monotype Sorts, Marlett, and Symbol. You can display the characters in these fonts by selecting the font in the Symbol dialog box.

5. Double-click the finger, or select it and click the Insert button
   [Insert].

6. Place the insertion point at the end of the title, and press the spacebar twice. Move the Symbol dialog box if necessary to see the end of the title.

7. Find the finger that points to the left ☜ (third row, sixth from the left).

8. Double-click the finger, or click it and click the Insert button
   [Insert].

9. Close the Symbol dialog box.

10. Save the document.

11. Print Preview and print the document.

12. Close the document, and exit Word unless you are continuing with the Exercise Directions.

In this exercise, you will add highlights, color, text enhancements, and symbols to an existing letter.

EXERCISE DIRECTIONS

Create the Letterhead

1. Open ☉ **06Coyote** from the data files.
2. Save the letter as **Coyote**.
3. Change *Today's Date* to the current date.
4. Center the first three lines (the company's name and address).
5. Insert the ⊠▷ (right-pointing checked arrow) Wingdings symbol before the word *Acme*.
6. Press the spacebar twice between the symbol and the word.
7. Press the spacebar twice after the word *Specialties* and insert the ◁⊠ (left-pointing checked arrow) Wingdings symbol.
8. Select the entire first line, and change the font size to 36 points.
9. Select each of the checked arrow symbols, and change the text color to red.
10. Select *Acme Specialties* and change the font color to blue.
11. Change the *Acme Specialties* font to Impact (if available), Arial Black (if available), or Arial bold.
12. Change the font effect of *Acme Specialties* to Shadow.
13. Change the address, city, and state to Comic Sans MS (if available); otherwise, use Arial 12-point bold. Make the text blue.
14. Save the document.

Call Attention to Text

1. In the first and second paragraphs of the letter, italicize the words:
   Acme Jet Powered Roller Skates.
2. Change the following words to blue and italic:
   your misuse of the skates
3. In the indented paragraph, use the yellow highlight color to highlight the words:
   utilization of skates for any other than recreational activities
4. Change the letters *yo* after the closing to your own initials.
5. Insert the smiley face symbol at the beginning and end of the PS: at the bottom of the letter.
6. Insert one space between each smiley face and the text.
7. Color the entire PS blue, and make it bold.
8. Save the document.

Spell and Grammar Check, Preview, and Print the Document

1. Spell and grammar check the letter.
2. Save the document.
3. Print Preview the letter.
4. Print one copy.
5. Compare your results with the letter shown in Illustration B on page 120.
6. Close the document, and exit Word.

Illustration A. Letter from Acme Specialties

Center all three lines.   *Insert checked arrow symbols.*

Acme Specialties   *Entire name and symbols 36 pt.*
911 Mayhem Lane   *Symbols red*
Williston Park, NY 11511   *Text blue, Impact font, shadow*

Comic Sans MS 12 pt., blue

Today's Date ——————— *Change to the current date.*

Mr. Wile E. Coyote
85 Roadrunner Chase
Arid Desert, AZ 85222

Dear Mr. Coyote: *Ital*

We are very sorry that you believe our Acme Jet Powered Roller Skates are defective. We hope you have recovered from the injuries you suffered in plunging from the mesa to the valley floor. Your injuries, however, were caused by your misuse of the skates rather than a defect in their manufacture.   *Ital*   *Blue, ital*

Your Acme Jet Powered Roller Skates Money-Back Warranty states, in part:

> Manufacturer is not liable for any damage caused by product abuse, by failure to heed all safety rules as outlined by the National Skating Association, or by utilization of skates for any other than recreational activities. Any violation of these limits makes this Warranty null and void.

Highlight (yellow)

Clearly, use of our skates on twisting mountain roads in pursuit of dinner is not a recreational activity; thus, we regret that we cannot honor your request for a new pair of skates.

Sincerely,

Allin Funn
Customer Service Manager

AF/yo —— *Change to your initials.*   *Blue and bold*

PS: Have you tried our Acme EZ-Ride Guided Missile?

Insert smiley face.

Acme Specialties

911 Mayhem Lane
Williston Park, NY 11511

Today's Date

Wile E. Coyote
85 Roadrunner Chase
Arid Desert, AZ 85222

Dear Mr. Coyote:

We are very sorry that you believe our *Acme Jet Powered Roller Skates* are defective. We hope you have recovered from the injuries you suffered in plunging from the mesa to the valley floor. Your injuries, however, were caused by *your misuse of the skates* rather than a defect in workmanship.

Your *Acme Jet Powered Roller Skates* Money-Back Guarantee states, in part:

> Manufacturer is not liable for any damage caused by product abuse, by failure to heed all safety rules as outlined by the National Skating Association, or by utilization of skates for any other than recreational activities. Any violation of these limits makes this Warranty null and void.

Clearly, use of our skates on twisting mountain roads in pursuit of dinner is not a recreational activity; thus, we regret that we cannot honor your request for a new pair of skates.

Sincerely,

Allin Funn
Customer Service Manager

af/yo

☺ **P. S. Have you tried our Acme EZ-Ride Guided Missile?** ☺

Exercise 7

Use Bullets and Numbers; Cut, Copy, and Paste
■ Introduction to Bullets and Numbering ■ Bullets ■ Numbering
■ Cut, Copy, and Paste

NOTES

Introduction to Bullets and Numbering

- To call readers' attention to lists of items, Word offers bullets and numbers. Use bullets to mark items in a list in which the order of the items is not important, as in a list of things you need to pack for a camping trip. Use numbers when the order is important, as in the steps for pitching a tent.

Bullets

- A **bullet** is a symbol that marks the beginning of a list item; the commonest bullet is a small, filled circle (●). Other common bullets are squares (■) and diamonds (◆).

Try It!

Create a Bulleted List

1. Start Word, and open a new document.

2. Type the following lines:

   Three important things to remember:
   Your name
   What you had for breakfast
   The date of the Norman Conquest (1066)

3. Select the last three paragraphs.

4. Click the Bullets button on the Formatting toolbar.

   The paragraphs are indented and preceded by a bullet.

Try It!

Change the Bullet Symbol

1. Select the bulleted paragraphs if they are not already selected.

2. Right-click the bulleted paragraphs.

3. Choose Bullets and Numbering from the shortcut menu to display the Bullets and Numbering dialog box, as shown in the illustration on the next page.

4. Select the bullet you wish to use from the list displayed.

5. Click OK.

   If you change the bullet symbol, the next time you click the Bullets button, Word uses the new symbol.

Bullet
Symbol used to mark an item in a list where the order of the items is not important.

The term **bullet** refers to the appearance of the common symbol (●), which resembles a bullet hole.

Select Paragraphs
To format a paragraph, you can select any part of it or simply place the insertion point within the paragraph. You do not need to select the entire paragraph.

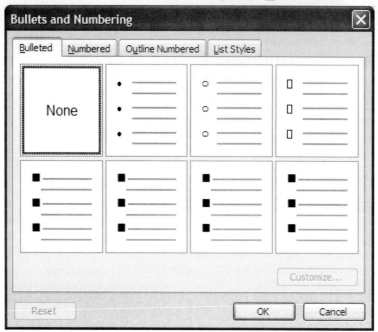

⌨ **Try It!**

Choose Your Own Bullet Symbol

1. Select the bulleted paragraphs and right-click.

2. Choose Bullets and Numbering from the shortcut menu to display the Bullets and Numbering dialog box, as shown in the illustration above.

3. Click the Customize button [Customize...] to display the Customize Bulleted List dialog box, as shown in the illustration on the next page.

4. Click the Character button [Character...] to display the Symbol dialog box.

5. Select the font and character you want to use as a bullet symbol.

6. Click OK twice.

Customize Bulleted List Dialog Box

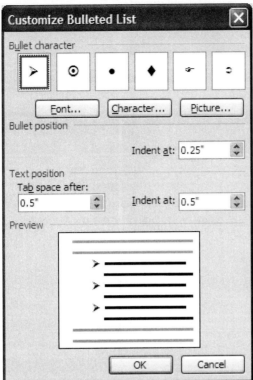

Numbering

🖳 Try It!

Create a Numbered List

1. Select the bulleted paragraphs.

2. Click the Numbering button ⊞ on the Formatting toolbar.

🖳 Try It!

Change from Numbers to Letters

1. Select the numbered paragraphs and right-click.

2. Choose Bullets and Numbering from the shortcut menu to display the Bullets and Numbering dialog box, as shown in the illustration on the next page.

3. Click the Numbered tab.

4. Select the letter format you wish to use.

5. Click the OK button ⌷ OK ⌷ .

Bullets and Numbering Dialog Box, <u>N</u>umbered Tab

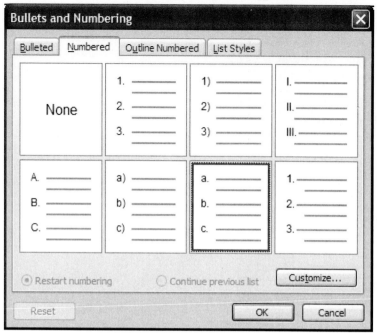

Try It!

Alter the Look of the Letter or Number

You can create your own numbering and lettering style. For example, you may wish to begin the list with a lowercase letter followed by a colon rather than a period.

1. Select the lettered paragraphs and right-click.
2. Choose Bullets and <u>N</u>umbering from the shortcut menu to display the Bullets and Numbering dialog box, as shown in the illustration above.
3. Click the Cus<u>t</u>omize button Customize... to display the Customize Numbered List dialog box, as shown in the illustration on the next page.
4. Edit the appearance of the letter in the Number f<u>o</u>rmat box. For example, delete the period and insert a colon.
5. Click OK.

Customize Numbered List

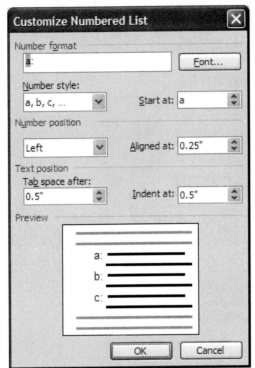

Try It!

Restart Numbering

If you have more than one numbered list in a document, you may find that the numbers continue in sequence from one list to the next. You can restart the numbering at the beginning of a new list.

1. Right-click on the first paragraph where you want the numbering to restart. In this case, use *The date of the Norman Conquest (1066)*.

2. Click the Restart numbering option

   Restart Numbering .

   The last item should now begin with a:.

Cut, Copy, and Paste

- You can cut and paste text to move it from one place to another. You can copy text to place a copy of the text in another spot.

Try It!

1. Select the last paragraph (*The date of the Norman …*).

   Include the paragraph mark ¶ if it is displayed. If the paragraph mark is displayed and you do not include it, you will copy or move just the text and not the formatting.

   If you select the paragraph when the paragraph mark is not displayed, Word will copy the formatting.

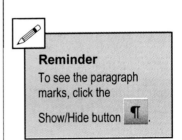

Reminder
To see the paragraph marks, click the

Show/Hide button ¶ .

• → The·date·of·the·Norman·Conquest·(1066)¶ ——— Text only selected

• → The·date·of·the·Norman·Conquest·(1066)¶ ——— Paragraph selected

2. **Move:** Click the Cut button ✂ to place the selection on the Windows Clipboard.

   The text disappears from its original location.

   OR

   Copy: Click the Copy button 📄 to place a copy of the selection on the Windows Clipboard.

   The text remains in its original location.

3. Place the insertion point just before *Your name.*

4. Click the Paste button 📋.

   The cut or copied text appears at the insertion point and the letters correct themselves. If the text does not appear as you expect when you paste it, click the Undo button to undo the copy or move and try again.

   The text remains on the Clipboard. Up to twenty-four copied items remain available until you copy the twenty-fifth. Then, the new item replaces the first item copied. You can use the Clipboard contents as many times as you wish.

5. Close the file without saving the changes. Leave Word open if you are continuing with the Exercise Directions.

In this exercise, you will create a bulleted list and a numbered list from a list of common rules and phrases that you may have heard around your house.

EXERCISE DIRECTIONS

Create a Bulleted List

1. Open ⊙ **07Rules** from the data files, or create a new document.
2. Save the file as **Rules1**.
3. Choose ten rules from the list (see Illustration A).
   - If you are using the data file, delete the rules you do not want.
   - If you are typing, type the heading and just the rules you want.
4. Create a bulleted list of the ten rules. Use any order you wish.
   If you select all the paragraphs at once, you can click the Bullets button once to format all of them at the same time.
5. Change the size of the bulleted text to 18 points.
6. Save the document.

Format the Heading and Spell Check

1. Go to the top of the document and select the heading.
2. Choose a font for the heading and use a font size of 36 points.
3. Insert a symbol of your choice before and after the heading (see Illustration B on page 129 for an example). You may wish to use a different symbol in each place.
   Symbols usually look better when they are not treated with special effects such as shadow or outline.
4. Spell check the document.
5. Save the document.

Save, Print Preview, and Print

1. Save the document.
2. Print Preview the document.
3. Print one copy.
4. Close the document, but leave Word open.
   A sample solution is shown in Illustration B.

Create a Numbered List

1. Open ⊙ **07Rules** from the data files, or create a new document.
2. Save the file as **Rules2**.

3. From the list, choose ten rules that you believe are good study habits (see Illustration A).
   - If you are using the data file, delete the rules you do not want.
   - If you are typing, type the heading and just the rules you want.
4. Select the rules and set the font size to 18 points.
5. Create a numbered list of the ten rules.
   Hint: If the Numbering button formats the paragraphs with letters, right-click, select Bullets and Numbering, and select the number format you want from the dialog box.
   Hint: If you select all the paragraphs at once, you can click the Numbering button once to format all of them at the same time.
6. Use Cut and Paste to put the rules in the order of their importance to you. Make the most important habit number 1; make the least important habit number 10.
   Hint: Move the rules as necessary to put them in the order you want.
7. Select all the numbered items.
8. Open the Bullets and Numbering dialog box (F̲ormat, Bullets and N̲umbering).
9. Click the Cus̲tomize button.
10. In the N̲umber position box, click the drop-down list and choose Right.
11. Click the OK button.
    The numbers are now properly aligned.
12. Save the document.

Format the Heading and Spell Check

1. Go to the top of the document.
2. Insert the following three words to the left of the heading:
   My Top Ten
3. Choose a font for the heading and use a font size of 22 points.
4. Insert one or more symbols of your choice before and after the heading. You may wish to use a different symbol in each place.
5. If the heading with symbols does not fit on one line, decrease the point size until the heading is on one line.
6. Spell check the document.

Save, Print Preview, and Print

1. Save the document.
2. Print Preview the document.
3. Print one copy.
4. Close the document, and exit Word.

   A sample solution is shown in Illustration C on page 129.

Illustration A. Study Habits List

Good Study Habits

Take notes in class.
Don't sleep during lectures.
Do your homework every night.
Read all your assignments before class.
Look up words you don't understand.
Have conferences with your teachers.
Form a study group.
Underline only key points.
Test yourself before a test.
Memorize important names and dates.
Tear ideas apart to see what makes them tick.
Dispute a theory with your own idea.
Back up your opinions with facts.
Debate new ideas with friends.
Defend an idea you don't believe in.
Don't watch TV while reading.
If you don't understand something, don't be afraid to ask questions.

Illustration B. Sample Bulleted List of Study Habits

➲ Good Study Habits ➾

- Don't sleep during lectures.
- Do your homework every night.
- Read all your assignments before class.
- Look up words you don't understand.
- Form a study group.
- Underline only key points.
- Test yourself before a test.
- Memorize important names and dates.
- Back up your opinions with facts.
- If you don't understand something, don't be afraid to ask questions.

Illustration C. Sample Numbered List of Study Habits

☆☆ My Top Ten Good Study Habits ☆☆

1. Do your homework every night.
2. Read all your assignments before class.
3. Look up words you don't understand.
4. Form a study group.
5. Test yourself before a test.
6. Tear ideas apart to see what makes them tick.
7. Dispute a theory with your own idea.
8. Back up your opinions with facts.
9. Debate new ideas with friends.
10. Defend an idea you don't believe in.

Exercise 8

Format Paragraphs

■ Change Line Spacing ■ Control Spacing between Paragraphs
■ Create Indented Paragraphs ■ Use Format Painter ■ Use the New Line Key

NOTES

Change Line Spacing

- The distance between lines within a paragraph is controlled by the line spacing option. You can set line spacing through:

  - Line Spacing button on the Formatting toolbar
  - Paragraph dialog box

- When you rest your mouse pointer on the Line Spacing button, a ScreenTip displays the current setting. If you click the button, the current selection (paragraph with the insertion point or all selected paragraphs) is formatted with the current line spacing.

Line Spacing Button ScreenTip

- You can specify a different line spacing value for the current selection by clicking the drop-down arrow of the Line Spacing button and selecting the desired value.

Line Spacing Drop-Down List

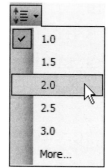

> **Line Spacing**
> Line spacing, also called **leading**, is the amount of vertical space on the page that a line of text occupies. Typographers use symbols like 12/14 to indicate that the text is 12 points and the leading or line spacing is 14 points.

💻**Try It!**

1. Open 💿 **08Marianne** from the data files.
2. Save the file as **Marianne**.
3. Select all paragraphs except the last.
4. Click the drop-down arrow of the Line Spacing button.

5. Click 2.0.

   The paragraphs are now double spaced.

6. Repeat steps 4 and 5, but select 1.5.

   The paragraphs now have a line spacing of one and a half lines.

- The Paragraph dialog box offers additional line spacing options. To display the Paragraph dialog box:

  - Click F<u>o</u>rmat, <u>P</u>aragraph (Alt+O, P).

  - Click the Line Spacing button  drop-down arrow and click the More option (see the illustration on the preceding page).

Paragraph Dialog Box

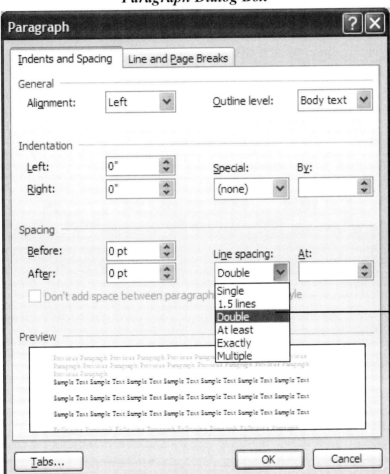

Choose Line spacing option.

Option	Description
Single	Space used for each line is large enough for the tallest character in the line, plus a small amount of extra space. The amount of extra space varies depending on the font size used.
1.5 lines	Each line is 1.5 times the height of the tallest character in the line.
Double	Each line is twice the height of the tallest character in the line. Use this setting for documents that should be double-spaced.
At least	Each line is at least as tall as the value specified in the <u>A</u>t box. If an object or character is taller than the value, the line spacing is larger. If the tallest character is less than the value in the <u>A</u>t box, the value in the box is used.

Option	Description
Exactly	Each line is exactly the height specified in the At box, regardless of the size of the tallest character in the line.
Multiple	Line spacing is increased or decreased by a percentage that you specify in the At box. For example, if you select Multiple and enter 1.2 in the At box, the line spacing is 20 percent taller than the tallest character. 0.8 in the At box makes the line 20 percent smaller than the tallest character. Setting Multiple with 2 in the At box is the same as setting Line spacing at Double. Setting Multiple with 3 in the At box sets triple line spacing.

🖥 Try It!

1. With all paragraphs except the last selected, open the Paragraph dialog box.
2. Change Line spacing to Single (Alt+N, choose Single).
3. Click OK.
4. Save the file.
5. Leave the document open.

Control Spacing between Paragraphs

- To control the distance between paragraphs, Word uses the Before and After options of the Paragraph dialog box.

Spacing, Before and After

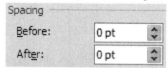

- The value in the Before box tells how many points to insert before the paragraph. The value in the After box tells how many points to insert after the paragraph. If you are using a font size of 10 or 12 points, 12 points before or after is about one line, as shown below.

Sample of Spacing After

The distance between this paragraph and the next is controlled by the After option, which has been set to 12 points.

This paragraph is defined with 0 points before and 12 points after, so it is about one line below the preceding paragraph.

This third paragraph is formatted the same as the second.

Spacing After = 12 pt. for these paragraphs.

🖥 Try It!

1. Select all paragraphs in **Marianne** except the last.
2. Click Format, Paragraph (Alt+O, P).
3. Enter 12 in the After text box `After: [12 pt] ⬍` (Alt+E, type 12 or click the Increase arrow ⬍). — Increase arrow

4. Click OK.

The selected paragraphs now have the equivalent of one line between them while their spacing remains single.

5. Leave the document open.

Create Indented Paragraphs

■ Indented paragraphs are commonly used to set information apart. Note the kinds of indenting shown below.

Indented Paragraphs

> The first line of this paragraph is indented from the left while the rest of the lines begin at the left margin. This format is often used to indicate paragraphing when no extra space between paragraphs is specified.
>
> • This bulleted paragraph is specified as a hanging indent. When it is longer than one line, the second line begins at the same position as the text of the first.
>
> > This paragraph is indented from the left by 1". All lines begin 1" from the left margin and wrap at the right margin.
> >
> > This paragraph is indented from the left by 1" and from the right by 1". All lines begin 1" from the left margin and wrap 1" from the right margin.
>
> This paragraph has a hanging indent. Its first line starts at the left margin and all others are indented by 0.5". Hanging indents of this type are often used for bibliographic entries in reports and papers.

■ Indented paragraphs can be formatted using the Indentation section of the Paragraph dialog box, as shown in the illustration that follows.

Left, Right, and Special Indentation Options

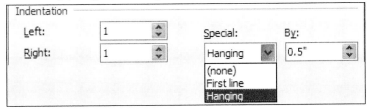

🖳Try It!

First-Line Indent

1. Select all paragraphs in **Marianne** except the last.

2. Click F**o**rmat, **P**aragraph to display the Paragraph dialog box (Alt+O, P).

3. Click the **S**pecial drop-down arrow.

4. Select First line.

0.5" appears in the By box.

5. Click OK.

   The selected paragraphs now have a first-line indent.

6. Leave the document open.

Hanging Indents

- For bulleted and numbered paragraphs, Word uses a **hanging indent**. In a hanging indent, the first line of the paragraph extends to the left of the remaining lines. If the text extends beyond one line in a bulleted or numbered list, the second line is indented to line up with the text in the first line, as shown in the illustration that follows.

Bulleted (Indented) Paragraph

•→ This·bulleted·paragraph·is·longer·than·one·line.·Its·second·line·begins·at·the·same·position·as·
   the·text·of·the·first.·The·paragraph,·therefore,·is·indented.¶

- Hanging indents are often used for bibliographies:

   White, Bailey. *Mama Makes Up Her Mind and Other Dangers of Southern Living.*
   Reading, MA: Addison-Wesley Publishing Company, 1993.

💻 Try It!

1. Select the last paragraph of the document.

2. Click F̲ormat, P̲aragraph to display the Paragraph dialog box (Alt+O, P).

3. Click the S̲pecial drop-down arrow.

4. Select Hanging.

   0.5" appears in the By box.

5. Click OK.

   The bibliographic entry is formatted with a hanging indent.

6. Leave the document open.

Left and Right Indents

- You may wish to indent a paragraph that is not bulleted or numbered. In reports and papers, for example, quotations longer than three lines are often indented from both the right and the left. In the letter from Acme Specialties (see Exercise 6), the quotation from the company's warranty was indented from the left.

💻 Try It!

1. Select the second paragraph in the document.

2. Click the Increase Indent button 📑 on the Formatting toolbar.

3. Click it again.

   Each time you click the button, the paragraph indent increases by 0.5", the distance of the default tab stops.

4. Click the Decrease Indent button 📑 once.

   The paragraph is now indented from the left by 0.5".

5. Click F<u>o</u>rmat, <u>P</u>aragraph to display the Paragraph dialog box.

6. Click the <u>S</u>pecial drop-down arrow.

7. Select (none).

8. Click the increase arrow next to the <u>R</u>ight text box. ⇕ — Increase arrow

9. Make the right indent 0.5".

10. Click OK.

   The first line indent has been removed and the paragraph is indented from the right by one-half inch (0.5").

   In Word, left indent and hanging indent are independent of each other. If you specify a left indent of 0.8" and a hanging indent of 0.4", the first line begins at 0.8" from the left margin and the second and subsequent lines begin at 1.2".

Use Format Painter

- Format Painter is a useful tool for copying paragraph and text formats from one place in a document to another.

🖥 Try It!

Paint Paragraph Format

1. Place the insertion point anywhere in the second paragraph.

   To copy the format of a paragraph, do not select any text or select the entire paragraph including the paragraph mark. If you select just some text, you will copy only the format of the selected text.

2. Double-click the Format Painter button 🖌 on the Standard toolbar.

   The mouse pointer becomes the Format Painter pointer 🖌I.

3. Move the mouse pointer to the fourth paragraph.

4. Click the left mouse button.

5. You can repeat steps 3 and 4 until you have formatted all the paragraphs you wish.

   If you single-click the button in step 2, you can use the painter only once.

6. Click the Format Painter button 🖌 to turn off Format Painter.

🖥 Try It!

Paint Text Format

1. Select at least three characters of the italicized book title *Sense and Sensibility* in the last paragraph.

2. Double-click the Format Painter button 🖌.

   The mouse pointer becomes the Format Painter pointer 🖌I.

3. Drag the pointer across the name *Lady Middleton* in the second paragraph.

   Lady Middleton is italicized.

4. Drag the pointer across the name *Colonel Brandon* in the third paragraph.

   Colonel Brandon is italicized.

5. Click the Format Painter button ✏ to turn off Format Painter.

6. Save the document and close it.

7. Exit Word unless you are continuing with the Exercise Directions.

Use the New Line Key

■ Pressing Shift+Enter, the New Line function, creates line breaks within a paragraph. The paragraph format remains the same. If you change the paragraph format, all lines in the paragraph are affected.

■ You use the line break in a paragraph when you want to end the line without ending the paragraph. The line break is often used in headings so that lines of the heading are about the same length.

■ A line break appears as a curved ↵ arrow when Show/Hide ¶ is on.

In this exercise, you will format a report on a story from a book. You will create indented paragraphs and use Format Painter to copy formats from one paragraph to another. You will also copy text formatting. And you will copy text and paste the copy to another part of the document. The resulting document will cover more than one page.

EXERCISE DIRECTIONS

Format the Title

1. Open 💿 **08Report** from the data files to display the document shown in Illustration A on page 138.
2. Save the document as **Report**.
3. Center the title.
4. Format the title to Times New Roman, 16-point bold.
5. Place the insertion point immediately before the word *from* in the title.
6. Press Shift+Enter to insert a line break.
7. Place the insertion point immediately before the word *by* in the title.
8. Press Shift+Enter to insert a line break.

   You now have a three-line title that is still only one paragraph.

9. Make the book title, *Mama Makes Up Her Mind*, italic.
10. Use Format, Paragraph to change the space After the title to 12 points.
11. Save the document.

Format the Body Paragraphs

1. Place the insertion point at the beginning of the first body paragraph.
2. Press the Tab key to indent the first line.

   Word automatically formats the paragraph as a First line indent usually of 0.5".

3. Use Format, Paragraph to set the space Before to 6 points and the space After to 6 points.
4. Use Format Painter to format the four other body paragraphs the same as the first.

   If you accidentally format an indented paragraph, use Undo to reverse the format. Do not format the last paragraph.

Format the Song

1. Select all nine lines of the song. (Each line is a paragraph.)
2. Indent each song paragraph 1" from the left margin.
3. Place the insertion point in the first line of the song (*William Matrimatoes*).

4. Set the space Before to 6 points.
5. Place the insertion point in the last line of the song (*You spell out and go*).
6. Change the space After to 6 points.

Format the Quotations

1. Place the insertion point in the paragraph that begins *The mare stood up high*.
2. Indent the paragraph 0.75" from the left margin and 0.75" from the right margin.
3. Set the space Before to 6 points and the space After to 6 points.
4. Use Format Painter to copy this format to the indented paragraph that begins *And I still miss him*.

Copy the Song

1. Select the entire song, including all paragraph marks.
2. Click the Copy button ▣ to copy the song.
3. Move the insertion point to the left of the first character of the last paragraph, which begins *White, Bailey*.
4. Click the Paste button ▣ to insert the song.

Format the Bibliography Paragraph

1. Click anywhere in the final paragraph (the one that identifies the author).
2. Change the format to a Special Hanging indent of 0.5".
3. Set the space Before to 6 points and the space After to 6 points.

Italicize the Name of the Book

1. In the last paragraph, italicize the title of the book, *Mama Makes Up Her Mind and Other Dangers of Southern Living*.
2. Select some of the italicized text (at least three characters).
3. Use Format Painter to copy the text format to the book title in the first body paragraph.

Save, Print Preview, Print

1. Save the document.
2. Print Preview the document.
3. Print one copy.
4. Compare your results with those shown in Illustration B on pages 139 and 140.
5. Close the document, and exit Word.

Illustration A: Report Data File (Line Spacing Added for Ease of Reading)

Insert line break.

Ital

Insert line break.

Center and make Times New Roman 16-pt. bold. Set space after to 12 pt.

Indent first line.

Report on "Joe King" from Mama Makes Up Her Mind by Bailey White

Ital

In her book, Mama Makes Up Her Mind and Other Dangers of Southern Living, Bailey White tells the story of Joe King, the man who allowed her to ride an old horse named Tony. The story tells of the song she and Joe King used to sing as she rode Tony, while Joe King rode a younger, more spirited Kentucky mare.

Set space Before to 6 pt. and space After to 6 pt.

Indent 1" from left.

Copy entire song.

William Matrimatoes
He's a good fisherman
Catches hens
Puts 'em in pens
Wire bright
Clock fell down
Little mice run around
Old dirty dishrag
You spell out and go

Set space Before to 6 pt.

Set space After to 6 pt.

Use Format Painter to copy format from paragraph 1 to these paragraphs.

She and Joe didn't understand the song. "Something wrong with that song," Joe King would say. "Sure is something wrong with that song." They couldn't figure out what was wrong, but Bailey liked it anyway, especially the "tap-tap-tapping part in the chorus."

One day Tony the horse got so old that he dwindled away and died. As they dragged his carcass away,

Indent .75" from left and .75" from right.

The mare stood up high on her feet and stared down the road where they had dragged Tony. She was trembling and shaking. Then she lifted her head and gave out a high, blowing whistle. It was almost like a cry. Joe King slapped her on the shoulder. "He's gone," Joe King said. "He ain't never coming back." The horse whistled again and Joe King gave her another comforting slap. "He's dead and gone, and you ain't never gon' see him no more."

Set space Before to 6 pt. and space After to 6 pt.

Joe King died soon after. Bailey White went to his funeral, her first. She was more surprised at Joe's being dressed in clothes she had never seen before than by the spectacle of the funeral, with his relatives and their sorrowful grief.

Copy format.

When spring came again, Ms. White missed Joe King for the first time. He didn't come driving up in his "powdery blue pickup truck smelling like horses and saddles and axle grease and Prince Albert." Ms. White concludes:

And I still miss him…. I think about Joe King. I remember the elegant grieving of the Kentucky mare, and the eerie, high, blowing whistle she gave. That's how I would like to mourn. But I don't have that much style. Instead, I like to take a little walk in the spring sunshine, and I say to myself:

Paste copied song.

Ital

White, Bailey. Mama Makes Up Her Mind and Other Dangers of Southern Living, Reading, MA: Addison-Wesley Publishing Company, 1993.

Hanging indent of 0.5"

Set space Before to 6 pt. and space After to 6 pt.

Illustration B. Desired Result

Report on "Joe King"
from *Mama Makes Up Her Mind*
by Bailey White

In her book, *Mama Makes Up Her Mind and Other Dangers of Southern Living*, Bailey White tells the story of Joe King, the man who allowed her to ride an old horse named Tony. The story tells of the song she and Joe King used to sing as she rode Tony, while Joe King rode a younger, more spirited Kentucky mare.

> William Matrimatoes
> He's a good fisherman
> Catches hens
> Puts 'em in pens
> Wire bright
> Clock fell down
> Little mice run around
> Old dirty dishrag
> You spell out and go.

She and Joe didn't understand the song. "Something wrong with that song," Joe King would say. "Sure is something wrong with that song." They couldn't figure out what was wrong, but Bailey liked it anyway, especially the "tap-tap-tapping part in the chorus."

One day Tony the horse got so old that he dwindled away and died. As they dragged his carcass away,

> The mare stood up high on her feet and stared down the road
> where they had dragged Tony. She was trembling and shaking.
> Then she lifted her head and gave out a high, blowing whistle. It
> was almost like a cry. Joe King slapped her on the shoulder. "He's
> gone," Joe King said. "He ain't never coming back." The horse
> whistled again and Joe King gave her another comforting slap.
> "He's dead and gone, and you ain't never gon' see him no more."

Joe King died soon after. Bailey White went to his funeral, her first. She was more surprised at Joe's being dressed in clothes she had never seen before than by the spectacle of the funeral, with his relatives and their sorrowful grief.

When spring came again, Ms. White missed Joe King for the first time. He didn't come driving up in his "powdery blue pickup truck smelling like horses and saddles and axle grease and Prince Albert." Ms. White concludes:

> And I still miss him…. I think about Joe King. I remember the
> elegant grieving of the Kentucky mare, and the eerie, high,
> blowing whistle she gave. That's how I would like to mourn. But I

don't have that much style. Instead, I like to take a little walk in the spring sunshine, and I say to myself:

William Matrimatoes
He's a good fisherman
Catches hens
Puts 'em in pens
Wire bright
Clock fell down
Little mice run around
Old dirty dishrag
You spell out and go.

White, Bailey. *Mama Makes Up Her Mind and Other Dangers of Southern Living.* Reading, MA: Addison-Wesley Publishing Company, 1993.

Exercise 9

Manage Multi-page Documents
■ Insert Page Breaks ■ Use Headers and Footers
■ Use Page Setup ■ Set Margins

NOTES

Insert Page Breaks

■ Word provides three types of page breaks: automatic, manual, and forced.

- Word inserts an **automatic page break** when it reaches the bottom margin of a page. In Normal view, it shows the page break by placing a dotted line across the window as illustrated below.

Automatic Page Break in Normal View

And I still miss him.... I think about Joe King. I remember the elegant grieving of the Kentucky mare, and the eerie, high, blowing whistle she gave. That's how I would like to mourn. But I don't have that much style. Instead, I like to take a little walk in the spring sunshine, and I say to myself:

—— Automatic page break

- If you do not like where the automatic page break occurs, you can insert a **manual page break** to start a new page where you wish.

- If you have a paragraph, such as the title of a chapter or part, which should always begin on a new page, you can create a **forced page break**, using paragraph formatting.

🖥 Try It!

Manual Page Break

1. Open 💿 **09Web_Page** from the data files.
2. Save the document as **Web_Page9**.
3. Scroll down, if necessary, to find the automatic page break.
   It is in the paragraph after the heading Allow *for easy navigation.*
4. Place your insertion point at the beginning of the heading before the word *Allow*.
5. Press Ctrl+Enter
   or
   Click Insert, Break, Page break (Alt+I, B, P), and click OK.
   A manual page break appears before the heading, as shown in the illustration on the following page.
6. Print Preview the document to review the page break.
7. Close Print Preview, but leave the document open.
8. Save the document.

> people to click elsewhere rather than wait to see what your page has to offer. Choose
> your graphics carefully for best results.
>
> ···Page Break············· — Manual page break
>
> **Allow for easy navigation**
>
> Whenever you have an option for people to click to a new page or a bookmark
> within the same page, it's always a good idea to make it easy to get back to the home
> page or the top of the page. You can do this in a couple of ways: You can either create

⌨ Try It!

Forced Page Break

1. Place the insertion point on the manual page break.
2. Press the Delete key.

   The manual page break disappears and the automatic page break reappears.
3. Place the insertion point at the beginning of the word *Allow* in the heading.
4. Click F̲ormat, P̲aragraph (Alt+O, P).
5. Click the Line and P̲age Breaks tab, as shown below.

Paragraph Dialog Box, Line and P̲age Breaks Tab

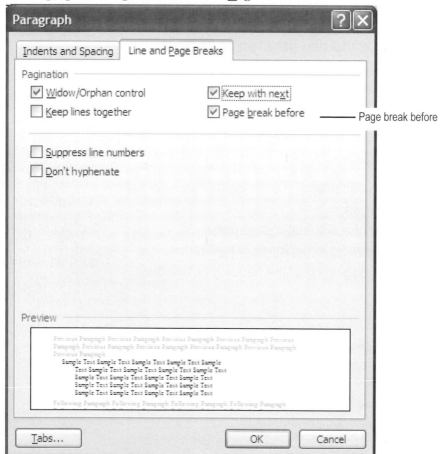

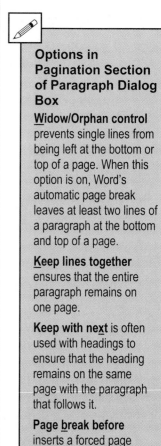

Options in Pagination Section of Paragraph Dialog Box

W̲idow/Orphan control prevents single lines from being left at the bottom or top of a page. When this option is on, Word's automatic page break leaves at least two lines of a paragraph at the bottom and top of a page.

K̲eep lines together ensures that the entire paragraph remains on one page.

Keep with ne̲xt is often used with headings to ensure that the heading remains on the same page with the paragraph that follows it.

Page b̲reak before inserts a forced page break before the paragraph.

6. Select Page b̲reak before.

7. Click OK.
8. Print Preview the document to review the page break.
9. Close Print Preview, save the document, but leave it open.

Use Headers and Footers

■ Headers and footers are used to insert information that appears at the top or bottom of every page. For example, in a multiple-page report, you may use headers and footers to insert your name and the page number at the top or bottom of every page.

Try It!

1. Press Ctrl+Home to return to the start of the document.
2. Click View, Header and Footer (Alt+V, H).

    The Header and Footer toolbar appears and the Header pane opens as shown in the illustration that follows. (Only the buttons used in this exercise are pointed out.)

Header Pane and Header and Footer Toolbar

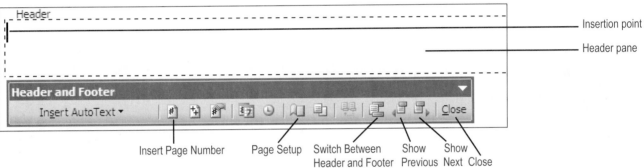

The insertion point is in the Header pane ready for you to type text. The toolbar may appear below the Header pane.

3. Type your last name followed by one space.

4. Click the Insert Page Number button.
    The text and paragraph in the Header pane can be formatted like any other text or paragraph.

5. Click the Align Right button on the Formatting toolbar.
    Your name and the page number now are aligned right.

6. Click the Close button on the Header and Footer toolbar.
7. Print Preview the document to review the headers.
8. Close Print Preview, save the document, but leave it open.

Use Page Setup

■ You may not want a header or footer to appear on the first page. For example, many reports and essays do not have the page number on the first page. The Page Setup options let you specify a different header and footer for the first page.

✓

Switch Between Header and Footer

If you want the page number (or other text) to appear at the bottom of every page, click the Switch Between Header and Footer button to display the Footer pane.

This button lets you switch between the Header and Footer panes as necessary.

Try It!

1. Click <u>V</u>iew, <u>H</u>eader and Footer (Alt+V, H).

2. Click the Page Setup button 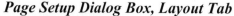 on the Header and Footer toolbar.
   OR
   Click <u>F</u>ile, Page Set<u>u</u>p (Alt+F, U).

3. Click the Layout tab, if necessary.
   The Page Setup dialog box appears as shown below.

Page Setup Dialog Box, Layout Tab

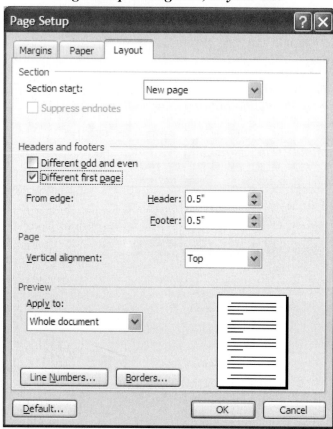

4. Select Different first <u>p</u>age.

5. Click OK.
   The First Page Header pane appears.
   If the First Page Header pane does not appear, click the Show
   Previous button to display it. The Show Previous button and
   Show Next button let you review all headers and footers in your
   document.

6. If text appears in the First Page Header pane, delete it so that no header appears on the first page.

7. Click the <u>C</u>lose button `Close` on the Header and Footer toolbar.

8. Print Preview the document to review the headers.

9. Close Print Preview, save the document, but leave it open.

Page Setup

You can use **<u>F</u>ile, <u>P</u>age Setup** without opening the header and footer pane. To edit the header or footer text, however, you must view the Header and Footer panes.

You can view the Header and Footer toolbar and panes by displaying the document in **<u>P</u>rint Layout** view and double-clicking the header or footer.

Different <u>o</u>dd and even

Select **Different <u>o</u>dd and even** to have different headers and footers on odd- and even-numbered pages. This option is used, as in the footers in this book, to maintain page numbers on the outside margins and to specify different kinds of identifying information on each page.

<u>H</u>eader specifies the distance from the top of the page to the header text. **<u>F</u>ooter** specifies the distance from the bottom of the page to the footer text.

Set Margins

■ For many of your documents, Word's default margins are appropriate. Sometimes, however, you may wish a page to include more (or less) text than the default margins allow. To increase the amount of text a page can hold, you make the margins smaller. To decrease the amount of text a page can hold, you make the margins larger.

■ The Page Setup dialog box Margins tab contains options for setting margins and the distance of headers and footers from the top and bottom edges of the paper, as shown in the following illustration.

Page Setup Dialog Box, Margins Tab

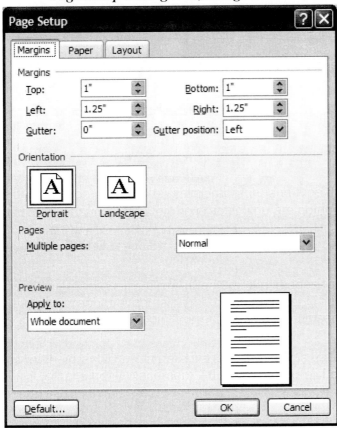

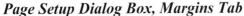

Margins

For all margins, the value in inches represents the distance from the edge of the paper to the body of the text.

Gutter specifies how much extra room to leave at the left or top of a page to allow for binding.

Gutter position specifies whether the extra space is at the left or top.

Multiple pages lets you choose from:

● **Normal** is the normal single page layout.

● **Mirror margins** is used for facing-page layout so that inside and outside margins are correct when the document is reproduced and bound like a book. This book, for example, was laid out in Word, using Mirror margins of 0.7" inside, 0.5" outside, and a gutter of 0.2" on the left.

● The other two options are for special booklet layouts.

Try It!

1. Click File, Page Setup (Alt + F, U).
2. Click the Margins tab, if necessary.
3. Change the Left margin to 1".
4. Change the Right margin to 1".
5. Make sure that Apply to specifies Whole document.
6. Leave the Top and Bottom margins at 1".
7. Click OK.
8. Print Preview the document.
9. Close Print Preview, save and close the document, and exit Word unless you are continuing with the Exercise Directions.

In this exercise, you will use Page Setup, insert your name and the page number in the footer, and insert a manual page break to alter the format of the report you formatted in the previous exercise.

EXERCISE DIRECTIONS

Open the File and Change the Margins

1. Open ⌨Report, or open 💿09Report from the data files.
2. Save the document as **Report2**.
3. Click View, Header and Footer to display the Header pane and the Header and Footer toolbar.
4. Click the Page Setup button 📖 to display the Page Setup dialog box.
5. Click the Margins tab.
6. Set the margins as follows to Apply to Whole document:
   - Top = 1.5"
   - Bottom = 1"
   - Left = 1"
   - Right = 1"
   - Gutter = 0"
   - Gutter position = Left
7. Click the Layout tab, and be sure the header and footer are set as follows:
   - Header = 0.5"
   - Footer = 0.5"
8. Be sure that neither *Different odd and even* nor *Different first page* is selected.
9. Click OK to close the Page Setup dialog box and return to the Header pane.
10. Save the document.

Insert Text in Header and Footer

1. Type your name in the Header pane.
2. Right-align the paragraph.
3. Click the Switch Between Header and Footer button 📑 to go to the Footer pane.
4. Type - (hyphen, space).
5. Click the Insert Page Number button 🔢.
6. Type - (space, hyphen).

7. Click the Center button ≡ on the Formatting toolbar to center the paragraph.

   The left half of the Footer pane should look similar to the following (your number may be -2-):

   ### Footer Pane

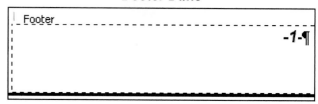

8. Save the document.

Format the Footer

1. Select the text (page number and hyphens) in the footer.
2. Change the font to Times New Roman.
3. Remove both the bold and italic. (Click the Bold and Italic buttons to turn off the emphasis formatting.)
4. Close the Header and Footer toolbar.
5. Save the document.

Insert a Manual Page Break

1. Place the insertion point to the left of the first word in the paragraph that begins *When spring came again*, as indicated in Illustration A on the next page.
2. Insert a manual page break (Ctrl+Enter or Insert, Break, and click Page Break [Alt+I, B, P], and then click OK).

Save, Print Preview, Print

1. Save the document.
2. Print Preview the document.
3. Print the document.
4. Compare your results to Illustration B on pages 148 and 149.
5. Close the document, and exit Word.

Illustration A. Page 1 (cropped at the top)

Wire bright
Clock fell down
Little mice run around
Old dirty dishrag
You spell out and go.

She and Joe didn't understand the song. "Something wrong with that song," Joe King would say. "Sure is something wrong with that song." They couldn't figure out what was wrong, but Bailey liked it anyway, especially the "tap-tap-tapping part in the chorus."

One day Tony the horse got so old that he dwindled away and died. As they dragged his carcass away,

> The mare stood up high on her feet and stared down the road where they had dragged Tony. She was trembling and shaking. Then she lifted her head and gave out a high, blowing whistle. It was almost like a cry. Joe King slapped her on the shoulder. "He's gone," Joe King said. "He ain't never coming back." The horse whistled again and Joe King gave her another comforting slap. "He's dead and gone, and you ain't never gon' see him no more."

Joe King died soon after. Bailey White went to his funeral, her first. She was more surprised at Joe's being dressed in clothes she had never seen before than by the spectacle of the funeral, with his relatives and their sorrowful grief.

Insert manual page break.

When spring came again, Ms. White missed Joe King for the first time. He didn't come driving up in his "powdery blue pickup truck smelling like horses and saddles and axle grease and Prince Albert." Ms. White concludes:

> And I still miss him…. I think about Joe King. I remember the elegant grieving of the Kentucky mare, and the eerie, high, blowing whistle she gave. That's how I would like to mourn. But I don't have that much style.

Your name

Report on "Joe King"
from *Mama Makes Up Her Mind*
by Bailey White

In her book, *Mama Makes Up Her Mind and Other Dangers of Southern Living*, Bailey White tells the story of Joe King, the man who allowed her to ride an old horse named Tony. The story tells of the song she and Joe King used to sing as she rode Tony, while Joe King rode a younger, more spirited Kentucky mare.

> William Matrimatoes
> He's a good fisherman
> Catches hens
> Puts 'em in pens
> Wire bright
> Clock fell down
> Little mice run around
> Old dirty dishrag
> You spell out and go.

She and Joe didn't understand the song. "Something wrong with that song," Joe King would say. "Sure is something wrong with that song." They couldn't figure out what was wrong, but Bailey liked it anyway, especially the "tap-tap-tapping part in the chorus."

One day Tony the horse got so old that he dwindled away and died. As they dragged his carcass away,

> The mare stood up high on her feet and stared down the road where they
> had dragged Tony. She was trembling and shaking. Then she lifted her
> head and gave out a high, blowing whistle. It was almost like a cry. Joe
> King slapped her on the shoulder. "He's gone," Joe King said. "He ain't
> never coming back." The horse whistled again and Joe King gave her
> another comforting slap. "He's dead and gone, and you ain't never gon'
> see him no more."

Joe King died soon after. Bailey White went to his funeral, her first. She was more surprised at Joe's being dressed in clothes she had never seen before than by the spectacle of the funeral, with his relatives and their sorrowful grief.

- 1 -

Illustration B. Desired Result, Page 2

Your name

When spring came again, Ms. White missed Joe King for the first time. He didn't come driving up in his "powdery blue pickup truck smelling like horses and saddles and axle grease and Prince Albert." Ms. White concludes:

> And I still miss him…. I think about Joe King. I remember the elegant grieving of the Kentucky mare, and the eerie, high, blowing whistle she gave. That's how I would like to mourn. But I don't have that much style. Instead, I like to take a little walk in the spring sunshine, and I say to myself:
>
> > William Matrimatoes
> > He's a good fisherman
> > Catches hens
> > Puts 'em in pens
> > Wire bright
> > Clock fell down
> > Little mice run around
> > Old dirty dishrag
> > You spell out and go.

White, Bailey. *Mama Makes Up Her Mind and Other Dangers of Southern Living.* Reading, MA: Addison-Wesley Publishing Company, 1993.

Exercise 10

Find and Replace Text
■ Use the Thesaurus ■ Find and Replace Text

NOTES

Use the Thesaurus

■ Word 2003 offers a synonym dictionary called a **Thesaurus**. The Thesaurus can help you find the right word, and it can help you avoid repeating a word over and over in a document.

💻 Try It!

1. Open 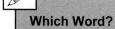**10Words** from the data files.
2. Save the document as **Words1**.
3. Point to the word *svelte*, and right-click.
4. On the shortcut menu, point to Synonyms.
5. Click *willowy* to replace the word *svelte*.
6. Right-click the word *willowy*, point to Synonyms, and then click Look Up on the shortcut menu.

   The Research task pane displays, as shown below.

Research Pane

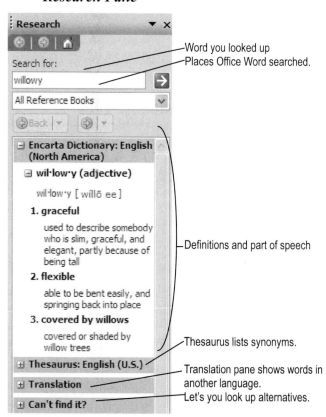

Which Word?

The Thesaurus cannot tell you whether the word is one that you should use. You have to know enough about the word to use it correctly. Choosing a word from the Thesaurus without knowing its meaning and connotation can make your document sound pretentious or silly.

Start Thesaurus

You can also open the Thesaurus by doing either of the following:

- Press **Shift+F7**.
- Click **Tools, Language, Thesaurus** (Alt+T, L, T) on the menu bar.

🖥️**Try It!**

Use the Thesaurus

1. Click the Close button ☒ on the Research pane.
2. Place the insertion point in the word *willowy*.
3. Press Shift+F7, or click <u>T</u>ools, <u>L</u>anguage, <u>T</u>hesaurus (Alt+T, L, T).

    The Research pane opens with the Thesaurus section expanded as shown in the following illustration.

    Thesaurus Section of Research Pane

    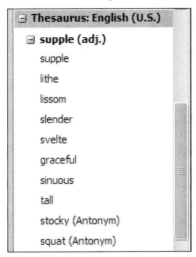

4. Point to the word *graceful*.

    The word is surrounded by a box with a drop-down arrow | graceful ▼ |.

    A list of synonyms for graceful *appears.*

5. Click the Back button | ⊕ Back ▼ |.

    The synonyms for willowy *reappear.*

6. Point to *graceful* again, click the drop-down button, and click the <u>I</u>nsert option.

    The word graceful replaces willowy.

    You can display the synonyms and antonyms for several words to find the one that you want.

🖥️**Try It!**

Word Forms and the Thesaurus

It is important to pay attention to the part of speech of the word you are looking up.

1. Press Ctrl+End to go to the end of the document.
2. Type **Godzilla fires the imagination.**
3. Place the insertion point in the word *fires*, and press Shift+F7.

    The Thesaurus displays in the task pane, as shown in the illustration that follows.

Sometimes the Thesaurus displays Related Words, a list of words that have related meanings.

Research Pane for fires

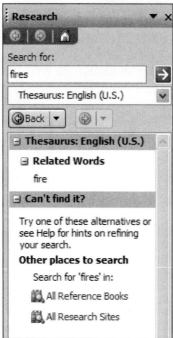

4. Under Related Words, point to fire, click the drop-down arrow, and click the Look Up option.

Choose Look Up Option

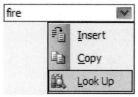

The resulting list (see the illustration that follows) contains several synonyms. Since the Godzilla sentence uses fires as a verb, you need to look up a verb form.

5. Scroll down to show the list of verbs under the word **inspire (v.)**.

List of Verb Synonyms for Fire

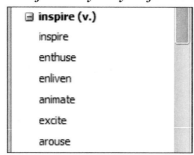

6. Insert the word *excite* to replace *fires*.

   The sentence now reads as follows: Godzilla excite the imagination.

   The verb has lost its "s" which indicates the tense and person.

7. Type the "**s**" to make the sentence correct.

8. Save and close the document, but do not exit Word.

As these steps show, you sometimes have to be careful and persistent to find a good replacement for the word you are looking up.

Find and Replace Text

- A useful tool for finding text and changing it is the Find and Replace feature. You can use it to look for an occurrence of a word or phrase, or you can use it to replace the word or phrase with another.

Try It!

1. Open ⊙ **10Godzilla** from the data files.

2. Save the document as **Godzilla1**.

3. Press Ctrl+F, or click <u>E</u>dit, <u>F</u>ind (Alt+E, F).
   The Find and Replace dialog box appears, as shown in the illustration on the next page.

4. Type the word **inspire** in the Fi<u>n</u>d what text box.

Find and Replace, Fin<u>d</u> Tab

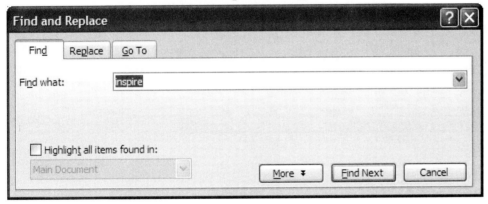

5. Click the <u>F</u>ind Next button [<u>F</u>ind Next].
   Word finds the first occurrence of the string of characters in the first sentence: inspires.

6. Click the <u>F</u>ind Next button [<u>F</u>ind Next].
   Word locates the word inspired.

7. Click the <u>F</u>ind Next button [<u>F</u>ind Next].
   Word locates the word inspire.

8. Click the Cancel button [Cancel] or press the Esc key to close the Find and Replace dialog box.

Try It!

Limit the Search

To prevent Word from finding words that you do not want, you can limit the search.

1. Press Ctrl+Home to go to the start of the document.

2. Open the Find and Replace dialog box (Ctrl+F or <u>E</u>dit, <u>F</u>ind).

3. Click the More button [More ▼] to display the Find and Replace dialog box with the additional options described below.

   Match case tells Word to look for the word or phrase capitalized exactly as you typed it in the Find what box.

   Find whole words only tells Word to look only for the word, not any variations of it.

Find and Replace after More is Selected

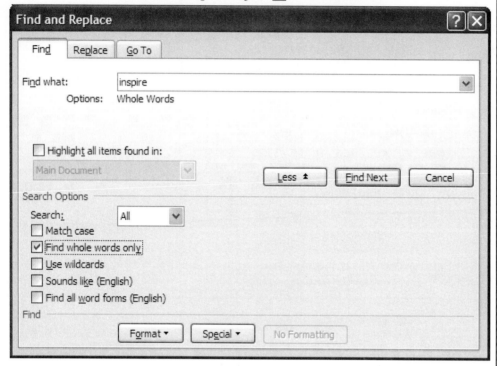

4. Select Find whole words only.
5. Click the Find Next button [Find Next].

   Word finds the word inspire *in the last sentence, but does not find* inspired *or* inspires *as it did before.*

6. Click the Cancel button [Cancel].
7. Leave the document open.

💻 **Try It!**

Replace a Word

1. Press Ctrl+Home to return to the start of the document.
2. Click the Replace tab if the Find and Replace dialog box is open.
   OR
   Press Ctrl+H, or click Edit, Replace (Alt+E, E).

   The Find and Replace dialog box appears with the Replace tab selected, as shown in the illustration on the next page.

Find and Replace with Replace Tab Selected

Find and Replace ? X

| Find | Replace | Go To |

Find what: `inspires`

Options: Whole Words

Replace with: `spurs`

[Less ▲] [Replace] [Replace All] [Find Next] [Cancel]

Search Options

Search: [All ▼]

☐ Match case
☑ Find whole words only
☐ Use wildcards
☐ Sounds like (English)
☐ Find all word forms (English)

Replace

[Format ▼] [Special ▼] [No Formatting]

3. In the Find what box, type the word **inspires**.

4. In the Replace with box, type the word **spurs**.
   Make sure that Find whole words only is checked.

5. Click the Find Next button [Find Next].
   Word selects the word inspires in the first sentence.

6. Click the Replace button [Replace].
   Word replaces the word and looks for it again. Since no other occurrences of inspires are found, Word tells you that it has completed searching the document.

7. Click OK, if available, or click the Find and Replace dialog box.

8. Save the document.

Try It!

1. Deselect Find whole words only (remove the check mark).

2. In the Find what box, type the word *inspire*.

3. In the Replace with box, type the word *excite*.

4. Click the Find Next button [Find Next].
   Word finds the word inspired in the last sentence. You do not want to replace this word.

5. Click the Find Next button [Find Next].
   Word finds the word inspire in the last sentence.

6. Click the Replace button [Replace].
   Word replaces the word and tells you that it has completed searching the document.

7. Click OK, if available, or click the Find and Replace dialog box.

8. Save the document.

155

🖥 Try It!

1. In the Find what box, type the word **gargantuan**.

2. In the Replace with box, type the word **huge**.

3. Click the Replace All button [Replace All].

   Word changes the word gargantuan in the second sentence, tells you that it has completed searching the document, and that it has made one replacement.

Find and Replace Results Message

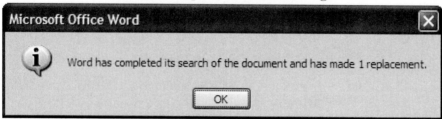

4. Click OK to turn off the message.

5. Click the Close button [Close], or click the Close button ☒ to close the Find and Replace dialog box.

6. Save and close the document, and exit Word unless you are continuing with the Exercise Directions.

In this exercise, you will use the Thesaurus and Find and Replace to change two names in a document.

EXERCISE DIRECTIONS

Open or Type the Document

1. Create a new document and type the text shown in Illustration A, or open 💿 **10Synonym** from the data files.

   If you type the document, you do not need to highlight the words that are highlighted in the illustration.

2. Save the document as **Synonym**.

3. Spell check the document.

Use the Thesaurus

1. Place the insertion point in each highlighted word shown in the illustration.

2. Use the Thesaurus feature to replace each word with a suitable synonym. Pay attention to the form of the verbs that are highlighted.

   For the word said, you may find it useful to look up related words to find declare and other synonyms.

3. Save the document.

Use Find and Replace

1. Return the insertion point to the top of the document.
2. Display the Find and Replace dialog box.
3. Use the Replace <u>A</u>ll button [Replace <u>A</u>ll] to change each occurrence of *Olivia* to *Terri*.

4. Save the document.
5. Print Preview the document.
6. Print one copy.
7. Close the document, and exit Word.

Illustration A. Paragraph with Words to Change

My willowy friend Olivia is a master of the enigmatic art of legerdemain. When she asked me to help her perform a particularly gruesome trick, I said that I was reluctant to appear on-stage because I am too meek and afraid to be cut in half, even in fun. Once I asked her, "How do you make a delicious triple fudge sundae disappear?" "I eat it!" she said.

Exercise 11

Create Tables

■ Introduction to Tables ■ Create a Table ■ Move within a Table
■ Enter Text in a Table ■ Use the Tables and Borders Toolbar

NOTES

Introduction to Tables

- Tables let you organize information in columns and rows without using tabs. The junction between the row and column is called a cell, as shown in the illustration below.

Table Structure

	Column 1	Column 2	Column 3	End of Row marker
Row 1	Cell (Row 1, Col 1)¤	Cell (Row 1, Col 2)¤	Cell (Row 1, Col 3)¤	¤
Row 2	Cell (Row 2, Col 1)¤	Cell (Row 2, Col 2)¤	Cell (Row 2, Col 3)¤	¤
Row 3	Cell (Row 3, Col 1)¤	Cell (Row 3, Col 2)¤	Cell (Row 3, Col 3)¤	¤

End of Cell marker

Create a Table

- Word offers several ways to create a table.

💻 **Try It!**

Insert Table Button

1. Start Word and create a new document.

2. Save the document as **Tables1**.

3. Click the Show/Hide button **¶** , if it is not already on.

4. Click the Insert Table button 🔳 on the Standard toolbar. Word displays a drop-down grid, as shown in the illustration that follows.

5. Move the mouse pointer to the third row and third column and click. *Word inserts a three-column, three-row table in the document.*

Insert Table Drop-Down Grid

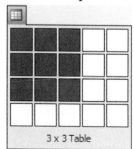

3 x 3 Table

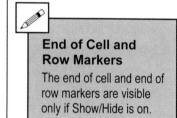

End of Cell and Row Markers

The end of cell and end of row markers are visible only if Show/Hide is on.

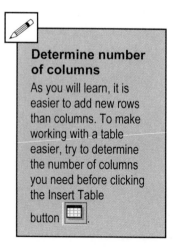

Determine number of columns

As you will learn, it is easier to add new rows than columns. To make working with a table easier, try to determine the number of columns you need before clicking the Insert Table button 🔳 .

🖥️**Try It!**

Table Menu

1. Go to the end of the document, and press the Enter key twice.

2. Click T̲able, I̲nsert, T̲able (Alt+A, I, T).

3. Word displays the Insert Table dialog box, as shown below.

4. Specify 2 in Number of c̲olumns and 2 in Number of r̲ows.

5. For AutoFit behavior, leave Fixed column w̲idth and Auto.

   AutoFit behavior controls whether columns adjust automatically to the length of the text entered.

6. Click the OK button [OK].

   Word inserts a two-column, two-row table in the document.

Insert Table Dialog Box

🖥️**Try It!**

Draw a Table

1. Go to the end of the document, and press the Enter key twice.

2. Click the Tables and Borders button 🖉 on the Standard toolbar.

   Word enters Print Layout view, the Tables and Borders toolbar appears (see page 161), and the mouse pointer turns into a pencil ✎.

3. Drag the pencil to form a dotted rectangle about an inch high and about half the width of the page, as shown in the illustration on the following page.

Drawing a Table

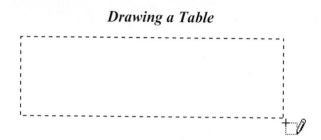

When you release the mouse button, Word inserts a one-column, one-row table the size of the rectangle you drew.

4. Place the pointer ✐ about halfway down the left side of the rectangle, and drag it across the rectangle to create two rows.

5. Place the pointer ✐ on the top line of the rectangle about halfway across the box, and drag the pointer down to the bottom line to create two columns.

   You have drawn a table with two rows and two columns.

6. Click the Draw Table button ✐ on the Tables and Borders toolbar to turn off the table drawing feature.

   The new document should now be similar to the one shown in the illustration that follows.

Blank Tables Created

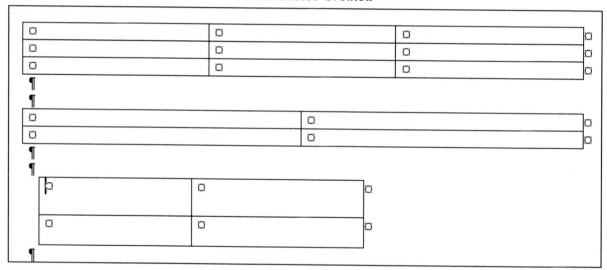

Move within a Table

💻 **Try It!**

1. Place the insertion point in the upper-left cell of the top table.
2. Press the Tab key.

   The insertion point moves to the next cell in the same row.

3. Press the Tab key twice.

   The insertion point moves to the first cell in the second row.

4. Press Shift+Tab.

   The insertion point moves back to the third cell in the first row.

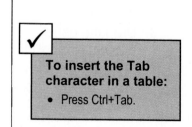

To insert the Tab character in a table:
- Press Ctrl+Tab.

5. Move the mouse pointer to the third cell in the third row.
6. Press the Tab key.

   Word inserts a new row in the table.

Enter Text in a Table

- You can have as many paragraphs in a table cell as you wish. The paragraphs can have different formats. The paragraphs can be aligned as you wish, just like paragraphs that are not in a table.

🖥 Try It!

1. Use the mouse to place the insertion point in column 1, row 1 of the second table.
2. Type the following text:

   Now is the winter of our discontent made glorious summer by this son of York.¶

3. Position the insertion point at the beginning of the sentence, and press Ctrl+Tab to indent the first line.
4. Tab to the next cell and type the following text:

   But soft! What light through yonder window breaks? It is the East, and Juliet is the sun.

5. Click Format, Paragraph and indent the paragraph 0.5" from the left and from the right.
6. Tab to the next cell and type the following text:

   Sunny days, sweeping the clouds away,¶
   On my way to where the air is free.¶
   Can you tell me how to get,¶
   How to get to Sesame Street?

7. Tab to the next cell and type the following text:

   The light that reaches us from the sun is already about eight minutes old.

Use the Tables and Borders Toolbar

- The Tables and Borders toolbar provides ways to enhance the appearance of a table.

🖥 Try It!

1. If the Tables and Borders toolbar is not displayed, click the Tables and Borders button  on the Standard toolbar.

   OR

   Click View, Toolbars (Alt+V, T) and select Tables and Borders.

Tables and Borders Toolbar

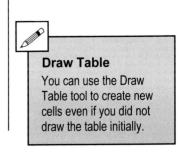

Draw Table
You can use the Draw Table tool to create new cells even if you did not draw the table initially.

2. Click the Draw Table button . If the mouse pointer is already a pencil, do not click the Draw Table button.

3. Draw a vertical line in the bottom table to split the first column into two new columns, as shown below.

Draw New Columns

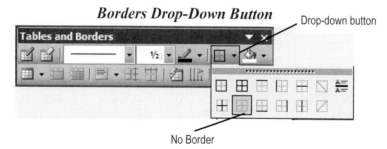

4. Click the Eraser button and drag it down the line you just created.

   Word erases the line and merges the cells (makes them into one).

5. Click the Eraser button again when finished.

⌨ Try It!

Cell Borders

By default, Word places a border around each cell of a table. If you do not wish to have a border on the table, you can eliminate the borders.

1. Click anywhere inside the middle table.

2. Select the entire table by clicking Table, Select, Table (Alt+A, C, T).

3. Click the Borders drop-down button (see below) on the Tables and Borders toolbar.

Borders Drop-Down Button

Drop-down button

No Border

The dark lines on the buttons show the border area controlled by the button. The grid with no dark line specifies a table with no borders.

4. Click the No Border button ⊞ to remove all borders from the table.

   If you wish to remove borders only from some cells, select the cell or cells and click the appropriate borders button from the drop-down list.

5. Print Preview the document.

   Note how the four paragraphs appear without borders.

6. Save and close the document, and exit Word unless you are continuing with the Exercise Directions.

Borders Button
The Borders button with its drop-down arrow also appears on the Standard toolbar when you are working with tables.

In this exercise, you will create a four-row, three-column table and enter text into its cells.

EXERCISE DIRECTIONS

Create a Table

1. Create a new document.
2. Save the document as **Tapes**.
3. Use the Insert Table button ▦ to create a 4 x 3 table (four rows, three columns).
4. Enter the text shown in Illustration A into the table.
5. Use the Tab key to move from cell to cell.
6. Save the document.

Format the Table

1. Select the first row of the table.
   a. Place the insertion point anywhere in the row.
   b. Click Table, Select, Row.
2. Make the text bold.
3. Select the paragraph in row 2, column 2 with the title *Evolution*.
4. Indent the paragraph from the left 0.2".
5. Use Format Painter to format the other episode titles with a 0.2" left indent.
6. Save the document.
7. Print Preview the document.
8. Print one copy.
9. Compare your results with Illustration B.
10. Close the document, and exit Word.

Illustration A. 4 × 3 Table with Text

Tape#	Contents	Condition
001	Start Trek: Next Generation Episodes: Evolution Ensigns of Command The Price High Ground The Offspring	Fair
002	X-Files, Season Premiere, 1998	Good
003	A Man for All Seasons	Good

Illustration B. Desired Result

Tape#	**Contents**	**Condition**
001	Start Trek: Next Generation Episodes: Evolution Ensigns of Command The Price High Ground The Offspring	Fair
002	X-Files, Season Premiere, 1998	Good
003	A Man for All Seasons	Good

Exercise 12

Format Tables

■ Insert and Delete Columns and Rows ■ Adjust Column Widths
■ Position a Table Horizontally ■ Add Shading to a Cell ■ Use Table AutoFormat

NOTES

Insert and Delete Columns and Rows

💻 **Try It!**

Insert a Column

1. Open 💿 **12Games** from the data files.

2. Save the document as **Games**.

3. Place the insertion point anywhere in the second column of the table, and click Table, Select, Column (Alt+A, C, C).

   OR

   a. Let the mouse pointer rest above the top margin of the second column.

      The pointer turns into a bold, black down-pointing arrow ↓ *.*

   b. Click to select the column.

4. Click Table, Insert, Columns to the Left (Alt+A, I, L).

   Word inserts a column of the same width to the left of the selected column.

5. With the new column selected, Click Table, Insert, Columns to the Left (Alt+A, I, L).

   Word inserts another column, making a four-column table.

💻 **Try It!**

Delete a Column

• With the second new column selected, click Table, Delete, Columns (Alt+A, D, C).

   The table now has three columns.

💻 **Try It!**

Insert a Row

1. Point to the selection area to the left of the Darts row of the table. (The selection area is at the left side of the Word workspace.)

   The pointer turns into a right-slanting arrow 𝄃.

2. Click to select the Darts row.

   OR

Place the insertion point anywhere in the Darts row, and click T<u>a</u>ble, Sele<u>c</u>t, <u>R</u>ow (Alt+A, C, R).

3. Click T<u>a</u>ble, <u>I</u>nsert, Rows <u>A</u>bove (Alt+A, I, A).

    Word inserts a row above the Darts row.

4. Click T<u>a</u>ble, <u>I</u>nsert, Rows <u>A</u>bove (Alt+A, I, A).

    Word inserts another row above the selected row.

Try It!

Delete a Row

- With the new row selected, click T<u>a</u>ble, <u>D</u>elete, <u>R</u>ows (Alt+A, D, R).

Try It!

Insert Text

1. In the remaining blank row, type the following entries.

Chess	Two	Chessboard Chess pieces Flat surface Timer (optional)

2. In the top row, middle column, type **Number of Players**.

3. In the second row (Dominoes), type **Two to Six**.

4. For Checkers, type **Two**.

5. For Darts, type **Two or more**.

6. For Scrabble, type **Two to Four**.

7. Save the document.

8. Leave the document open.

Adjust Column Widths

- When the insertion point is anywhere in a table, the ruler looks like the one shown in the illustration that follows. The small dotted squares mark the boundaries between columns.

Ruler Line for Table

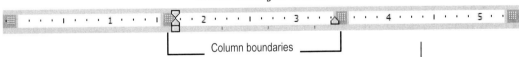

Column boundaries

Try It!

Adjust Width Manually

1. Place the insertion point anywhere in the table, but do not select any text.

2. Place the mouse pointer on the column boundary closest to the 4 on the ruler.

    The mouse pointer becomes a two-headed arrow .

3. Click and drag the column boundary to the left or right to adjust the width of the column.

    Word extends a dotted, vertical line through the table to show where the boundary is being moved.

✓

To delete text from a cell, row, or column:

1. Select the cell, row, or column.

2. Press the Delete key.

---

4. Drag the boundary to the left until it nearly reaches the end-of-cell marker for Number of Players, as shown below.

5. Save the document.

Column boundary
marker extended

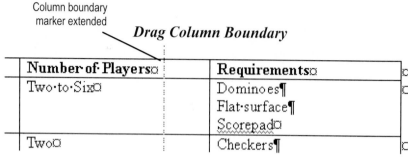

Drag Column Boundary

Number of Players¤	Requirements¤	¤
Two·to·Six¤	Dominoes¶ Flat·surface¶ Scorepad¤	¤
Two¤	Checkers¶	¤

💻 **Try It!**

Adjust Width with AutoFit

The AutoFit feature adjusts the width of a column to the longest text entry in the column:

1. Select the entire table by dragging the mouse pointer or by clicking, Table, Select, Table (Alt+A, C, T).

2. Place the mouse pointer on a boundary between two columns.

   The mouse pointer turns into a double-headed arrow with a double vertical bar ┿.

3. Double-click.

   All column widths adjust to the longest text entry.

4. Save the document.

• To AutoFit the width of a single column, double-click on the column boundary to the right of the column.

Position a Table Horizontally

■ Tables can be left-aligned with an indent, right-aligned, or centered.

💻 **Try It!**

1. Place the insertion point in the table, but do not select any text.
2. Click Table, Table Properties (Alt+A, R).
3. Select the Table tab if it is not selected (Alt+T or T).

   Word displays the Table Properties dialog box, as shown in the illustration that follows.

4. In the Alignment section, select Center to center the table under the title of the document.

   Left aligns the table at the left margin. Right aligns the table at the right margin. If you choose Left, you can enter an Indent from left to position the table a specific distance from the left margin.

5. Click the OK button [OK], or press Enter.
6. Save the document.

✓

Another Way to Select an Entire Table

1. Point to the upper-left corner of the table.

   Word displays the table selector

2. Click the table selector.

Table Properties Dialog Box, Table Tab

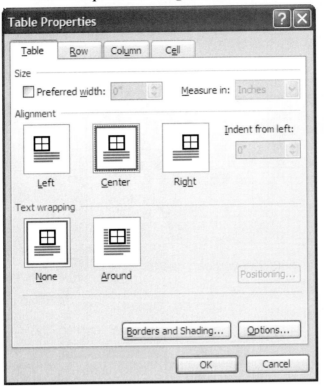

Add Shading to a Cell

- Word lets you shade individual cells, a group of cells, whole rows, and entire columns. Shading is often used to call attention to important information in a table. It is also frequently used in headings to distinguish the heading row from other rows.

Try It!

1. Select the top row of the table.
2. Click the drop-down arrow next to the Shading Color button on the Tables and Borders toolbar, as shown on the next page.
3. Click the black color box.
4. Click outside the row.
   The cells turn black, and the text turns white.
5. Save the document.

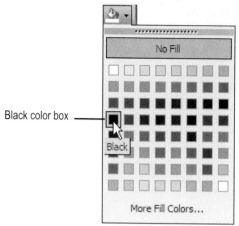

Shading Color Drop-Down Options

Black color box

No Fill

Black

More Fill Colors...

Use Table AutoFormat

- Word provides a number of predefined formats that you can use to format tables.

💻 Try It!

1. Place the insertion point in any cell of the table.

2. Click the Table AutoFormat button on the Tables and Borders toolbar.

   OR

   Click T<u>a</u>ble, Table Auto<u>F</u>ormat (Alt+A, F).

   Word displays the Table AutoFormat dialog box, as shown in the illustration that follows.

3. Select Table Colorful 3 from the <u>T</u>able styles box.

4. Under Apply special formats to, select Heading <u>r</u>ows.

5. Click the <u>A</u>pply button [Apply].

   Word applies the format as specified. You can adjust the format after applying it.

6. Click T<u>a</u>ble, Table P<u>r</u>operties, and click the <u>T</u>ables tab. Select <u>C</u>enter to center the table, and click the OK button [OK], or press Enter.

7. Select the heading row, and change the text color to white using the Font Color button drop-down arrow on the Formatting toolbar.

   The desired result is shown in the illustration on page 169.

8. Save the document, close it, and exit Word unless you are continuing with the Exercise Directions.

AutoFormat Options

In the Formats to apply section of the Table AutoFormat dialog box, you can deselect any option that you do not want to apply.

You can also adjust the colors, borders, and shading formats after applying the AutoFormat.

Table AutoFormat Dialog Box

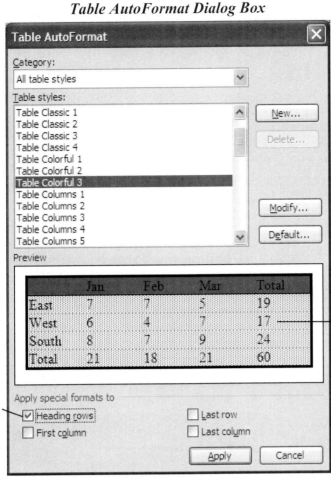

Select this option to shade heading row darker.

Word shows a sample table in the lower part of the dialog box to help you choose a suitable format.

Desired Result

Some Games and Their Requirements

Game	Number of Players	Requirements
Dominoes	Two to Six	Dominoes Flat surface Scorepad
Checkers	Two	Checkers Checkerboard Flat surface
Chess	Two	Chessboard Chess pieces Flat surface Timer (Optional)
Darts	Two or more	Dartboard Darts Unobstructed path from shooting line to board
Scrabble®	Two to four	Scrabble board Scrabble tiles Flat surface Scorepad

In this exercise, you will insert rows in a table, adjust the column widths, position the table horizontally, and shade the table headings.

EXERCISE DIRECTIONS

Insert a Row and Add a Row to the Table

1. Open ⌨ **Tapes**, or open 💿 **12Tapes** from the data files.
2. Save the file as **Tapes2**.
3. Place the insertion point in the row of the table that has *002* in the first column.
4. Insert a new row (T̲able, I̲nsert, Row A̲bove).
5. Type the following text in the three cells.

006	Rocky and Bullwinkle	Good

6. Place the insertion point in the rightmost cell of the last row.
7. Press the Tab key to add a row at the bottom of the table.
8. Enter the following text in the three cells.

020	Star Wars: The Empire Strikes Back	Fair

9. Save the document.

Adjust the Column Widths

1. Click anywhere in the table. Be sure that no text is selected.
2. AutoFit the first column by double-clicking on the boundary line between between columns 1 and 2.
3. On the ruler, select the marker for the column boundary between columns 2 and 3.
4. AutoFit column 2 to allow the word *Episodes* to be on the same line as *Star Trek: Next Generation*.

5. Select the boundary marker for the last column

       ————— Boundary marker for last column

You can drag this boundary marker just as you can drag the boundary marker for an inside column.

6. Drag it to the left, almost to the end-of-cell marker for Condition.
7. Save the document.

Position the Table Horizontally and Shade the Heading Row

1. Click anywhere in the table. Be sure that no text is selected.
2. Center the table between the margins.
   Hint: Use the T̲able menu, Table P̲roperties, T̲able tab.
3. Select the heading row.
4. Use the Shading Color drop-down menu on the Tables and Borders toolbar to select Dark Red (fourth row from the bottom in the first column).
5. Save the document.

Print Preview, and Print

1. Print Preview the file.
2. Print one copy.
3. Compare your results with Illustration A.
4. Save the document.
5. Close the document, and exit Word.

Illustration A. Desired Result (Tapes2)

Tape #	Contents	Condition
001	Star Trek: Next Generation Episodes Evolution Ensigns of Command The Price High Ground The Offspring	Fair
006	Rocky and Bullwinkle	Good
002	X-Files, Season Premiere, 1998	Good
003	A Man for All Seasons	Good
020	Star Wars: The Empire Strikes Back	Fair

Exercise 13

Challenge Exercises

EXERCISE DIRECTIONS

Format a Story

1. Open 💿 **13Fairmaiden** from the data files.
2. Save the document as **Fairmaiden**.
3. Double-space the document.
4. Change the font size for all text to 11 points.
5. Insert a title at the top of the document:
   The Fair Maiden
6. Center the title.
7. Make it Arial, 24-point bold, italic.
8. Leave 36 points (three lines) after the title paragraph.
   Hint: *Because Line spacing is already set to double, one blank line (24 points) follows the title. You need to specify enough space after the title to bring the total to 36 points.*
9. Save the document.
10. Center a page number at the bottom of each page.
11. Print Preview the document.
12. Spell check the document.
13. Save the document.
14. Print one copy.
15. Close the document, and exit Word unless you are continuing with the Challenge Exercises.

Create a Memorandum

1. Start Word and create a new document.
2. Press Enter three times.
3. Place the insertion point in the first paragraph and type the memorandum shown in Illustration A on the next page.
4. Center the word *Memorandum*, use Times New Roman, 24-point bold.
5. Save the memorandum as **Latin Club**.
6. Place a double underline under the word *Memorandum*.
   Hint: *Use Format, Font and locate the double underline option.*
7. Type the remaining text in the document.
8. Use Times New Roman, 12 point for all text.
9. Format the bullets and indents using the appropriate buttons on the Formatting toolbar.
10. Use blank paragraphs to separate the body paragraphs.
11. Italicize the Latin words as shown in Illustration A.
12. Spell check the document.
13. Print Preview the document.
14. Save the document.
15. Print one copy.
16. Close the document, and exit Word unless you are continuing with the Challenge Exercises.

Memorandum

To: Members of Latin Club

From: Your name

Date: Today's date

Subject: Installation of New Officers

Ave, amici.

The year-end meeting of the Latin Club will be held on Thursday, June 4, at 3:30 in Room 225. At that time, we will officially install the following new Latin Club officers:

- Miguel Palacio, President
- Mary Jane Pastore, Vice-President
- Allison Clarke, Secretary
- Hanover Chase, Treasurer

Refreshments will be served at the end of the installation. Outgoing officers will express their appreciation to Mr. Cato, our club sponsor, and plans for travel to next year's state Junior Classical League conference will be discussed.

It has been a great year. *Gratias.*

Vale, amici.

Format a Letter

1. Open ⊙ **13Gourmet** from the data disk. Create the result shown in Illustration B by following the steps below.
2. Save the document as **Gourmet**.
3. At the top of the document, insert a table of one row and three columns.
4. Move the writer's name to the first column; move the street address to the second column; move the city, state, and ZIP Code to the third column.
5. Select the table; remove the border; shade the entire row with a dark color such as navy blue or dark red.
6. Change the font in the table to Arial, 14-point bold, italic.
7. Format the paragraphs in the table with 12 points Before and 12 points After.
8. Center the paragraph in column 2.
9. Right align the paragraph in column 3.
10. Insert today's date.
11. Click the Show/Hide button, if necessary, to hide Word's nonprinting paragraph symbols.
12. Press Enter for each paragraph symbol in **Gourmet**, and delete the symbol.
13. Save the document.
14. Print Preview the document.
15. Print one copy.
16. Close the document, and exit Word.

Phineas Bream   **814 Court Street**   **Scott City, KS 67871**

Today's date

Hake Sturgeon
The E-Z Gourmet
1234 Lobster Lane
Cabot Cove, ME 01333

Dear Mr. Sturgeon:

On your January 16 TV show, seen in this area on KGLD in Garden City, KS, you demonstrated how to prepare creamy clam chowder. Fresh clams not being available here on the plains of Kansas, I substituted canned oyster. What a treat the dish turned out to be!

When I served it to my family, accompanied by a cucumber and tomato salad, the raves were long and as hearty as the chowder itself.

Thanks for such a tasty recipe.

Sincerely,

Phineas Bream

Lesson 5: Desktop Publishing

Exercise 1: Begin Using Clip Art
- About Desktop Publishing
- Insert Microsoft Clip Art
- Use the Clip Art Task Pane
- Size a Graphic Using the Mouse

Exercise 2: Insert Graphics from a File
- Insert a Graphic from a File
- Size a Graphic Using the Format Picture Dialog Box

Exercise 3: Use Floating Graphics
- Create a Floating Graphic
- Use Other Text Wrapping Options
- Size a Graphic Using the Dialog Box
- Align Floating Graphics Independently
- Align Floating Graphics in Relation to One Another
- Add a Border to a Page

Exercise 4: Create a Newsletter
- Multiple Column Formats
- Insert Section Breaks
- Put a Border Around a Graphic
- Border/Shade a Paragraph
- Insert a File

Exercise 1

Begin Using Clip Art
■ About Desktop Publishing ■ Insert Microsoft Clip Art
■ Use the Clip Art Task Pane ■ Size a Graphic Using the Mouse

NOTES

About Desktop Publishing

- Using desktop publishing, you can create documents that combine text and graphics. Desktop publishing applications, such as Adobe PageMaker, Quark XPress, Corel Ventura, and Microsoft Publisher were created specifically to make combining text and graphics easy because early word processing applications could not combine graphics and text very well. Recent versions of word processors, however, offer many of the features that used to belong solely to desktop publishing applications.

- Although Word 2003 was not specifically designed to perform desktop publishing, it has many desktop publishing features. You can combine text and graphics to create documents that look attractive and professional.

> **Image, Graphic, Picture**
> As used in this book, the three terms—**image**, **graphic**, **picture**—have the same meaning and are used interchangeably.

Organize Microsoft Clip Art

- Microsoft Office can organize clip art and other graphics on your computer automatically. The first time you try to insert clip art after installing Microsoft Office 2003, a message like the following appears.

Add Clips to Organizer

- To allow Microsoft Office to organize the clip art on your computer, click the Now button [Now]. Microsoft Office searches your hard drive for graphics that it can use and incorporates them into the Microsoft Clip Art Organizer.

- If the message does not appear, your clip art has probably already been organized.

Insert Microsoft Clip Art

- In Word, you insert graphics directly into the word processing file. To make it easy to create documents with graphics, Microsoft Office provides a number of clip art images that you can use in your documents.

- Some of these images are installed on your hard drive with Microsoft Office. Others are available through Microsoft's Web site. If you have a constant high-speed Internet connection (cable modem, DSL, T1 line, or other fast connection), you may wish to use images from the Web. Microsoft Web-based images are indicated by a small globe in the lower-left corner of the graphic. If you cannot find the graphic shown in this text, substitute any appropriate available image; you need not feel obliged to find the exact image referred to in an exercise.

Try It!

Prepare the Document and Create a Caption

1. Start Word and create a new document.

2. Click the Show/Hide button **¶** to display the formatting characters. *You may find it easier to work with the paragraph symbols visible.*

3. Press the Enter key twice.

4. Place the insertion point in the first paragraph, and type the word **Tiger** to serve as a caption for the graphic you are going to insert.

5. Format the word as 22-point bold, italic, and center the paragraph.

6. Save the document as **Tiger1**.

- When you work with Microsoft's Clip Art feature, the images (graphics) are inserted in the paragraph that contains the insertion point. Thus, it is important to place the insertion point correctly before you insert the clip art graphic.

- The insertion of the graphic into a paragraph in this way is called **in-line** placement. The other kind of placement—**float over text** or **floating**—you will learn about later in this lesson.

Try It!

Prepare the Document and Create a Caption

1. Position the insertion point in the last blank line.

2. Click Insert, Picture, Clip Art (Alt+I, P, C). *The task pane displays the Clip Art search options, as shown in the illustration that follows. This feature works in a similar way in the other Microsoft Office applications.*

Clip Art Sources

Many software applications include graphics that can be incorporated into your documents. In addition, CDs with images are widely available in software outlets, bookstores, and music stores.

Also, if you have access to the Internet, you can find graphic images available for downloading. Be sure that you have permission to use any images you download if you plan to distribute the document you create.

Graphic Placement

With **In-line** placement, the graphic is inserted in a paragraph. Its horizontal alignment and vertical position are controlled by paragraph formatting techniques.

Float-over-text (floating) graphics are positioned by independently of the text in the document by use of picture layout options.

Clip Art Task Pane Search Options

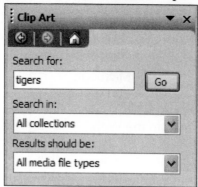

3. In the Search for text box, type **tigers**.
4. In the Search in box, click the drop-down arrow and select Everywhere so that the clip art feature searches all available sources for images.

    If your searches take too long, limit the search to Office Collections.

Clip Art Task Pane Search in Options

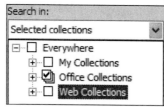

5. In the Results should be box, click the drop-down arrow and select Clip Art and Photographs.

Clip Art Task Pane Results should be Options

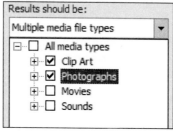

6. Click the Go button Go .

    The task pane displays a group of images that match the search text entered, in this case: tigers.

7. Click any appropriate image of a tiger.

    The image appears in the document in the paragraph that contains the insertion point.

8. Click the graphic or place the insertion point to the right or left of the image but within the paragraph where it is inserted.

9. Click the Center button .

    The graphic is centered under the caption you created with a blank line between the caption and the graphic.

10. Save the document.

Web Collections

If you have constant access to the World Wide Web (Internet), Office can automatically search the Microsoft Office clip art Web site for images that match your search criteria.

Clip Art Search Results

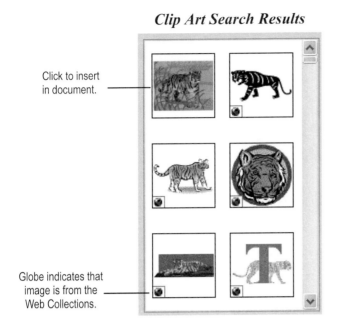

Click to insert in document.

Globe indicates that image is from the Web Collections.

Use the Clip Art Task Pane

- The Clip Art task pane appears when you click Insert, Picture, Clip Art, and it remains displayed so that you can continue to use it. The following options can help.

  - Point to an image to view a ScreenTip with information about the graphic—search categories, size, and format.

  - At the bottom of the task pane, the Organize clips, Clip art on Office Online, and Tips for finding clips can help you make efficient use of the clip art feature. These options are not described in this book.

Try It!

Insert another Image

1. Press Ctrl+End to go to the last line of the document.

2. Press the Enter key twice.

   You have two blank paragraphs under the tiger image.

3. In the Search text box, type **cat**, and press the Enter key or click the Search button Go.

   The task pane displays images that include cats.

4. Point to the image in the upper left to display the ScreenTip, as shown in the following illustration.

   The ScreenTip gives the categories—animals, cats, children, dogs— which can be entered as Search criteria to locate this image. It also gives the size in pixels (one dot on the monitor screen), size in kilobytes (KB), and the format (WMF, the file extension, which means Windows metafile).

   Note that a scroll bar may appear to indicate that more images are available than those displayed.

Clip Art ScreenTip

animals, cats, children, dogs...
210 (w) x 264 (h) pixels, 24 KB, WMF

5. Point to the image of the veterinarian and the girl with the cat.
6. Right-click the image.

A menu appears, as shown in the following illustration.

Clip Art Menu

7. Click the <u>I</u>nsert option to place the image in the document.

The image appears in the document in the last paragraph.

Size a Graphic Using the Mouse

■ The proportions of an image—the relationship between its height and width—are called its **aspect ratio**. When you change the size of a graphic, you can maintain its aspect ratio or distort the image's proportions, as described in the Try It! activities that follow.

 Try It!

Enlarge an Image and Maintain its Aspect Ratio

1. Click the tiger image to select it.

*The image is surrounded by a black border with small black squares called **sizing handles**, and the Picture toolbar appears.*

If the Picture toolbar does not appear automatically when you select the picture, click <u>V</u>iew, <u>T</u>oolbars, Picture (Alt+V, T, Picture).

Use Keyboard to Select a Toolbar

To select an option from a menu such as the list of toolbars where no letters are underlined:

1. Use the down and up arrow keys to highlight the option you want.

2. Press the Enter key.

Note that you can use the down and up arrow keys and Enter on any menu to select an option.

Sizing Handles

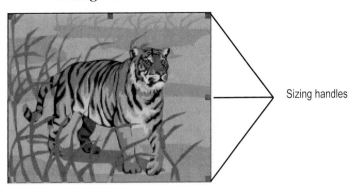

Sizing handles

2. Place the mouse pointer on the upper-right corner sizing handle.

   The mouse pointer turns into a two-headed arrow ⤢.

3. Click on the sizing handle, and hold down the left mouse button.

   The mouse pointer turns into a crosshair ✛, and a dotted line surrounds the image.

4. Drag the crosshair and dotted line in the direction which will enlarge the image, as shown in the illustration below.

   The arrow is part of the illustration, not part of the graphic. Note also that the Show/Hide button has been pressed so paragraph marks are visible.

5. When you have enlarged the image by about 50%, release the mouse button.

   Dragging a corner of an image maintains its aspect ratio.

Enlarge a Graphic

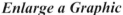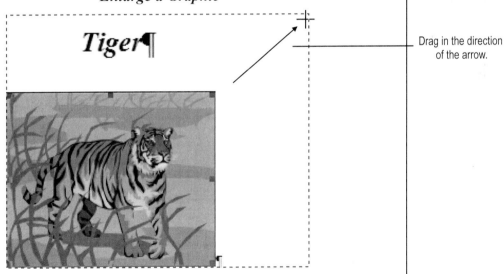

Drag in the direction of the arrow.

🖥️**Try It!**

Shrink an Image and Maintain its Aspect Ratio

1. Place the mouse pointer on the upper-right corner sizing handle of the tiger image.

2. Drag the handle in the direction that will shrink the image, as shown in the following illustration.

3. When you have shrunk the image to about one-half its previous size, release the mouse button.

4. Save the document.

Shrink a Graphic

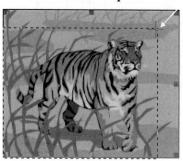

Drag in the direction of the arrow.

🖥 Try It!

Enlarge an Image and Distort its Aspect Ratio

1. Select the tiger graphic.

2. Place the mouse pointer on the sizing handle in the middle of the right side of the graphic.

   The mouse pointer turns into a two-headed arrow ↔.

3. Click on the sizing handle and hold down the mouse button.

4. Drag the handle toward the right to increase the width of the original image, as shown in the illustration below.

   The resulting image is wider and its original aspect ratio has changed.

Stretch a Graphic Image

Stretching   **Stretched**

Drag to the right.

🖥 Try It!

Shrink an Image and Distort its Aspect Ratio

1. Select the image of the tiger.

2. Place the mouse pointer on the sizing handle in the middle of the right side of the graphic.

   The mouse pointer turns into a two-headed arrow ↔.

3. Click on the sizing handle and hold down the mouse button.

4. Drag the handle toward the left until the image is narrower than the original, as shown in the following illustration.

The resulting image is narrower and its original aspect ratio has changed.

5. Save and close the document, and exit Word unless you are continuing with the Exercise Directions.

Squeeze a Graphic

Squeezing

← Drag to the left.

Squeezed

As a member of the Lightwood family, you want to create a flyer announcing the next family reunion. The text of the flyer has been created but not formatted. In this exercise, you will format the text and add some graphics. In the next exercise, you will complete the flyer with different graphics.

EXERCISE DIRECTIONS

Format the Title and Subtitle

1. Open 💿 **01Flyer** from the data files.
2. Save the document as **Flyer1**.
3. Use File, Page Setup to change the margins to:
   Top: 0.75", Bottom: 0.75", Left: 0.75", Right: 0.75"
4. Use <u>E</u>dit, Select A<u>l</u>l (Ctrl+A) to select the entire document.
5. Center all paragraphs.
6. Place the insertion point at the beginning of the document.
7. Insert a symbol from the Symbol dialog box and a space before the title *We are Family!* Insert a space and the same symbol after the title.
8. Insert a different symbol before and after the subtitle *Lightwood Family Reunion*.
9. Select both the title and subtitle and set the font to a decorative font, such as Market or Broadway, 28-point blue.

   If you do not have Market or Broadway on your system, use another decorative font, or choose Arial Black. (Illustrations A use the Market font.)

10. Reduce the point size of the subtitle, if necessary, so that it fits on one line.

    With Broadway, for example, reduce the subtitle font size to 24 points.

11. Place the insertion point anywhere in the subtitle, and set the spacing before to 12 points.
12. Save the document.

Format the Text

1. Change the year (yyyy) to the year of next August, and format the date to Arial, 22-point bold.
2. Set the spacing before the paragraph to 18 points.
3. Use Format Painter and select the entire date paragraph.
4. Drag Format Painter across the next line—*Floyd & Leona Riverside Park.*

   The line should now be Arial, 22-point bold with 18 points before it.

5. Select the line you just formatted and change the font size to 18 points.
6. Format *Chaffin Shelter House* to Arial, 16-point bold.
7. Set the two address lines to Arial, 12 point.

183

8. Format *What Fun!* to Arial Black, 24-point, blue. Set the spacing before to 18 points.

9. Format *Baked Macaroni and Cheese Contest* to Arial, 14-point.

10. Use Format Painter to make the phrases that begin with Scrabble and Horseshoe look the same as Baked Macaroni and Cheese.

11. Save the document.

12. Format the *Play ball, swim...* paragraph to Times New Roman, 14 point.

13. Specify 24 points before the paragraph.

14. At the beginning of the last sentence, insert the Wingdings symbol ⊠ and a space. At the end of the last sentence insert a space and the Wingdings symbol ⊠.

15. Format the last paragraph to Times New Roman, 22-point bold, blue.

16. Specify 24 points before the paragraph.
    Save the document.

Insert and Size a Graphic

1. Place the insertion point in the blank paragraph above *Baked Macaroni and Cheese Contest.*

2. Click Insert, Picture, Clip Art and insert the following graphic or any suitable substitute.
   Hint: Search for family.

The graphic appears on the page.

3. Use the mouse on a corner-sizing handle to shrink the image without distorting it to about 1" tall.

4. Click anywhere outside the graphic.

5. Copy the graphic and paste it into the paragraph just above *Scrabble, Trivial Pursuit, Pitch Tournaments.*

6. Paste it again into the paragraph just above *Horseshoe, Log splitting, Softball Competitions.*
   The flyer should now look similar to the one shown in Illustration A.

7. If the graphics cause the last lines of text to move to the next page, resize them until all the text fits on one page.
   You will resize graphics more exactly in the next exercise.

8. Print Preview and print the document.

9. Save the document.

10. Close the document, and exit Word.

Illustration A. Flyer1 with Graphics

❋ WE ARE FAMILY! ❋

❖ Lightwood Family Reunion ❖

August 9-11, yyyy

Floyd & Leona Riverside Park
Chaffin Shelter House
20 North Shore Drive
Thompson Falls, MT 59873

What Fun!

Baked Macaroni and Cheese Contest

Scrabble, Trivial Pursuit, Pitch Tournaments

Horseshoe Pitching, Log Splitting, Softball Competitions

Play ball, swim, go canoeing, sit and talk, or sit and sit.

⊠ **Come! Help Us Celebrate a Great Family** ⊠

Exercise 2

Insert Graphics from a File

■ Insert a Graphic from a File ■ Size a Graphic Using the Format Picture Dialog Box

NOTES

Insert a Graphic from a File

■ Through the Clip Art task pane, Microsoft Office offers a variety of graphics. You can retrieve images from any location, however, so long as Microsoft Office recognizes the file type of the graphic. Popular graphics types include BMP, GIF, JPG (JPEG), PCX, TIF (TIFF), and .WMF. .JPG and .GIF files are often used in Web pages. The other formats have been in use in PCs for a number of years.

💻 Try It!

1. Create a new document.

2. Click Insert, Picture, From File (Alt+I, P, F).

   The Insert Picture dialog box appears. The illustrations that follow show the Graphics folder from the data files for this book. In Windows XP, the dialog box normally opens in Thumbnails view. Some formats, such as .PCX files, display only as icons in Thumbnails view.

3. To switch to Thumbnails view, click the Views button and select Thumbnails.

Graphics Types

Over time, a variety of graphics formats have been developed. Each structures the information about the image in a different way, and experts argue over which type works best for a particular use.

As a result of this variety, desktop publishing programs, including Word, can recognize and display a wide variety of graphic image types.

Insert Picture Dialog Box, Thumbnails View

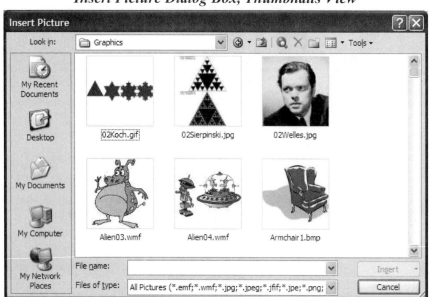

186

4. In the Look in drop-down list, change to the location of the data files for this book, and open the Graphics folder.

5. Double-click ◎ **Alien04.wmf**, or select it and click the Insert button

   [Insert ▾] .

   The picture is inserted into the document.

6. Center the paragraph that contains the graphic.

7. Save the document as **Aliens**.

Size a Graphic Using the Format Picture Dialog Box

■ In Exercise 1, you used the mouse to resize an image. To more precisely size an image, you can use the Format, Picture command. You can make an image a specific size or a specific percentage using this command.

🖳 Try It!

1. Select the graphic in **Aliens**.

2. Click the Format Picture button 🖼 on the Picture toolbar, or click Format, Picture (Alt+O, I).

3. Click the Size tab to display the Format Picture dialog box as shown in the following illustration.

Format Picture Dialog Box, Size Tab

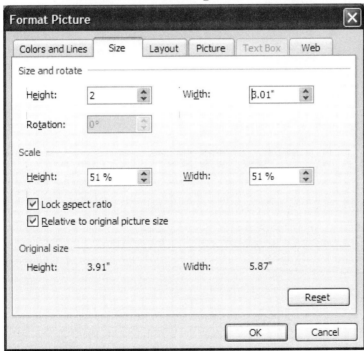

4. In the Size and rotate section, change the Height to 2".

5. Press the Tab key.

   The other three values—Size and rotate Width, Scale Height, and Scale Width—change proportionally so long as Lock aspect ratio is selected.

6. Click the OK button [OK] or press Enter.

7. Move the insertion point to the end of the paragraph, and press the Spacebar three times.

   *You should have three spaces after the **Alien04** image.*

8. Use Insert, Picture, From File, to insert the graphic ◉ **Alien03.pcx** from the Graphics folder in the data files.

9. Select the **Alien03** graphic and size it to 2" in height using the Format Picture dialog box.

   The alien jumps to the same line as the first image because both are in the same paragraph. Your document should resemble the one shown in the illustration that follows.

10. Save and close the document, and exit Word unless you are continuing with the Exercise Directions.

Aliens Document

You have reviewed the flyer you created in the previous exercise. You are now ready to incorporate different graphics and to size them to the same height. You will use two graphics from the data files and one from Microsoft clip art, and you will print the completed flyer.

EXERCISE DIRECTIONS

Replace the First Graphic with Diploma

1. Open ⌨Flyer1, or open 💿02Flyer1 from the data files.
2. Save the document as **Flyer2**.
3. Select the graphic above *Baked Macaroni and Cheese Contest*.
4. Use Insert, Picture, From File to insert one of the following images from the Graphics folder of the data files: 💿**Chef01.bmp**, 💿**Chef02.bmp**, 💿**Chef03.bmp**, or 💿**Chef04.bmp**.
5. If necessary, delete the original graphic. (Select it and press the Delete key.)
6. Select the graphic and use the Format Picture dialog box Size tab to make it 1" high. (**Chef02.bmp** is shown below; Illustration A uses **Chef04.bmp**.)

7. Save the document.

Replace a Graphic with Scrabble® Tiles

1. Select the graphic above *Scrabble, Trivial ....*
2. Use Insert, Picture, From File to insert the graphic 💿**Scrabble.bmp**.
3. If necessary, delete the original graphic. (Select it and press the Delete key.)
4. Select the graphic and use the Format Picture dialog box Size tab to make it 1" high.

5. Save the document

Replace the Third Graphic with Horseshoe

1. Select the graphic above *Horseshoe pitching....*
2. Use Insert, Picture, From File to insert 💿**Horseshoe.bmp** from the data files.
3. If necessary, delete the original graphic. (Select it and press the Delete key.)
4. Select the graphic and use the Format Picture dialog box Size tab to make it 1" high.

5. Save the document.

Save, Print Preview, and Print the Document

1. Print Preview the document.
2. Print one copy of the document.
3. Compare your results with Illustration A.
4. Save the document.
5. Close the document, and exit Word.

✳ WE ARE FAMILY! ✳

❖ Lightwood Family Reunion ❖

August 9-11, yyyy

Floyd & Leona Riverside Park
Chaffin Shelter House
20 North Shore Drive
Thompson Falls, MT 59873

What Fun!

Baked Macaroni and Cheese Contest

Scrabble, Trivial Pursuit, Pitch Tournaments

Horseshoe Pitching, Log Splitting, Softball Competitions

Fish, swim, go canoeing, sit and talk, or sit and sit.

⊠ Come! Help Us Celebrate a Great Family ⊠

Exercise 3

Use Floating Graphics
■ Create a Floating Graphic ■ Use Other Text Wrapping Options
■ Size a Graphic Using the Dialog Box ■ Align Floating Graphics Independently
■ Align Floating Graphics in Relation to One Another ■ Add a Border to a Page

NOTES

Create a Floating Graphic

■ In the previous two exercises, you inserted images directly into a paragraph. The horizontal and vertical positions of the graphics were determined by the paragraph into which they were inserted. Word, however, allows you to create graphics that float over the text. That is, they are not part of a paragraph, but can be positioned by dragging.

■ The float-over-text objects are often used in newsletters and similar documents so that text surrounds the picture on all sides rather than just above or below as in the flyer you created.

■ **Note:** Float-over-text objects require that you be in Print Layout view. When you specify an object as float-over-text, Word automatically enters Print Layout view. If you cannot see the objects, click View, Print Layout, or click the Print Layout View button in the lower left of the Word window.

💻 Try It!

Create Float-Over-Text Picture

1. Open 💿 **03Lion** from the data files.

2. Save the document as **Lion3**.

3. Read the first two paragraphs, which tell you a little about what you are going to do.

4. Select the lion graphic.

   • You can use the Picture toolbar to open the Format Picture (or Format Object) dialog box and to redefine the wrapping option for a float-over-text graphic.

Picture Toolbar

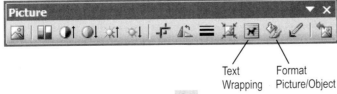

Text
Wrapping

Format
Picture/Object

5. Click the Format Picture button 🖫 on the Picture toolbar.

   OR

   Click Format, Picture on the main menu (Alt+O, I).

The Format Picture dialog box appears.

6. Click the Layout tab to view the Wrapping style options, as shown in the following illustration.

Format Picture Dialog Box, Layout Tab

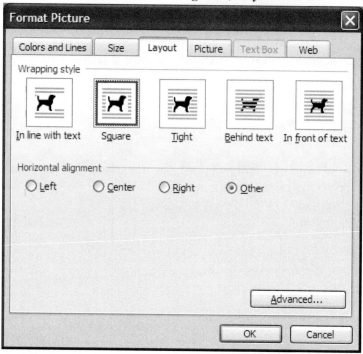

7. Select Square (Alt+Q), and click the OK button .

The lion is now surrounded by white, circular sizing handles rather than black.

*A picture formatted in this way is defined as **Float-over-text** or floating, which means you can position it by dragging it with the mouse and cause the text around it to move.*

🖥 Try It!

Rotate and Move a Picture

The green dot above the upper center-sizing handle is the **rotate handle**.

Floating Graphic with Sizing and Rotate Handles

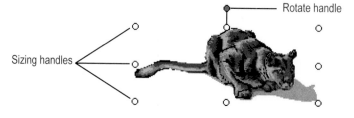

1. Point to the rotate handle.

The mouse pointer changes to a rotation symbol ↻.

2. Click and drag the rotate handle left or right.

As you drag, the rotate handle becomes a complete circle of arrows ↻, and the graphic rotates in the direction you drag.

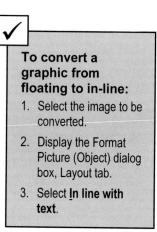

To convert a graphic from floating to in-line:

1. Select the image to be converted.

2. Display the Format Picture (Object) dialog box, Layout tab.

3. Select **In line with text**.

Picture or Object
Sometimes Word treats inserted graphics as objects and changes the name of the button to Format Object and the menu option to Format, Object. The dialog boxes for both pictures and objects offer the same options.

3. Release the mouse button, and review the results.

4. Click the Undo button to return the graphic to its original orientation.

5. If necessary, click the picture to select.

6. Point to the picture.

   The mouse pointer turns into a four-headed arrow ✛.

7. Click and drag the picture to the left into the text.

   The text is displaced and wraps around the graphic in a rectangle, as shown in the following illustration.

   Your lion may be in a different location from the one illustrated.

Square Wrapping Option

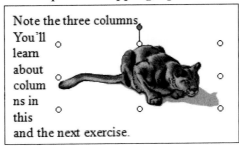

8. Save the document.

💻 Try It!

Use Tight Wrapping and Size the Graphic

1. Select the lion picture.

   The Picture toolbar re-appears. If it is not displayed, click View, Toolbars, Picture (Alt+V, T, Picture).

2. Click the Text Wrapping button.

3. The menu of Text Wrapping options appears as shown in the following illustration.

Text Wrapping Options

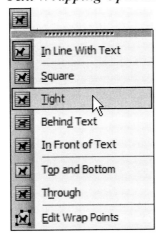

4. Select Tight (T), as shown in the illustration.

Text Wrapping Options

For some reason, two options—Square and In Front of Text—have different underlined, quick key letters on the Layout tab and the Text Wrapping menu.

Note that the text now wraps closer to the lion's tail.

Tight Wrapping Option

5. Use the mouse to shrink the lion proportionally and drag it into the second paragraph until it appears as close to the illustration below as you can make it.

   Sizing with the mouse works the same as with an in-line graphic.

Shrunk and Repositioned Lion

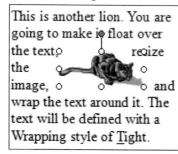

6. When you are satisfied with the size and position of the image, click anywhere outside the graphic to deselect it.

7. Save the document.

Use Other Text Wrapping Options

Try It!

Place an Image Behind Text

1. Select the horseshoe graphic in the lower part of the document.

2. Click the Text Wrapping button on the Picture toolbar, and select a Wrapping style of Behi<u>n</u>d Text.

3. Drag the horseshoe image up until it is behind the two words, as shown in the following illustration.

Image Behind Text

Horseshoe Pitching

✓ To position a graphic with the arrow keys:

1. Use the mouse to place the graphic close to where you want it.

2. With the image selected, press the up, down, left, or right arrow.

   The image is nudged in the direction of the key you press.

   Hold down the arrow key to move (nudge) the image repeatedly.

---

4. Click the Text Wrapping button [image] on the Picture toolbar and select the In Front of Text option.

    Part of the text is now obscured by the graphic.

5. Press Ctrl+Z or click the Undo button [image] to place the graphic behind the text again.

    OR

    Click the Text Wrapping button [image] on the Picture toolbar, and choose Behind Text.

    As nearly as possible, center the horseshoe image over the two words as shown in the previous illustration.

6. Save and close the document.

Size a Graphic Using the Dialog Box

■ If you are sizing one graphic in a document, you can manage quite well simply by specifying the Wrapping options and using the mouse to size the image. If you want several images to be the same height or width, use the Format Picture/Object dialog box, Size tab to specify the dimensions.

🖥 Try It!

1. Open ⊙ **03Animals** from the data files.
2. Save the document as **Animals**.
3. Select the bull and change its layout from In Line With Text to Square. (Use the Text Wrapping button [image] on the Picture toolbar or the Layout tab of the Format Object dialog box.)
    The bull is surrounded by white, circular sizing handles indicating that it is now a floating object. Note also that it does not have a rotate handle.
4. Repeat step 3 for the elephant and the bear.
5. Select all three objects. (Hold down the Shift key and click on each object.)
    All three objects are selected. (You cannot select more than one in-line object at a time; you can, however, select more than one floating object at the same time.)
6. Click the Format Object button [image] on the Picture toolbar, or right-click any of the objects and select Format Object from the shortcut menu, or click Format, Object (Alt+O, O).
7. Click the Size tab.
    Note that the Size and rotate Height and Width and the Scale Height and Width boxes are blank.
8. In the Size and rotate section, change the Height to 2".
9. Click the OK button [OK].
    All three images are now the same height.
10. Save the document.

Align Floating Graphics Independently

- You can align floating graphics using the Format Picture/Object dialog box Layout tab.

🖳Try It!

1. Select the bull.
2. Display the Format Object dialog box, and click the Size tab.
3. Change the Size and rotate Height to 1". DO NOT close the dialog box.
4. Click the Layout tab.
5. Click the Left option ⦿Left , and click the OK button [OK].

   You can specify the options on more than one tab at a time when you use a dialog box. Thus, you can size and align a floating object without closing the dialog box.
6. Format the elephant to 2.5" in height, and center it using the Center option ⦿Center.
7. Format the bear to 1.5" in height, and align it at the right margin using the Right option ⦿Right .
8. Save the document.

Align Floating Graphics in Relation to One Another

- If you are positioning one floating graphic in a document, you may be able to manage quite well simply by specifying the Wrapping options and using the mouse to position the image. If you want several images to be aligned vertically or horizontally, use the Drawing Toolbar Draw menu.

🖳Try It!

Activate the Drawing toolbar:

- Click the Drawing button 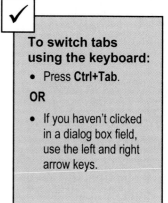 on the Standard toolbar.

OR

- Click View, Toolbars, Drawing (Alt+V, T, Drawing).

  The Drawing toolbar displays at the bottom of the Word window.

  You will use the options on the Draw menu shown in the following illustration.

✓

To switch tabs using the keyboard:

- Press **Ctrl+Tab**.

OR

- If you haven't clicked in a dialog box field, use the left and right arrow keys.

Draw Menu

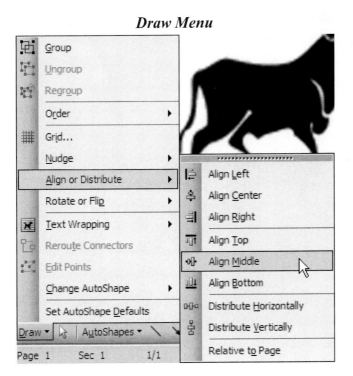

💻 Try It!

Line up Floating Pictures in a Row

1. Select all three images.
2. Click the Draw menu (Alt+D) on the Drawing toolbar.
3. Slide to Align or Distribute (A), and select Align Middle (M).

    The three images are aligned vertically at their centers.

4. With the three images selected, click Draw, Align or Distribute, Align Bottom (Alt+D, A, B).

    The three images are aligned vertically at their lower edges.

5. Align the three images by their top edges using the Draw menu.

💻 Try It!

Line up Floating Pictures in a Column

1. Click anywhere on a blank area of the document to deselect the images.
2. Select the elephant and drag it down and to the left to position it below the bull. You don't need to try to line it up with the bull.
3. Select the bear and position it below the elephant. Use the following illustration as a guide.

Animals Ready to Align in a Column

4. Select all three animals.

5. Click <u>D</u>raw, <u>A</u>lign or Distribute, Align <u>C</u>enter (Alt+D, A, C).

   The images are aligned in a column at their centers.

6. Click <u>D</u>raw, <u>A</u>lign or Distribute, Align <u>R</u>ight (Alt+D, A, R).

   The images are aligned in a column at their right edges.

7. Click <u>D</u>raw, <u>A</u>lign or Distribute, Align <u>L</u>eft (Alt+D, A, L).

   The images are aligned in a column at their left edges.

8. Save the document.

🖥 Try It!

Distribute Images

1. Click on any blank area of the document to deselect the images.

2. Select the bear and drag it toward the bottom of the page. Place it as close to the bottom margin as you can.

3. Select the bull and drag it toward the top of the page. Place it as close to the top margin as you can.

4. Change the Zoom factor on your screen to Whole Page so you can see the effects of the next steps.

5. Hold down the Shift key and select all three images.

6. Click <u>D</u>raw, <u>A</u>lign or Distribute, Distribute <u>V</u>ertically (Alt+D, A, V).

   The elephant is placed so that it is equidistant from the other two images. If you have more images, the inside images will be equidistant from each other and from the two outermost images. If you have images in a row that you'd like to distribute across the page, use Distribute Horizontally.

   Images need not be aligned for distribution to work.

7. Click on the page to deselect the object.

8. Save the document.

Add a Border to a Page

- Word provides a way for you to create a border around an entire page. Page borders are useful for decorating flyers and announcements.

🖥 Try It!

1. Click Format, Borders and Shading (Alt+O, B).
2. Click the Page Border tab on the Borders and Shading dialog box, as shown in the following illustration.

Borders and Shading Dialog Box, Page Border Tab

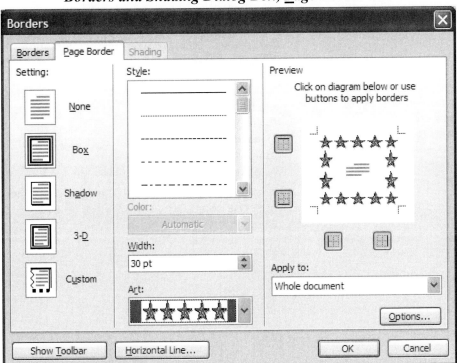

3. Under Setting, select Box.
4. Click the drop-down arrow in the Art field.
5. Scroll down and select the third set of stars.

   Make sure that Apply to is set to Whole document.

6. Click the OK button [OK].
7. Print Preview the document.
8. Save the document.
9. Close the document, and exit Word unless you are continuing with the Exercise Directions.

Four families in your neighborhood are having a garage sale. They have asked you to create a flyer to advertise this sale. They want you to use graphics and to make the flyer attractive.

EXERCISE DIRECTIONS

Open the Data File and Review It

1. Open ⊙ **03GarageSale** from the data files.
2. Save the file as **GarageSale**.

   The file contains a garage sale graphic and some text. You are going to position the text and insert, size, position, and align images as necessary to create your own flyer.

3. Set all margins to 0.75".

   You MUST retain all the text EXCEPT Furniture, Toys, Appliances, Clothes, and And more…! You may retain some or all of these words or you can delete them all and rely on the images you insert to indicate that all these types of items and more are included in the garage sale.

   You may delete the Garage Sale graphic and use text instead, as in Illustration A.

   Use a mix of graphics from the Clip Art task pane and from the Datafiles\Graphics folder on the CD-ROM. You can also use appropriate images from other sources if you have them.

4. Review Illustrations A and B for ideas. They were created with images exclusively from the Graphics folder.

   In Illustration A, the bicycle and coffee maker are both in-line graphics while the others are floating. You can mix the two types in any way you wish.

   Note also that Illustration A has a page border; Illustration B does not.

5. Use the sizing, positioning, and aligning techniques you have learned in this lesson. Use the text formatting you learned in the Word lesson to create your flyer.
6. Use Print Preview and Zoom to help you adjust the positions and sizes of images.
7. Save the document frequently.
8. When you are satisfied with the flyer, save and print one copy.
9. Close the document and exit Word.

Illustration A. Example 1

Four-Family Garage Sale

2222 Sharkfin Circle
Whitefish Bay, WI

Saturday, August 4
8:30 am until 3:30 pm

Furniture Toys
Appliances Clothes

☞ See you there! ☜

Four-Family

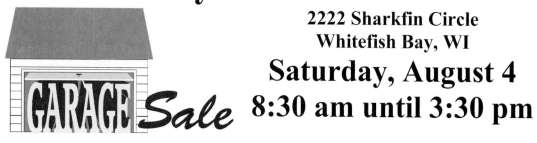

2222 Sharkfin Circle
Whitefish Bay, WI

Saturday, August 4
8:30 am until 3:30 pm

☞ **See you there!** ☜

Exercise 4

Create a Newsletter
■ Multiple Column Formats ■ Insert Section Breaks
■ Put a Border Around a Graphic ■ Border/Shade a Paragraph ■ Insert a File

NOTES

Multiple Column Formats

- For information to be read in rows, use Word's table feature. For information to be read in columns, like a newspaper or magazine, you divide the page into columns. Text begins in one column and flows into the next column when the first column fills up.

🖥 Try It!

1. Open ⊙ **04Extreme** from the data files.

2. Save the document as **Extreme**.

3. Click F̲ormat, C̲olumns (Alt+O, C).

   The Columns dialog box appears, as shown below.

   Columns Dialog Box

   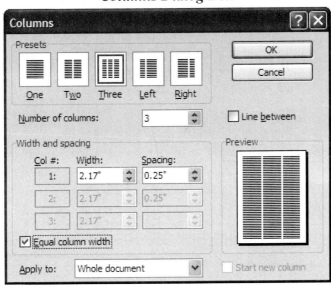

4. Click the T̲hree icon, or type **3** in the N̲umber of columns box.

5. Do not select Line b̲etween.

6. Select E̲qual column width.

7. Click S̲pacing and specify **0.25"** to put one-fourth of an inch between columns.

8. Click the OK button ⌈ OK ⌉.

   The document is reformatted into three columns.

9. Save the document.

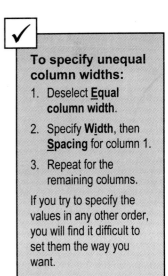

✓

To specify unequal column widths:

1. Deselect **Equal column width**.

2. Specify **Width**, then **Spacing** for column 1.

3. Repeat for the remaining columns.

If you try to specify the values in any other order, you will find it difficult to set them the way you want.

Insert Section Breaks

- To use multiple columns in documents, you need to use Word sections. Sections are codes that let you use different layouts within the same document. Each section can have different margins, headers/footers, and column layouts.

- Word's section formats control paragraphs above the position where the section code is inserted, as shown below.

Section Break Codes, Show/Hide On

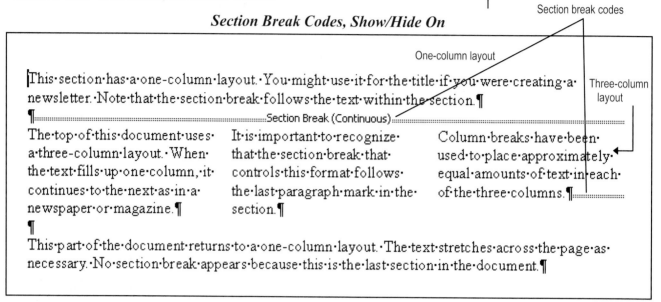

This·section·has·a·one-column·layout.·You·might·use·it·for·the·title·if·you·were·creating·a· newsletter.·Note·that·the·section·break·follows·the·text·within·the·section.¶

¶━━━━━━━━━━━━━━━Section Break (Continuous)━━━━━━━━━━━━━━━

The·top·of·this·document·uses· a·three-column·layout.·When· the·text·fills·up·one·column,·it· continues·to·the·next·as·in·a· newspaper·or·magazine.¶

It·is·important·to·recognize· that·the·section·break·that· controls·this·format·follows· the·last·paragraph·mark·in·the· section.¶

Column·breaks·have·been· used·to·place·approximately· equal·amounts·of·text·in·each· of·the·three·columns.¶

¶

This·part·of·the·document·returns·to·a·one-column·layout.·The·text·stretches·across·the·page·as· necessary.·No·section·break·appears·because·this·is·the·last·section·in·the·document.¶

Section break codes

One-column layout

Three-column layout

🖥 Try It!

1. Place the insertion point to the left of the tab that begins the first body paragraph of the essay. (The insertion point must be to the left of the tab.) You may wish to display nonprinting characters to see the tab.

2. Click Insert, Break (Alt+I, B).
   The Break dialog box appears, as shown below.

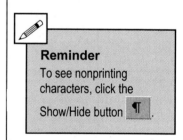

Reminder

To see nonprinting characters, click the Show/Hide button ¶.

Break Dialog Box

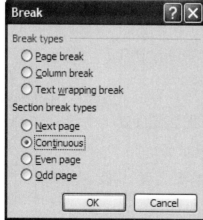

3. Click Continuous.

204

4. Click the OK button .

   Word inserts a section break immediately between the tab and the preceding paragraph mark (the one that creates a blank line after the heading).

   The heading The Adventure of Extreme Sports is now split across two of the three columns.

5. Move the insertion point into the heading, and click the Columns

   button 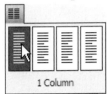 on the Standard toolbar.

6. Select and click the left-most option (1 Column) of the drop-down display, as shown below.

Columns Button Drop-down Display

1 Column

The heading is centered across the three columns.

Put a Border Around a Graphic

- You can easily place a border around a graphic.

💻 Try It!

Insert a Graphic

1. Place the insertion point at the beginning of the first paragraph of the Mountain Biking section. Be sure the insertion point is to the left of the tab.

2. Press the Enter key to insert a new paragraph.

3. In the new paragraph, insert the file ✪ **Mountain Bike.jpg** from the Graphics folder of the data files.

4. Shrink it to about half its original size, center the paragraph, and format it with 2 points before and 6 points after.

   The image is now centered within the column, and the beginning of the Mountain Biking section should look as shown below.

5. Save the document.

Picture Inserted in Paragraph

> **To put a border on a floating graphic:**
> 1. Click the Line Style
>
>   button ☰ on the Picture toolbar to display a drop-down list of line widths.
>
> 2. Click the line width you wish to use for the border.

🖳 Try It!

Put a Border Around the Graphic

1. Select the image of the mountain biker.
2. Click Format, Borders and Shading (Alt+O, B).
   Word displays the Borders dialog box, as shown in the illustration that follows.
3. Select Box, select the solid line under Style, and select a Width of ¾ point.
4. Click the OK button [OK].
   The graphic has a border with a width of ¾ point.
5. Print Preview the document to see the border.
6. Close Print Preview, but leave the document open.
7. Save the document.

Borders Dialog Box, Borders Tab

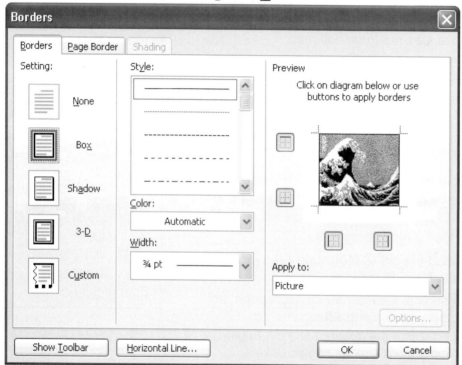

Border/Shade a Paragraph

- You can put a border around a paragraph or shade the paragraph. In a newsletter, for example, you may wish to call attention to a paragraph by putting a border around it or shading it, as shown on the right.

🖳 Try It!

1. Place the insertion point in the paragraph under *Skysurfing*.
2. Click Format, Borders and Shading (Alt+O, B) to display the Borders and Shading dialog box, as shown in the following illustration.
3. Click the Shading tab.
4. Select turquoise as the Fill color.

Border or Shade a Paragraph

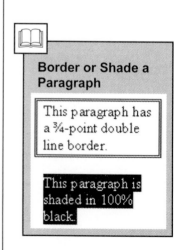

This paragraph has a ¾-point double line border.

This paragraph is shaded in 100% black.

5. Click the OK button [OK]
6. Save the document.

Borders and Shading Dialog Box, Shading Tab

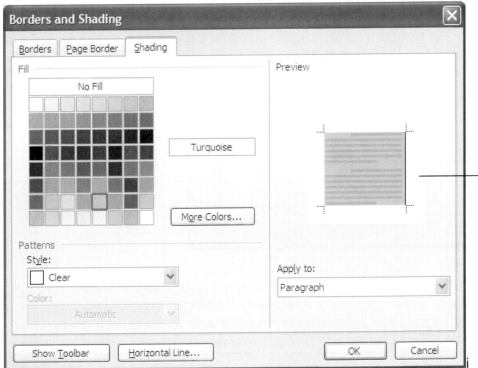

— Preview box.

Border a Paragraph
To put a border around
the paragraph, select the
Borders tab, click Box,
and select a Style, Color,
and Width for the line. The
Preview box shows what
the border will look like.

Insert a File

■ When you work in desktop publishing, the text often comes from other writers. You need to bring their files into your document.

⌨ Try It!

1. Place the insertion point at the end of the document.
2. Click Insert, File (Alt+I, L).
   Word displays the Insert File dialog box, as shown in the following illustration.
3. Select the file ⊙ **04Wakeboard** from the data files.
4. Click the Insert button [Insert ▾].
   Word inserts the file. The file is now part of the document and can be formatted and edited.
5. Save the document.
6. To balance the columns on the second page, insert another section break at the end of the document. Balancing the columns causes the text to be equally distributed among the three columns.
7. Close the document, and exit Word unless you are continuing with the Exercise Directions.

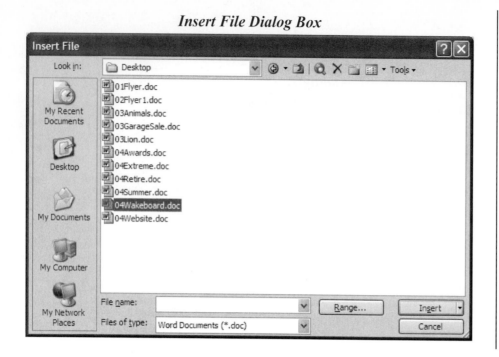

Insert File Dialog Box

In this exercise, you will create a three-column newsletter for Ulysses Middle School, using files provided. You will insert graphics and apply borders and shading to enhance the appeal of the newsletter. Note that laying out and formatting a newsletter takes time. You may not be able to complete this project in one class period.

EXERCISE DIRECTIONS

Set Up the Page Layout

1. Start Word and create a new document.
2. Display the Drawing toolbar if it is not already displayed (View, Toolbars, Drawing).
3. Use File, Page Setup to set the top, bottom, left, and right margins to 0.75".
4. Press the Enter key three times.
5. Save the document as **UMSNews**.
6. Use Insert, Break, Continuous to insert a continuous section break.
7. Turn Show/Hide on to see the section break code.
   You should have three blank lines above the section break and one below.
8. Place the insertion point below the section break.
9. Use Format, Columns to set the layout to three equal columns with 0.2" Spacing.
10. Make sure that Line between is deselected.
11. Save the document.

Create the Newsletter Main Title

1. Place the insertion point in the first paragraph of the document (above the section break).
2. Type the following text:
   UMS News & Views
3. Format the text to Arial Black, 28 point, and center the paragraph.
4. Save the document.
5. Using the Clip Art task pane, insert the light bulb shown in Illustration A.
   *Hint: Search for **light bulb**.*

Illustration A. Light Bulb

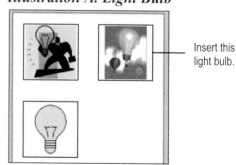

Insert this light bulb.

a. Set the Wrap option to Behind Text.
b. Shrink the light bulb and drag it to the left of the title.
c. Copy and paste the light bulb.
d. Drag the copy of the light bulb to the right of the title.
e. Select the light bulb to the left of the title.
f. Click the <u>D</u>raw, Rotate or Flip, Flip <u>H</u>orizontal, as shown in Illustration B.

Illustration B. Flip a Graphic

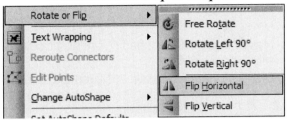

g. Use the Format Picture dialog box to position the left image at the left margin and the right image at the right margin.
h. Use the <u>D</u>raw menu to align the images at the top.
6. Save the document.

Put a Border around the Title

1. Select the title and the blank line that follows it.
2. Use F<u>o</u>rmat, <u>B</u>orders and Shading to place a border around the two paragraphs.
   - For line style, choose a double-line border with one line thicker than the other.
   - For color, choose blue.
   - Choose a width of 1½ points, as shown in Illustration C.

Illustration C. Border Style

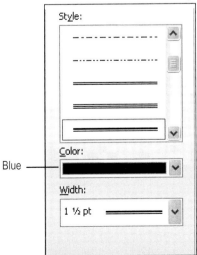

3. Save the document.

Add the Publication Information

1. Position the Insertion point in the blank paragraph within the border.
2. Type the following text: **Produced by Technology Classes**
3. Select the entire paragraph, including the paragraph mark.
4. Left-align the paragraph, and format the font to Times New Roman, 12 point.
5. Go to the end of the paragraph.
6. Press the Tab key.
7. Type the following text. For yyyy, substitute this year: **June 1, yyyy**
8. Set a right tab of 7", as outlined below and shown in Illustration D.
   a. Click F<u>o</u>rmat, <u>T</u>abs.
   b. In the <u>T</u>ab stop position box, type 7.
   c. In the Alignment section, click <u>R</u>ight.
   d. Click the <u>S</u>et button [Set].
   e. Click the OK button [OK].
9. Save the document.

Illustration D. Tabs Dialog Box

Save and Print Preview

1. Print Preview the document.
2. Compare your document with Illustration E to see whether you have completed the title correctly.

Illustration E. Newsletter Title

 # UMS News & Views

Produced by Technology Classes   June 1, yyyy

Insert and Format the Awards Story

1. Place the insertion point in the first paragraph below the section break.
2. Insert the file 04Awards from the data files.
3. Center the headline (*Principal...*). Make its text Arial, 12-point bold.
4. Format the paragraph with 6 points after.
5. Make sure that the first body paragraph is Times New Roman, 10 point.
6. Format the paragraph as justified.

   The body paragraphs throughout this newsletter will be justified so that they begin at the left and right column boundaries. To keep justified paragraphs from having large gaps, the text should be hyphenated. To make this easy, Word offers automatic hyphenation, which you are now going to activate.

7. Click Tools, Language, Hyphenation to display the Hyphenation dialog box.
8. Set the options as shown in Illustration F, and click OK.

Illustration F. Hyphenation Dialog Box

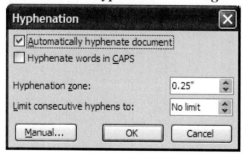

9. Make the awards subheadings Arial, 11-point bold with 6 points Before.

   Hint: Format Academic Achievement, *and then use Format Painter to format* Outstanding Citizenship *and* Athletic Excellence.

10. Make each grade heading Times New Roman, 10-point bold.
11. Format the paragraphs with names as Times New Roman, 8 point.
12. From the graphics data files, insert the images Diploma.wmf, Ribbon.wmf, and Trophy.wmf.
13. Make them float over the text, with Square wrapping.
14. Position and size them as shown in Illustration G on the next page. If the names do not wrap exactly the same, that's all right. Your results may not match exactly, but make sure that no subheading is displaced.

    Hint: *You can use the Format Picture, Layout tab to align the images at left and right column boundaries. The Left and Right alignment options align the pictures with the column boundaries.*

15. Save and Print Preview the document.

Illustration G. Position of Images

Academic Achievement
Grade 7
Juan Guerra, Denise LeBihan, Anna Magilozzi, David Mistri, Cassandra Pierce, Walter Strate, Raisa Whittaker
Grade 8
Carlton Doermann, Northrop Frye, John Giambalvo, Miguel Palacio, Ganga Patel, Mary Jane Pastore, Daniel Wilson
Grade 9
Larry Bommer, Maria Daniw, Sabina Romanowska, Portia Smith, William Sonoma, John Steinhart, Jane Zakrewska

Outstanding Citizenship

Grade 7
Georgina Plum, David Mistri
Grade 8
Sandra Newcomer, Robert Plum, Mary Ellen Rhodes
Grade 9
Louise Lewis, Sonya Newcomer, Thomas Purma

Athletic Excellence
Grade 7
Maria Agnelli, Lawrence Berry, Karalea Bishop, Juan Guerra, Susan Knipp, Ronald Myrick, Harold Ohmart, Nancy VanAntwerp, Florence Wunderlich
Grade 8
Howard Beech, Michael O'Loughlin, Miguel Palacio, Carol Ann Paul, Frieda Payne, Suzanne Rodenbeek, Winston Salem, Robert Stewart, Rosemarie Winderlin
Grade 9
Natasha Borodin, Maria Daniw, Raleigh Durham, James Holmes, Thomas Purma, William Sonoma, Paul Stookey, Barbara Timmons, Dill VanAntwerp

Insert and Format the Retirement Story

1. Place the insertion point at the end of the document.
2. Click <u>I</u>nsert, <u>B</u>reak, <u>C</u>olumn Break, or press Ctrl+Shift+Enter to start a new column.
3. Insert the file 04Retire from the data files.
4. Use Format Painter to make the heading the same format as the title for the awards story.
5. Format the subheading the same as the awards subtitles, and then center the paragraph. (It begins *UMS Community Wishes….*)
6. Press Shift+Enter before the words *Dr. Griffith-* so that no words in the story title are hyphenated.
   In general, headlines should not be hyphenated.
7. Make sure all body paragraphs are justified using Times New Roman, 10 point.

8. Insert a blank paragraph before the first paragraph of the story.
9. Use <u>I</u>nsert, <u>P</u>icture, <u>C</u>lip Art to insert an appropriate picture to represent the principal, Dr. Griffith-Kimball.
10. Use Format Picture to change the height of the image to 1.5".
11. Center the paragraph that contains the picture, and change its first-line indentation to 0".
12. Shrink the image as necessary, so that the story fits within the middle column.
13. Save and Print Preview the document.

Insert and Format the Web Site Story

1. Place the insertion point in the blank paragraph following the story about the principal's retirement.
2. Click <u>I</u>nsert, <u>B</u>reak, <u>C</u>olumn Break, or press Ctrl+Shift+Enter.
3. Insert the file 04Website from the data files.
4. Use Format Painter to make the title the same as the title for the other two stories.
5. Press Shift+Enter before the word *Available* so that no words in the story title are hyphenated.
6. Use Format Painter to format all three body paragraphs the same as the body paragraphs in the other stories. (Justified, 0.2" first-line indent, Times New Roman, 10 point.)
7. Place the insertion point at the end of the document.
8. At the end of the story, insert a clip art graphic of a computer or a suitable graphic of your choice.
   Hint: The computer in Illustration H came from the Clip Art task pane. Search for **computer***.*
9. Make its height about 1".
10. Center the paragraph that contains the graphic.
11. Below the image create a new paragraph, and type the following Web address:
    http://www.ulyssesms.edu
    Word formats the address automatically as a hyperlink (link to the Internet).
12. Leave the color and underline, but make the text Arial, 12 point, and make sure the paragraph is centered.
13. Add 6 points after the paragraph.
14. Save and Print Preview the document.

Insert and Format the Summer Story

1. Insert a blank paragraph after the Web address.
2. Place the insertion point in the blank paragraph.
3. Insert the file ⊘ **04Summer** from the data files.
4. Format the title like the other story titles.
5. Format main body paragraph like the other body paragraphs.
6. Add 3 points after the paragraph.
7. Select the paragraphs with the results of the survey, and set the text to bold.
8. Set a right tab at 2.17".
   Hint: See the Tabs Dialog Box on page 209.
9. Select all the paragraphs in the story including the heading.
10. Use Format, Borders and Shading to apply turquoise shading.
    The entire Summer story is now shaded.
11. Save and Print Preview the document.

Add Filler at the Bottom of Column 1

When you create a newsletter, you want the three columns to have about equal amounts of information. Editors use material called **filler** *to fill up the columns. In this part of the exercise, you will add two filler paragraphs.*

1. At the bottom of the first column, insert a blank paragraph, if necessary.
2. Type the following text into the paragraph:

   Thought for the Day
   He who laughs last just takes longer to get the joke.
3. Format the text to Times New Roman, 10 point.
4. Make the title bold, and insert 6 points Before the paragraph.
5. Select both paragraphs, center them, and indent them 0.2" left and right.
6. With both paragraphs selected, place a solid, black, 2¼-point border around both paragraphs, as shown in Illustration H.
7. With both paragraphs selected, apply a turquoise shading to both paragraphs.
8. If necessary, place the insertion point in the last paragraph of the award winners story and press Enter to create a blank paragraph before the filler.

Add Filler at the Bottom of Column 3

1. In a blank, centered paragraph after the summer story, insert a clip art graphic of the sun or another symbol of summer.
2. Format the paragraph with 12 points Before 3 points After. Be sure there are no blank paragraphs between the shaded paragraph and the symbol of summer.
3. If necessary, use Format, Borders and Shading to remove any shading on the paragraph.
4. In a blank paragraph after the summer graphic, type **HAVE A GREAT SUMMER!**
5. Format the new text to Arial, 12-point bold and center the paragraph.
6. Shrink the graphic until the last sentence fits on the page.
7. Save, Print Preview, and print one copy of the document.
8. Compare your results with Illustration H.
9. Close the document, and exit Word.

Illustration H. Desired Result

UMS News & Views

Produced by Technology Classes   June 1, yyyy

Principal Griffith-Kimball Announces Annual Awards

This year's award winners in three categories were announced last week by Janet Griffith-Kimball, Principal. The awards, to be presented at the Annual Awards Assembly on June 10, "reward students who have shown outstanding academic, citizenship, and athletic abilities this year," said the principal. Award winners are listed below.

Academic Achievement
Grade 7
Juan Guerra, Denise LeBihan, Anna Magilozzi, David Mistri, Cassandra Pierce, Walter Strate, Raisa Whittaker

Grade 8
Carlton Doermann, Northrop Frye, John Giambalvo, Miguel Palacio, Ganga Patel, Mary Jane Pastore, Daniel Wilson

Grade 9
Larry Bommer, Maria Daniw, Sabina Romanowska, Portia Smith, William Sonoma, John Steinhart, Jane Zakrewska

Outstanding Citizenship

Grade 7
Georgina Plum, David Mistri
Grade 8
Sandra Newcomer, Robert Plum, Mary Ellen Rhodes
Grade 9
Louise Lewis, Sonya Newcomer, Thomas Purma

Athletic Excellence
Grade 7
Maria Agnelli, Lawrence Berry, Karalea Bishop, Juan Guerra, Susan Knipp, Ronald Myrick, Harold Ohmart, Nancy VanAntwerp, Florence Wunderlich

Grade 8
Howard Beech, Michael O'Loughlin, Miguel Palacio, Carol Ann Paul, Frieda Payne, Suzanne Rodenbeek, Winston Salem, Robert Stewart, Rosemarie Winderlin

Grade 9
Natasha Borodin, Maria Daniw, Raleigh Durham, James Holmes, Thomas Purma, William Sonoma, Paul Stookey, Barbara Timmons, Dill VanAntwerp

> **Thought for the Day**
> He who laughs last just takes
> longer to get the joke.

Principal Griffith-Kimball Plans to Retire

After serving Ulysses Middle School (UMS) for more than 25 years, Principal Janet Griffith-Kimball is retiring. She began her career at UMS as a mathematics teacher and 7th grade girls' basketball coach. Twenty years ago, she was appointed as principal.

"It will be odd," Dr. Griffith-Kimball says, "not to come to UMS after so many years of being here nearly every day. I'll miss the students, the teachers, and the staff, but I hope to keep busy in retirement. My husband and I plan to travel."

Dr. Griffith-Kimball urges current and former students, faculty, and staff to keep in touch through e-mail – jgkimball@ulyssesms.edu.

UMS Community Wishes Dr. Griffith-Kimball Well

"It won't be the same around here without Dr. Griffith-Kimball," said Student Council President, William Sonoma. "She will be missed, but I hope she is going to have a great retirement."

"It is hard to imagine UMS without Dr. Griffith-Kimball," said PTA president Judy Winderlin. "It seems only yesterday that she was my algebra teacher in 9th grade, and now she's old enough to retire."

Faculty Council President, Georgia Plum said that everyone will miss the support, kind words, and good leadership that Dr. Griffith-Kimball has provided.

UMS Web Site to be Available All Summer

Technology Department Head, Lynn Epler announced this week that with the help of student volunteers, the ATMS World Wide Web Site will be active and updated all summer.

Students can continue to get the latest schedule update, post questions for teachers and fellow students, and perform research in UMS's electronic library.

"We are pleased to be able to maintain the Web site rather than let it slide over the summer. The Parents for Technology Committee of the PTA found grants and gifts to support the effort. We are grateful for the support of such dedicated parents," said Mr. Epler.

http://www.ulyssesms.edu

Summer Activities Include Camp, Sports, Vacation

A survey of UMS students found that most students remain at home during the summer and participate in family activities and sports. The survey results are summarized below:

Sleepover Camp	3%
Day Camp	6%
Local Daytime Activities	30%
Summer with Relatives	2%
Vacation with Family	59%

HAVE A GREAT SUMMER!

Lesson 6: Microsoft Office Excel 2003

Exercise 1:   Get Started with Microsoft Office Excel

♦ What are Spreadsheets?
♦ Excel and Word
♦ The Excel Window
♦ Select a Cell and Enter Data
♦ Enter a Simple Addition Formula
♦ Enter Values and Labels
♦ Copy a Formula
♦ Print With or Without Gridlines

Exercise 2:   Work with Ranges and the SUM Function

♦ Select Rows or Columns
♦ Select a Range of Cells
♦ Use Auto Fill to Complete a Series
♦ The SUM Function
♦ Use AutoSum
♦ Copy a Formula to a Range
♦ Copy a Formula Using Auto Fill
♦ Ask a Question to Resolve Errors

Exercise 3:   Use the Toolbar and the AutoSum Drop-Down Menu

♦ Format Numbers
♦ Format Labels
♦ Align Labels
♦ Use Functions
♦ Use the AutoSum Drop-Down Menu

Exercise 4:   Manage Columns and Rows and Sort Data

♦ Adjust Column Widths
♦ Insert Rows or Columns
♦ Add a Title to a Worksheet
♦ Sort Data

Exercise 5:   Use Absolute References and the Print Dialog Box

♦ Relative and Absolute References
♦ Change Print Orientation
♦ Print to Fit on One Page

Exercise 6:   Use Chart Wizard I

♦ About Pie Charts
♦ Create a Pie Chart
♦ Other Pie Chart Options

Exercise 7:   Use Chart Wizard II

♦ Create a Bar Chart

Exercise 8:   Use Chart Wizard III

♦ Create a Line Graph
♦ Edit the Line Graph

Exercise 9:   Use Insert Function; Use the IF Function

♦ Use Insert Function Feature
♦ About the IF Function
♦ Understand Operators
♦ Insert the IF Function

Exercise 10: Integrate Excel and Word

♦ Insert an Excel Object into a Word Document
♦ Insert a Word Table into an Excel Worksheet

Exercise 11: Challenge Exercises

♦ Structure of a Checkbook Register
♦ Create a Checkbook Register
♦ Insert an Excel Spreadsheet into Word

Exercise 1

Get Started with Microsoft Office Excel

■ What are Spreadsheets? ■ Excel and Word ■ The Excel Window
■ Select a Cell and Enter Data ■ Enter a Simple Addition Formula
■ Enter Values and Labels ■ Copy a Formula
■ Print With or Without Gridlines

NOTES

What are Spreadsheets?

- Spreadsheets are used in business to plan and track budgets and projects and to perform financial analyses.

- Spreadsheets are tables. The box formed by the intersection of a column and row on the table is called a **cell**. To create a spreadsheet to solve a problem or provide information, you fill cells with either:

  - **Data**, which may be either text or numbers. Text data is called a **label**. Numeric data is called a **value**.

  - **Formulas**, which tell the spreadsheet program which data to use and how to calculate results. The cell containing the formula displays the results of the calculation. When the data in a cell changes, all the cells that rely on the data in that cell are updated. In spreadsheet terminology, these cells are said to **reference** one another.

- Excel, the spreadsheet application in Microsoft Office, organizes its spreadsheets into individual **worksheets**, which combine to make a **workbook**; the workbook is saved as a file.

- Cells in one worksheet can reference and use data from another worksheet in the same workbook. Cells in one workbook can reference and use data from other workbooks.

- Modern spreadsheet applications, like Excel, make it easy to provide visual representations of the data and results. They do this through the **chart** feature, which guides you step-by-step through the creation of a line graph, a pie chart, or bar chart that represents the spreadsheet pictorially.

Excel and Word

- Once you've created a spreadsheet and/or chart in Excel, it is easy to combine the spreadsheet information with text in a Word document. One of the aims of the Microsoft Office group of applications is this ability to use the output from one application as input to another.

- Letters, reports, and memoranda often are created in Word using charts or tables from Excel to help clarify and support the message in the document. Exercise 10 shows you how to integrate Word and Excel documents.

The Excel Window

- When you start Excel, a worksheet opens and the Excel window looks like the one shown below.

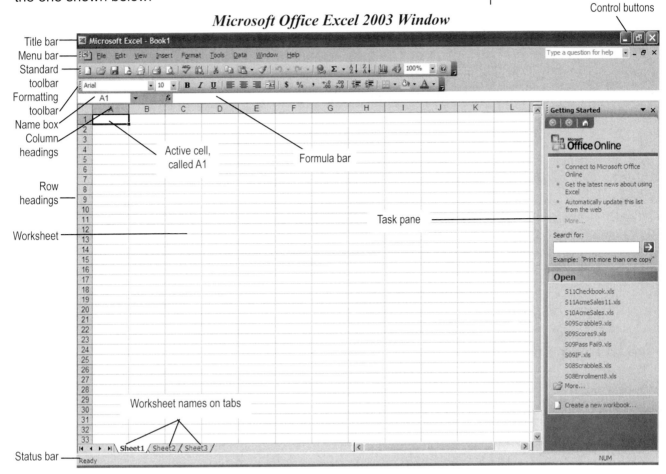

Microsoft Office Excel 2003 Window

- Excel creates a new workbook when it starts. Each new workbook contains three worksheets named Sheet1, Sheet2, and Sheet3, as shown at the bottom of the Excel window. You can add new worksheets, rename them, and delete them. The bar with the worksheet tabs contains four buttons that let you switch from worksheet to worksheet.

Worksheet Tabs

- Cells are named by their locations. For example, Cell A1 is the box at the intersection of column A and row 1. Cell B32 is column B, row 32.

- In addition to the usual set of window objects—title bar, toolbars, scroll bars, and status bar—Excel adds another line that includes the **Name box** and the **Formula bar**, as described below.

  - Name box, which tells you which cell is selected.

  - When the Formula bar is selected, three buttons used for editing appear, as shown on the next page.

- Formula area where cell contents appear. If the cell contains a number, the number appears; if the cell contains the result of a formula, the formula appears.

Formula Bar when Selected Cell can be Edited

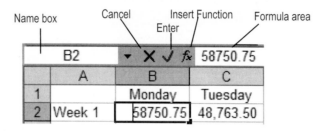

Select a Cell and Enter Data

- When a new workbook opens, cell A1 is the **active cell** as indicated by the A1 in the Name box and the bold outline around the cell on the worksheet itself. When a cell is **active**, you can enter data or edit the cell's contents.

Active Cell A1, Newly Opened Workbook

A1	▼
A	B
1	
2	

💻**Try It!**

1. Start Excel.
2. Type the number **38** in cell A1.
3. Press the Tab key.
   The number (value) 38 appears in cell A1 and cell B1 is selected.

   To select a cell with the mouse, point to the desired cell and click. When you move the mouse pointer over the worksheet, the pointer displays as a white cross ✚.

Active Cell B1, Reached by Pressing Tab

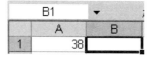

4. Type the number **62**, and press the Enter key.
   The value 62 appears in cell B1 and cell A2 is selected.
5. Save the workbook as **Practice1**.
   Save works the same in Excel as in Word.

Enter a Simple Addition Formula

💻**Try It!**

1. Move the mouse pointer.
2. Point to the middle of cell B2 and click.
   The cell is outlined in black and the entry in the Name box changes, as shown in the illustration on the next page.

Active Cell B2, Selected by a Click

	A	B
1	38	62
2		

3. Type the following formula **=a1+b1**.

All formulas begin with an equal sign (=) to tell Excel that the text that follows is a formula. a1 and b1 are cell references. The formula tells Excel to add the values in A1 and B1.

Enter a Formula

	A	B
1	38	62
2		=a1+b1
3		

4. Press the Enter key.

The result of the formula (100) appears in cell B2 and cell B3 is selected, as shown in the following illustration.

Cell B2 Completed with Result

	A	B
1	38	62
2		100
3		

5. Save the workbook.

Cell References

The column identifier in a cell reference can be upper or lowercase: A1 or a1. If you enter the reference in lowercase (a1) Excel converts it to uppercase when you press the Enter or Tab key.

💻 Try It!

To see what happens when you change data in a referenced cell:

1. Click in cell A1.

2. Type **138**, and press the Enter or Tab key.

If you select a cell that already has data, typing replaces existing data.

The result in cell B2 changes to 200.

3. Double-click cell B1, or select cell B1 and press the F2 key.

The insertion point appears in the cell so you can edit the data. You can position the insertion point using the cursor movement keys.

4. Change the number to **162**, and press Enter.

The result of the formula (300) appears in cell B2.

5. Save the workbook.

Edit in Formula Bar

You can also edit data by selecting the desired cell and then clicking in the Formula bar. Any data in the cell is displayed in the Formula bar and you can edit the data in the Formula bar.

This technique is useful if the formula is longer than the width of the cell.

Enter Values and Labels

- **Values** are entries in a cell that can be used in formulas; values include numbers, dates, and the results of formulas. When you begin typing in a cell with one of the digits 0-9, a period, or a $, Excel treats the entry as a value.

- **Labels** are text that is not used in a formula. When you begin typing with any alphabetic character or the ' (single quotation mark), Excel treats the entry as a label.

Enter* versus *Type

In these exercises, *enter* means to key the entry and press the Enter or Tab key.

Type means just to key the entry.

Try It!

1. Select cell A4, type **Cost**, and press Enter.
   The word is left-aligned, indicating that the cell contains a label.
2. In cell A5, enter **3855**.
   The number is right-aligned, indicating that the cell contains a value.
3. Select cell B4, and enter **Price**.
4. Select cell B5, and enter **2588**.
5. Select cell C4, and enter **Profit**.

   Your spreadsheet should look like the one shown below.

Spreadsheet with Labels and Values

	A	B	C
1	138	162	
2		300	
3			
4	Cost	Price	Profit
5	3855	2588	

6. Save the workbook.

Copy a Formula

- You can copy a formula from one cell to another. When the cell references are written as in the preceding example, Excel changes the cell references appropriately as you paste the formula into new cells.

Try It!

1. With cell C5 selected, enter the following formula: **=a5-b5**.
   The result 1267 appears in cell C5.
2. Select cell A6, and enter **2979**.
3. Select cell B6, and enter **1823**.
4. Select cell C5.
5. Click the Copy button , or press Ctrl+C.
   A blinking rectangle surrounds the copied cell.
6. Click cell C6 to select it.

   Click the Paste button , press Ctrl+V, or press the Enter key.

   If you click the Paste button or press Ctrl+V, you can continue to paste the formula into additional cells. If you press the Enter key, the formula is no longer on the Clipboard and cannot be pasted.

   If the blinking rectangle remains after pasting, press the Enter key or the Esc key.
7. Select cell C6, and look at the Formula bar near the top of the window.
   The formula reads =A6-B6. The cell references changed automatically when the formula was copied.
8. Save the workbook.

Print With or Without Gridlines

- You can print a worksheet with or without column and row numbers. You can also print with or without the lines that form the cells (called **gridlines**). Spreadsheet output is often easier to read if the gridlines are showing. And you may wish to see the column and row headings.

🖥 Try It!

1. Select a blank cell on the worksheet.
2. Click File, Page Setup to display the Page Setup dialog box, as shown in the following illustration.
3. Click the Sheet tab.
4. Select Gridlines to print gridlines.
5. Select Row and column headings to print the numbers and letters that identify rows and columns.
6. Click the Print button [Print...].
   The Print dialog box appears.
7. Click the OK button [OK] to print the spreadsheet created in these Try It! activities.
8. Save and close the workbook.
9. Exit Excel unless you are continuing with the Exercise Directions.

Page Setup Dialog Box, Sheet Tab

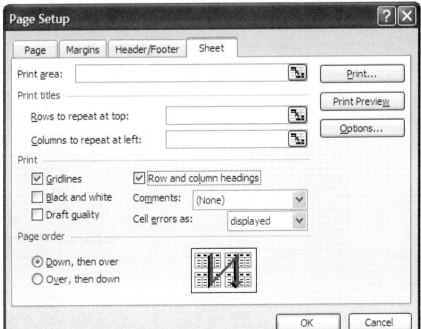

In this exercise, you will enter labels and values to create a spreadsheet that summarizes two shopping trips that a college student made to the store near her school. You will create a formula to add up how much she spent for chips on the two trips. You will then copy the formula to calculate how much she spent on cola and popcorn.

EXERCISE DIRECTIONS

Start Excel and Enter Labels and Values

1. Start Excel to create a new spreadsheet. If Excel is open, click the New button ⬜ to create a new workbook.
2. Save the workbook as **Shopping1**.
3. Close the task pane if you wish.
4. Enter the labels and values in the spreadsheet as shown in Illustration A.
   Be sure the entries are in the correct cells.

Illustration A. Spreadsheet Data

	A	B	C
1	ITEM	TRIP 1	TRIP 2
2	Chips	1.99	3.89
3	Cola	2.59	2.59
4	Popcorn	1.89	3.78

If you make a mistake, remember that you can double-click a cell to edit its contents.

5. Save the workbook.

Enter and Copy a Formula

1. Select cell D2.
2. Type the following formula and press Enter:
   =B2+C2
3. Select cell D2.
4. Copy its contents to D3 and D4.
   Your spreadsheet should now look like the one in Illustration B.

Illustration B. Spreadsheet with Formulas

	A	B	C	D
1	ITEM	TRIP 1	TRIP 2	
2	Chips	1.99	3.89	5.88
3	Cola	2.59	2.59	5.18
4	Popcorn	1.89	3.78	5.67

5. Press Enter to end the copy function if necessary.

Review the Formulas

1. Select cell D2.
   Look at the Formula bar and note that the result (which is a value) appears in the cell and the formula appears in the Formula bar, as shown in Illustration C.

Illustration C. Formula in Formula Bar

D2	▼		*fx* =B2+C2	
	A	B	C	D
1	ITEM	TRIP 1	TRIP 2	
2	Chips	1.99	3.89	5.88
3	Cola	2.59	2.59	5.18
4	Popcorn	1.89	3.78	5.67
5				

2. Select cell D3.
   Note that the formula has changed to =B3+C3. Excel has automatically adjusted the cell references.
3. Select cell D4 and note the change in the formula.
4. Double-click cell D2.
   The formula appears in the cell ready for editing and the two cells referenced in the formula are outlined as shown in Illustration D.
5. Press Enter to end edit mode.

Illustration D. Formula and Referenced Cells

SUM	▼	✗ ✓ *fx* =B2+C2		
	A	B	C	D
1	ITEM	TRIP 1	TRIP 2	
2	Chips	1.99	3.89	=B2+C2
3	Cola	2.59	2.59	5.18
4	Popcorn	1.89	3.78	5.67

Save, Print Preview, Print

1. Save the workbook.
2. Print Preview the document (the feature is similar to the one in Word).
3. Click the Setup button on the Print Preview toolbar to display the Page Setup dialog box.
   OR
   If you closed Print Preview, click File, Page Setup (on the menu bar).

4. Click the Sheet tab and set Gridlines and Row and column headings to print.
5. Click the Print button [Print...].
   It is on the Print Preview toolbar or on the Page Setup dialog box.
6. In the Print dialog box, click the OK button [OK] to print one copy of the workbook.
7. Save the workbook.
8. Close the workbook, and exit Excel.

Exercise 2

Work with Ranges and the SUM Function

■ Select Rows or Columns ■ Select a Range of Cells ■ Use Auto Fill to Complete a Series
■ The SUM Function ■ Use AutoSum ■ Copy a Formula to a Range
■ Copy a Formula Using Auto Fill ■ Ask a Question to Resolve Errors

NOTES

Select Rows or Columns

■ To operate on all entries in a column or row, you can select the entire column or row. For example, selecting a row or column makes it easier to insert a new one or to delete the one selected.

💻 Try It!

Select Columns

1. Open 💿 **02Select** from the data files.
2. Click on the identifier for column A. Drag the pointer across to column G.

   All six columns are selected as shown below.

Click here and drag right.

Columns A-G Selected

	A	B	C	D	E	F	G
1	Year	January	February	March	April	May	June
2	1996	5942	6345.4	7391	8423.3	6792.29	8941.88
3	1997	6090.5	6503.62	7575.77	8633.575	6961.8	9164
4	1998	6242.81	6666.21	7765	8849.414	7135.3	9393.6
5	1999	6398.8	6832.87	7959	9070.65	7314.24	9628.47
6	2000	6558.85	7003.6	8158.2	9297.416	7497.09	9869.2
7	2001	6722.43	7178.7	8362.25	9529.851	7684.52	10115.93

3. Click on the identifier for column B.
4. Hold the Ctrl key and click on columns D and F.

   Columns B, D, and F are selected as shown in the following illustration.

Columns B, D, and F Selected

	A	B	C	D	E	F	G
1	Year	January	February	March	April	May	June
2	1996	5942	6345.4	7391	8423.3	6792.29	8941.88
3	1997	6090.5	6503.62	7575.77	8633.575	6961.8	9164
4	1998	6242.81	6666.21	7765	8849.414	7135.3	9393.6
5	1999	6398.8	6832.87	7959	9070.65	7314.24	9628.47
6	2000	6558.85	7003.6	8158.2	9297.416	7497.09	9869.2
7	2001	6722.43	7178.7	8362.25	9529.851	7684.52	10115.93

🖥 **Try It!**

Select Rows

1. Click on the identifier for row 2. Hold down the left mouse button and drag the pointer down to row 6.

   Rows 2-6 are selected as shown below.

Rows 2-6 Selected

	A	B	C	D	E	F	G
1	Year	January	February	March	April	May	June
2	1996	5942	6345.4	7391	8423.3	6792.29	8941.88
3	1997	6090.5	6503.62	7575.77	8633.575	6961.8	9164
4	1998	6242.81	6666.21	7765	8849.414	7135.3	9393.6
5	1999	6398.8	6832.87	7959	9070.65	7314.24	9628.47
6	2000	6558.85	7003.6	8158.2	9297.416	7497.09	9869.2
7	2001	6722.43	7178.7	8362.25	9529.851	7684.52	10115.93

2. Click on the identifier for row 2.

3. Hold the Ctrl key and click on rows 4 and 6.

   Rows 2, 4, and 6 are selected as shown in the following illustration.

Rows 2, 4, and 6 Selected

	A	B	C	D	E	F	G
1	Year	January	February	March	April	May	June
2	1996	5942	6345.4	7391	8423.3	6792.29	8941.88
3	1997	6090.5	6503.62	7575.77	8633.575	6961.8	9164
4	1998	6242.81	6666.21	7765	8849.414	7135.3	9393.6
5	1999	6398.8	6832.87	7959	9070.65	7314.24	9628.47
6	2000	6558.85	7003.6	8158.2	9297.416	7497.09	9869.2
7	2001	6722.43	7178.7	8362.25	9529.851	7684.52	10115.93

Select a Range of Cells

- You can select a group of cells for formatting or for inclusion in a formula. The group is called a **range** and is identified by the cell in its upper-left corner and the cell in its lower-right corner separated by a colon.

🖥 **Try It!**

1. Click cell B2, hold the left mouse button, and drag the pointer to cell G7.

   The cell range B2:G7 is selected, with B2 remaining the active cell. The active cell is the cell from which you start the selection.

Cell Range, B2:G7 with B2 as Active Cell

	A	B	C	D	E	F	G
1	Year	January	February	March	April	May	June
2	1996	5942	6345.4	7391	8423.3	6792.29	8941.88
3	1997	6090.5	6503.62	7575.77	8633.575	6961.8	9164
4	1998	6242.81	6666.21	7765	8849.414	7135.3	9393.6
5	1999	6398.8	6832.87	7959	9070.65	7314.24	9628.47
6	2000	6558.85	7003.6	8158.2	9297.416	7497.09	9869.2
7	2001	6722.43	7178.7	8362.25	9529.851	7684.52	10115.93

⚠️

Click and Drag

Be careful when you click and drag to select. If you accidentally click to select, then click again and begin to drag, you will drag the contents of the selected cell.

If you move the cell contents, click the Undo button to undo the move, and then try selecting again.

2. Click cell F5, and drag the mouse up and to the left to cell C2.

The cell range C2:F5 is selected, with F5 as the active cell.

Cell Range F5:C2, with F5 as Active Cell

	A	B	C	D	E	F	G
1	Year	January	February	March	April	May	June
2	1996	5942	6345.4	7391	8423.3	6792.29	8941.88
3	1997	6090.5	6503.62	7575.77	8633.575	6961.8	9164
4	1998	6242.81	6666.21	7765	8849.414	7135.3	9393.6
5	1999	6398.8	6832.87	7959	9070.65	7314.24	9628.47
6	2000	6558.85	7003.6	8158.2	9297.416	7497.09	9869.2
7	2001	6722.43	7178.7	8362.25	9529.851	7684.52	10115.93

3. Close the workbook without saving it.

Use Auto Fill to Complete a Series

- The Auto Fill feature is used to complete a series of numbers, days, weeks, quarters, or years. To fill a series, you need two values that Excel can use to determine how the series is constructed.

- After creating a series, you can change it if necessary by using the in-document Auto Fill Options button 🔳.

💻 Try It!

1. Open 💿 **02Lunch** from the data files.

2. Save the workbook as **Lunch2**.

3. Select the range A2:A3.

4. Point to the small black square in the lower-right corner of cell A3.

   The pointer turns into a small black cross ✚ called the Auto Fill handle.

5. Click and drag down through cell A6.

   As you drag, the ScreenTip indicates the value Excel will place in each cell.

Fill Series

4	17-Aug
5	24-Aug
6	31-Aug
7	7-Sep
8	14-Sep
9	21-Sep
10	28-Sep
11	5-Oct
12	12-Oct

Auto Fill Series

	A	B	C
1	WEEK	MONDAY	TUESDAY
2	3-Aug	6.48	5.22
3	10-Aug	6.48	6.48
4			
5			
6			
7	31-Aug		
8			

6. Release the mouse button.

   The appropriate dates are filled in and the Auto Fill Options button 🔳 appears. When you point to the button, it displays a drop-down arrow 🔳▾.

Completed Fill Series with Auto Fill Options Button

	A	B	C
1	WEEK	MONDAY	TUESDAY
2	3-Aug	6.48	5.22
3	10-Aug	6.48	6.48
4	17-Aug		
5	24-Aug		
6	31-Aug		
7			

Auto Fill Options button

7. Click the Auto Fill Options button to see the Auto Fill options.

Auto Fill Options Menu

6	31-Aug
7	
8	
9	○ Copy Cells
10	◉ Fill Series
11	○ Fill Formatting Only
12	
13	○ Fill Without Formatting
14	○ Fill Days
15	○ Fill Weekdays
16	
17	○ Fill Months
18	○ Fill Years

Fill Series is selected. Because you selected two cells to start with, Excel assumes that you are completing a series.

The Auto Fill Options button appears immediately after you complete the Auto Fill action. It disappears from the cell when you perform an action elsewhere on the worksheet.

8. With the Auto Fill Options menu displayed, select Copy Cells rather than Fill Series.

   The series changes to a repetition of the two dates selected initially.

9. Click the Auto Fill Options button, and select Fill Series.

   The correct series reappears.

10. Save the workbook.

Try It!

1. Select the range B1:C1.

2. Drag the Auto Fill handle **+** to cell F1 to complete the series of weekdays through Friday.

3. Enter the data shown in the shaded areas in the illustration on the next page.

4. Save the workbook.

Data to Enter

	A	B	C	D	E	F
1	WEEK	MONDAY	TUESDAY	WEDNESDAY	THURSDAY	FRIDAY
2	3-Aug	6.48	5.22	6.48	7.59	3.6
3	10-Aug	6.48	6.48	4	6.72	4.98
4	17-Aug	6.48	10.69	3.75	6.48	2.34
5	24-Aug	6.48	6.48	7.59	4.5	3
6	31-Aug	6.48	7.3	5.22	6	7

The SUM Function

- You can create a formula for adding cells B2 through B6 by entering:

  =B2+B3+B4+B5

- If you have a large number of cells to be added, it quickly becomes cumbersome to type all the cell references. Excel, therefore, provides a shorthand way of adding the cells in a range—the **SUM function**.

- The SUM function lets you specify a range of cells to be added up, as shown below:

  =SUM(B2:B5)

- The formula begins with the equal sign followed by the function name SUM and the range of cells given in parentheses. All functions follow this format called the function **syntax**.

Try It!

1. With **Lunch2** open, click in cell B7.
2. Type the following formula: **=SUM(B2:B6)**
3. Press Enter.

   The results appear in cell B7.

4. Save the workbook.

Use AutoSum

- Rather than type the =SUM formula, you can use the AutoSum feature. You select the cell where you want the total to appear, and then click the AutoSum button **Σ** on the Standard toolbar. Excel surrounds a possible range of cells with a dotted blinking line and displays a formula in the cell. You can then accept the suggested range or select a new range for the SUM function.

Try It!

1. Select cell C7.

2. Click the AutoSum button .

   Because the selected cell is at the bottom of a column, Excel assumes that you want a total for the cells above. Excel analyzes the entries in the column and determines that numeric cells C2:C6 contain values that can be added and displays the potential formula. Note also that the syntax of the function is indicated in a ScreenTip.

3. Press Enter to accept the proposed formula.
4. Select cell G2.

Function

A predefined formula that performs simple or complex calculations.

Syntax

The order in which the elements of a formula are arranged and punctuated so that Excel can interpret and execute the elements successfully.

AutoSum

C	D
TUESDAY	WEDNESDAY
5.22	6.48
6.48	4
10.69	3.75
6.48	7.59
7.3	5.22
=SUM(C2:C6)	
SUM(**number1**, [number2], ...)	

In this exercise, you will add additional items that the college student purchased on her shopping trips. You will use AutoSum to calculate how much she spent on each trip, and you will format the values and some of the labels.

EXERCISE DIRECTIONS

Start Excel and Auto Fill a Series

1. Open 💿 **02Shopping1** from the data files.
2. Save the workbook as **Shopping2**.
3. Select the range B1:C1.
4. Use Auto Fill to complete the series to cell F1 for a total of five trips. (See Illustration A.)

Enter Labels and Values

1. Add the labels and values in the shaded areas shown in Illustration A.
   The 0 entries in column B make it easier to use AutoSum to create the totals.
2. Save the workbook.

Illustration A. Add Data to Shopping2

	A	B	C	D	E	F	G
1	ITEM	TRIP 1	TRIP 2	TRIP 3	TRIP 4	TRIP 5	TOTAL
2	Chips	1.99	3.89	1.99	1.99	3.89	
3	Cola	2.59	2.59	2.59	2.59	5.18	
4	Popcorn	1.89	3.78	0	2.29	1.89	
5	Bath Soap	0		1.99			
6	Shampoo	0		2.79			
7	Pens	1		2		0.5	
8	Paper	0.75		1.5	1.5	0.75	
9	TOTALS						

Use AutoSum

1. Select cell B9.
2. Click the AutoSum button **Σ**.
   Check that the range reads B2:B8.
3. Press Enter.
4. Use any method you know to copy the formula to the range C9:F9.

5. Use AutoSum in cell G2 to add the values in row 2 (range B2:F2).
6. Copy the formula from G2 to the range G3:G9.
7. Save the workbook.
   The worksheet should look like the one in Illustration B.
8. Close the workbook and exit Excel.

Illustration B. Totals Calculated

	A	B	C	D	E	F	G
1	ITEM	TRIP 1	TRIP 2	TRIP 3	TRIP 4	TRIP 5	TOTAL
2	Chips	1.99	3.89	1.99	1.99	3.89	13.75
3	Cola	2.59	2.59	2.59	2.59	5.18	15.54
4	Popcorn	1.89	3.78	0	2.29	1.89	9.85
5	Bath Soap	0		1.99			1.99
6	Shampoo	0		2.79			2.79
7	Pens	1		2		0.5	3.5
8	Paper	0.75		1.5	1.5	0.75	4.5
9	TOTALS	8.22	10.26	12.86	8.37	12.21	51.92

Exercise 3

Use the Toolbar and the AutoSum Drop-Down Menu
■ Format Numbers ■ Format Labels ■ Align Labels ■ Use Functions
■ Use the AutoSum Drop-Down Menu

NOTES

Format Numbers

■ By default, Excel uses a number format called **General**. If you type a non-zero decimal, Excel displays the decimal place. If you enter a whole number, only the whole number displays. For example, **113.1** displays as **113.1** while **113.0** displays as **113**.

■ To change the way numbers display, you use either:
  - Number formatting buttons on the Formatting toolbar
  - Format Cells dialog box, Number tab

■ **Understand Formatting Options.** As you work with number formats, you will learn that slight differences in number appearance depend on the options you apply when formatting numbers.

■ The **Excel Formatting toolbar** contains five buttons that are useful in formatting numbers in cells. These buttons are described below.

Important Note
The format of a number **does NOT affect its value** in calculations. For example, 6.239124 may be displayed 6.24 or 6.239. If multiplied by two, the value stored is 13.478248 even if it is displayed as 13.48 or 13.478.

Number Formatting Buttons

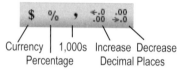

Currency | 1,000s Increase Decrease
Percentage   Decimal Places

Button	Dialog Box	Result
Currency Style **$**	Format, Cells, Number tab Category: Accounting Decimal places: 2 Symbol: $ Category: General Number Currency **Accounting** Date Time Percentage Sample Decimal places: 2 Symbol: $	In Accounting format, the numbers (negative and positive) align at the decimal and the $ signs align in a column. **H** Total $ (41,839.87) $ 46,926.26 $ 48,050.33 $ 49,202.98 $ (46,384.35) $ 51,594.68 $ 95,559.03

Button	Dialog Box	Result
(none)	Format, Cells, Number tab Category: Number Decimal places: 2 Use 1000 separator Negative numbers: -1234.10 Category: General Number Currency Accounting Date Time Percentage Fraction Scientific Text Special Custom Sample Decimal places: 2 ☑ Use 1000 Separator (,) Negative numbers: -1,234.10 1,234.10 (1,234.10) (1,234.10) 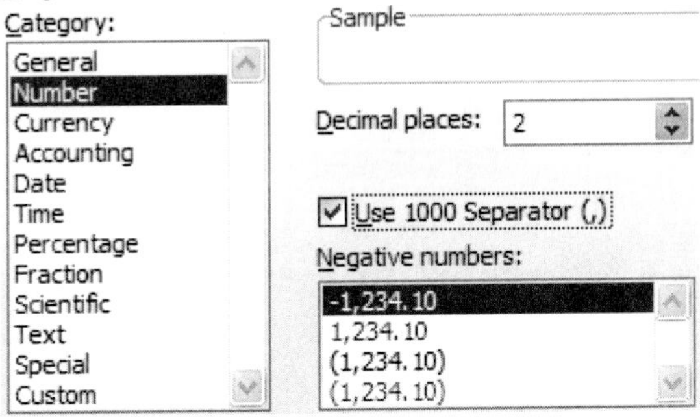	With Number, you can choose how negative numbers appear. The illustration below shows the first option, -1234.10. **D** March -7,391.00 7,575.77 7,765.00 7,959.00 -8,158.20 8,362.25 16,112.82
(none)	Format, Cells, Number tab Category: Currency Decimal places: 2 Symbol: $ Negative numbers: -$1234.10 Category: General Number Currency Accounting Date Time Percentage Fraction Scientific Text Special Custom Sample Decimal places: 2 Symbol: $ Negative numbers: -$1,234.10 $1,234.10 ($1,234.10) ($1,234.10)	Despite its name in the dialog box, the Currency category gives a different result from the Currency Style button. The dollar signs are just to the left of the number rather than aligned in a column. With Currency, you can choose the method for displaying negative numbers. The illustration below shows the first option, -$1234.10. **D** March -$7,391.00 $7,575.77 $7,765.00 $7,959.00 -$8,158.20 $8,362.25 $16,112.82
Percent Style  %	Format, Cells, Number tab Category: Percentage Decimal places: 0 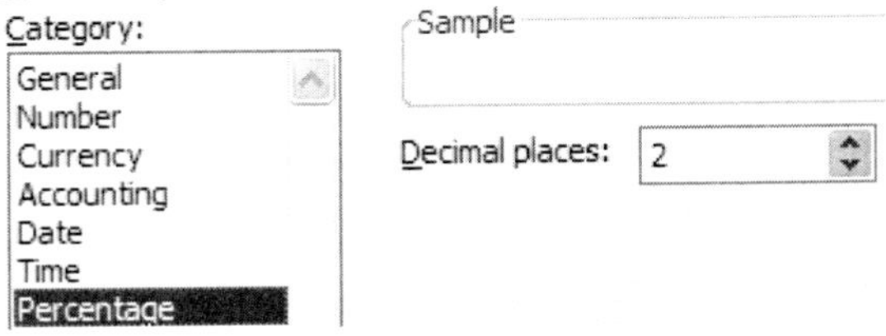 Category: General Number Currency Accounting Date Time Percentage Sample Decimal places: 2	The Percent format displays the value formatted as a percentage. For example, 0.50 displays as 50%. 0.35 displays as 35%. **I** Pctg. 14% 13% 13% 13% 14% 13% 14%

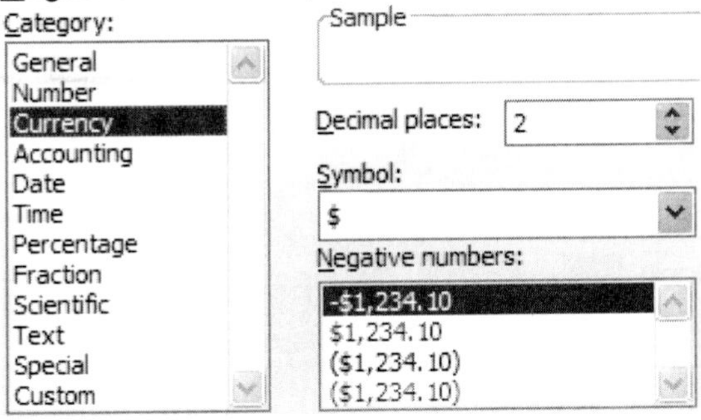

Button	Dialog Box	Result
Comma Style	Format, Cells, Number tab Category: Accounting Decimal places: 2 Symbol: None Category: General Number Currency **Accounting** Date Time Percentage Sample Decimal places: 2 Symbol: None	The Comma format sets off each thousand with a comma and applies the Accounting format without the $ decorator. C February (6,345.40) 6,503.62 6,666.21 6,832.87 (7,003.60) 7,178.70 13,832.40
Increase Decimal Decrease Decimal	Format, Cells, Number tab Decimal places: increase or decrease number If the number is in General format, Increase or Decrease Decimal applies 2 decimal places and formats negative numbers with a minus sign -1234.10. Otherwise, these buttons increase the number of Decimal places within the current format.	The Increase Decimal format adds one decimal place to the display. The Decrease Decimal format removes one decimal place from the display. D March -7391.00 7575.77 7765.00 7959.00 -8158.20 8362.25 16112.82

Try It!

Format a Range Using the Comma Style Button

1. Open ⊙ **03Align** from the data files. This workbook has some negative values.

2. Save the workbook as **Align3**.

3. Note the values for the year 1998.

   The General format displays a number as it was typed or calculated. If no decimal is typed, none is shown. If a decimal is typed, it is shown, and so on. If a calculated value has decimal places, up to nine are displayed. (The actual number of decimal places displayed depends on the width of the column.) For example, the calculated fractional values in row 11 in the illustration on the next page show a maximum of eight decimal places.

Number Alignment and Formats

	A	B	C	D	E	F	G	H
1	Year	January	February	March	April	May	June	Total
2	1996	-5942	-6345.4	-7391	-8423.3	-6792.29	-8941.88	-41839.87
3	1997	6090.5	6503.62	7575.77	8633.57	6961.8	9164	46926.26
4	1998	6242.81	6666.21	7765	8849.41	7135.3	9393.6	48050.33
5	1999	6398.8	6832.87	7959	9070.6	7314.24	9628.47	49202.98
6	2000	-6558.85	-7003.6	-8158.2	-9297.41	-7497.09	-9869.2	-46384.35
7	2001	6722.43	7178.7	8362.25	9529.85	7684.52	10115.93	51594.68
8								
9	TOTALS	12953.69	13832.4	16112.82	18362.72	14806.48	19490.92	95559.03
10								
11	Percentage	0.13555694	0.14475241	0.1686164	0.19216101	0.1549459	0.20396733	

4. Select the range B2:G7.

5. Click the Comma Style button ⟦,⟧ .

   All values in the range are displayed with two decimal places with the comma to indicate thousands; negative numbers are displayed in parentheses.

6. Save the workbook.

Comma Style Button Applied to Range B2:G7

	A	B	C	D	E	F	G	H
1	Year	January	February	March	April	May	June	Total
2	1996	(5,942.00)	(6,345.40)	(7,391.00)	(8,423.30)	(6,792.29)	(8,941.88)	-41839.87
3	1997	6,090.50	6,503.62	7,575.77	8,633.57	6,961.80	9,164.00	46926.26
4	1998	6,242.81	6,666.21	7,765.00	8,849.41	7,135.30	9,393.60	48050.33
5	1999	6,398.80	6,832.87	7,959.00	9,070.60	7,314.24	9,628.47	49202.98
6	2000	(6,558.85)	(7,003.60)	(8,158.20)	(9,297.41)	(7,497.09)	(9,869.20)	-46384.35
7	2001	6,722.43	7,178.70	8,362.25	9,529.85	7,684.52	10,115.93	51594.68
8								
9	TOTALS	12953.69	13832.4	16112.82	18362.72	14806.48	19490.92	95559.03
10								
11	Percentage	0.135556943	0.144752411	0.168616404	0.192161013	0.154945901	0.203967328	

⌨ **Try It!**

Format a Range using the Currency Style Button

1. Select the range B9:H9.

2. Hold down the Ctrl key, click in cell H9, and drag up to select the range H2:H9 with cell H9 as the active cell.

3. Click the Currency Style button ⟦$⟧ .

   This technique is a way to select and format nonadjacent ranges, as shown in the illustration on the next page. The values are formatted in Accounting format with the $ decorator and negative numbers shown in parentheses.

Nonadjacent Range: B9:H9, H2:H9
Currency Style Button Applied for Accounting Format

	A	B	C	D	E	F	G	H
1	Year	January	February	March	April	May	June	Total
2	1996	(5,942.00)	(6,345.40)	(7,391.00)	(8,423.30)	(6,792.29)	(8,941.88)	$ (41,839.87)
3	1997	6,090.50	6,503.62	7,575.77	8,633.57	6,961.80	9,164.00	$ 46,926.26
4	1998	6,242.81	6,666.21	7,765.00	8,849.41	7,135.30	9,393.60	$ 48,050.33
5	1999	6,398.80	6,832.87	7,959.00	9,070.60	7,314.24	9,628.47	$ 49,202.98
6	2000	(6,558.85)	(7,003.60)	(8,158.20)	(9,297.41)	(7,497.09)	(9,869.20)	$ (46,384.35)
7	2001	6,722.43	7,178.70	8,362.25	9,529.85	7,684.52	10,115.93	$ 51,594.68
8								
9	TOTALS	$12,953.69	$13,832.40	$16,112.82	$18,362.72	$14,806.48	$19,490.92	$ 95,559.03
10								
11	Percentage	0.13555694	0.14475241	0.1686164	0.19216101	0.1549459	0.20396733	

🖥 Try It!

Format a Range using the Percent Style Button

1. Select the range B11:G11.

2. Click the Percent Style button .

   The values are expressed as percentages without decimal places.

3. With the range still selected, click the Increase Decimal button ⬅.0 / .00 four times to increase the display to four decimal places.

4. With the range still selected, click the Decrease Decimal button .00 / ➡.0 once to decrease the display to three decimal places.

5. Save the workbook.

> **Decimal Display**
> If you format the display for two decimal places and type a number with four decimal places, only the first two (rounded as necessary) show up in the cell. All four decimal places, however, are included in calculations.

Percent Style with Decimal Increase/Decrease Applied

	A	B	C	D	E	F	G	H
1	Year	January	February	March	April	May	June	Total
2	1996	(5,942.00)	(6,345.40)	(7,391.00)	(8,423.30)	(6,792.29)	(8,941.88)	$ (41,839.87)
3	1997	6,090.50	6,503.62	7,575.77	8,633.57	6,961.80	9,164.00	$ 46,926.26
4	1998	6,242.81	6,666.21	7,765.00	8,849.41	7,135.30	9,393.60	$ 48,050.33
5	1999	6,398.80	6,832.87	7,959.00	9,070.60	7,314.24	9,628.47	$ 49,202.98
6	2000	(6,558.85)	(7,003.60)	(8,158.20)	(9,297.41)	(7,497.09)	(9,869.20)	$ (46,384.35)
7	2001	6,722.43	7,178.70	8,362.25	9,529.85	7,684.52	10,115.93	$ 51,594.68
8								
9	TOTALS	$12,953.69	$13,832.40	$16,112.82	$18,362.72	$14,806.48	$19,490.92	$ 95,559.03
10								
11	Percentage	13.556%	14.475%	16.862%	19.216%	15.495%	20.397%	

Format Labels

■ The Formatting toolbar lets you enhance the appearance of entries by making them bold, italic, or underlined. You can also change the font and font size using the Font and Font Size drop-down lists on the Formatting toolbar or the Font dialog box.

💻**Try It!**

Text Format Buttons

Bold Italic Underline

1. Select the range A1:H1.

2. Click the Bold button **B**.

3. Select cell A11, and click the Bold button **B** to format the label as bold.

4. Save the workbook.

💻**Try It!**

Font and Font Size Drop-down Lists

Arial Narrow ▼ 10 ▼

1. Select the range A1:H1.

2. Click the Font drop-down list and select Arial Narrow.

3. Click the Font size drop-down list and select 12. Leave the text bold.

4. Select cell A9 and format *TOTALS* as Arial Black (leave the font size as 10).

5. Save and close the workbook.

The worksheet should look as shown in the following illustration.

Font and Font Size Changes

	A	B	C	D	E	F	G	H
1	Year	January	February	March	April	May	June	Total
2	1996	(5,942.00)	(6,345.40)	(7,391.00)	(8,423.30)	(6,792.29)	(8,941.88)	$ (41,839.87)
3	1997	6,090.50	6,503.62	7,575.77	8,633.57	6,961.80	9,164.00	$ 46,926.26
4	1998	6,242.81	6,666.21	7,765.00	8,849.41	7,135.30	9,393.60	$ 48,050.33
5	1999	6,398.80	6,832.87	7,959.00	9,070.60	7,314.24	9,628.47	$ 49,202.98
6	2000	(6,558.85)	(7,003.60)	(8,158.20)	(9,297.41)	(7,497.09)	(9,869.20)	$ (46,384.35)
7	2001	6,722.43	7,178.70	8,362.25	9,529.85	7,684.52	10,115.93	$ 51,594.68
8								
9	**TOTALS**	$12,953.69	$13,832.40	$16,112.82	$18,362.72	$14,806.48	$19,490.92	$ 95,559.03
10								
11	Percentage	13.556%	14.475%	16.862%	19.216%	15.495%	20.397%	

Align Labels

- By default, Excel left-aligns labels and right-aligns values, as shown in the illustration on the next page.

- While you can align both labels and values in a worksheet, it is customary practice to format values using the number formatting techniques described earlier in this exercise, leaving them aligned at the decimal point.

	A	B	C	D	E	F	G
1	WEEK	MONDAY	TUESDAY	WEDNESDAY	THURSDAY	FRIDAY	TOTAL
2	3-Aug	6.48	5.22	6.48	7.59	3.6	29.37
3	10-Aug	6.48	6.48	4	6.72	4.98	28.66
4	17-Aug	6.48	10.69	3.75	6.48	2.34	29.74
5	24-Aug	6.48	6.48	7.59	4.5	3	28.05
6	31-Aug	6.48	7.3	5.22	6	7	32
7	TOTALS	32.4	36.17	27.04	31.29	20.92	147.82

- To align labels, select the cell with the label and click one of the alignment buttons on the Formatting toolbar.

Excel Text Alignment Buttons

Left Center Right

🖥 Try It!

1. Open 💿 **03Lunch2** from the data files.

2. Save it as **Lunch3**.

3. Select cell A1, and click the Center button ≣.

4. Select cells A1 through F1, and click the Center button ≣.
   The column headings are left-aligned.

5. Click the Center button ≣ again to center the headings.

6. Click the Align Right button ≣ to right-align the headings.

7. Click the Center button ≣ so that all column headings are centered.

8. Select cell A1 and right-align the column heading.

9. Format all column headings as Arial Narrow, 12-point bold.

10. Format the *TOTALS* label in cell A7 as Arial Black, 10 point.

11. Save and close the workbook.

>
>
> **Center Button Left-Aligned?**
> Because the text in cell A1 is centered, when you select the range A1:F1 and click the Center button, Excel turns off the centering on cell A1. That's why you have to click the Center button again to center the entire range.

Use Functions

- In Exercise 2, you used the SUM function to add up numbers in a column. Excel provides some other functions that you will find useful. In this exercise, you will work with the following:

  - **AVERAGE**, which adds all the values in the range and divides the total by the number of values; that is, it calculates an average.

  - **MAX**, which calculates the largest value in the range.

  - **MIN**, which calculates the smallest value in the range.

  - **COUNT**, which counts the number of cells in the range that contain numeric values.

  - **COUNTA**, which counts the number cells in the range that contain data of any type—numeric values or alphabetic labels.

💻**Try It!**

1. Open 💿**03Students** from the data files.
2. Save the workbook as **Students3**.
3. Enter the following label in cell A12: **GREATEST**.
4. Select cell B12.
5. Enter the following formula **=MAX(B2:B10)**.
   The result is 6.00 for Bruce, the tallest in the group of students.
6. Copy the formula to the range C12:D12.
7. Save the workbook.

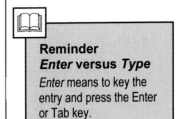

Reminder
Enter* versus *Type
Enter means to key the entry and press the Enter or Tab key.

Use the AutoSum Drop-Down Menu

■ The AutoSum button **Σ ▾** has a drop-down button. When you click the drop-down arrow, a menu offers additional functions.

AutoSum Drop-Down Menu

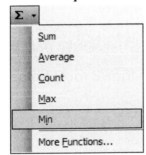

💻**Try It!**

1. Enter the following label in cell A13: **LEAST**.
2. Select cell B13.
3. Click the AutoSum button **Σ ▾** drop-down arrow.
4. Select Min.
   Excel highlights cell B12 as the possible argument for the function.
5. Select the range B2:B10 to indicate the correct values to include in the function, as shown in the following illustration.

Select Correct Range for Function

	A	B	C	D	
1	STUDENT	HEIGHT	WEIGHT	AGE	
2	LAMONT	5.42	143	14	Select the correct
3	ALLAN	5.25	103	13	range.
4	FRANK	5.92	175	13	
5	MELISSA	5.64	120	12	
6	LAYLA	5.17	95	15	
7	CARA	5.67	134	16	
8	ZENA	5.83	160	13	
9	PHILOMELA	5.33	143	13	
10	BRUCE	6.00	180	15	
11					
12	GREATEST	6.00	180.00	16.00	
13	LEAST	=MIN(B2:B10)			
14	AVERAGE	MIN(**number1**, [number2], ...)			

6. Press the Enter key.
7. Copy the formula to the range C13:D13.
8. Save the workbook.

💻 Try It!

1. Enter the following label in cell A14: **AVERAGE**.
2. Select cell B14.
3. Click the AutoSum button Σ ▾ drop-down arrow.
4. Select *A*verage.

   Excel highlights the range B12:B13 as the possible argument for the function.
5. Select the range B2:B10, and press the Enter key.
6. Copy the formula to C14:D14.
7. Format as bold the column headings and the labels you entered.
8. Center the *Height*, *Weight*, and *Age* headings.

   Your worksheet should look like the one in the following illustration.
9. Save the workbook. Close the workbook and exit Excel unless you are continuing with the Exercise Directions.

Completed Students3 Worksheet

	A	B	C	D
1	STUDENT	HEIGHT	WEIGHT	AGE
2	LAMONT	5.42	143	14
3	ALLAN	5.25	103	13
4	FRANK	5.92	175	13
5	MELISSA	5.64	120	12
6	LAYLA	5.17	95	15
7	CARA	5.67	134	16
8	ZENA	5.83	160	13
9	PHILOMELA	5.33	143	13
10	BRUCE	6.00	180	15
11				
12	GREATEST	6.00	180.00	16.00
13	LEAST	5.17	95.00	12.00
14	AVERAGE	5.58	139.22	13.78

In this exercise, you will build a worksheet that contains Scrabble® scores for several people. You will calculate the average score for each player. For each round, you will determine the highest score, the lowest score, and the average score.

EXERCISE DIRECTIONS

Open the Workbook and Enter Scores for Round 3

1. Open ⊙ **03Scrabble** from the data files.
2. Save the workbook as **Scrabble3**.
3. Add the labels and values in the shaded areas shown in Illustration A.

Illustration A. Add Data to Scrabble

	A	B	C	D	E
1	PLAYER	ROUND 1	ROUND 2	ROUND 3	AVERAGE
2	Bossman	275	355	307	
3	Castillo	316	345	320	
4	Chien	295	325	301	
5	Chin, S.	295	318	307	
6	Chin, Y.	297	317	306	
7	Kardash	340	323	298	
8	Kern	283	295	303	
9	Kudja	395	370	356	
10	LeBihan	307	308	288	
11	Perro	402	299	336	
12	Rhodes	322	316	304	
13	Veach	378	279	346	
14	Wang	324	339	364	
15					
16	Highest				
17	Lowest				
18	Average				

Calculate the Average for Each Player

1. Select cell E2.
2. Click the AutoSum button drop-down arrow Σ ▾.
3. Select Average.
4. Check that the range reads B2:D2. Select the range if necessary.
5. Copy the result in E2 to the range E3:E14.
   Your worksheet should now look like the one in Illustration B.

Illustration B. Average for Each Player

	A	B	C	D	E
1	PLAYER	ROUND 1	ROUND 2	ROUND 3	AVERAGE
2	Bossman	275	355	307	312.33333
3	Castillo	316	345	320	327
4	Chien	295	325	301	307
5	Chin, S.	295	318	307	306.66667
6	Chin, Y.	297	317	306	306.66667
7	Kardash	340	323	298	320.33333
8	Kern	283	295	303	293.66667
9	Kudja	395	370	356	373.66667
10	LeBihan	307	308	288	301
11	Perro	402	299	336	345.66667
12	Rhodes	322	316	304	314
13	Veach	378	279	346	334.33333
14	Wang	324	339	364	342.33333
15					
16	Highest				
17	Lowest				
18	Average				

Calculate the Highest, Lowest, and Average Score for Round 1

1. Select cell B16.
2. Click the AutoSum button Σ ▾ drop-down arrow.
3. Select Max.
4. Select the range B2:B14, and press the Enter key.
5. Select cell B17, and repeat steps 2-4, but use the Min function.
6. Select cell B18, and repeat steps 2-4, but use the Average function.
7. Save the workbook.

   Your worksheet should now look like the one in Illustration C. Note that Excel automatically added decimals for some averages.

Illustration C. Highest, Lowest, and Average for Round 1

	A	B	C	D	E
1	PLAYER	ROUND 1	ROUND 2	ROUND 3	AVERAGE
2	Bossman	275	355	307	312.33333
3	Castillo	316	345	320	327
4	Chien	295	325	301	307
5	Chin, S.	295	318	307	306.66667
6	Chin, Y.	297	317	306	306.66667
7	Kardash	340	323	298	320.33333
8	Kern	283	295	303	293.66667
9	Kudja	395	370	356	373.66667
10	LeBihan	307	308	288	301
11	Perro	402	299	336	345.66667
12	Rhodes	322	316	304	314
13	Veach	378	279	346	334.33333
14	Wang	324	339	364	342.33333
15					
16	Highest	402			
17	Lowest	275			
18	Average	325.3077			

Copy Highest, Lowest, and Average Formulas to the Other Rounds

1. Select range B16:B18.
2. Copy the formulas to the range C16:E18. You can copy all three at once using the AutoFill method.
3. Delete the value in cell E18. (The average of the averages is not very useful information.)
4. Save the workbook.

   Your worksheet should now look like the one in Illustration D.

Illustration D. All Rounds Calculated

	A	B	C	D	E
1	PLAYER	ROUND 1	ROUND 2	ROUND 3	AVERAGE
2	Bossman	275	355	307	312.33333
3	Castillo	316	345	320	327
4	Chien	295	325	301	307
5	Chin, S.	295	318	307	306.66667
6	Chin, Y.	297	317	306	306.66667
7	Kardash	340	323	298	320.33333
8	Kern	283	295	303	293.66667
9	Kudja	395	370	356	373.66667
10	LeBihan	307	308	288	301
11	Perro	402	299	336	345.66667
12	Rhodes	322	316	304	314
13	Veach	378	279	346	334.33333
14	Wang	324	339	364	342.33333
15					
16	Highest	402	370	364	373.66667
17	Lowest	275	279	288	293.66667
18	Average	325.3077	322.2308	318.1538	

Format the Averages

1. Select the range E2:E17.
2. Click the Increase Decimal button ⬅.0/.00 once.

   ##### signs may display in the cells because the data is too long for the column width.

3. Click the Decrease Decimal button .00/➡.0 twice.

   All values in the range should now have four decimal places.

4. Use Format Painter to format the values in the range B18:D18.

   The Format Painter works the same in Excel as in Word. Double-click the button to format more than one value. Then click it again (or press Esc) after you have completed the formatting.

   Even though these averages may display decimal places, they retain the General format until you change them.

5. Save the workbook.

Format the Column and Row Headings

1. Select the range A1:E1.
2. Center and bold the column headings.
3. Select the range A16:A18.
4. Bold the row headings.
5. Save the workbook.

   Your worksheet should now look like the one shown in Illustration E.

Save, Print Preview, Print

1. Print Preview the document.
2. Print one copy with gridlines but without row and column headings.
3. Close the workbook, and exit Excel.

Illustration E. Finished Scrabble® Worksheet

	A	B	C	D	E
1	PLAYER	ROUND 1	ROUND 2	ROUND 3	AVERAGE
2	Bossman	275	355	307	312.3333
3	Castillo	316	345	320	327.0000
4	Chien	295	325	301	307.0000
5	Chin, S.	295	318	307	306.6667
6	Chin, Y.	297	317	306	306.6667
7	Kardash	340	323	298	320.3333
8	Kern	283	295	303	293.6667
9	Kudja	395	370	356	373.6667
10	LeBihan	307	308	288	301.0000
11	Perro	402	299	336	345.6667
12	Rhodes	322	316	304	314.0000
13	Veach	378	279	346	334.3333
14	Wang	324	339	364	342.3333
15					
16	**Highest**	402	370	364	373.6667
17	**Lowest**	275	279	288	293.6667
18	**Average**	325.3077	322.2308	318.1538	

Manage Columns and Rows and Sort Data
■ Adjust Column Widths ■ Insert Rows or Columns
■ Add a Title to a Worksheet ■ Sort Data

NOTES

Adjust Column Widths

- If a label (text entry) is too long to fit in a cell, Excel allows it to display in the cell to its right if the adjacent cell contains no data.

- Excel provides several ways to adjust the width of a column, as you will learn in the Try It! activities in this section.

🖥 Try It!

1. Start Excel.

2. In the new worksheet, enter the names as shown below.

Text Too Long for Column B

	A	B	C
1	Suzanne	Rodenbeek	
2	Della	VanValkenberg	
3	Jane	Zakrsewski	
4	Sabina	Romanowska	

Parts of the labels in B1:B4 display in C1:C4. It is important to understand that the longer entries are entirely within column B. They partly display in column C, but the entry is only in column B. To edit or delete Rodenbeek, for example, you must select cell B1.

3. Save the workbook as **Perfect**.

🖥 Try It!

Drag the Column Boundary

1. Place the mouse on the boundary between the identifiers of columns B and C as shown below.

   The pointer turns into a two-headed arrow.

2. Click and drag the border right to expand the column so that all of VanValkenberg displays in column B.

Drag with Mouse to Adjust Column Width

	C4	▾	Width: 8.43 (64 pixels)	
	A	B ↔ C	D	
1	Suzanne	Rodenbeek		
2	Della	VanValkenberg		
3	Jane	Zakrsewski		
4	Sabina	Romanowska		

Numbers Too Wide

If a number is too wide to display in a column, Excel displays ###### in the cell to indicate that the column is too small to display the value.

Widen the column to make the number appear.

AutoComplete

As you begin typing, Excel automatically tries to complete the text with an existing entry that starts with the same characters. This feature, called **AutoComplete**, is useful when you are repeating text entries.

3. Click the Undo button to return the column to its original width.

Undo in Excel works the same as in Word. You can undo one action with a click of the button or Ctrl+Z. You can click the drop-down arrow and select to undo more than one action.

4. Save the workbook.

Try It!

Use the AutoFit Feature—Click Column Boundary

The **AutoFit** feature adjusts the column to fit the longest entry in the column or the longest entry in the selection.

- Double-click the border to the right of the letter identifying the column to be adjusted. Try it with the boundary between columns B and C.

  With this method you can adjust the width of one column at a time.

OR

1. Select columns A and B (the columns whose width is to be adjusted).

2. Double-click the border of any selected column. Try it with the boundary between columns A and B.

   The columns adjust to fit the longer name in each column. With this method you can adjust the width of all selected columns at the same time.

3. Click the Undo button to return the columns to their original widths.

Multi-Column Width Adjustment

Try It!

Use the AutoFit Feature—Menu Method

1. Select columns A and B, and click F<u>o</u>rmat, <u>C</u>olumn, <u>A</u>utoFit Selection (Alt+O, C, A).

   The columns adjust to fit the longer name in each column.

2. Click the Undo button to return the columns to their original widths.

3. Select cells A2 and B2 (Della VanValkenberg).

4. Click F<u>o</u>rmat, <u>C</u>olumn, <u>A</u>utoFit Selection (Alt+O, C, A).

   Column A adjusts to fit the width of Della, and parts of Suzanne (cell A1) and Sabina (cell A4) are hidden.

5. Use any method you have learned to adjust the widths so that all first and last names are visible.

6. Save the workbook.

🖥️Try It!

Specify a Column Width

By default, Excel uses a column width of 8.43, which represents how many characters can be displayed in the cell using the standard font (Arial, 10 point). You can specify a column width.

1. Select column B.
2. Click F*o*rmat, *C*olumn, *W*idth (Alt+O, C, W).
   Excel displays the Column Width dialog box, as shown below. (Your AutoFit column width may differ from the one shown.)

Column Width after AutoFit   *Column Width Specified*

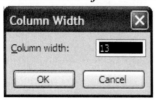   

3. Type **15** and click OK.
   Column B is now about two characters wider than VanValkenberg.
4. Set the width of column A to 10.
5. Save the workbook.

Insert Rows or Columns

■ Sometimes you need to insert new rows or columns into your worksheet. Excel inserts new columns to the left of the column selected when you perform the insert procedure. It inserts new rows above the selected row.

🖥️Try It!

1. Select cell A1 or click the row selector for row 1.
2. Click *I*nsert, *R*ows on the menu (Alt+I, R).
   Excel inserts a new row 1.
3. Select column A.
4. Click *I*nsert, *C*olumns (Alt+I, C).
   Excel inserts a new column A.
5. Click the Undo button ↩ to remove the new column, but leave the new row.
6. Save the workbook.

Add a Title to a Worksheet

■ The top rows of a worksheet are often used to display a title. You should add a title after you have adjusted the column widths for the body of the spreadsheet, especially if you use the AutoFit feature. If you use AutoFit after adding the title, the cell containing the title may expand too much for the rest of the entries in the column to appear attractive.

1. Select cell B1.
2. Type **Students with Perfect Attendance**.
3. Use the AutoFit Feature to adjust the width of column B.

The column is now considerably wider than VanValkenberg, the longest name, as shown below.

Column Widths Adjusted by AutoFit with Title Entered

	A	B	C
1		Students with Perfect Attendance	
2	Suzanne	Rodenbeek	
3	Della	VanValkenberg	
4	Jane	Zakrsewski	
5	Sabina	Romanowska	

4. Click the Undo button 🔄 to return the column to its previous width.

5. Save the workbook.

🖥Try It!

Center the Title Across Several Columns

1. Select cell A1.

2. Insert a new row.

3. Select cell B2.

4. Click the Cut button ✂.

5. Select cell A1.

6. Press Enter to paste the title into cell A1.

   The title is now in cell A1. It is a good idea to insert the title in cell A1 and then center it across the columns as described below.

7. Select range A1:D1 (the range across which you want to center the title).

8. Click the Merge and Center button 🔳 on the Formatting toolbar.

   The title is centered and the range A1:D1 is merged so that it forms a single cell A1.

Centered Across the Range A1:D1

	A	B	C	D
1	Students with Perfect Attendance			
2				
3	Suzanne	Rodenbeek		
4	Della	VanValkenberg		
5	Jane	Zakrsewski		
6	Sabina	Romanowska		

9. Format the title to Arial Black, 12 point.

10. Save the workbook.

Sort Data

■ You may find it useful to arrange data in alphabetical or numeric order to make information easier to find.

1. Enter the additional names and the school grades shown in the shaded portion of the following illustration.

Additional Names and School Grade

	A	B	C	D
1	**Students with Perfect Attendance**			
2				
3	Suzanne	Rodenbeek	7	
4	Della	VanValkenberg	8	
5	Jane	Zakrsewski	8	
6	Sabina	Romanowska	9	
7	Fredrich	Bachmann	6	
8	Marianne	Dashwood	6	
9	Alain	Delouche	7	
10	William	FitzMorris	6	

2. Select range A3:C10.

3. Click <u>D</u>ata, <u>S</u>ort (Alt+D, S).

   Excel displays the Sort dialog box shown below.

Sort Dialog Box

4. In the Sort by drop-down list, select Column B.

5. Select <u>A</u>scending, if necessary.

6. Click No header ro<u>w</u>, if necessary.

7. Click the OK button ▭ OK ▭ .

   The names are sorted alphabetically in ascending order by last name (column B).

8. Save the workbook.

Select Data to Sort

1. Add the following three names to the list in the cells shown. When you start to type the last name, press the Tab key to accept the AutoComplete suggestion from Excel.

Three New Names and School Grades

11	Wanda	FitzMorris	7
12	Walker	FitzMorris	8
13	Erin	FitzMorris	9

2. Select the range B3:B13.

3. Click Data, Sort (Alt+D, S).

   Excel displays the Sort Warning shown below.

Sort Warning

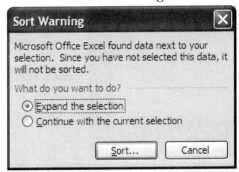

Excel warns that the data on either side of the selected column will not be sorted with the data in the column. In this example, the first names and grades may not end up with the correct last names.

4. Select Expand the selection.

5. Click the Sort button [Sort...].

   Excel expands the selection to all three columns and displays the Sort dialog box.

6. Make sure that No header row is selected.

7. In the Sort by section, select Column B and Ascending.

8. Click the OK button [OK].

   The list is sorted alphabetically by last name (column B). Excel reselects the original range.

   Note that the FitzMorris names are not alphabetical by first name. Later in this exercise, you will sort the list so that the names appear in the correct alphabetical order.

9. Save the workbook.

🖥 **Try It!**

Data with Header Rows

1. Insert a new row above the current row 3.

2. Enter the headings shown shaded in the illustration on the next page.

   The headings are formatted like the title. Excel assumes that the previous formatting should be continued.

3. Format the headings as left-aligned, Arial Narrow, 10 point, bold.

Header Row (Column Titles)

	A	B	C	D
1	**Students with Perfect Attendance**			
2				
3	First	Last	Grade	
4	Fredrich	Bachmann	6	

4. Add the names and grades shown below in rows 15-17.

Additional Names and Grades

15	Judy	Shuler	7
16	James	Griffith	7
17	Michael	Kimball	7

5. Select range A3:C17.

6. Click <u>D</u>ata, <u>S</u>ort (Alt+D, S).

    Excel detects a header row, changes the range to A4:C17, and displays the Sort dialog box.

7. In the Sort by section, select Grade, and <u>A</u>scending.

    Verify that Header row is selected.

Sort Dialog Box with Header Row Selected

8. Click the OK button [OK].

    The list is sorted by Grade, and Excel reselects the original range.

9. Save the workbook.

⌨ Try It!

Sort by More than One Column

1. Select range A3:C17.

2. Click <u>D</u>ata, <u>S</u>ort (Alt+D, S).

    Excel detects a header row, changes the range to A4:C17, and displays the Sort dialog box.

3. In the Sort by section, select Last and <u>A</u>scending.

4. In the first Then by section, select First and Ascending.

    This is called a secondary sort or subsort. Note that the FitzMorris entries are listed alphabetically by first name.

    ### Sort Dialog Box with Secondary Sort

5. Click the OK button [OK].

    The list is sorted by last name and by first name within last name, and Excel reselects the original range. The FitzMorris students are now listed alphabetically by first name.

    ### Spreadsheet after Sorting by Last Name and First Name

	A	B	C	D
1	**Students with Perfect Attendance**			
2				
3	**First**	**Last**	**Grade**	
4	Fredrich	Bachmann	6	
5	Marianne	Dashwood	6	
6	Alain	Delouche	7	
7	Erin	FitzMorris	9	
8	Walker	FitzMorris	8	
9	Wanda	FitzMorris	7	
10	William	FitzMorris	6	
11	James	Griffith	7	
12	Michael	Kimball	7	
13	Suzanne	Rodenbeek	7	
14	Sabina	Romanowska	9	
15	Judy	Shuler	7	
16	Della	VanValkenberg	8	
17	Jane	Zakrsewski	8	

6. Save and close the workbook, and exit Excel unless you are continuing with the Exercise Directions.

In this exercise, you will add players and their scores to the Scrabble® worksheet. You will also format and sort the data.

EXERCISE DIRECTIONS

Open the Workbook and Add New Players

1. Open 🖳Scrabble3, or open 💿04Scrabble3 from the data files.
2. Save the workbook as **Scrabble4**.
3. Select row 15.
4. Insert three rows.
5. Add the labels in the shaded areas shown in Illustration A.

Illustration A. Add Data to Scrabble

	A	B	C	D	E
1	PLAYER	ROUND 1	ROUND 2	ROUND 3	AVERAGE
2	Bossman	275	355	307	312.3333
3	Castillo	316	345	320	327.0000
4	Chien	295	325	301	307.0000
5	Chin, S.	295	318	307	306.6667
6	Chin, Y.	297	317	306	306.6667
7	Kardash	340	323	298	320.3333
8	Kern	283	295	303	293.6667
9	Kudja	395	370	356	373.6667
10	LeBihan	307	308	288	301.0000
11	Perro	402	299	336	345.6667
12	Rhodes	322	316	304	314.0000
13	Veach	378	279	346	334.3333
14	Wang	324	339	364	342.3333
15	VanderHoffen				
16	Reifschneider				
17	Cruz-Guerra				
18					
19	Highest	402	370	364	373.6667
20	Lowest	275	279	288	293.6667
21	Average	325.3077	322.2308	318.1538	

Adjust the Column Widths

1. Use AutoFit to adjust the width of column A.
2. Select all the remaining columns and use Format, Column, Width to define their widths as 10.5.

Add a Title

3. Insert two rows above existing row 1.
4. Select cell A1.
5. Type the following title:
   Scrabble Scores
6. Select the range A1:E1.
7. Click the Merge and Center button 🔳 to merge and center the title across the columns.
8. Format the text to Arial Black, 14 point.

Your worksheet should look like the one in Illustration B.

Illustration B. Scrabble Worksheet with Title

	A	B	C	D	E
1			Scrabble Scores		
2					
3	PLAYER	ROUND 1	ROUND 2	ROUND 3	AVERAGE
4	Bossman	275	355	307	312.3333
5	Castillo	316	345	320	327.0000
6	Chien	295	325	301	307.0000
7	Chin, S.	295	318	307	306.6667
8	Chin, Y.	297	317	306	306.6667
9	Kardash	340	323	298	320.3333
10	Kern	283	295	303	293.6667
11	Kudja	395	370	356	373.6667
12	LeBihan	307	308	288	301.0000
13	Perro	402	299	336	345.6667
14	Rhodes	322	316	304	314.0000
15	Veach	378	279	346	334.3333
16	Wang	324	339	364	342.3333
17	VanderHoffen				
18	Reifschneider				
19	Cruz-Guerra				
20					
21	Highest	402	370	364	373.6667
22	Lowest	275	279	288	293.6667
23	Average	325.3077	322.2308	318.1538	

Enter Scores for the Additional Players

1. Enter the following scores for the players just added, as shown in Illustration C.

Illustration C. Additional Scores

	A	B	C	D
17	VanderHoffen	377	422	355
18	Reifschneider	415	332	345
19	Cruz-Guerra	303	366	325

As you move from cell to cell, Excel automatically completes the formulas in column E and rows 21 through 23.

2. If Excel does not automatically update the Average column, copy the formula for the player average to cells E17:E19.

   Note that Reifschneider now has the highest score in Round 1. The Highest value in cell B21 changed automatically.

   Sometimes, however, when you insert rows or columns between a formula and its referenced cells, Excel may not automatically adjust the formula references because it cannot be certain you want to include the new rows in the formula. You may need to edit the cells with references.

3. Save the workbook.

Sort the List

1. Select the range A3:E19.
2. Click <u>D</u>ata, <u>S</u>ort and Sort by PLAYER in <u>A</u>scending order.
3. Click OK.

   Your worksheet should now look like the one in Illustration D.

Save, Print Preview, Print

1. Save the workbook.
2. Print Preview the document.
3. Print one copy with gridlines but without row and column headings.
4. Close the workbook, and exit Excel.

Illustration D. Completed Spreadsheet

	A	B	C	D	E
1			**Scrabble Scores**		
2					
3	PLAYER	ROUND 1	ROUND 2	ROUND 3	AVERAGE
4	Bossman	275	355	307	312.3333
5	Castillo	316	345	320	327.0000
6	Chien	295	325	301	307.0000
7	Chin, S.	295	318	307	306.6667
8	Chin, Y.	297	317	306	306.6667
9	Cruz-Guerra	303	366	325	331.3333
10	Kardash	340	323	298	320.3333
11	Kern	283	295	303	293.6667
12	Kudja	395	370	356	373.6667
13	LeBihan	307	308	288	301.0000
14	Perro	402	299	336	345.6667
15	Reifschneider	415	332	345	364.0000
16	Rhodes	322	316	304	314.0000
17	VanderHoffen	377	422	355	384.6667
18	Veach	378	279	346	334.3333
19	Wang	324	339	364	342.3333
20					
21	**Highest**	415	422	364	384.6667
22	**Lowest**	275	279	288	293.6667
23	**Average**	332.7500	331.8125	322.5625	

Exercise 5

Use Absolute References and the Print Dialog Box
■ Relative and Absolute References
■ Change Print Orientation ■ Print to Fit on One Page

NOTES

Relative and Absolute References

- So far in these exercises, you have used **relative** references when building formulas. For example, when you enter a formula in cell D2 and then copy it to cells D3:D8, the cell references change automatically as the row numbers change. The reference in cell D2 is relative: when it is copied to a new row its references change according to its new location.

- Sometimes, however, you want to refer to the same cell in several other cells. To keep a reference from changing when a formula is copied, place a $ before the part of the reference that should not change. This is called making the reference **absolute**; the reference does not change as the location of the formula changes. In this exercise, you'll learn the value of absolute references in calculating percentages.

🖳Try It!

Enter Totals and Average Stock Value

1. Open ⊙ **05Stocks** from the data files.

2. Save the workbook as **Stocks**.

3. Select cell A12, and enter the label **TOTAL**, and format it as bold.

4. Select cell C12, and use the AutoSum button Σ to find the total number of stocks.

5. Copy the formula to cell E12.

6. Select cell E12, and click the Currency button $ to format the value.

7. Select cell D12, and use the AutoSum button Σ ▾ drop-down arrow to enter a formula for the average price of the stocks.

   Click the warning button and tell Excel to ignore the error. The warning appears because the formulas in C12 and E12 use the SUM function while D12 uses AVERAGE.

   The last row of the worksheet should look like the one shown below.

   Rows 10-12 of Sample Stock Portfolio Worksheet

10	SLB	SCHLUMBERGER LTD	500	51.60	25,800
11					
12	**TOTAL**		6200	46.80	$283,972.00

⌨ **Try It!**

Calculate Percentages

1. Select cell F3, and enter the label **% of Stocks**. Format the label as bold, and adjust the column width as necessary to display the label within the cell.

2. Select cell G3, and enter the label **% of Value**. Format the label as bold, and adjust the column width as necessary to display the label within the cell.

3. Select cell F4, and enter the following formula to find what percentage AIG represents of total number of stocks. (Percent = Quantity divided by TOTAL Quantity.)

   =C4/C12

4. Copy the formula to cell F5.
   Cell F5 displays the error #DIV/0!, as shown below.

Divide by 0 Error

Value	% of Stocks
72,900	0.14516129
2⟨⟩⟩8	#DIV/0!

5. Edit the formula in cell F4 to read: **=C4/$C$12**
   The dollar signs tell Excel that you are making an absolute reference to cell C12.

6. Copy the formula to range F5:F10.
   The references in the first part of the formula (C4) change but the reference to cell C12 remains the same.

7. Select cell G4, and enter the formula: **=E4/$E$12**
   The formula calculates the percentage of total portfolio value represented by AIG stock.

8. Copy the formula to range G5:G10.

9. Select range F4:G10.

10. Click the Percent button .
    Percentages are displayed as whole numbers.

11. Click the Increase Decimal button until two decimal places are showing.
    The worksheet should look like the one shown on the next page.

12. Save the workbook.

✏️

Use the F4 Key

You can change from a relative to an absolute reference and back again by using the F4 key.

1. Display the formula you want to change.

% of Stocks
=C4/C12

2. Move the insertion point to any part of the reference to be changed.

% of Stocks
=C4/C1|2

3. Press the **F4** key.

% of Stocks
=C4/▮$C$12

   Pressing the F4 key cycles through $C$12, C$12, $C12, C12, and back to $C$12. Thus, an absolute reference may be to both the column and row ($C$12), just the row (C$12), just the column ($C12), or entirely relative (C12).

Completed Sample Stock Portfolio Worksheet

	A	B	C	D	E	F	G
1		SAMPLE STOCK PORTFOLIO					
2							
3	Symbol	Company	Quantity	Price	Value	% of Stocks	% of Value
4	AIG	American International Group, Inc.	900	81.00	72,900	14.52%	25.67%
5	XOM	Exxon-Mobil Corporation, Common Stock	600	40.68	24,408	9.68%	8.60%
6	GE	General Electric	2,000	37.43	74,860	32.26%	26.36%
7	HD	Home Depot, Inc.	200	38.62	7,724	3.23%	2.72%
8	JPM	J P Morgan Chase and Company	1,000	35.71	35,710	16.13%	12.58%
9	PFE	Pfizer, Inc. del PV$0.05	1,000	42.57	42,570	16.13%	14.99%
10	SLB	Schlumberger, Ltd.	500	51.60	25,800	8.06%	9.09%
11							
12	TOTAL		6200	46.80	$283,972.00		

Change Print Orientation

- By default, Excel prints in **Portrait** orientation (8½" x 11"). When a spreadsheet is wide, it prints part of the sheet on a second page. You can often cause a worksheet to print on one page by changing its print orientation to **Landscape** orientation (11" x 8½ ").

Try It!

1. Print Preview the worksheet.
2. Press the Page Down key.
   Note that at least one column of the worksheet appears on page 2.
3. Close Print Preview.
4. Click File, Page Setup (Alt+F, U).
5. Click the Sheet tab and select Gridlines and Row and column headings, if not already selected.
6. Click the Page tab.
7. Select Landscape.
8. Click the Print Preview button ⬚ Print Preview ⬚.
   The worksheet fits on one Landscape page (11" x 8½").
9. Print the worksheet.
10. Save the workbook.

Print to Fit on One Page

- Rather than change orientation, you can specify that Excel fit the worksheet on a single portrait page.

Try It!

1. Click File, Page Setup (Alt+F, U).
2. Click the Page tab.
3. Select Portrait.
4. Select Fit to, and check that each box contains a 1, as shown on the next page.

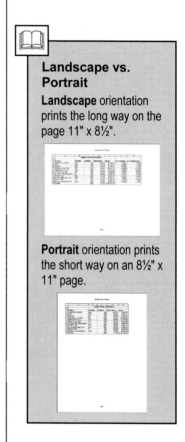

Landscape vs. Portrait

Landscape orientation prints the long way on the page 11" x 8½".

Portrait orientation prints the short way on an 8½" x 11" page.

Fit to 1 Page Wide by 1 Page Tall

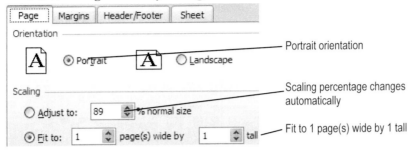

5. Click the Print Preview button [Print Preview].

   The worksheet is reduced so that it fits on one Portrait page.

6. Print the worksheet.

7. Save and close the workbook, and exit Excel unless you are continuing with the Exercise Directions.

In this exercise, you will use an absolute reference to calculate what percentage of the team total each basketball player's score represents.

EXERCISE DIRECTIONS

Open the Workbook and Enter New Labels

1. Open 💿 **05Basketball** from the data files.

2. Save the workbook as **Basketball5**.

3. Add the labels and values in the shaded areas shown in Illustration A.

Illustration A. Add Scores to Basketball

	A	B	C
1	Player	Score	Percent
2	Bretz	2	
3	Brokofsky	10	
4	Castillo	6	
5	Holmes	9	
6	Rhodes	15	
7	Rodriguez	7	
8	Thompson	1	
9	Veach	13	
10	Yuan	8	
11			
12	TOTAL		

4. Select cell B12 and enter a formula to calculate the total score for the team.

5. Save the workbook.

Calculate the Percentage of the Total for Each Player

1. Select cell C2.

2. Enter the formula to calculate the percentage of the total score that Bretz contributed.

   Hint: *Divide Bretz's score by the total score and use an absolute reference to ensure that the reference does not change when the formula is copied.*

3. Copy the formula to the remaining players (range C3:C10).

4. Select the range C2:C10.

5. Click the Percent button **%** on the Formatting toolbar.

6. Increase the decimal display to two decimal places.

Add a Title and Format Headings

1. Insert two rows above existing row 1.
2. Type the following title in cell A1:

    Basketball Scores

3. Center the title across columns A, B, and C.
4. Format the title as Arial 12-point bold, italic.
5. Format *Player*, *Score*, *Percent*, and *TOTAL* as bold.

    Your worksheet should look like the one shown in Illustration B.

Illustration B. Completed Worksheet

	A	B	C
1	***Basketball Scores***		
2			
3	**Player**	**Score**	**Percent**
4	Bretz	2	2.82%
5	Brokofsky	10	14.08%
6	Castillo	6	8.45%
7	Holmes	9	12.68%
8	Rhodes	15	21.13%
9	Rodriguez	7	9.86%
10	Thompson	1	1.41%
11	Veach	13	18.31%
12	Yuan	8	11.27%
13			
14	**TOTAL**	71	

Save, Print Preview, Print

1. Save the workbook.
2. Print Preview the document.
3. Print one copy in Portrait orientation.
4. Close the workbook, and exit Excel.

Use Chart Wizard I
■ About Pie Charts ■ Create a Pie Chart ■ Other Pie Chart Options

NOTES

About Pie Charts

■ A pie chart is a circle divided into segments. Each slice of the pie represents one column or row of data. The parts of a pie chart are labeled in the illustration below.

Parts of a Pie Chart (with Legend)

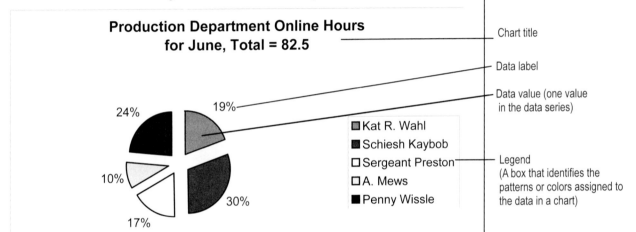

■ When you communicate the results of your work with spreadsheets, you can increase the impact of your message by including pictorial representations of your spreadsheet data. Excel makes creating charts and graphs easy with its **Chart Wizard**.

Create a Pie Chart

■ The Chart Wizard guides you through the creation of a chart, step-by-step, until the chart is complete. After the creation, Excel lets you edit the chart so that you end up with a picture that clearly represents the data.

🖥️ Try It!

Step 1: Select the Data to be Charted and the Chart Type

1. Open 💿 **06Online** from the data files.

2. Save the workbook as **Online6**.

3. Select range A4:B9, as shown in the illustration on the next page.
   In a pie chart, Excel works with one data series, the data in one row or one column.

Spreadsheet for Production Department Online Usage

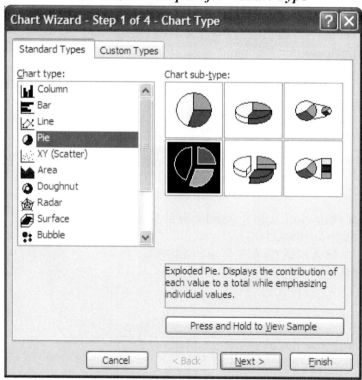

	A	B	C	D	E
1	Online Hours -- Production Department				
2	Month of June				
3					
4	User	Hours Online	Percent of Total		
5	Kat R. Wahl	16.0	19.39%		
6	Schiesh Kaybob	25.0	30.30%		
7	Sergeant Preston	14.0	16.97%		
8	A. Mews	8.0	9.70%		
9	Penny Wissle	19.5	23.64%		
10	TOTALS	82.5			

Data labels

Data series (values to be charted)

4. Click the Chart Wizard button on the Standard toolbar.

   The Chart Wizard starts and displays the Chart Type dialog box shown below. If the Office Assistant asks if you want help with this feature, click No, don't provide help now.

Chart Wizard - Step 1 of 4 - Chart Type

5. Select Pie for Chart type, and select the exploded pie for Chart sub-type, as shown in the illustration.

   An exploded pie chart separates out the slices to show them individually.

Chart sub-type

When you click on a chart sub-type, Excel displays an explanation of the sub-type in the lower right of the wizard dialog box.

🖳**Try It!**

Step 2: Specify the Chart Source Data Range

1. Click the <u>N</u>ext button [<u>N</u>ext >].

   Excel displays the Chart Source Data dialog box shown below.

   In creating a chart, the Chart Wizard tries to figure out whether you want to chart the data in rows or columns. The values to be charted are called a data series and the text that identifies each value is called a data label.

2. Accept the <u>D</u>ata range, and select Co<u>l</u>umns if it is not already selected.

Chart Wizard - Step 2 of 4 - Chart Source Data

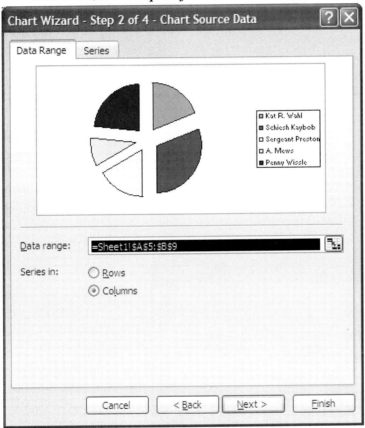

🖳**Try It!**

Step 3: Specify Chart Options

1. Click the <u>N</u>ext button [<u>N</u>ext >].

2. Click the Titles tab if it is not already selected.

   Excel displays the Chart Options dialog box shown in the illustration on the next page. Note the sample chart displayed in the right side of the dialog box.

Chart Wizard - Step 3 of 4 - Chart Options, Titles Tab

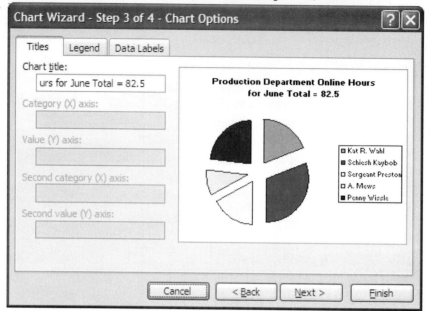

3. Click the Chart title box.

4. Delete the current title and enter the following text:

   Production Department Online Hours for June, Total = 82.5

5. Click the Legend tab. (Your title may appear on three lines.)

   Excel displays the Chart Options dialog box shown below.

Chart Wizard - Step 3 of 4 - Chart Options, Legend Tab

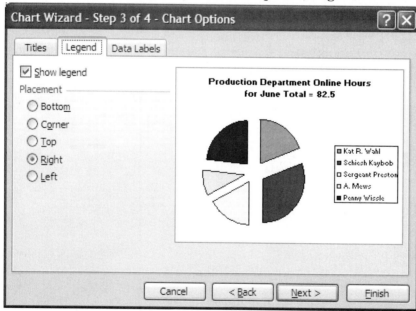

6. Select Show legend and Right if they are not already selected.

7. Click the Data Labels tab.

   Excel displays the Chart Options dialog box shown in the illustration on the next page.

Chart Wizard - Step 3 of 4 - Chart Options, Data Labels Page

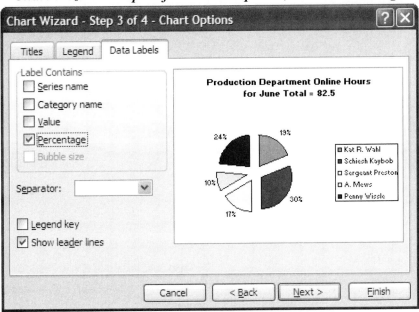

8. Select Percentage, as shown in the illustration.

9. Select Show leader lines if it is not already selected.

Try It!

Step 4: Specify Chart Location

1. Click the Next button [Next >].

   Excel displays the Chart Location dialog box shown below.

2. Select As object in and Sheet1 if they are not already selected.

Chart Wizard - Step 4 of 4 - Chart Location

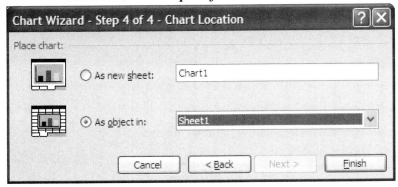

3. Click the Finish button [Finish].

   The pie chart appears in the worksheet as an object that floats over the grid, and the Chart toolbar displays.

4. Click a blank area of the chart and drag the chart to position it underneath the spreadsheet data.

5. If necessary, click the center sizing handle on the bottom edge of the chart, and drag until the chart covers row 28.

   The text and pie slices change size as you drag.

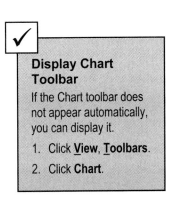

Display Chart Toolbar

If the Chart toolbar does not appear automatically, you can display it.

1. Click **View**, **Toolbars**.
2. Click **Chart**.

6. If necessary, click the center sizing handle on the right edge of the chart, and drag it until it covers column G.

   The text and pie slices change size as you drag.

7. Save the workbook.

🖥 Try It!

Edit the Chart Title

If necessary, you can format the chart title so that the lines are closer to the same length.

1. Click the title.

   A gray box surrounds the title.

2. Click inside the box.

   The insertion point appears where you clicked.

3. Press the Enter key just before the word *for.*

   Your worksheet should look like the one in the illustration below.

4. Save the workbook.

5. Print one copy in Landscape orientation.

6. Close the workbook, and exit Excel unless you are continuing with the Exercise Directions after reviewing the explanation of other options on the next page.

Completed Worksheet with Pie Chart

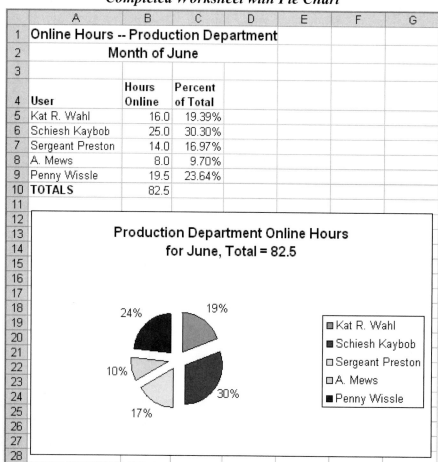

	A	B	C	D	E	F	G
1	Online Hours -- Production Department						
2	Month of June						
3							
4	User	Hours Online	Percent of Total				
5	Kat R. Wahl	16.0	19.39%				
6	Schiesh Kaybob	25.0	30.30%				
7	Sergeant Preston	14.0	16.97%				
8	A. Mews	8.0	9.70%				
9	Penny Wissle	19.5	23.64%				
10	TOTALS	82.5					
11							

Production Department Online Hours
for June, Total = 82.5

24%   19%

10%

30%

17%

- ■ Kat R. Wahl
- ■ Schiesh Kaybob
- ☐ Sergeant Preston
- ☐ A. Mews
- ■ Penny Wissle

Other Pie Chart Options

- You can create a pie chart that has no legend but includes the labels and the percentages on the pie.

- In Step 3 of the Chart Wizard or on the Chart Options dialog box (see margin note at the right) :

  - Deselect <u>S</u>how legend in the Legend tab.

  - Select Cate<u>g</u>ory name and <u>P</u>ercentage on the Data Labels page.

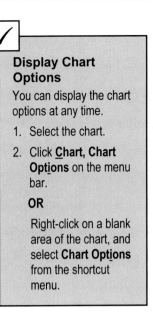

Display Chart Options

You can display the chart options at any time.

1. Select the chart.

2. Click **Chart, Chart Options** on the menu bar.

   OR

   Right-click on a blank area of the chart, and select **Chart Options** from the shortcut menu.

Chart Wizard - Chart Options, Legend and Data Labels Pages

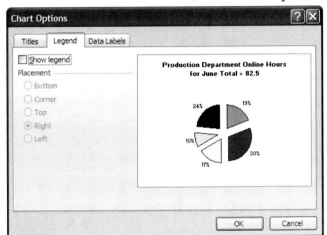

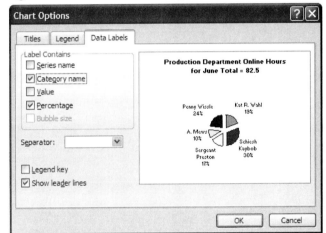

Exploded Pie Chart with Category Names and Percentages

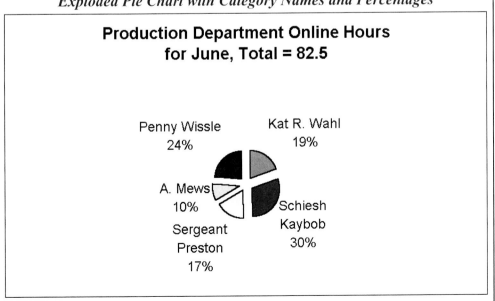

Production Department Online Hours for June, Total = 82.5

> *In this exercise, you will use the Chart Wizard to create an exploded 3-D pie chart from basketball scores.*

EXERCISE DIRECTIONS

Open the Workbook and Select the Data to Include in Chart

1. Open 🖫 **Basketball5**, or open 💿 **06Basketball5** from the data files.
2. Save the workbook as **Basketball6**.
3. Select the range A4:B12.

Start the Chart Wizard and Select Pie Chart

1. Click the Chart Wizard button 📊 to start the Chart Wizard.

   The dialog box shown in Illustration A appears.
2. Select Pie.
3. Select the exploded 3-D pie chart in the middle of the bottom row, as shown in the illustration.
4. Click the Next button ⟨ Next > ⟩.

   The dialog box shown in Illustration B appears.

Illustration A. Chart Wizard, Choose a Chart Type

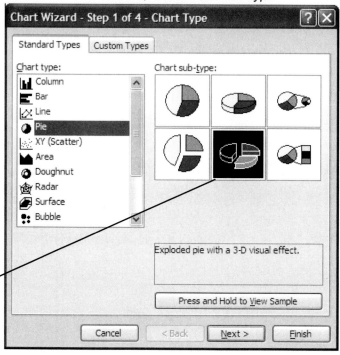

Verify that the Selected Range is Correct

1. Check that the Data range is correct.
2. Since you want to chart the data series in the column rather than the row, leave Columns selected for Series in.
3. Click the Next button ⟨ Next > ⟩.

   The dialog box shown in Illustration C (next page) appears.

Illustration B. Chart Wizard, Chart Source Data

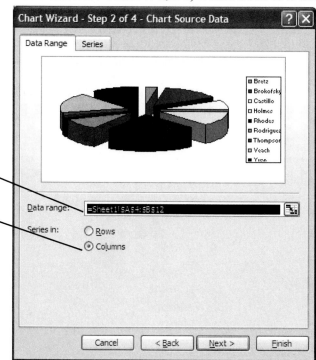

Illustration C. Chart Wizard, Chart Options, Titles

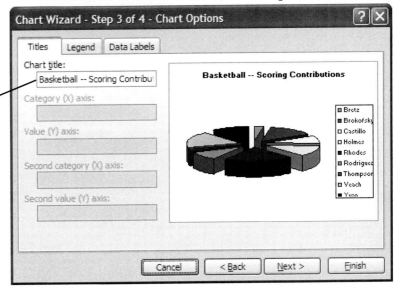

Enter a Title for the Chart

1. If it is not already selected, click the Titles tab, as shown in Illustration C.
2. Type the following title in the Chart title text box:

   Basketball -- Scoring Contributions
3. Click the Legend tab.

   The dialog box shown in Illustration D appears.

Choose Not to Display a Legend

1. Deselect Show legend.
2. Click the Data Labels tab.

   The dialog box shown in Illustration E (next page) appears.

Illustration D. Chart Wizard, Chart Options, Legend

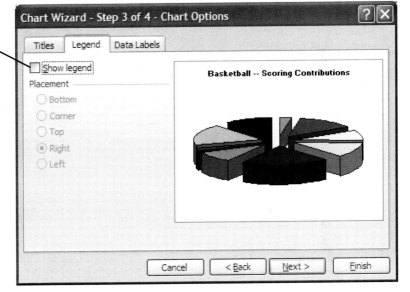

Choose to Show Label and Percentage

1. Select Category name and Percentage.
2. Click the Next button ⌈ Next > ⌉.

   The dialog box shown in Illustration F appears.

Illustration E. Chart Wizard, Chart Options, Data Labels

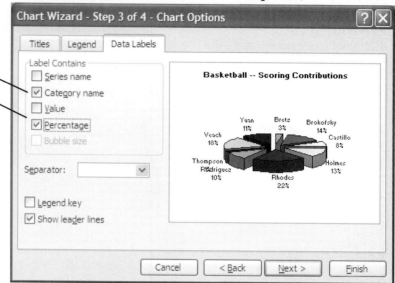

Illustration E. Chart Wizard, Chart Options, Data Labels

Choose to Keep the Chart on the Current Worksheet

1. If it is not already selected, click As object in and make sure that the drop-down box says Sheet1.
2. Click the Finish button ⌈ Finish ⌉.

   The chart appears on the worksheet, as shown in Illustration G.

Illustration F. Chart Wizard, Chart Location

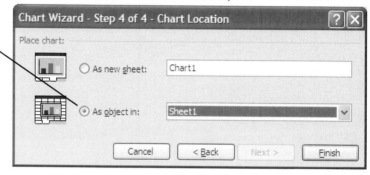

3. If necessary, select the chart and drag it to the location shown in the illustration.
4. Stretch the chart horizontally and vertically so that the right side reaches column H and the bottom reaches row 31.

   As you can see, the data label for Thompson is partially hiding the data label for Rodriguez. You need to edit the Thompson data label so that both data labels can be seen clearly.

5. Save the workbook.

Illustration G. Chart in Worksheet

	A	B	C	D	E	F	G	H
1	**Basketball Scores**							
2								
3	**Player**	**Score**	**Percent**					
4	Bretz	2	2.82%					
5	Brokofsky	10	14.08%					
6	Castillo	6	8.45%					
7	Holmes	9	12.68%					
8	Rhodes	15	21.13%					
9	Rodriguez	7	9.86%					
10	Thompson	1	1.41%					
11	Veach	13	18.31%					
12	Yuan	8	11.27%					
13								
14	**TOTAL**	71						
15								
16								
17								
18								
19								
20								
21								
22								
23								
24								
25								
26								
27								
28								
29								
30								
31								

Basketball -- Scoring Contributions

Edit the Chart Elements

1. Select the data label for Thompson.
   Each data label is marked by sizing handles (black squares).
2. Click Thompson's name again.

Illustration H. Edit the Chart, Step 1

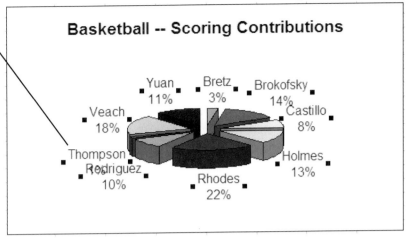

A gray border surrounds the data label as shown in Illustration I.

If you accidentally double-click the data label, Excel lets you edit the text. Click outside the chart, then repeat steps 1 and 2.

3. Move the mouse pointer to the top or bottom line of the gray square.
4. Click and drag the data label up until Thompson's data label no longer hides any part of Rodriguez's, as shown in Illustration J. If necessary, move Rodriguez's label as well. You may also wish to move Castillo's label to separate it from Brokofsky.
5. If a small line leads from the data label to the pie slice, you may choose to leave it. If you want to remove it, click the line and press the Delete key.

   Your completed worksheet with the chart should now look like the one shown in Illustration K on the next page.

Save, Print Preview, Print

1. Save the workbook.
2. Print Preview the document.
3. Print one copy in Landscape orientation.
4. Close the workbook, and exit Excel.

Illustration I. Edit the Chart, Step 2

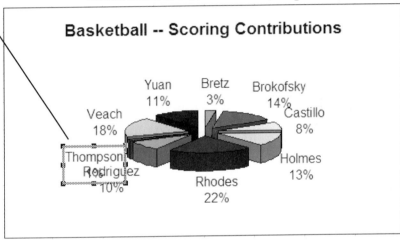

Illustration J. Edit the Chart, Steps 3 and 4

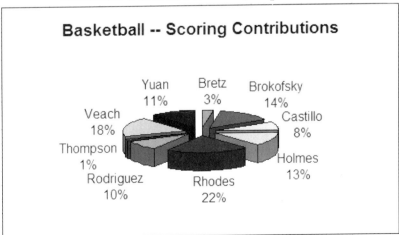

Illustration K. Desired Result

	A	B	C	D	E	F	G	H
1	*Basketball Scores*							
2								
3	**Player**	**Score**	**Percent**					
4	Bretz	2	2.82%					
5	Brokofsky	10	14.08%					
6	Castillo	6	8.45%					
7	Holmes	9	12.68%					
8	Rhodes	15	21.13%					
9	Rodriguez	7	9.86%					
10	Thompson	1	1.41%					
11	Veach	13	18.31%					
12	Yuan	8	11.27%					
13								
14	**TOTAL**	71						
15								

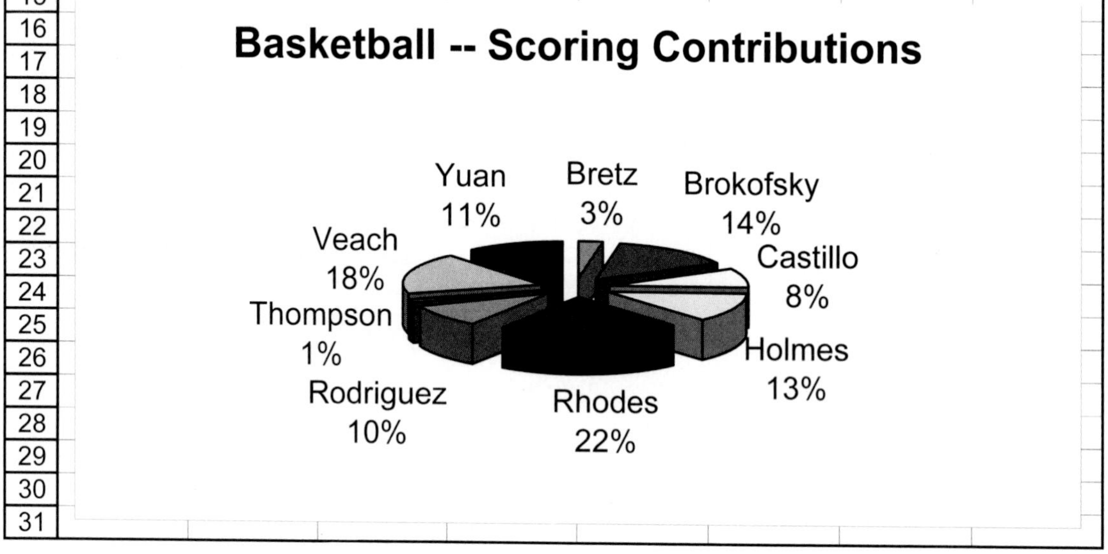

Basketball -- Scoring Contributions

Yuan 11%
Bretz 3%
Brokofsky 14%
Veach 18%
Castillo 8%
Thompson 1%
Holmes 13%
Rodriguez 10%
Rhodes 22%

Exercise 7

Use Chart Wizard II
■ Create a Bar Chart

NOTES

Create a Bar Chart

- Bar and column charts are good tools for illustrating comparisons of data.
- When building a bar or column chart, Excel works with two data series. One series is shown along the **x-axis (horizontal)**; Excel calls this the **Category (X) Axis** because the labels for the chart appear along this axis.
- The other data series is shown along the **y-axis (vertical)**; Excel calls this the **Value (Y) Axis** because the scale for the values selected for the chart appear along this axis.

> 📖 **Bar or Column Chart**
> Excel distinguishes between **column charts**, in which the bars rise from the x-axis, and **bar charts**, in which the bars extend from the y-axis. Most users call both types bar charts.

Bar/Column Chart (Data Series in Rows)

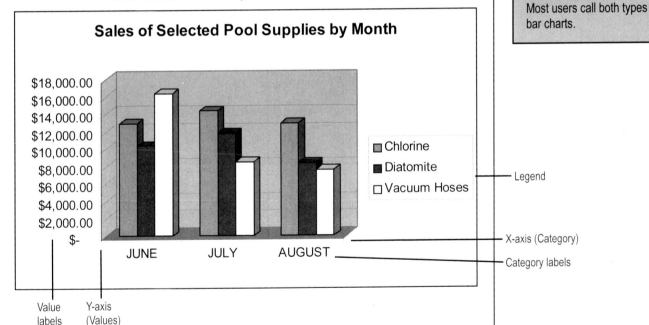

Sales of Selected Pool Supplies by Month

Legend — Chlorine, Diatomite, Vacuum Hoses

X-axis (Category)

Category labels

Value labels

Y-axis (Values)

🖳 Try It!

1. Open 🖸 **07Pool** from the data files to display the spreadsheet shown on the next page.
2. Save the workbook as **Pool7**.
3. Select the range A4:D7.

273

Sales of Pool Supplies Worksheet

	A	B	C	D
1	SALES OF POOL SUPPLIES			
2	THREE MONTHS			
3				
4	PRODUCT	JUNE	JULY	AUGUST
5	Chlorine	$ 12,896.56	$ 14,344.92	$ 12,946.22
6	Diatomite	$ 10,375.44	$ 11,795.62	$ 8,345.18
7	Vacuum Hoses	$ 16,384.95	$ 8,492.33	$ 7,543.95

4. Click the Chart Wizard button ![Chart Wizard icon] to start the Chart Wizard.

5. In the Chart Type dialog box, select Column chart and Clustered column with a 3-D effect, as shown below.

Column and Clustered Column with 3-D Effect Selected

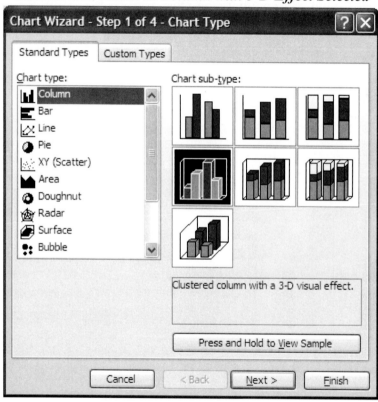

6. Click the Next button [Next >].

   Excel displays the Source Data dialog box shown in the illustration on the next page.

7. Click the Data Range tab if it is not already selected.

8. Click the Collapse button ![Collapse icon] at the right of the Data range box.

   You can review the selected range or change it if necessary. If you are sure the range is correct, you can skip this step and the next.

9. Click the Expand button ![Expand icon].

Source Data, Series in Rows

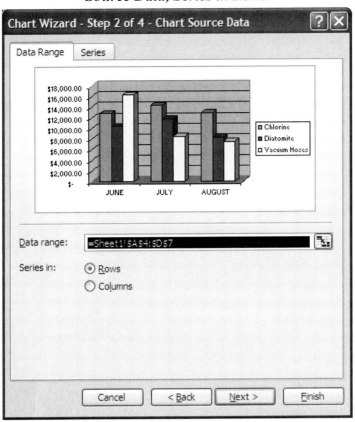

Try It!

Data Series in Rows or Columns

1. Select Rows.

   The months are displayed as the Category labels, and the Legend displays the products. With this option, you can easily see which product sold the most for each month.

2. Select Columns.

   The products are displayed as the Category labels, and the Legend displays the months. With this option, you can easily see in which month each product sold best. You can choose which way you want to view the data by setting this option.

3. Select Rows again.

   The months are displayed as the Category labels, and the Legend displays the products.

4. Click the Next button ⟨ Next > ⟩ .

   Excel displays the Chart Options dialog box.

5. Click the Titles tab if it is not already displayed.

6. For Chart title, type **Sales of Selected Pool Supplies by Month**.

7. Click the Next button ⟨ Next > ⟩ .

   Excel displays the Chart Location dialog box.

8. Select As object in and Sheet1.

9. Click the Finish button [Finish].

Your chart should look similar to the one shown below. The scale on your Y-axis may be different. You will adjust the look of the chart in the next few steps.

Bar/Column Chart (Data Series in Rows)

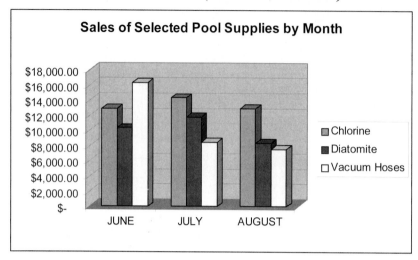

10. Position the chart below the spreadsheet data.

11. Select the center-sizing handle on the lower edge of the chart, and drag until the bottom covers row 28.

    The chart stretches vertically and more scale increments appear.

12. Click the center sizing handle on the right edge of the chart, and drag until the right edge covers column G.

    The chart stretches and the names of the months adjust position.

13. Save the workbook.

14. Close the workbook, and exit Excel unless you are continuing with the Exercise Directions.

If you had selected Columns in the Chart Source Data dialog box, the chart would appear like the one in the following illustration. The chart has been stretched to display all elements clearly.

Bar/Column Chart (Data Series in Columns)

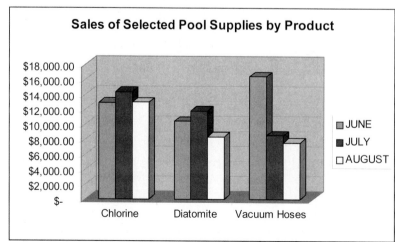

In this exercise, you will create a column chart using the Chart Wizard.

EXERCISE DIRECTIONS

Open the Workbook and Select the Rows for the Column Chart

1. Open 🖫Scrabble4, or open
   💿07Scrabble4 from the data files.
2. Save the workbook as **Scrabble7**
3. Select the range A21:D23, as shown in Illustration A.

Start the Chart Wizard

1. Click the Chart Wizard button 📊.

   The Chart Wizard starts and displays the dialog box shown in Illustration B.

2. Select Column for Chart type.
3. For Chart sub-type, select Clustered column with a 3-D visual effect (first option in second row).
4. Click the Next button [Next >].
   The dialog box shown in Illustration C appears.

Illustration A. Data Series to be Included in Chart

21	Highest	415	422	364
22	Lowest	275	279	288
23	Average	332.7500	331.8125	322.5625

Illustration B. Chart Wizard for Column Chart

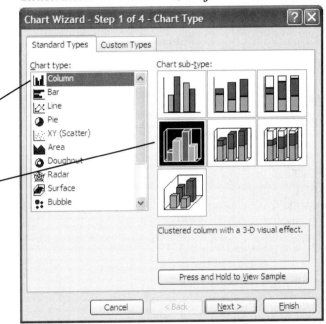

Verify the Data Range and Series Values and Labels

1. Check that the Data range is correct.
2. Select Rows for Series in.
3. Click the Series tab.

Illustration C. Column Chart, Data Range Tab

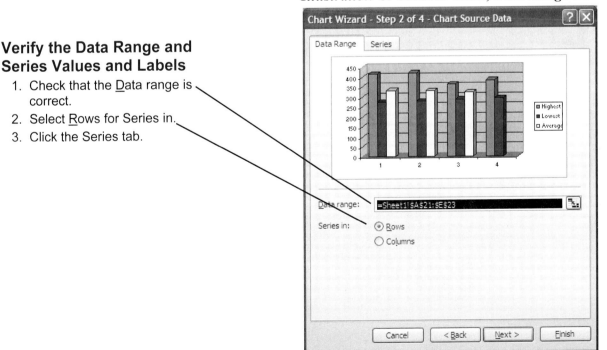

*The dialog box shown in
Illustration D appears.*

4. Verify that the Series list box shows
   Highest, *Lowest*, and *Average*.

   *If it shows some other text, click
   the Data Range tab and make sure
   that Rows is selected for Series in.*

   *Note the range in the Name box. It
   lists the cell from which Excel is
   getting the Name (data label) for
   the Values.*

   *=Sheet1!$A$21 is Excel's way of
   ensuring that it knows on which
   worksheet the series resides.*

5. Select *Lowest* in the Series list box.

   *Note that the Name and Values
   boxes now list the cell locations of
   the data label and range for the
   Lowest series.*

   *As you can see from the chart in
   the upper part of the dialog box, the
   X-axis labels are numbers. You
   want them to read Round 1, Round
   2, and Round 3.*

6. Click on the title bar of the Chart
   Source Data dialog box and drag
   the dialog box to the right so that it
   does not obscure any of the
   worksheet data.

7. Place the insertion point in the
   Category (X) axis labels text box.

8. Select the range B3:D3, as shown
   in Illustration E.

   *The dialog box collapses when you
   click in cell B3 and expands when
   you release the mouse button in
   cell D3.*

Illustration D. Column Chart, Series Tab

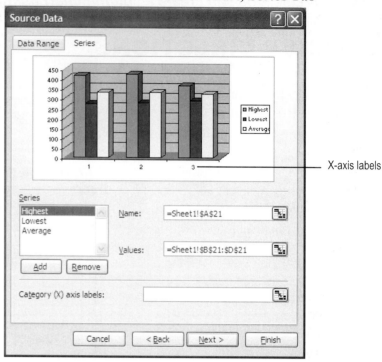

X-axis labels

Illustration E. Collapsed Dialog Box when Selecting Data

	A	B	C	D	E	F	G	H	I	J	K	L
1		**Scrabble Scores**										
2												
3	PLAYER	ROUND 1	ROUND 2	ROUND 3	AVERAGE	Source Data - Category (X) axis labels:						
4	Bossman	275	355	307	312.3333	=Sheet1!$B$3:$D$3						
5	Castillo	216	345	320	227.0000							

The completed Chart Source Data dialog box with the Category (X) axis labels text box completed is shown in Illustration F.

Note that the proper labels now appear in the chart illustration in the upper half of the box.

Add a Title to the Chart

1. Click the Next button 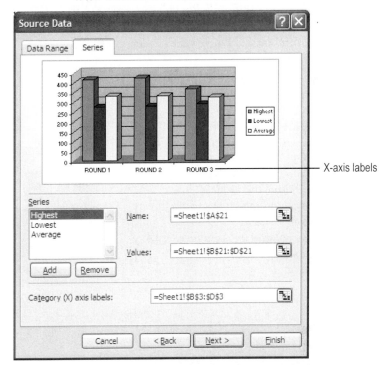.

   The dialog box shown in Illustration G appears. (Your Chart title box will be different from the one shown.)

2. Click in the Chart title text box and type the following title:

   Highest, Lowest, & Average Scores for Each Round

3. Click the Next button.

4. Click the Finish button.

Illustration F. Expanded Dialog Box with Selected X-axis Labels

Illustration G. Column Chart, Titles Tab

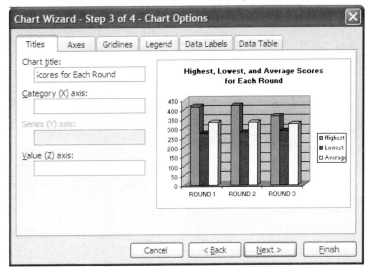

Edit the Title

1. Click the title once.

   A gray border surrounds the title as shown in Illustration H.

2. Click just in front of the word *Scores*.

3. Press Enter to make the two lines of the title more nearly the same length.

4. Click anywhere outside the chart.

   Your chart title should now look like the one in Illustration I.

5. Click on a blank area of the chart and drag until the chart is positioned directly underneath the spreadsheet data.

   Your completed worksheet should now look like the one in Illustration J.

Save, Print Preview, Print

1. Save the workbook.

2. Print Preview the document.

3. Print one copy in Portrait orientation.

4. Close the workbook, and exit Excel.

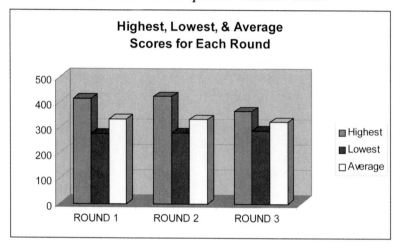

Illustration H. Select Title for Editing

Highest, Lowest, & Average Scores for Each Round

Click here and press Enter.

Illustration I. Completed Column Chart

Illustration J. Desired Result

	A	B	C	D	E	F	G
1	**Scrabble Scores**						
2							
3	**PLAYER**	**ROUND 1**	**ROUND 2**	**ROUND 3**	**AVERAGE**		
4	Bossman	275	355	307	312.3333		
5	Castillo	316	345	320	327.0000		
6	Chien	295	325	301	307.0000		
7	Chin, S.	295	318	307	306.6667		
8	Chin, Y.	297	317	306	306.6667		
9	Cruz-Guerra	303	366	325	331.3333		
10	Kardash	340	323	298	320.3333		
11	Kern	283	295	303	293.6667		
12	Kudja	395	370	356	373.6667		
13	LeBihan	307	308	288	301.0000		
14	Perro	402	299	336	345.6667		
15	Reifschneider	415	332	345	364.0000		
16	Rhodes	322	316	304	314.0000		
17	VanderHoffen	377	422	355	384.6667		
18	Veach	378	279	346	334.3333		
19	Wang	324	339	364	342.3333		
20							
21	**Highest**	415	422	364	384.6667		
22	**Lowest**	275	279	288	293.6667		
23	**Average**	332.7500	331.8125	322.5625			
24							
25							
26		Highest, Lowest, & Average					
27		Scores for Each Round					
28							
29							
30							
31							
32							
33							
34							
35							
36							
37							
38							
39							
40							

Use Chart Wizard III
■ Create a Line Graph ■ Edit the Line Graph

NOTES

Create a Line Graph

■ A line graph is a good tool to illustrate a trend or the changes in values through time. For example, the changes in a school's enrollment over several years make a good candidate for a line graph. Weekly changes in the price of oil for a couple of months also can be illustrated well by a line graph.

⌨ Try It!

Open File and Select Data and Chart Type

1. Open ⊚ **08Enrollment** from the data files.

2. Save the workbook as **Enrollment8**.

3. Select range A3:F7, as shown below.

Enrollment Figures for Ulysses Middle School

	A	B	C	D	E	F
1	**Ulysses Middle School Enrollment**					
2						
3		1997	1998	1999	2000	2001
4	Sixth	325	342	345	350	360
5	Seventh	295	302	317	325	340
6	Eighth	263	272	296	320	330
7	Ninth	252	261	285	315	320
8	TOTALS	1135	1177	1243	1310	1350

4. Click the Chart Wizard button 📊.

   The Chart Type dialog box appears.

5. For Chart type, select Line.

6. For Chart sub-type, select Line with markers displayed at each data value, as shown in the illustration on the next page. (Note only the upper portion of the dialog box is shown on the next page.)

Chart type, Line; Sub-type, Line with Markers

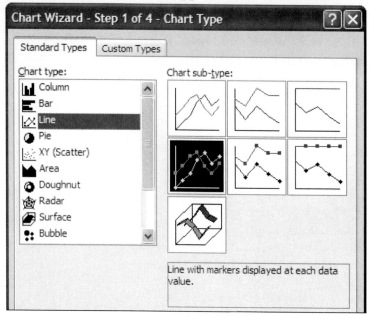

Try It!

Check Data Range and Enter Title and Category (X) Axis Label

1. Click the Next button [Next >].

   Excel displays the Chart Source Data dialog box. Check the Data range to be sure it is $A$3:$F$7. Correct it if necessary.

2. For Series in, select Rows.

Series in Rows

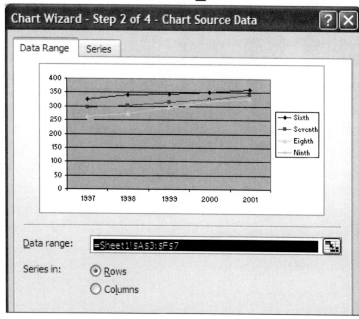

3. Click the Next button [Next >].

   Excel displays the Chart Options dialog box.

4. Click the Titles tab if it is not already displayed.
5. For Chart title, type: **Ulysses Middle School Enrollment**
6. For Category (X) axis, type: **Year**

Title and Category (X) Axis Label

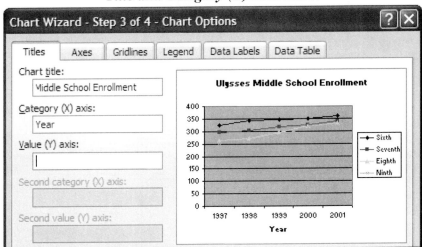

Try It!

Finish and Review Graph

1. Click the Next button [Next >].

   Excel displays the Chart Location dialog box.

2. Select As object in and Sheet1.

3. Click the Finish button [Finish].

4. Position the chart below the spreadsheet data, and stretch it so that the right side covers most of column H and the bottom reaches row 27.

5. Save the workbook.

   Your chart should look like the one shown below.

Line Graph Showing Enrollment Trends

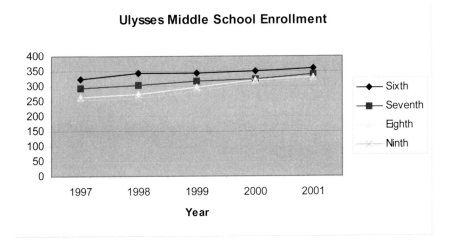

Edit the Line Graph

- The values on the y-axis run from 0 to 400. The Sixth, Seventh, Eighth, and Ninth lines run together, making them hard to distinguish. You can edit the y-axis to change its beginning and ending numbers.

ScreenTip for Value Axis

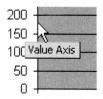

💻Try It!

1. Point at the line that marks the Value Axis (vertical or y-axis).
   A ScreenTip appears as shown at the right.

2. Right-click on the Value axis.
   A shortcut menu appears.

Value Axis Shortcut Menu

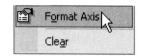

3. Click Format Axis.
   The Format Axis dialog box appears, as shown in the illustration that follows.

4. Click the Scale tab.

Format Axis Dialog Box, Scale Tab

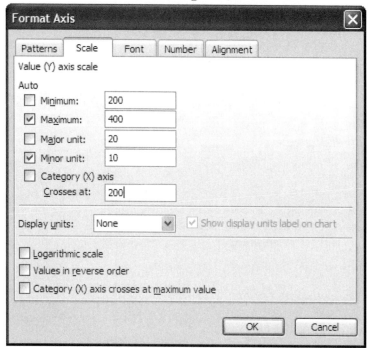

5. Type **200** in the Minimum box.

6. Leave Maximum unchanged at 400. If it is not 400, change it to **400**, and make sure the check box remains selected.

7. Type **20** in the Major unit box.

8. Leave Minor unit unchanged at 10. If it is not 10, change it to **10**.

9. Deselect Category (X) axis Crosses at, and type **200** in the box.

10. Click the OK button [OK].
    The line graph should look like the one shown in the illustration on the next page.

11. Save the workbook, close the workbook, and exit Excel unless you are continuing with the Exercise Directions.

Enrollment Trends by Class

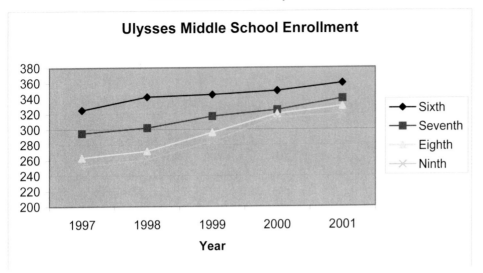

Ulysses Middle School Enrollment

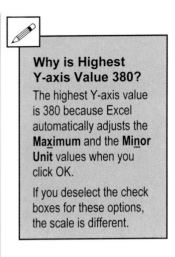

Why is Highest Y-axis Value 380?

The highest Y-axis value is 380 because Excel automatically adjusts the **Maximum** and the **Minor Unit** values when you click OK.

If you deselect the check boxes for these options, the scale is different.

In this exercise, you will create a line graph using the Chart Wizard.

EXERCISE DIRECTIONS

Open the Workbook and Select the Rows for the Line Graph

1. Open 📖**Scrabble7**, or open 💿**08Scrabble7** from the data files.

2. Save the workbook as **Scrabble8**.

3. Locate the players who scored highest in each round (Reifschneider, VanderHoffen, Wang).

4. Select the range A-D for each of these players (A15:D15, A17:D17, A19:D19), as shown in Illustration A.

   Hint: Hold down the Ctrl key while selecting the ranges for VanderHoffen and Wang.

Start the Chart Wizard and Select Line Graph

1. Click the Chart Wizard button 📊 to start the Chart Wizard.

2. Select Line for Chart type.

3. Select *Line with markers displayed at each data value* (first option in second row), as shown in Illustration B.

4. Click the **N**ext button.

Illustration A. Ranges for Players with Highest Scores

13	LeBihan	307	308	288	301.0000
14	Perro	402	299	336	345.6667
15	Reifschneider	415	332	345	364.0000
16	Rhodes	322	316	304	314.0000
17	VanderHoffen	377	422	355	384.6667
18	Veach	378	279	346	334.3333
19	Wang	324	339	364	342.3333
20					

Illustration B. Chart Wizard, Line Graph, Specify Chart Type

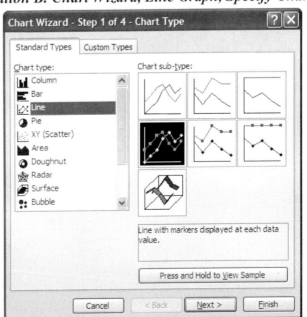

The dialog box shown in Illustration C appears.

Verify the Ranges and Make Sure that Rows is Selected

1. Click the Data Range tab, if necessary.
2. Verify that Rows is selected and that the Data range box specifies the three ranges you selected.

   If the data ranges are incorrect, use the Collapse button to select the data ranges correctly.
3. Click the Series tab.

   The dialog box shown in Illustration D appears.

Illustration C. Line Graph, Verify Data Ranges

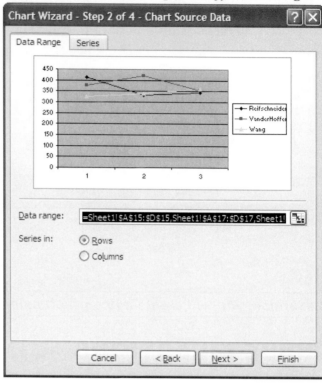

Select the Range for the X-axis Labels

1. Verify that the data labels for each Series are correct.
2. Place the insertion point in the Category (X) axis labels text box.
3. Click the title bar of the dialog box and move it to the right so that it does not obscure any of the data.
4. Select the range B3:D3.

   The dialog box collapses to a single line then expands.

   The dialog box should now look as shown in Illustration D.
5. Click the Next button Next >

Illustration D. Line Graph, Ensure Accuracy of Data Labels

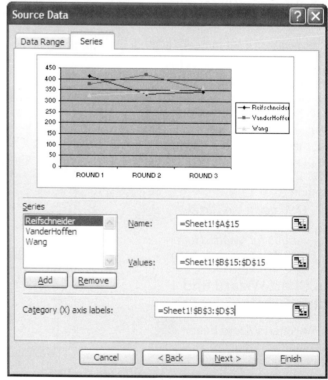

The dialog box shown in Illustration E appears.

Specify the Chart Title

1. Click the Titles tab.
2. Click in the Chart <u>t</u>itle text box.
3. Type the following title:

   Scores for Players with Highest Score in Each Round
4. Review the results in the box that shows the chart so far.
5. Click the <u>N</u>ext button [<u>N</u>ext >].

   The dialog box shown in Illustration F appears.

Illustration E. Specify Chart Title

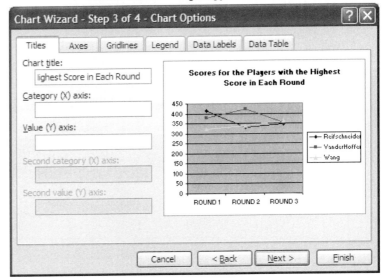

Place Chart on Separate Worksheet

1. Click As new <u>s</u>heet to place the graph on a new worksheet.
2. Click the <u>F</u>inish button [<u>F</u>inish].

   Excel creates a new worksheet named Chart1, activates it, and displays the line graph, as shown in Illustration G on the next page.
3. Save the workbook.

Illustration F. Specify Chart Location

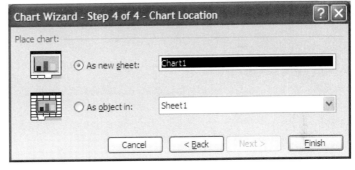

Illustration G. Line Graph on Chart1 Worksheet

Microsoft Excel - Scrabble8.xls

File Edit View Insert Format Tools Chart Window Help

Type a question for help

Arial   10   B I U

Chart Area

Scores for the Players with the Highest Score in Each Round

- ◆ Reifschneider
- ■ VanderHoffen
- Wang

ROUND 1   ROUND 2   ROUND 3

Chart

Chart Area

◄ ► ►│ \ **Chart1** / Sheet1 / Sheet2 / Sheet3 /

Ready   NUM

Adjust the Y-axis (Vertical) Scale

Note the sheet names at the bottom of the Excel Window. Chart1 has been inserted before Sheet1. See Illustration H.

1. Click the Sheet1 tab to display the spreadsheet and the column chart.

2. Click the Chart1 tab to return to the line graph.

    The scale of the vertical axis runs from 0 to 450. Change this scale to make the graph easier to read and to show the changes in scores more dramatically.

3. Place the mouse pointer on the vertical axis line.

    The ScreenTip Value Axis appears under the mouse pointer, as shown in Illustration H.

4. Double-click the Value axis.

Illustration H. Mouse Pointer on Value (Y) Axis

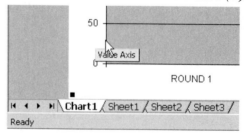

50

Value Axis

0

ROUND 1

│◄ ◄ ► ►│ \ **Chart1** / Sheet1 / Sheet2 / Sheet3 /

Ready

The Format Axis dialog box appears as shown in Illustration I.

5. Click the Scale tab.
6. Deselect each Auto option and change the values as follows.

Minimum	**250**
Maximum	**450**
Major unit	**25**
Minor unit	**5**
Category (X) axis Crosses at	**250**

These values establish a scale that crosses the X-axis at 250 and rises in units of 25 to reach 450.

7. Click the OK button OK .

The line graph changes and appears as shown in Illustration J.

Illustration I. Format Axis Dialog Box, Scale Tab

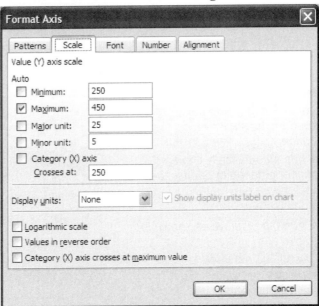

Illustration J. Completed Line Graph with Adjusted Scale

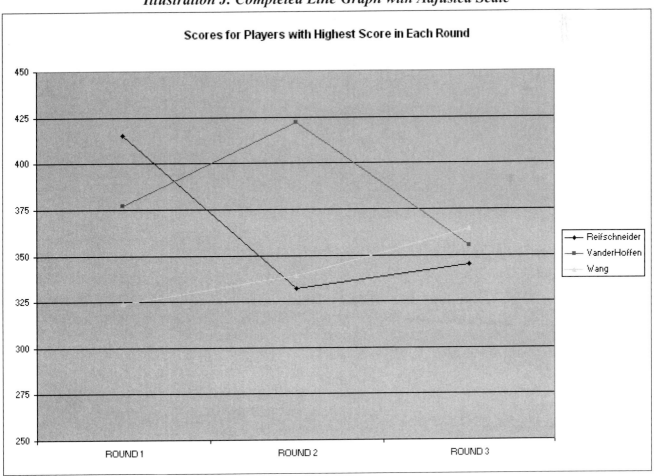

Save, Print Preview, Print

1. Save the workbook.
2. Print Preview the Chart1.
3. Close Print Preview.
4. Click File, Page Setup and click the Page tab, if it is not already selected.

   The Page Setup dialog box, Page tab appears, as shown in Illustration K.

   Excel has automatically changed the print orientation to Landscape.

5. Click the Chart tab.

   The Chart tab displays as shown in Illustration L.

   You usually do not need to make any changes on this tab. On a black and white printer, the colors print in shades of gray.

6. Click the Print button [Print...].

Illustration K. Page Setup, Page Tab for Line Graph

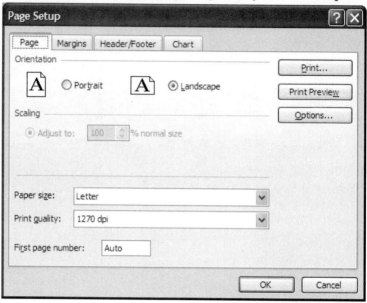

Illustration L. Page Setup, Chart Tab for Line Graph

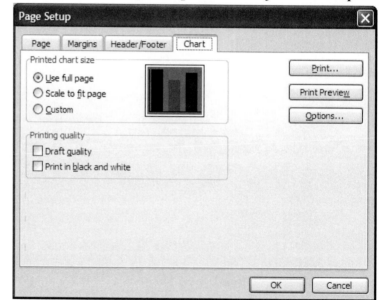

The Print dialog box appears, as shown in Illustration M.

7. To print just the Chart1 sheet, click Active sheet(s). To print the line graph and the spreadsheet with the column chart, click Entire workbook.

8. Print one copy of the line graph or of the entire workbook.

9. Close the workbook, and exit Excel.

Illustration M. Print Dialog Box for Line Graph

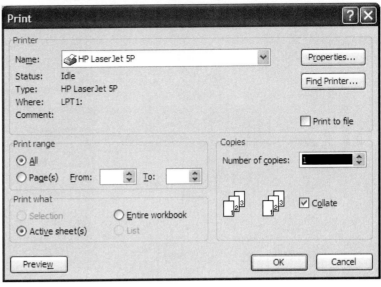

Exercise 9

Use Insert Function; Use the IF Function
■ Use Insert Function Feature ■ About the IF Function
■ Understand Operators ■ Insert the IF Function

NOTES

Use Insert Function Feature

- The Insert Function feature provides guidance in completing the arguments (syntax) of a function. You can start the Insert Function feature in two different ways:

  - Click the Insert function button *fx* just to the left of the Formula bar.

  - Select More Functions from the AutoSum button Σ ▾ drop-down menu.

- In the following Try It! activity, you will use the Insert Function feature to count the number of players in the Scrabble worksheet.

💻Try It!

1. Open 💿**09Scrabble4**.
2. Save the file as **Scrabble9**.
3. Select cell A24, and enter the following label: **Total Players**.
   The text is formatted automatically like the label in A23 because that label was previously formatted.
4. Adjust the width of column A as necessary so that the entire label is visible.
5. Select cell B24. Using either method described at the beginning of this exercise, start the Insert Function feature to display the Insert Function dialog box shown in the following illustration.

More Functions Option

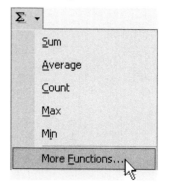

COUNT
The COUNT function is on the AutoSum drop-down list, but this exercise shows you how to use the Insert Function feature. That is why you are not simply selecting COUNT from the list.

Insert Function Dialog Box

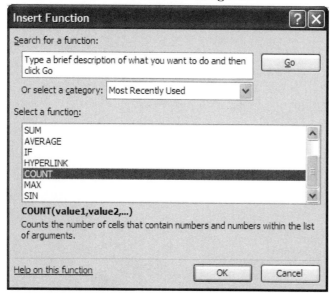

In the Search for a function text box, you describe the function you need. You can look for functions in different categories using the Or select a category drop-down list. You can also select a function from the list in the Select a function list.

6. In the Select a function list, select COUNT.

   If COUNT is not in the list, type **COUNT** in the *Search for a function* text box, and click the Go button 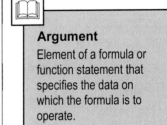.

   The COUNT function can also be located in the Statistical category in the Select a category drop-down list.

7. Click the OK button ⌷ OK ⌷.

   Excel displays the Function Arguments dialog box shown in the following illustration, with a suggested range in the Value1 field.

   The suggested range is not correct. You will correct it.

Argument
Element of a formula or function statement that specifies the data on which the formula is to operate.

Function Arguments Dialog Box

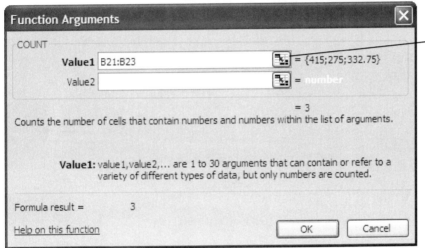

Collapse button

8. Click the Collapse button 📲 at the right end of the Value1 text box.

   The Function Arguments dialog box collapses to a single line.

9. Click and drag through the range B4:B19 (the correct range for the function), as shown in the illustration on the next page.

Collapsed Function Arguments Dialog Box with Selected Range

	COUNT	▾ X ✓ ƒx	=COUNT(B4:B19)			

Function Arguments ✕

B4:B19| 🔲 ——— Expand button

	PLAYER	ROUND 1	ROUND 2	ROUND 3	AVERAGE
3	PLAYER	ROUND 1	ROUND 2	ROUND 3	AVERAGE
4	Bossman	275	355	307	312.3333
5	Castillo	316	345	320	327.0000
6	Chien	295	325	301	307.0000
7	Chin, S.	295	318	307	306.6667
8	Chin, Y.	297	317	306	306.6667
9	Cruz-Guerra	303	366	325	331.3333
10	Kardash	340	323	298	320.3333
11	Kern	283	295	303	293.6667
12	Kudja	395	370	356	373.6667
13	LeBihan	307	308	288	301.0000
14	Perro	402	299	336	345.6667
15	Reifschneider	415	332	345	364.0000
16	Rhodes	322	316	304	314.0000
17	VanderHoffen	377	422	355	384.6667
18	Veach	378	279	346	334.3333
19	Wang	324	339	364	342.3333
20					
21	Highest	415	422	364	384.6667
22	Lowest	275	279	288	293.6667
23	Average	332.7500	331.8125	322.5625	
24	Total Players	B4:B19)			

10. Click the Expand button at the right end of the collapsed dialog box.

11. Click the OK button [OK].

    Excel counts the number of scores in the range B4:B19 and displays 16 in cell B24.

12. Save the workbook.

13. Print one copy with gridlines and row and column headings.

14. Close the workbook.

About the IF Function

- One of the most useful functions in a spreadsheet is the IF function. The IF function lets you ask a question of data and make the result **conditional** on that data.

💻 **Try It!**

1. Click the New button 🗋 to create a new workbook.

2. Save the new workbook as **IF**.

3. In cell A1, enter **6**.

Conditional Result

A conditional result is one that can change depending on the data (or result) in another cell. An IF function sets a condition. If the condition is met, one result is used; if the condition is not met, a different result is used.

4. In cell B1, enter the following formula; be sure to type it exactly as shown below, and press Enter. (A ScreenTip appears as you type to show you the correct syntax.)

   =IF(A1=6,"YES","NO")

   The word YES appears in cell B1.

5. In cell A2, type **5**.

6. Copy the formula from B1 to B2.

   The word NO appears in cell B2.

- In this example, you entered a formula that is the equivalent of the English sentence:

   If cell A1 is equal to 6, then display YES, otherwise display NO.

- The parts of an IF statement are labeled below.

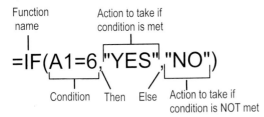

- The commas in the statement separate the phrases of the IF function. The first comma means THEN; the second means ELSE. As with other functions, the arguments are enclosed in parentheses.

- If you can phrase the IF statement in English, you can turn it into a formula that Excel can calculate. So, when you want to fill a cell with a conditional result, phrase the IF statement in English first, then think about how that translates into an Excel formula.

Try It!

1. Select cell A6, and enter **3842**.

2. Select cell B6, and enter **3795**.

3. Select cell C6, and enter the following IF statement:

   =IF(A6>B6,A6-B6,A6+B6)

   The symbol > means greater than. The IF statement says, "If the value in cell A6 is greater than the value in cell B6, subtract the value in B6 from A6, else add the two values."

   The number 47 appears in cell C6.

4. Select cell A7, and enter **3795**.

5. Select cell B7, and enter **3842**.

6. Copy the formula from C6 to C7.

   The number 7637 appears in cell C7.

7. Save and close the workbook.

Formula Bar

Try typing the formula in the Formula bar. It is easier to see the entire IF statement in that way.

Why Quotation Marks?

The quotation marks tell Excel that the word is to be treated as a word and not as the name of an object.

Understand Operators

- Excel uses symbols to perform common arithmetic and comparison calculations. These symbols are called **operators**. The arithmetic and comparison operators are listed and described in the table below.

Operator	Action	Sample Use
+	Addition	=B2+C2
-	Subtraction	=B2-C2
* (asterisk)	Multiplication	=B2*C2
/ (forward slash)	Division	=B2/C2
% (percent sign)	Percent	=B2%
^ (caret)	Exponentiation	=B2^C2. For example, if B2 is 4 and C2 is 2, the result is 16 (4^2 or 4*4).
=	Equal to	=IF(A1=B1,A1+B1,A1-B1)
>	Greater than	=IF(A1>B1,A1-B1,B1-A1)
<	Less than	=IF(A1<B1,B1-A1,A1-B1)
>=	Greater than or equal to	=IF(A1>=B1,A1+B1,B1-A1)
<=	Less than or equal to	=IF(A1<=B1,A1+B1,A1-B1)
<>	Not equal to	=IF(A1<>B1,"Unequal", "Equal")

Insert the IF Function

- You can use the Insert Function feature to create an IF statement.

🖥 Try It!

Build the Excel equivalent of the following English statement:

If the value in the Score column is greater than or equal to 45, then display the word Qualifies, else display the phrase TOO LOW!

1. Open 💿 **09Scores** from the data files.
2. Save the workbook as **Scores9**.
3. Select cell C2.
4. Start the Insert Function feature, and select the IF function.
   If the Select a function box does not contain the IF function, search for IF or look in the Logical category.
5. Click the OK button [OK].
6. When the Function Arguments dialog box appears, click the Collapse button 🔲 on the Logical_test box.
7. Click cell B2 (the first cell to be used as an argument for the function).
8. Type the operator and value for the condition: **>=45**

Logical test
Excel's term for the condition to be met.

Formula Palette Collapsed, IF Function

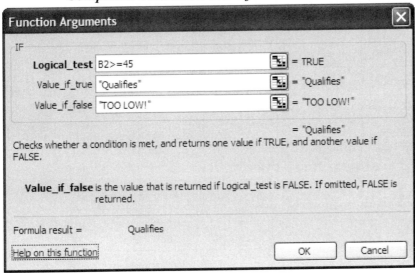

9. Click the Expand button 🔄.

10. Press the Tab key or click in the Value_if_true box.

11. Type **Qualifies**, as shown in the following illustration.
    You do not need to enter the quotation marks. Excel enters them for you when you move to the next field.

12. In the Value_if_false box, and type **TOO LOW!**, as shown in the illustration that follows.

Completed Formula Palette for IF Function

13. Click the OK button.

14. Copy the IF statement in C2 to the range C3:C12.

15. Adjust the width of column C as necessary so that all text is visible.

16. Save the workbook.

17. Close the workbook, and exit Excel unless you are continuing with the Exercise Directions.

In this exercise, you will use the IF function to determine whether students in a Computer Essentials class receive a PASS or FAIL grade.

EXERCISE DIRECTIONS

Open the Workbook and Enter Scores for Test 4

1. Open ⊙ **09Pass Fail** from the data files.
2. Save the workbook as **Pass Fail9**.
3. Use the AutoFill feature to complete cells E1:F1 with TEST 3 and TEST 4.
4. Add the labels and values in the shaded areas shown in Illustration A.
5. Save the workbook.

Calculate the Average for Each Student

1. In cell G2, use the Insert Function feature to calculate the average test score for Howard Beech.
2. Copy the formula to the remaining players.
3. Display two decimal places for all averages. *Your worksheet should now look like the one in Illustration B.*
4. Save the workbook.

Illustration A. Add Data to Pass Fail

	A	B	C	D	E	F	G	H
1	LAST NAME	FIRST NAME	TEST 1	TEST 2	TEST 3	TEST 4	AVERAGE	PASS/FAIL
2	Beech	Howard	78	58	79	65		
3	Doermann	Carlton	70	85	82	63		
4	Frye	Northrop	95	100	99	92		
5	Giambalvo	John	52	64	55	48		
6	Newcomer	Sandra	100	95	94	98		
7	O'Loughlin	Michael	90	88	92	91		
8	Palacio	Miguel	100	100	100	100		
9	Pastore	Mary Jane	60	65	43	55		
10	Patel	Ganga	98	97	96	93		
11	Paul	Carol Ann	87	77	83	91		
12	Payne	Frieda	67	73	84	75		
13	Plum	Robert	60	65	73	76		
14	Rhodes	Mary Ellen	88	87	86	85		
15	Rodenbeek	Suzanne	100	100	100	100		
16	Salem	Winston	63	72	78	69		
17	Stewart	Robert	54	48	62	70		
18	Wilson	Daniel	78	84	83	80		
19	Winderlin	Rosemarie	84	83	78	82		

Illustration B. Worksheet with Averages Calculated

	A	B	C	D	E	F	G	H
1	LAST NAME	FIRST NAME	TEST 1	TEST 2	TEST 3	TEST 4	AVERAGE	PASS/FAIL
2	Beech	Howard	78	58	79	65	70.00	
3	Doermann	Carlton	70	85	82	63	75.00	
4	Frye	Northrop	95	100	99	92	96.50	
5	Giambalvo	John	52	64	55	48	54.75	
6	Newcomer	Sandra	100	95	94	98	96.75	
7	O'Loughlin	Michael	90	88	92	91	90.25	
8	Palacio	Miguel	100	100	100	100	100.00	
9	Pastore	Mary Jane	60	65	43	55	55.75	
10	Patel	Ganga	98	97	96	93	96.00	
11	Paul	Carol Ann	87	77	83	91	84.50	
12	Payne	Frieda	67	73	84	75	74.75	
13	Plum	Robert	60	65	73	76	68.50	
14	Rhodes	Mary Ellen	88	87	86	85	86.50	
15	Rodenbeek	Suzanne	100	100	100	100	100.00	
16	Salem	Winston	63	72	78	69	70.50	
17	Stewart	Robert	54	48	62	70	58.50	
18	Wilson	Daniel	78	84	83	80	81.25	
19	Winderlin	Rosemarie	84	83	78	82	81.75	

Use Insert Function to Insert IF Function for PASS/FAIL

The statement in English is "If the test average is greater than or equal to 70, the student passes; otherwise, the student fails." When completed, the Excel IF statement will read:

=IF(G2>=70,"PASS","FAIL")

1. Select cell H2.
2. Start the Insert Function feature.
3. Select IF, and click OK.
4. Click the Logical_test Collapse button .
5. Select cell G2.
6. Type >=70.
7. Click the Expand button .
8. In the Value_if_true box, type **PASS**.
9. In the Value_if_false box, type **FAIL**.

Illustration C. Completed Function Arguments

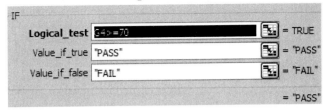

10. Click OK.

    The word PASS should appear in the cell. If it does not, complete the following steps:

    a. Select cell G2 and look at the Formula bar.

    b. Click in the Formula bar to edit the IF statement.

    c. Be sure the IF statement reads exactly as follows, with the commas, quotation marks, and parentheses as shown.

    =IF(G2>=70,"PASS","FAIL")

    d. When it is correct, press Enter.

11. Copy the IF statement to cells H3 through H19.

    Your worksheet should look like the one shown in Illustration D.

12. Save the workbook.

Illustration D. IF Function Specified for Each Student

	A	B	C	D	E	F	G	H
1	LAST NAME	FIRST NAME	TEST 1	TEST 2	TEST 3	TEST 4	AVERAGE	PASS/FAIL
2	Beech	Howard	78	58	79	65	70.00	PASS
3	Doermann	Carlton	70	85	82	63	75.00	PASS
4	Frye	Northrop	95	100	99	92	96.50	PASS
5	Giambalvo	John	52	64	55	48	54.75	FAIL
6	Newcomer	Sandra	100	95	94	98	96.75	PASS
7	O'Loughlin	Michael	90	88	92	91	90.25	PASS
8	Palacio	Miguel	100	100	100	100	100.00	PASS
9	Pastore	Mary Jane	60	65	43	55	55.75	FAIL
10	Patel	Ganga	98	97	96	93	96.00	PASS
11	Paul	Carol Ann	87	77	83	91	84.50	PASS
12	Payne	Frieda	67	73	84	75	74.75	PASS
13	Plum	Robert	60	65	73	76	68.50	FAIL
14	Rhodes	Mary Ellen	88	87	86	85	86.50	PASS
15	Rodenbeek	Suzanne	100	100	100	100	100.00	PASS
16	Salem	Winston	63	72	78	69	70.50	PASS
17	Stewart	Robert	54	48	62	70	58.50	FAIL
18	Wilson	Daniel	78	84	83	80	81.25	PASS
19	Winderlin	Rosemarie	84	83	78	82	81.75	PASS

Format the Column Headings

1. Center and bold the headings over each column.
2. Center all entries in the PASS/FAIL column.
3. Save the workbook.

Add a Title

1. Insert two rows above existing row 1.
2. Select cell A1.
3. Type the following title:
   Computer Essentials -- 4th Period
4. Select the range A1:H1.
5. Click the Merge and Center button ⊞.
6. Format the text to Arial Black, 14 point.
7. Click Format, Row, AutoFit.

   Row, AutoFit works just like Column, AutoFit to adjust the height of the row to the largest character in the row.

   Your worksheet should look like the one in Illustration E.

Save, Print Preview, Print

1. Save the workbook.
2. Print Preview the document.
3. Print one copy with gridlines only.
4. Save and close the workbook unless you are going to complete the challenge on the following page.

Illustration E. Desired Result

	A	B	C	D	E	F	G	H
1	**Computer Essentials – 4th Period**							
2								
3	**LAST NAME**	**FIRST NAME**	**TEST 1**	**TEST 2**	**TEST 3**	**TEST 4**	**AVERAGE**	**PASS/FAIL**
4	Beech	Howard	78	58	79	65	70.00	PASS
5	Doermann	Carlton	70	85	82	63	75.00	PASS
6	Frye	Northrop	95	100	99	92	96.50	PASS
7	Giambalvo	John	52	64	55	48	54.75	FAIL
8	Newcomer	Sandra	100	95	94	98	96.75	PASS
9	O'Loughlin	Michael	90	88	92	91	90.25	PASS
10	Palacio	Miguel	100	100	100	100	100.00	PASS
11	Pastore	Mary Jane	60	65	43	55	55.75	FAIL
12	Patel	Ganga	98	97	96	93	96.00	PASS
13	Paul	Carol Ann	87	77	83	91	84.50	PASS
14	Payne	Frieda	67	73	84	75	74.75	PASS
15	Plum	Robert	60	65	73	76	68.50	FAIL
16	Rhodes	Mary Ellen	88	87	86	85	86.50	PASS
17	Rodenbeek	Suzanne	100	100	100	100	100.00	PASS
18	Salem	Winston	63	72	78	69	70.50	PASS
19	Stewart	Robert	54	48	62	70	58.50	FAIL
20	Wilson	Daniel	78	84	83	80	81.25	PASS
21	Winderlin	Rosemarie	84	83	78	82	81.75	PASS

Challenge

1. Calculate an average, the highest, and lowest score for each test.
2. Insert a Count function to show the number of students, as shown in Illustration F.
3. Use the Insert Function feature to add CountIF functions in cell H27 and H28 to show the number who passed and the number who failed.

Illustration F. Challenge Results

21	Winderlin	Rosemarie	84	83	78	82	81.75	PASS
22								
23		Average	79.11	80.06	81.50	79.61		
24		Highest	100	100	100	100	100	
25		Lowest	52	48	43	48	54.75	
26		Count	18					
27							Passed	14
28							Failed	4

Exercise 10

Integrate Excel and Word
- Insert an Excel Object into a Word Document
- Insert a Word Table into an Excel Worksheet

NOTES

Insert an Excel Object into a Word Document

- As parts of Microsoft Office 2003, Excel and Word are designed to work well together. You can create a table in Word and import it into Excel. You can create a spreadsheet or chart in Excel and insert it into Word.

💻Try It!

1. Start Excel and open 💿**10Enrollment8** from the data files.
2. Start Word and open 💿**10Memo1** from the data files.
3. Save the Word document as **Memo1**.
4. Go to the end of the memo.
5. Switch to Excel.

   To switch to Excel, click the workbook's icon on the taskbar.

6. Click the white area of the chart to select it, and click the Copy button 📋.
7. Switch back to the Word document.
8. Click the Paste button 📋.

   The graph is inserted as an in-line object. Note that you can also use Edit, Paste Special, Microsoft Office Excel Chart Object to paste the chart.

9. Click the Center button ≡ to center the paragraph with the chart.
10. Save the document.
11. Print Preview the document.
12. Print one copy.
13. Close the file, but leave Word open.
14. Switch to Excel, and close **10Enrollment8** without saving it.

Insert a Word Table into an Excel Worksheet

- You can create a table in Word and insert it into an Excel worksheet.

💻Try It!

1. Open the Word file 💿**10Acme** from the data files.
2. Select the entire table.

   If you haven't worked with tables up to now:

   a. Place the insertion point anywhere inside the table.

b. Click T<u>a</u>ble, Sele<u>c</u>t, <u>T</u>able (Alt+A, C, T).
   The entire table is selected.

3. Click the Copy button 📋 .

4. Switch to Excel, and click the New button 🗋 to create a new workbook.

5. Select cell A1.

6. Click <u>E</u>dit, Paste <u>S</u>pecial, select Text, and click the OK button
   [OK] .

   Excel converts the table into labels and numbers based on the contents of each cell, as shown below.

   ### A Word Table Converted to Excel Spreadsheet

	A	B	C	D	E	F
1		Monday	Tuesday	Wednesda	Thursday	Friday
2	Week 1	58,750.75	48,763.50	44,378.65	34,832.67	59,432.18
3	Week 2	55,562.87	47,332.91	36,753.52	37,812.03	46,739.83
4	Week 3	52,374.61	50,328.40	40,293.38	40,374.72	52,983.26
5	Week 4	62,278.10	54,974.98	48,374.65	42,746.32	63,374.45

7. Set all column widths to 10.25 if they are not already.
   Note: *If you use the Paste button, the table is pasted into Excel, but you have to use AutoFit to adjust both the column widths and row heights.*

8. Save the workbook as **AcmeSales**.

9. Close the workbook, and exit Excel unless you are continuing with the Exercise Directions.

10. Close the Word document, and exit Word.

In this exercise, you will work on the memo about Ulysses Middle School enrollment. To do so, you will create a new Excel chart and insert it into an existing Word document.

EXERCISE DIRECTIONS

Create an Excel Chart

1. In Excel, open 🖉 **10Enrollment8** from the data files.

2. Save the workbook as **Enrollment10**.

3. Select ranges A3:F3 and A8:F8.

4. Click the Chart Wizard button 📊 .

5. In Step 1, select a Chart type of Line and a Chart sub-type of Line with markers displayed at each data value.

6. In step 2 in the Data Range tab, select <u>R</u>ows.

7. In step 3 in the Titles tab, enter the following Chart title: **UMS Middle School Total Enrollment**

8. Enter the following <u>C</u>ategory (X) axis title: **Year**

9. On the Legend tab, deselect <u>S</u>how legend.

10. In step 4, select As <u>o</u>bject in Sheet1.

11. Position the new chart below the existing chart, and make it the same size.

12. Save the workbook.

Edit a Word Document

1. Open the Word file 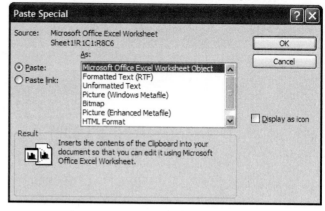**10Memo2** from the data files.
2. Save the document as **Memo2**.
3. Place the insertion point at the end of the document.
4. Insert a new paragraph after the chart, left-align it and enter:

   The chart below shows the trend for total enrollment for the same five years.

5. Insert another new paragraph, left-align it, and enter:

   These charts are based on the data shown below.

Insert an Excel Chart

1. Switch to Excel.
2. Select the line graph that shows the trend of total enrollment (the chart you just created).
3. Copy it.
4. Switch to Word.
5. Insert it as an in-line object in a new paragraph between the two final text paragraphs.
6. Center the paragraph that contains the chart.

Insert a Range from an Excel Worksheet

1. Save the document.
2. Switch to Excel.
3. Click anywhere on the worksheet except on a chart.
4. Use File, Page Setup to ensure that gridlines and row and column headings are set to print.
5. Select range A1:F8 and copy it.
6. Switch to Word.
7. Use Paste Special to insert the copied data as a Microsoft Office Excel Worksheet Object into a new paragraph at the end of the document.

Illustration A. Paste Special Microsoft Office Excel Worksheet Object

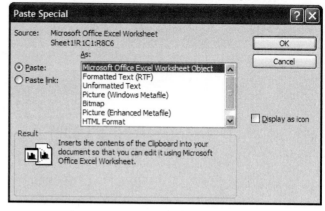

8. Format the table as an in-line object.
9. Center the paragraph with the inserted table.
10. Save the document, but leave it open.

Finish Formatting the Memo

1. Make sure there is one blank paragraph before and after each illustration.
2. Insert a manual page break before the second body paragraph.
3. Insert a footer with the page number and the number of pages following the steps below.
   a. Click View, Header and Footer.
   b. Switch to the Footer pane.
   c. Type **Page**
   d. Press the spacebar.
   e. Click the Insert Page Number button .
   f. Press the spacebar and type: **of**
   g. Press the spacebar.
   h. Click the Insert Number of Pages button .
   i. Close the Header and Footer dialog box.
4. Save the document.
5. Print Preview the document.
6. Print one copy.

   Your word document should now look like the one shown in Illustration B on the next page.

7. Close the document, and exit Word.
8. Switch to Excel, close the workbook and exit Excel.

Illustration B. Memo2

MEMORANDUM

To: Ulysses Middle School Faculty

From: Janet Griffith-Kimball

Subject: Enrollment Trends

Date: Today's Date

At the request of Robert Plum, president of the Grant County Board of Education, we have prepared a look at recent enrollment figures here at UMS. The chart below shows enrollment trends by class for five recent years.

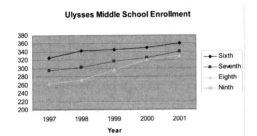

Page 1 of 2

The chart below shows the trend for total enrollment for the same five years.

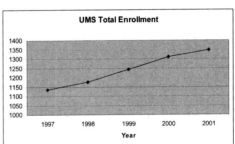

These charts are based on the data shown below.

	A	B	C	D	E	F
1	**Ulysses Middle School Enrollment**					
2						
3		**1997**	**1998**	**1999**	**2000**	**2001**
4	Sixth	325	342	345	350	360
5	Seventh	295	302	317	325	340
6	Eighth	263	272	296	320	330
7	Ninth	252	261	285	315	320
8	**TOTALS**	1135	1177	1243	1310	1350

Page 2 of 2

Exercise 11

Challenge Exercises
■ Structure of a Checkbook Register ■ Create a Checkbook Register
■ Insert an Excel Spreadsheet into Word

NOTES

Structure of a Checkbook Register

■ A checkbook register, like a spreadsheet, consists of rows and columns that form a grid. The checkbook register usually looks like the following:

DATE	TRANS ID	PAYEE	TYPE	AMOUNT	BALANCE
		Brought Forward			2403.46
1/3/05	2421	Mortgage	W	1,582.10	821.36

■ The columns in the grid are described below.

DATE	Date of the transaction.
TRANS ID	Identifier of the transaction. Usually this is a check number. With online banking, however, this may be an identifier assigned by the bank.
PAYEE	Name of the person or company involved in the transaction.
TYPE	Type of transaction: W = Withdrawal, D = Deposit.
AMOUNT	Amount of the transaction.
BALANCE	Amount in the account after the transaction.

■ In a checkbook register kept by hand, these columns may vary. Sometimes the manual register has two rows in the balance column to make subtraction and addition easier. In an electronic register, however, you can write an IF function to handle the calculation automatically.

■ The IF statement in the BALANCE column, in English, is:

If the transaction TYPE is W, subtract the AMOUNT from the previous BALANCE; otherwise, add the AMOUNT to the previous BALANCE.

Sample Electronic Check Register

	A	B	C	D	E	F
1			Checking -- Account # 12345678			
2	DATE	TRANS ID	PAYEE	TYPE	AMOUNT	BALANCE
3			Balance Brought Forward			2403.46
4	1/3/2002	10344	Mortgage	W	1582.10	821.36
5	1/3/2002	10345	Electric Company	W	340.89	480.47
6	1/3/2002	10346	Telephone Company	W	54.97	425.50
7	1/31/2002		Salary from School	D	2674.36	3099.86
8	1/27/2002		ATM Cash - First National Bank	W	300.00	2799.86

- Before starting the Exercise Directions, try to construct the IF statement for the BALANCE cell F4 in the Check Register on the previous page. Remember that text entries in the statement must be enclosed in double quotation marks. Use the questions below to help you.

Condition =IF(cell="text",

_____ Which cell contains the data to determine whether the amount should be added to or subtracted from the balance?

_____ What text indicates that the amount is to be subtracted from the balance?

Result if true(... ,balance-amount

_____ Which cell contains the balance from which the amount should subtracted?

_____ Which cell contains the amount?

Result if false(... , ... , balance+amount

_____ Which cell contains the balance to which the amount should added?

_____ Which cell contains the amount?

- The answers to these questions should help you correctly structure the IF statement for cell F4. You can then copy that formula to all the other cells.

- Write your proposed IF statement on the blank below.

_____

In this exercise, you will use the IF function to create a checkbook register.

EXERCISE DIRECTIONS

Create a Checkbook Register

Start a New Workbook and Enter the Title and Column Headings

1. Start Excel and use the new workbook that Excel creates.
2. Save the workbook as **Checkbook**.
3. In cell C1, type:
   Checking -- Account # 12345678
4. In cell A2, enter **DATE**
5. In cell B2, enter **TRANS ID**
6. In cell C2, enter **PAYEE**
7. In cell D2, enter **TYPE**
8. In cell E2, enter **AMOUNT**
9. In cell F2, enter **BALANCE**
10. Center and bold all headings in row 2.
11. In cell C3, enter:
    Balance Brought Forward
12. Use AutoFit to set all column widths.

    The worksheet should now look like the one in Illustration A.
13. Save the workbook.

Enter the Balance Brought Forward and Enter Some Transactions

1. In cell F3, enter the following value as the balance brought forward:
   2403.46
2. Format the dates in range A4:A18 dates with the format m/dd/yyyy (3/14/2001), as shown in Illustration B.
3. Format the range D4:D18 as centered text.
4. Complete the range A4:E7 with the data shown in Illustration C.
5. Select the range E3:F25, and click the Comma Style button ![comma] to format the values as accounting with no symbol.

Illustration A. Checkbook Register Headings

	A	B	C	D	E	F
1			Checking -- Account # 12345678			
2	DATE	TRANS ID	PAYEE	TYPE	AMOUNT	BALANCE
3			Balance Brought Forward			
4						
5						
6						
7						
8						
9						
10						
11						
12						
13						
14						
15						

Illustration B. Date Format

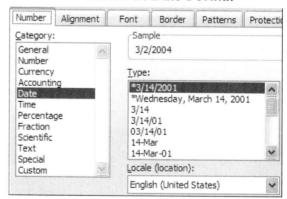

Illustration C. Transactions for Rows 4 - 7

	A	B	C	D	E	F
1			Checking -- Account # 12345678			
2	DATE	TRANS ID	PAYEE	TYPE	AMOUNT	BALANCE
3			Balance Brought Forward			2,403.46
4	1/3/2002	10344	Mortgage	W	1,582.10	
5	1/3/2002	10345	Electric Company	W	340.89	
6	1/3/2002	10346	Telephone Company	W	54.97	
7	1/31/2002		Salary from School	D	2,874.36	

Enter the IF Statement in Cell F4

1. Select cell F4.
2. Use the Insert Function feature to create the IF statement.
3. In the Insert Function dialog box, select the IF function to display the IF Function Arguments dialog box.
4. Complete the function arguments as shown in Illustration D.
5. Check your formula (look at the Formula bar) against the one shown below:

    =IF(D4="W",F3-E4,F3+E4)

    Did the formula you created match the one shown above?
6. Copy the formula to the range F5:F25.

    When you add entries in rows 8 - 25, the formulas in column F will be calculated automatically.
7. Add the two new transactions in the shaded area of Illustration E.

    Did the values update correctly?
8. Save and close the workbook.

    You now have a checkbook register and the knowledge to use it. You can use this register to track your own banking transactions or those of someone you know who trusts you with financial information.
9. Exit Excel, unless you are continuing with the Challenge Exercises.

Illustration D. Function Arguments for IF Function

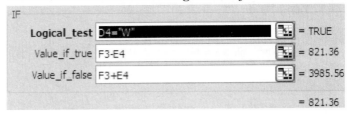

Logical_test	D4="W"	= TRUE
Value_if_true	F3-E4	= 821.36
Value_if_false	F3+E4	= 3985.56
	= 821.36

Illustration E. Completed Checkbook Register

	A	B	C	D	E	F
1			Checking -- Account # 12345678			
2	DATE	TRANS ID	PAYEE	TYPE	AMOUNT	BALANCE
3			Balance Brought Forward			2,403.46
4	1/3/2002	10344	Mortgage	W	1,582.10	821.36
5	1/3/2002	10345	Electric Company	W	340.89	480.47
6	1/3/2002	10346	Telephone Company	W	54.97	425.50
7	1/31/2002		Salary from School	D	2,874.36	3,299.86
8	1/27/2002		ATM Cash - 1st National Bank	W	300.00	2,999.86
9	2/4/2002		Milburn Stone, M.D.	W	220.00	2,779.86
10						2,779.86
11						2,779.86
12						2,779.86
13						2,779.86
14						2,779.86

In this exercise, you will add formulas to an Excel spreadsheet and insert the worksheet into a Word document.

EXERCISE DIRECTIONS

Insert an Excel Spreadsheet into Word

Format a Spreadsheet

1. Open the 📁AcmeSales, or open
   💿11AcmeSales from the data files.
2. Save the workbook as **AcmeSales11**.
3. Bold and center the days of the week in row 1.
4. Bold the week numbers in column A.
5. Select the range B2:F5, and click the Comma
   Style button [,] to format the values as
   accounting with no symbol.
6. Select range B5:F5.
7. Click Format, Cells and select the Border tab to
   display the dialog box shown in Illustration F.
8. In the Style box, click the double line.
9. In the Border box, click the bottom of the box as
   shown in the illustration.
10. Click the OK button [OK].

Enter Labels

1. In cell A7, enter the label **TOTALS**. Make it bold.
2. In cell A8, enter the label **AVERAGES**. Make it bold.
3. In cell A10, enter the label **GRAND TOTAL**. Make it bold.
4. In cell A11, enter the label **DAILY AVERAGE**. Make it bold.
5. Adjust the column width to display the labels within column A.
6. Format all the weekday columns (B through F) to a specific width of 11.
7. Save the workbook.

Calculate Totals and Averages

1. In cell B7, enter a formula to calculate the total sales for Monday.
2. Copy the formula in B7 to the remaining columns.
3. In cell B8, enter a formula to calculate the average sales for Monday.
4. Copy the formula in B8 to the remaining columns.
5. In cell B10, calculate the total for all days for all weeks.
   Hint: Use AutoSum, and select B2:F5 or B7:F7 as the range.
6. In cell B11, calculate the daily average.
   Hint: Select B2:F5 or B8:F8 as the range.
7. Use the Currency Style button [$] to format all totals and averages as accounting format.
8. Adjust column widths as necessary to eliminate ####### displays.
9. Save the workbook.
10. Print Preview the worksheet.
11. Print the worksheet with gridlines and row and column headings.
    The worksheet should look like the one shown in Illustration G on the next page.

Illustration F.
Format Cells Dialog Box, Border Tab

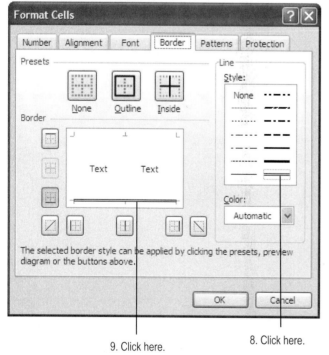

9. Click here.   8. Click here.

Illustration G. Desired Result

	A	B	C	D	E	F
1		**Monday**	**Tuesday**	**Wednesday**	**Thursday**	**Friday**
2	**Week 1**	58,750.75	48,763.50	44,378.65	34,832.67	59,432.18
3	**Week 2**	55,562.87	47,332.91	36,753.52	37,812.03	46,739.83
4	**Week 3**	52,374.61	50,328.40	40,293.38	40,374.72	52,983.26
5	**Week 4**	62,278.10	54,974.98	48,374.65	42,746.32	63,374.45
6						
7	**TOTALS**	$ 228,966.33	$ 201,399.79	$ 169,800.20	$ 155,765.74	$ 222,529.72
8	**AVERAGES**	$ 57,241.58	$ 50,349.95	$ 42,450.05	$ 38,941.44	$ 55,632.43
9						
10	**GRAND TOTAL**	$ 978,461.78				
11	**DAILY AVERAGE**	$ 48,923.09				

Insert the Worksheet
into a Word Document

1. Start Word and open the document ⊙ **11Impost** from the data files.
2. Save the document as **Impost**.
3. Place the insertion point at the end of the document.
4. Switch to Excel and copy the entire **AcmeSales11** worksheet.
5. Switch back to Word.

6. Use Paste Special to paste the worksheet table into the Word document as a Microsoft Office Excel Worksheet Object.
7. Save the document.
8. Print Preview the document.
9. Print a copy of the memo and compare it to the one shown in Illustration H on the following page.
10. Close the document, and exit Word.
11. Switch back to the workbook.
12. Close the workbook, and exit Excel.

Illustration H. Desired Result

Impost Banking Interoffice Memorandum

To: L. Pound Sterling

From: Plusier D'Argent

Subject: Acme Specialties Income

Date: Today's Date

The spreadsheet illustration below summarizes the sales figures for Acme Specialties. These figures should help you decide on an appropriate credit line for the company.

	A	B	C	D	E	F
1		**Monday**	**Tuesday**	**Wednesday**	**Thursday**	**Friday**
2	**Week 1**	58,750.75	48,763.50	44,378.65	34,832.67	59,432.18
3	**Week 2**	55,562.87	47,332.91	36,753.52	37,812.03	46,739.83
4	**Week 3**	52,374.61	50,328.40	40,293.38	40,374.72	52,983.26
5	**Week 4**	62,278.10	54,974.98	48,374.65	42,746.32	63,374.45
6						
7	**TOTALS**	$ 228,966.33	$ 201,399.79	$ 169,800.20	$ 155,765.74	$ 222,529.72
8	**AVERAGES**	$ 57,241.58	$ 50,349.95	$ 42,450.05	$ 38,941.44	$ 55,632.43
9						
10	**GRAND TOTAL**	$ 978,461.78				
11	**DAILY AVERAGE**	$ 48,923.09				

Lesson 7: Microsoft Office PowerPoint 2003

Exercise 1: Getting Started with PowerPoint 2003
- About PowerPoint
- The PowerPoint Window
- Add Text
- Save the Presentation
- Choose a Design Template
- Print the Presentation
- Start a New Presentation

Exercise 2: Add to an Existing Presentation
- Open a PowerPoint Presentation
- Add a Title and Text Slide
- Add Speaker Notes
- Review the Outline
- Add Content (Graphics)

Exercise 3: Review and Enhance a Presentation
- Review a Presentation
- Use PowerPoint Views
- Add a Title and Content Slide
- Insert a Slide from Another Presentation
- Edit a Slide
- Print a Presentation from the Print Dialog Box

Exercise 4: Create a Slide Show
- About Slide Shows
- Create Slide Transitions
- Add Animation
- Summary of Animation Procedures

Exercise 1

Getting Started with PowerPoint 2003
■ About PowerPoint ■ The PowerPoint Window ■ Add Text
■ Save the Presentation ■ Choose a Design Template
■ Print the Presentation ■ Start a New Presentation

NOTES

About PowerPoint

■ PowerPoint is a presentations application. It lets you build presentations that you can display on a computer or computer projection system, publish on the World Wide Web, print as overhead transparencies, or produce as 35mm slides (with the appropriate software). It is often used to create marketing, sales, and other business reports and presentations.

The PowerPoint Window

■ When PowerPoint starts, it first displays the PowerPoint window in Normal view. The PowerPoint window, illustrated on the next page, includes elements common to all Microsoft Office 2003 windows—title bar, menu bar, toolbars, and status bar. As with other Microsoft Office 2003 applications, you can drag the toolbars to new positions on the screen or use View, Toolbars, Customize, Options to make more of their buttons visible.

■ In Normal view, the PowerPoint window has the following working areas:

- **Outline/Slides pane** is an area at the left of the window that has two tabs: Outline and Slides. The Slides tab shows thumbnail images of the slides in the presentation. The Outline tab shows the text of your presentation in outline form. You can switch from one tab to the other at any time, and you can click a slide in either pane to move to that slide.

- **Slide pane** shows the slide as it will appear when displayed or printed. You can use this pane to add and edit text and graphics.

- **Notes pane** lets you add notes that you can use as reminders of important points you want to make when giving the presentation.

- **Task pane**, as in other Microsoft Office 2003 applications, offers important startup and formatting options.

■ These areas and the options on the toolbars are described as necessary in the exercises in this lesson.

Slide
A PowerPoint page is called a *slide*, a common term in business for overhead transparencies as well as 35mm slides.

PowerPoint Window

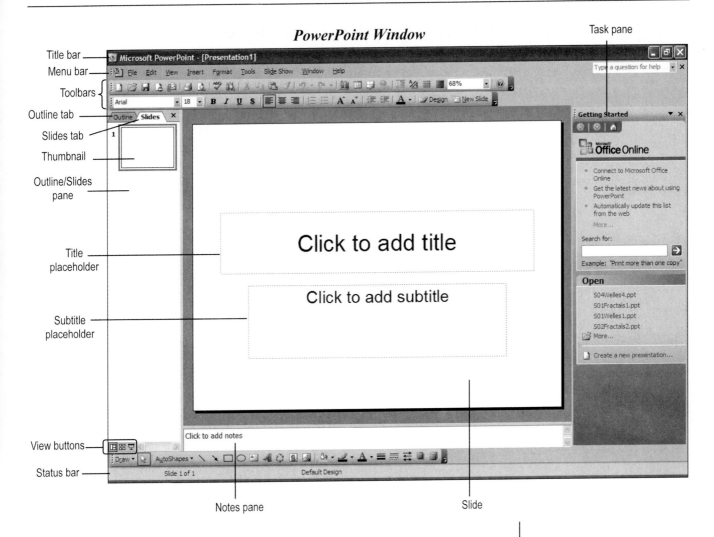

Title bar — Microsoft PowerPoint - [Presentation1]

Menu bar — File Edit View Insert Format Tools Slide Show Window Help

Toolbars

Outline tab

Slides tab

Thumbnail

Outline/Slides pane

Title placeholder — Click to add title

Subtitle placeholder — Click to add subtitle

Task pane

View buttons

Status bar — Slide 1 of 1 — Default Design

Notes pane — Click to add notes

Slide

Add Text

- PowerPoint provides **placeholders** into which you type text or insert pictures. The placeholders that appear vary with the type of slide layout you choose. The **Title Slide** layout, shown in the preceding illustration, appears automatically when you start a new presentation. The title layout has placeholders for a title and subtitle. You need not use every placeholder on a slide, but PowerPoint provides them as aids in creating your presentation.

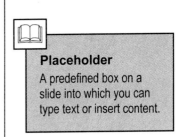

Placeholder
A predefined box on a slide into which you can type text or insert content.

📖 Try It!

1. Start PowerPoint.

2. Click the text *Click to add title*.

   The text disappears, and a gray border surrounds the placeholder. The insertion point appears centered in the box, as shown below.

Title Text Box Ready for Typing

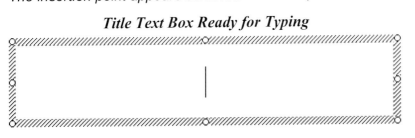

3. Type the following text (do not press the Enter key): **Orson Welles**.

Title Completed

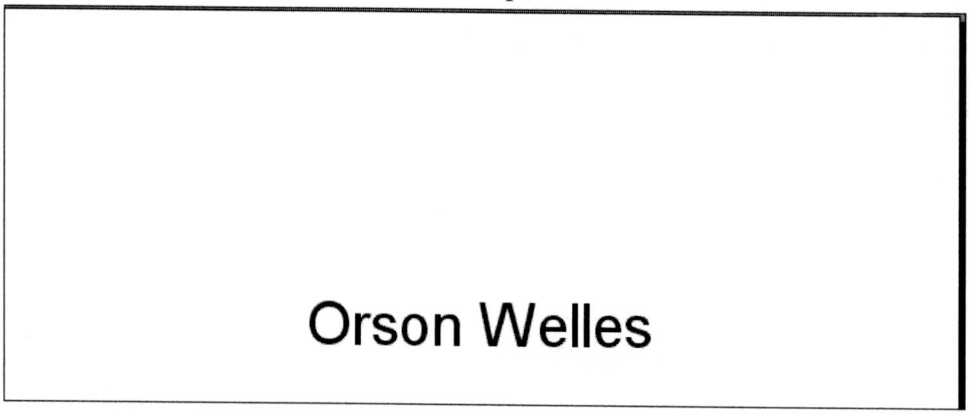

Orson Welles

4. Click the text *Click here to add subtitle*, and type the following text without pressing the Enter key: **Writer, Director, Star**, and click outside the placeholder.

   The slide should now look like the one shown below.

Title Slide Completed

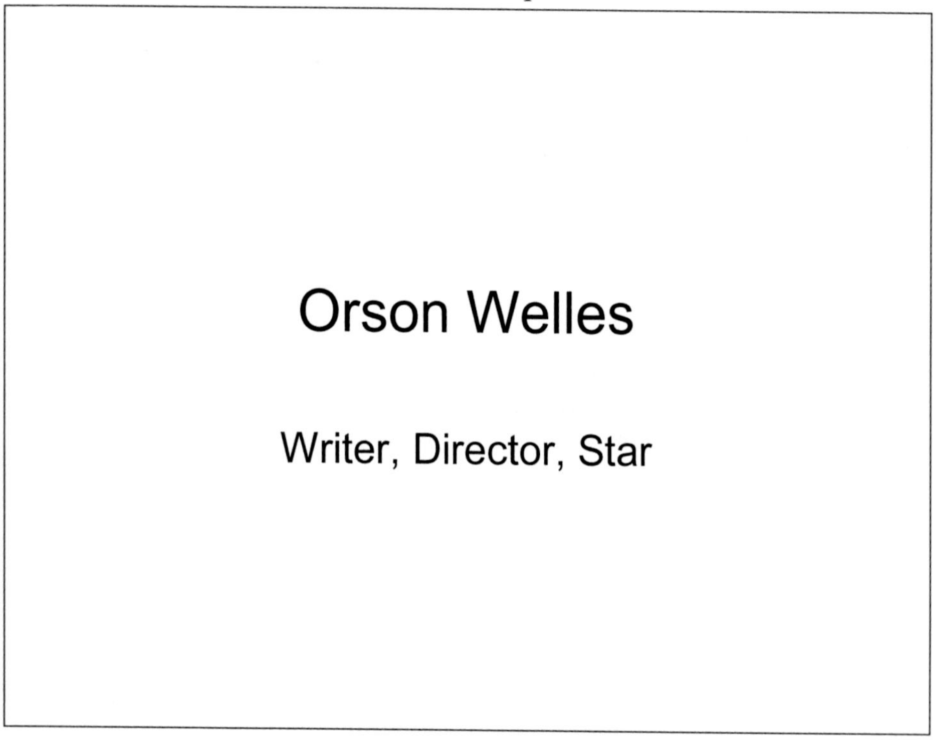

Orson Welles

Writer, Director, Star

Save the Presentation

- Once you have entered text into your presentation, you should save it.

Try It!

1. Click the Save button on the Standard toolbar.

   PowerPoint displays the Save As dialog box. This Save As dialog box is just like the others you have used throughout your work with Microsoft Office.

2. Locate the folder where you want to save the presentation.

3. Name the presentation **Welles1**.

4. Click the <u>S</u>ave button in the dialog box, or press the Enter key.

Choose a Design Template

- When you start a new presentation, you can begin creating it immediately. At some point, however, you need to establish the look of your presentation. PowerPoint makes it easy to create attractive presentations by offering a number of slide designs that you can use. These are called **design templates**.

- A design template provides a color scheme and overall look to your presentation. When you use a design template provided by PowerPoint, you can select a different design template at any time and quickly change the look of your presentation.

⌨Try It!

1. Click F<u>o</u>rmat, Slide <u>D</u>esign (Alt+O, D).

2. The task pane displays thumbnail images of the design templates grouped by color. Linger on a thumbnail image to see the template's name.

3. Under *Apply a Design Template*, scroll down to locate the template Studio.pot, which is among the templates with white backgrounds.

Studio.pot

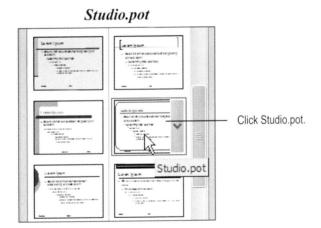

Click Studio.pot.

The template is applied and the title slide looks like the one in the following illustration.

Design Template
A predefined set of colors and fonts that PowerPoint provides to make it simple to create attractive presentations.

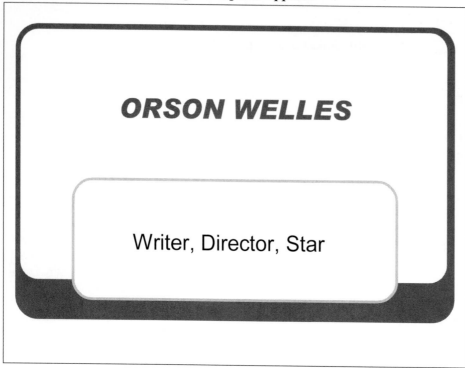
Design Template Applied

Print the Presentation

- You can print the presentation by clicking the Print button 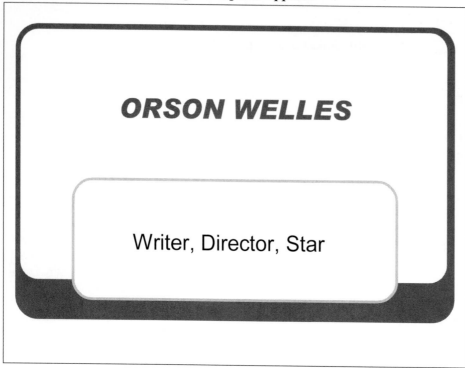 on the Standard toolbar. If you are connected to a color printer, the presentation prints in color; on a black-and-white printer, colors print in shades of gray.

💻 Try It!

1. Click the Print button to print the presentation.
2. Click the document Close button ✕ to close the presentation.
3. Answer *Yes* if PowerPoint asks whether you want to save the presentation.
4. Exit PowerPoint unless you are continuing with the Exercise Directions.

Start a New Presentation

- When PowerPoint is already running, to create a new presentation, either:
   1. Click File, New on the menu bar.

      The New Presentation task pane displays a number of options, as shown in the illustration on the next page.

   2. Click the *From design template* option under New to start by choosing a design template.

New Presentation

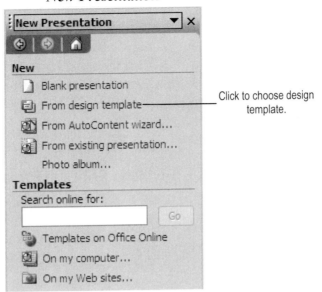

Click to choose design template.

3. In the Slide Design task pane, click the design template you want.

OR

1. Click the New button 📄 on the Standard toolbar.
2. In the Slide Layout task pane, select an AutoLayout for the first slide and click OK.
3. Click F<u>o</u>rmat, Slide <u>D</u>esign on the menu bar.
4. In the Slide Design task pane, click the design template you want.

In this exercise, you will create the title slide for a presentation about fractals—geometrical shapes created by repeatedly applying a formula to a shape.

EXERCISE DIRECTIONS

Select the Design Template

1. If PowerPoint is running, click the New button 📄 on the Standard toolbar.

   OR

   Start PowerPoint.
2. Click F<u>o</u>rmat, Slide <u>D</u>esign.
3. In the Slide Design task pane, click the **Cliff.pot** design (it's among the green backgrounds), as shown in Illustration A.

Illustration A. Select Cliff.pot

PowerPoint displays the title slide format with the Cliff design applied, as shown in Illustration B.

Illustration B. PowerPoint Window for Cliff.pot

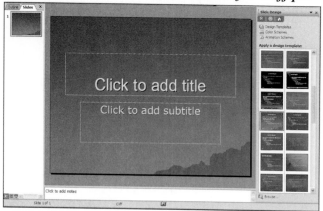

Add the Title and Subtitle

1. Click the title placeholder.
2. Type **Fractal Facts**.
   Remember not to press Enter.
3. Click the subtitle placeholder.
4. Type **Brief Introduction to the Beauty of Fractal Geometry**, and click outside the placeholder.
   Your slide should look like the one shown in Illustration C.

Save and Print the Presentation

1. Click the Save button ![save icon] on the Standard toolbar.
2. Save the presentation as **Fractals1**.
3. Click the Print button ![print icon] on the Standard toolbar to print the presentation.
4. Close the presentation, and exit PowerPoint.

Illustration C. Completed Title Slide

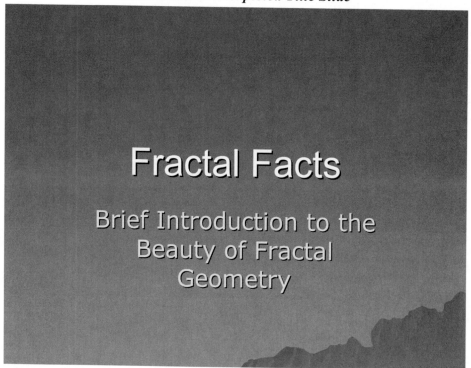

Exercise 2

Add to an Existing Presentation

■ Open a PowerPoint Presentation ■ Add a Title and Text Slide
■ Add Speaker Notes ■ Review the Outline ■ Add Content (Graphics)

NOTES

Open a PowerPoint Presentation

■ To open an existing presentation, start PowerPoint and select the presentation you want from the *Open* list in the Getting Started task pane, or click File, Open on the menu bar.

🖳Try It!

1. Start PowerPoint.

   PowerPoint starts and displays a list of recently opened presentations in the Getting Started task pane, as shown in the following illustration.

   Task Pane List of Recently Opened Presentations

   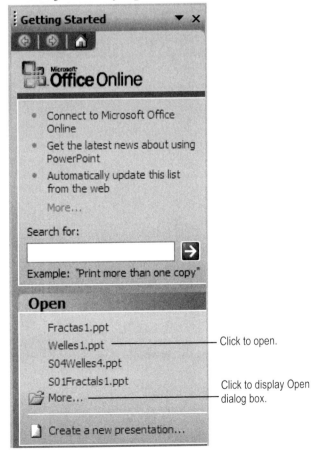

2. Click 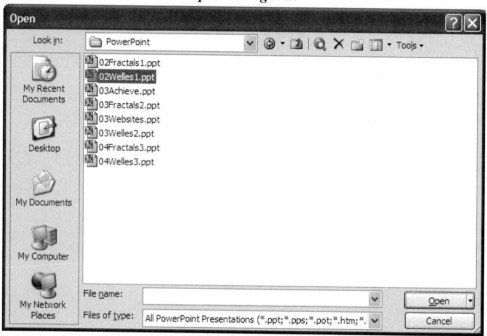**Welles1.ppt** if it is listed.

   The presentation opens and you are ready to edit it.

3. If **Welles1** is not listed or you want to use ⊙ **02Welles1** from the data files:

   - Click [📂 More...] at the bottom of the list.

   OR

   - Click the Open button 📂 on the Standard toolbar.

   OR

   - Click <u>F</u>ile, <u>O</u>pen.

   PowerPoint displays the Open dialog box, as shown in the following illustration.

Open Dialog Box

4. Locate the file you want to open (Welles1 or ⊙ **02Welles1**) and double-click its name or select it and click the <u>O</u>pen button [<u>O</u>pen |▼].

   PowerPoint opens the presentation.

5. Save the presentation as **Welles2**.

Add a Title and Text Slide

■ To add information to the presentation, you insert a new slide.

💻**Try It!**

1. Click the <u>N</u>ew Slide button  on the Formatting toolbar.
   PowerPoint inserts a Title and Text slide and displays the Slide Layout options in the task pane, as shown in the illustration on the next page.

   As you perform the steps outlined in this Try It! activity, check your progress against the completed slide illustrated on page 324.

2. Click the slide title placeholder.
3. Type **Major Milestones** (remember not to press Enter).
4. Click the text placeholder.
5. Type **War of the Worlds radio broadcast (1938)**.
   The text appears as a bullet list item on the slide.

6. Press the Enter key.
7. Type **Citizen Kane movie (1941)**, and press Enter.
   The second bullet list item appears.

8. Type **Lifetime Achievement Awards**, and press Enter.
   The third bullet list item appears.

Insert New Slide
- Click **New Slide**
  button ![New Slide].
  OR
- Press **Alt+N**.
  OR
- Press **Ctrl+M**.
  OR
- Click **Insert, New Slide** on the menu bar (**Alt+I, N**).

Title and Text Slide Inserted

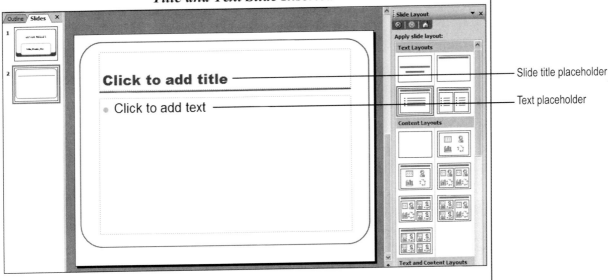

Slide title placeholder
Text placeholder

💻**Try It!**

Add Two Sub-Bullets

1. Press the Tab key to create a second-level bullet under *Lifetime Achievement Awards*.

2. Type **Academy of Motion Picture Arts and Sciences (1970)**, and press Enter.

3. Type **American Film Institute (1975)**, and click outside the placeholder.

4. Compare your results with the completed slide, and save the presentation.

Completed Major Milestones Slide

Major Milestones

- War of the Worlds radio broadcast (1938)
- Citizen Kane movie (1941)
- Lifetime Achievement Awards
  - Academy of Motion Picture Arts and Sciences (1970)
  - American Film Institute (1975)

Add Speaker Notes

- The Notes pane at the bottom of the window offers a place to add reminders of things you want to say when you display a slide. You can print the speaker notes separately to have them in hand when you make the presentation.

- You can enlarge and shrink the Notes pane by dragging the bar that separates the Notes pane from the main slide pane, as shown in the following illustration.

Resize Notes Pane

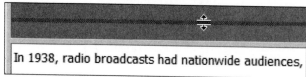

🖥 Try It!

1. Click in the Notes pane.
2. Type **In 1938, radio broadcasts had nationwide audiences, just as television shows do today.**
3. Resize the Notes pane as necessary to see the text easily.
4. Save the presentation.

Review the Outline

- The left pane of the PowerPoint window in Normal view has two tabs: *Outline* and *Slides*. The default display is slides, but you can easily switch to the outline by clicking the Outline tab.

🖥 **Try It!**

1. On the left side of the PowerPoint window, click the Outline tab.

   PowerPoint displays the presentation in outline form, as shown in the following illustration.

2. Review the outline so far.

   As you add text to slides, the outline displays the text. You can also edit the text in the outline pane.

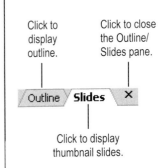

Click to display outline.

Click to close the Outline/ Slides pane.

Click to display thumbnail slides.

Outline Pane for First Two Slides

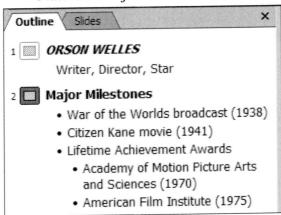

3. Click the Slides tab if you wish to return the left pane to Slides tab view.

Add Content (Graphics)

- PowerPoint offers slide layouts with placeholders for graphics. You add visual interest by including a graphic.

🖥 **Try It!**

Insert a Title, Text, and Content Slide

1. Insert a new slide.
2. In the task pane, click the *Title, Text, and Content* layout under Text and Content Layouts.

   PowerPoint displays the slide layout with placeholders for the slide title, text, and a graphic, as shown in the illustration on the following page. Note that each icon in the content placeholder represents a different type of illustration.

Title, Text, and Content Layout

🖥 Try It!

As you perform the steps outlined in this Try It! activity, check your progress against the illustration of the completed slide on page 327.

1. Click the title placeholder.

2. Type **War of the Worlds (1938 radio)** *(remember not to press Enter).*

3. Click the text placeholder.

4. Add the bullets shown below. Press Enter after typing each item except the last.

    - **Presented by Mercury Theater as if an emergency news broadcast**
    - **Based on 1901 novel by H. G. Wells**
    - **Caused widespread panic**

5. Click in the Notes pane.

6. Type the following two notes:

    Welles was founder and director of Mercury Theater.

    Story is that Martians had landed in New Jersey in an effort to take over the earth.

7. Resize the Notes pane if necessary.

8. Save the presentation.

Completed Title, Text, and Content Slide

War of the Worlds (1938 radio)

- Presented by Mercury Theater as if an emergency news broadcast
- Based on 1901 novel by H. G. Wells
- Caused widespread panic

🖥 Try It!

Add a Graphic

1. Click the Insert Picture icon in the content placeholder.
   PowerPoint opens the Insert Picture dialog box. This is the same dialog box used for inserting pictures from files in Word.

2. Locate the drive and folder that contains the data files for this book, and open the Graphics folder.

3. Insert the file ✐ **02Welles.jpg**.
   PowerPoint inserts the photograph into the placeholder and sizes it automatically.

4. Save the presentation.

> **Clip Art**
> If you click the Insert Clip Art icon, PowerPoint displays a box with clip art images that come with Microsoft Office.

Insert Picture Dialog Box

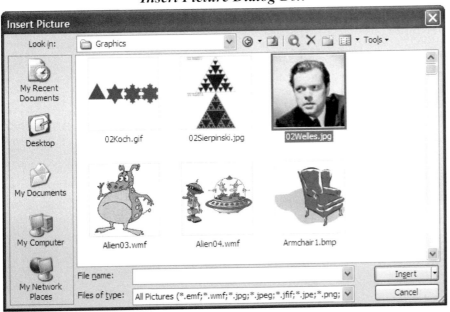

🖥️ Try It!

Insert a Title, Content, and Text Slide

1. Insert a new slide.

2. In the task pane under Text and Content Layouts, click the *Title, Content and Text* layout.

   PowerPoint displays a slide with the content placeholder on the left and the text placeholder on the right.

3. Click the Insert Picture icon 🖼️ in the content placeholder.

   PowerPoint opens the Insert Picture dialog box.

4. Locate the drive and folder that contains the data files for this book, and open the Graphics folder.

5. Insert either 💿 **Kane3.jpg** or 💿 **Kane4.gif**.

   PowerPoint inserts the photograph into the placeholder but does not automatically resize it because the graphic is smaller than the placeholder. Sizing handles and a rotation handle are displayed, as shown in the illustration at the right.

6. Save the presentation.

🖥️ Try It!

Adjust the Size and Position the Photograph

1. Resize the photograph until is about the same height as the text placeholder.

   Refer to the desktop publishing section for information on resizing pictures.

2. Click and drag to position it in the area of the content placeholder.

   The completed content area should look like the one in the slide illustrated below.

3. Save the presentation.

🖥️ Try It!

Add the Title and Text for the Slide

1. In the title placeholder, type **Citizen Kane (1941 movie)**.

2. In the text placeholder, insert the following three bullet paragraphs.

   - **Widely considered the best American movie ever**
   - **Used members of Mercury Theater**
   - **Eight Academy Award nominations; won for Best Screenplay**

3. Compare your results with the illustration below.

4. Add the following in the Notes pane. Resize the Notes pane if necessary.

   Welles took the Mercury Theater group from New York to Hollywood to make Citizen Kane.

Title, Content and Text Layout

Kane4.gif with Sizing and Rotation Handles

Written by Welles and Herman J. Mankiewicz, the story parallels career of William Randolph Hearst, well-known newspaper and magazine publisher.

5. Save the presentation.

6. Close the presentation. Exit PowerPoint unless you are continuing with the Exercise Directions.

Completed Title, Content and Text Slide

Citizen Kane (1941 movie)

In time, Citizen Kane would be recognized as a cinematic masterpiece.

- Widely considered the best American movie ever
- Used members of Mercury Theater
- Eight Academy Award nominations; won for Best Screenplay

In this exercise, you will add three slides to the Fractal Facts presentation.

EXERCISE DIRECTIONS

Open the Presentation

1. Open ⌨️**Fractals1** from your saved files, or open 💿**02Fractals1** from the data files.
2. Save the presentation as **Fractals2**.

Add a Title and Text Slide

As you create this slide, check your progress against the completed slide shown in Illustration A.

1. Insert a new slide.
2. Click the title placeholder and type **Fractal Properties**.

3. Click the text placeholder and create the following bullet points.
   - **Geometric shapes generated from formula**
   - **Iteration: repeated application of a formula to all parts of the shape**
   - **Self-similarity: each small portion is a miniature of the whole**
   - **Fractional dimension: see http://math.rice.edu/~lanius/frac**

PowerPoint automatically formats the URL (Web address) as a hyperlink when you press Enter at the end of the paragraph. (You will learn more about the use of hyperlinks in Lesson 9.) If PowerPoint fails to format the URL, leave the bullet as typed.

4. In the Notes pane, add the following text: **See also http://www.best.com/~ejad/java/fractals /intro.shtml.**
5. Save the presentation.

Illustration A. Completed Title and Text Slide

Fractal Properties

- Geometric shapes generated from formula
- Iteration: repeated application of a formula to all parts of the shape
- Self-similarity: each small portion is a miniature of the whole
- Fractional dimension: see http://math.rice.edu/~lanius/frac

Add a Title, Text, and Content Slide

As you create this slide, check your progress against the completed slide shown in Illustration B.

1. Insert a new slide.
2. Apply the Title, Text, and Content layout to it.
   PowerPoint displays the slide with placeholders for the slide title, text, and content (graphic).
3. In the title placeholder, type **Sierpinski Triangle**.
4. Click the text placeholder and add the following bullet and sub-bullet points:
   - **Create half-size triangle on each side of a triangle**
   - **Apply each iteration to all triangles**
     To create the following sub-bullets, press the Tab key before typing.
     - **Top picture shows iteration 3**
     - **Bottom picture shows iteration 5**
5. Save the presentation.

Insert a Picture and Notes

1. Double-click the Insert Picture icon in the content placeholder.
2. Locate the data files for this book and open the Graphics folder.
3. Insert the file ⊚ **02Sierpinski.jpg**.
   PowerPoint automatically adjusts the illustration to fit the content placeholder.
4. Check your text against the text in Illustration B.
5. Add the following text in the Notes pane: **Illustration shows equilateral triangle, but any type of triangle type can be used.**
6. Save the presentation.

Illustration B. Completed Title, Text, and Content Slide

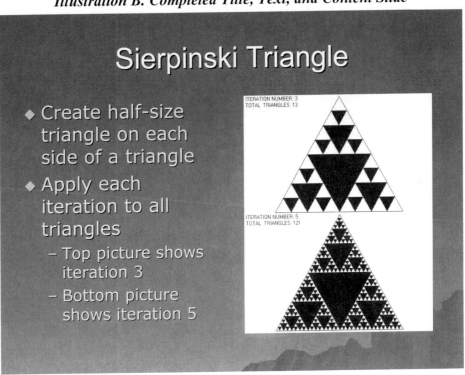

Add a Title, 2 Content, and Text Slide

As you create this slide, check your progress against the completed slide shown in Illustration D on the next page.

1. Insert a new slide.
2. Apply the *Title, 2 Content and Text* slide layout. (See Illustration C.)

Illustration C. Title, 2 Content and Text Layout

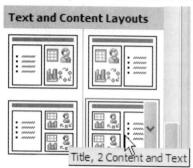

PowerPoint displays a slide with two content placeholders on the left side.

3. Click the title placeholder and type **Koch Snowflake**.
4. Click the Insert Picture icon in the upper-content placeholder.
5. Locate and insert the file 💿 **02Koch.gif**.
6. Click the Insert Picture icon in the lower-content placeholder.
7. Locate and insert the file 💿 **Kochcolor.gif**.
8. Enlarge the graphic slightly if you wish. The illustration shows the graphic at 120% of its original size.
9. Save the presentation.

Add Text and Notes

1. Click the text placeholder and add the following bullet and sub-bullet points:
   - **Start with triangle**
   - **Make a kink on each side**
   - **Iterate**
     To create the following sub-bullets, press the Tab key before typing.
     - **Top picture shows iterations 1-4**
     - **Bottom shows flake with triangles in different colors**
2. Save the presentation.
3. Compare your results with Illustration D.
4. Click the Outline tab in the left pane of the PowerPoint window, and review the outline of the presentation so far.
5. After reviewing the outline, return to the Slides tab if you wish.
6. Add the following in the Notes pane: **Start with straight line to create only top part of snowflake**.
7. Print the presentation.
8. Close the presentation, and exit PowerPoint.

Illustration D. Completed Title, 2 Content and Text Slide

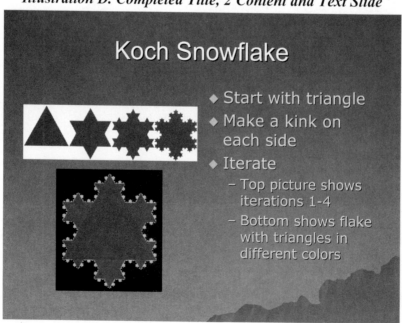

Exercise 3

Review and Enhance a Presentation
■ Review a Presentation ■ Use PowerPoint Views ■ Add a Title and Content Slide
■ Insert a Slide from Another Presentation ■ Edit a Slide
■ Print a Presentation from the Print Dialog Box

NOTES

Review a Presentation

■ PowerPoint provides several ways to view the presentation, so you can verify the order of the slides, the organization of the content, and the presentation's visual appeal. To review a presentation, you use the View buttons in the lower left of the PowerPoint window.

View Buttons

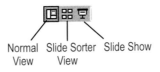

Normal   Slide Sorter   Slide Show
View   View

Normal View 🔲	Displays the outline, slide, and notes panes.
Slide Sorter View ⊞	Displays all slides in miniature. In this view, you can rearrange slide order or select a slide for viewing in Normal view.
Slide Show 🖵	Displays the presentation as a slide show, starting at the current slide. (Slide shows are discussed in the next exercise.)

■ When you enter Slide Sorter view, PowerPoint adds a Slide Sorter toolbar at the right end of the Standard toolbar.

Slide Sorter Toolbar

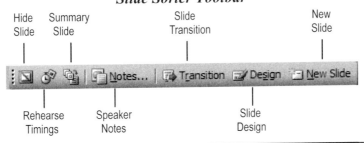

Hide Summary   Slide   New
Slide Slide   Transition   Slide

Rehearse   Speaker   Slide
Timings   Notes   Design

Button	Action
Hide Slide 🔲	Lets you hide a slide to prevent it from displaying.
Rehearse Timings ⏱	Lets you review the automatic timings for a slide show.
Summary Slide 🗇	Creates a slide that summarizes the presentation.

Button	Action
Speaker Notes Notes...	Opens a text entry dialog box so that you can add speaker notes to the selected slide without changing views.
Slide Transition Transition	Lets you select a method for switching from one slide to another in a slide show.
Slide Design Design	Lets you choose a new design template for the presentation.
New Slide New Slide	Inserts a new slide after the selected slide.

Try It!

Review Slide Order in Slide Sorter View

1. Open Welles2, or open 03Welles2 from the data files.
2. Save the presentation as Welles3.
3. Click the Slide Sorter View button.

   PowerPoint displays all four slides in miniature across the top of the window, as shown in the following illustration.

   Note the bold border around slide 1. The border indicates that the slide is selected.

4. Click to select slide 3.
5. Press the Enter key to switch to Normal view with slide 3 displayed.
6. Click the Slide Sorter View button.

Slide Sorter View

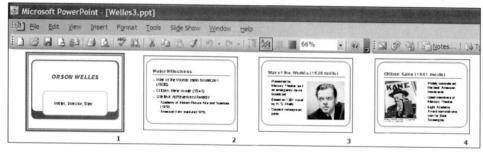

Use PowerPoint Views

- The techniques for moving from slide to slide and from area to area within a slide work in both Normal view and Slide Sorter view. You can switch from one view to another until you find the view that is easiest for you to use for any task in creating a presentation.

Try It!

Navigate the Views

1. Click the Normal View button to view the Outline/Slides, Slide, Notes as well as the task pane.
2. In the Outline/Slides pane, click the Outline tab.

3. Click the icon for the title of slide 4.

   The entire outline entry for slide 4 is selected and slide 4 appears in the Slide pane.

4. Press the Page Up key to display slide 3.

5. Press the Page Up key again.

   Slide 2 appears in the Slide pane and the insertion point is in the title of slide 2.

6. Press the down arrow key.

   The insertion point moves down one line.

7. Press the down arrow key until slide 3 appears.

8. Click the Slides tab in the Outline/Slides pane.

   Thumbnail slides appear in the pane.

9. Click the thumbnail of slide 1.

   Slide 1 is displayed.

10. Click the thumbnail of slide 4 to display slide 4.

11. Click the Slide Sorter View button ⊞ to return to Slide Sorter view.

Add a Title and Content Slide

■ The Welles presentation needs a good closing slide to make it complete.

💻 Try It!

1. Click slide 4.

2. Insert a new slide.

3. From the Content Layouts section of the task pane, apply the *Title and Content* layout to the new slide.

Title and Content Layout

4. Double-click the new slide to switch to Normal view.

5. In the title placeholder, type **Orson Welles 1915-1985**.

6. In the content placeholder, click the Insert Picture icon 🖾 .

7. Locate the graphics data files and insert 💿 **Director chair.jpg**, and click outside the placeholder.

   The slide should look like the one in the illustration on the next page.

8. Save the presentation.

Insert a Slide from Another Presentation

- You can copy and paste slides from one presentation to another. PowerPoint automatically applies the slide design of the receiving presentation. You can copy and paste in Normal view or Slide Sorter view.

💻 Try It!

1. With **Welles3.ppt** open, click the Slide Sorter View button 🔲.

   The five slides appear in Slide Sorter view.

2. Open 💿 **03Achieve.ppt** from the data files.

3. In Normal view, click the Slides tab to display thumbnail slides in the Outline/Slides pane.

4. Click to select slide 3, and do one of the following to copy it:

   - Click the Copy button 📋 on the Standard toolbar.
   - Press Ctrl+C.
   - Click <u>E</u>dit, <u>C</u>opy (Alt+E, C).

5. Switch to **Welles3** using one of the following methods.

   - Click **Welles3.ppt** button 📄 Welles3.ppt on the Windows taskbar.
   - Press Ctrl+F6.
   - Click <u>W</u>indow, <u>2</u> Welles3.ppt (Alt+W, 2).

6. Select slide 4.

   You are choosing the slide after which you want to insert the slide from another presentation.

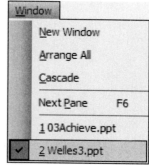

Window Menu

Window
<u>N</u>ew Window
<u>A</u>rrange All
<u>C</u>ascade
Next <u>P</u>ane   F6
<u>1</u> 03Achieve.ppt
✓   <u>2</u> Welles3.ppt

336

7. Do one of the following to paste the copied slide into **Welles3**.

   - Click the Paste button 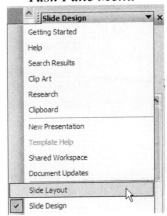 on the Standard toolbar.
   - Press Ctrl+V.
   - Click <u>E</u>dit, <u>P</u>aste (Alt+E, P).

   The pasted slide becomes slide 5, and PowerPoint applies the design of Welles3.ppt, as shown in the following illustration.

8. Save the presentation.

Welles3.ppt after Slide is Pasted

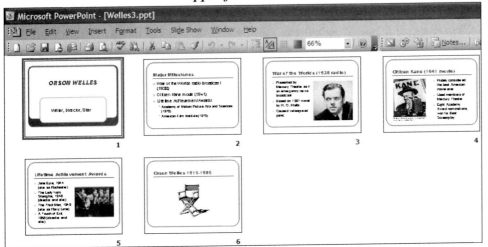

Edit a Slide

- You can edit text or change the layout of any slide.

🖵 Try It!

Edit the Pasted Slide

1. Double-click slide 5 to display the presentation in Normal view.
2. Display the Slide Layout options in the task pane by doing one of the following:

   Task Pane Menu

   - Click the drop-down arrow on the task pane and select Slide Layout, as shown at the right.

   - Click the Back or Forward button on the Task Pane to return to the Slide Layout options.
     Back   Forward

   - Click F<u>o</u>rmat, Slide <u>L</u>ayout (Alt+O, L).
3. Select the *Title, Text, and 2 Content* layout.

   PowerPoint applies the layout, placing the text on the left and two content placeholders on the right.

4. In the text placeholder, place the insertion point at the beginning of the *A Touch of Evil* bullet point.
5. Press the Enter key to create a new bullet.
6. Type the text **The Third Man, 1949 (star as Harry Lime)**.

💻 Try It!

Insert Two Pictures

1. In the bottom content placeholder, insert the picture 🎞 **Shanghai.jpg** from the graphics data files.

2. In the top content placeholder, click the Insert Clip Art icon .

   PowerPoint displays the Select Picture dialog box.

3. In the Search field, type **movies**, and press the Enter key or click the Go button [Go].

4. Insert any appropriate image.

   See the desktop publishing section for information on inserting clip art.

5. Save the presentation, and print it.

💻 Try It!

Change the Layout

1. Delete the upper picture in the Lifetime Achievement Awards slide.

2. Apply the *Title, Text, and Content* layout.

   The resulting slide should look as shown in the following illustration.

Completed Lifetime Achievement Awards Slide

Lifetime Achievement Awards

- Jane Eyre, 1944 (star as Rochester)
- The Lady from Shanghai, 1948 (director and star)
- The Third Man, 1949 (star as Harry Lime)
- A Touch of Evil, 1958 (director and star)

3. Switch to Slide Sorter view.

4. With the Lifetime Achievement Awards slide selected, click the <u>N</u>otes button [📋 <u>N</u>otes...].

5. Add the following two speaker notes in the Speaker Notes dialog box:

   Lady from Shanghai includes famous scene with shoot-out in hall of mirrors.

Select Picture

Third Man concerns villainy in post-World War II Vienna.

Speaker Notes Dialog Box (Slide Sorter View)

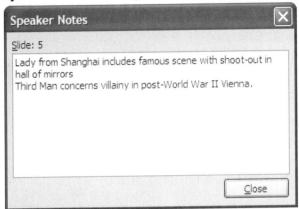

6. Save the presentation.

Print a Presentation from the Print Dialog Box

■ PowerPoint lets you print the presentation in a variety of ways through the Print dialog box.

🖥 Try It!

1. Press Ctrl+P.

   PowerPoint displays the Print dialog box shown in the following illustration.

PowerPoint Print Dialog Box

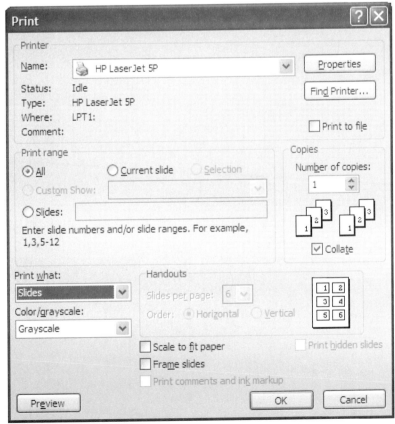

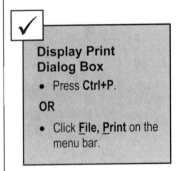

✓

Display Print Dialog Box

- Press **Ctrl+P**.

OR

- Click **File, Print** on the menu bar.

Note the options displayed in the Print what drop-down list shown at the right. You can print:

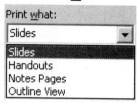

- *Slides, just as you have done using the Print button.*
- *Handouts for the audience. When you select this option, you can choose to print 1, 2, 3, 4, 6, or 9 slides per page.*
- *Notes Pages that include the information form the Notes pane.*
- *Presentation in Outline View.*

2. In the Print what drop-down list, select Handouts.

3. In the Slides per page drop-down list, select 6. Next to Order, select Horizontal.

4. In the Color/grayscale drop-down list, select Pure Black and White.

   The bottom of the Print dialog box should look as shown in the illustration on the next page.

Print Handouts – 6 Per Page

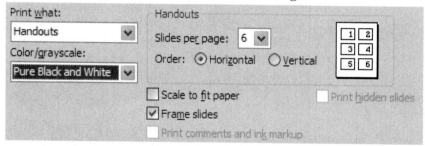

5. Click the OK button OK to print the handouts.

   The result should look similar to the illustration on the next page.

6. Save and close both presentations. Exit PowerPoint unless you are continuing with the Exercise Directions.

Printed Handouts (6 slides per page)

ORSON WELLES

Writer, Director, Star

Major Milestones

- War of the Worlds radio broadcast (1938)
- Citizen Kane movie (1941)
- Lifetime Achievement Awards
  - Academy of Motion Picture Arts and Sciences (1970)
  - American Film Institute (1975)

War of the Worlds (1938 radio)

- Presented by Mercury Theater as if an emergency news broadcast
- Based on 1901 novel by H. G. Wells
- Caused widespread panic

Citizen Kane (1941 movie)

In time, Citizen Kane would be recognized as a cinematic masterpiece.

- Widely considered the best American movie ever
- Used members of Mercury Theater
- Eight Academy Award nominations; won for Best Screenplay

Lifetime Achievement Awards

- Jane Eyre, 1944 (star as Rochester)
- The Lady from Shanghai, 1948 (director and star)
- The Third Man, 1949 (star as Harry Lime)
- A Touch of Evil, 1958 (director and star)

Orson Welles 1915-1985

1

> *In this exercise, you will review the Fractals presentation, add three slides, and print notes and handouts.*

EXERCISE DIRECTIONS

Open the Presentation

1. Open 🖼Fractals2, or open 💿03Fractals2 from the data files.
2. Save the presentation as **Fractals3**.

Review the Presentation

1. Review the appearance of the presentation title slide.
2. Display the presentation in Normal view.
3. Click the Outline tab in the Outline/Slides pane.
4. Click the icon for slide 2.
5. Review its appearance.
6. Click the Slides tab to display thumbnails in the Outline/Slides pane.
7. Select slide 3 and review it.
8. Select and review slide 4.
9. Switch to Slide Sorter view.

Copy Two Slides

1. Open 💿**03Websites**.
2. Copy slides 2 and 3 from **03Websites** and paste them at the end of **Fractals3**, as shown in Illustration A.
3. Save the presentation.

Illustration A. Fractals3 in Slide Sorter View after Slides are Pasted

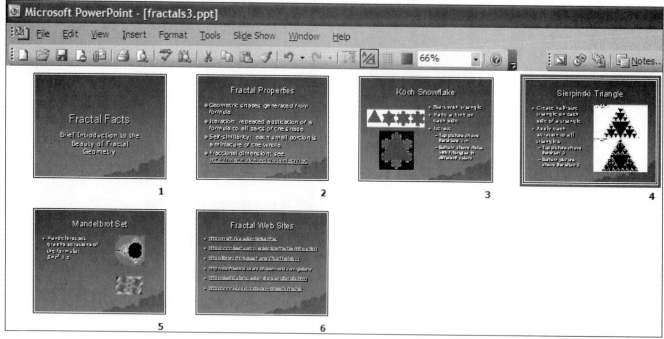

Add Text and Notes

1. Double-click slide 5 to display it in Normal view.
2. Click at the end of the bulleted paragraph and then press Enter.
3. Type the following text: **Named for Benoit Mandelbrot who first used the formula in a computer**
4. In the Notes pane, add the following two notes:

   Top image from http://aleph0.clarku.edu/~djoyce/julia/julia.html

   Bottom image from http://klein.math.okstate.edu/IndrasPearls/cover-art/.
5. Display slide 6, and add the following text in the Notes pane:

   All sites include links to other sites.
6. Save the presentation.

Add a Title and 4 Content Slide

1. Display slide 5.
2. Insert a new slide.
3. Apply the layout *Title and 4 Content* from the Content Layouts section of the Slide Layout task pane.
4. In the Graphics data files, locate and insert any four of the files that begin with **Fractal**.
5. Save the presentation.

Print Notes Pages and Handouts

1. Press Ctrl+P to display the Print dialog box.
2. Click the drop-down list arrow on the Print what box. Select Notes Pages.
3. In the Color/grayscale drop-down list, select Pure Black and White. Select the Frame slides check box, as shown in Illustration B.

   Illustration D on the next page shows the Notes page for slide 5.
4. Click the OK button OK .

Illustration B. Print Notes

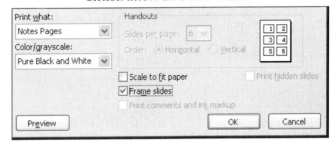

5. Press Ctrl+P to display the Print dialog box.
6. Click the drop-down list arrow on the Print what box.
7. Select Handouts, Slides per page 4, Pure Black and White, and Frame slides as shown in Illustration C.
8. Click the OK button OK .

Illustration C. Print Handouts

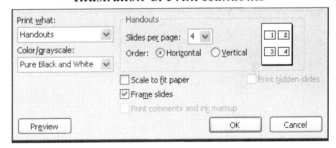

Illustration E shows the Handouts pages.

9. Close both presentations, saving them if requested, and exit PowerPoint.

Mandelbrot Set

◆ Mandelbrot set graphs iterations of the formula: $Z = z^Z + c$

◆ Named for Benoit Mandelbrot who first used the formula in a computer

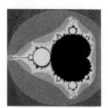

Top image from http://aleph0.clarku.edu/~djoyce/julia/julia.html

Bottom image from http://www.deepleaf.com/fractal/

5

Illustration E. Handouts for Fractals3

Fractal Facts

Brief Introduction to the Beauty of Fractal Geometry

Fractal Properties

- ◆ Geometric shapes generated from formula
- ◆ Iteration: repeated application of a formula to all parts of the shape
- ◆ Self-similarity: each small portion is a miniature of the whole
- ◆ Fractional dimension: see http://math.rice.edu/~lanius/frac

Sierpinski Triangle

- ◆ Create half-size triangle on each side of a triangle
- ◆ Apply each iteration to all triangles
  - Top picture shows iteration 3
  - Bottom shows iteration 5

Koch Snowflake

- ◆ Start with triangle
- ◆ Make a kink on each side
- ◆ Iterate
  - Top picture shows iterations 1-4
  - Bottom shows flake with triangles in different colors

Mandelbrot Set

- ◆ Mandelbrot set graphs iterations of the formula: $Z=z^z + c$
- ◆ Named for Benoit Mandelbrot who first used the formula in a computer

Sample Fractal Images

Fractal Web Sites

- • http://math.rice.edu/~lanius/frac
- • http://www.best.com/~ejad/java/fractals/intro.shtml
- • http://library.thinkquest.org/3703/?tgskip=1
- • http://www.deepleaf.com/fractal/
- • http://aleph0.clarku.edu/~djoyce/julia/julia.html
- • http://www.kcsd.k12.pa.us/~projects/fractal/

2

Exercise 4

Create a Slide Show
■ About Slide Shows ■ Create Slide Transitions
■ Add Animation ■ Summary of Animation Procedures

NOTES

About Slide Shows

■ PowerPoint provides a number of options that allow you to build a slide show that you can run on your computer or on a computer projection system. The options include:

- Transitions from slide to slide to vary the way a slide is displayed when you run the slide show.

- A number of animation techniques for controlling when and how slide elements appear.

- Sound to call attention to slide elements. (Sound is outside the scope of this book.)

Create Slide Transitions

■ Slide transitions let you determine the way in which a slide is first displayed when you run a slide show. You can make a slide appear as if it were enlarged or shrunk, as if it were revealed by opening blinds, or in a variety of other ways.

🖳Try It!

Create Transitions for All Slides

1. Open 📻**Welles3**, or open 💿**04Welles3** from the data files.

2. Save the presentation as **Welles4**.

3. Display the presentation in Slide Sorter view.

4. Select any slide.

5. Click the Transition button 📑 Transition on the Slide Sorter toolbar.
   OR
   Click Slide Show, Slide Transition (Alt+D, T) on the menu bar.

   PowerPoint displays the Slide Transition options in the task pane, as shown in the illustration at the right.

6. Select any option in the list (except No Transition or Random Transition) to see the effect on the selected slide.

   You can specify a different transition for each slide in the show. You can choose one transition to use for all slides. You can choose No Transition (the first option in the list) for any or all slides. Or, you can choose Random Transition (the last option in the list) for any or all slides.

7. Select *Random Transition*.

*Slide Transition
Options*

8. In Modify transition, select *Speed: Medium.*

9. In Advance slide, be sure the *On mouse click* option is selected.

10. Click the Apply to All Slides button Apply to All Slides .

11. Make sure the On mouse click option is selected.
    The lower portion of the task pane is shown below.

12. Save the presentation.

Completed Task Pane

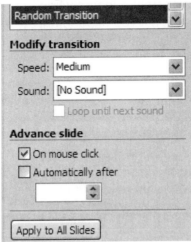

Try It!

Run the Slide Show

1. Select the title slide (slide 1).

2. Click the Slide Show button 🖳 in the lower left of the window.
   The title slide appears with the effect specified.

3. Press the Enter key or click the left mouse button to advance through the show.

4. After the last slide, click again, press the Enter key, or press the Esc key to end the slide show.

5. Click the Slide Show button 🖳 again.

6. Press Enter or click to advance through the show. Note that the transitions are different for this show.

7. After the last slide, click again, press the Enter key, or press the Esc key to end the slide show.

Add Animation

- Animation effects control how individual elements on a slide appear during a slide show. Slide elements are animated in one or more of the following ways:

  - Entrance, which specifies when and how the element first appears during the slide show.

  - Emphasis, which specifies changes in the element's appearance on entrance or exit.

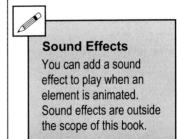

Sound Effects
You can add a sound effect to play when an element is animated. Sound effects are outside the scope of this book.

- Exit, which specifies when and how the element is treated when the slide show moves to the next slide.
- Motion Paths, which specify how the element moves on entrance or exit.

■ You can specify an Entrance and/or Exit for each element on a slide, and you can add Emphasis and/or Motion Paths to each element on Entrance or Exit.

■ To animate a slide's elements quickly, you can apply an **Animation Scheme**, which affects only the text on a slide; the content appears when the slide is displayed. Animation schemes, as you'll see if you experiment with them, may apply a combination of Entrance, Emphasis, Exit, and Motion Paths. (Animation schemes also provide slide transitions.)

■ You can use **Custom Animation** to animate the text and content (graphics).

■ To specify Custom Animation:
- Select the element you want to animate.
- Specify the desired animation effects.
- Use the Re-Order buttons ⬆ Re-Order ⬇ to change the order in which elements appear during a slide show.

🖥 Try It!

Use an Animation Scheme for the Title Slide
1. Click the Normal View button 🖽 to switch to Normal view.
2. Select the title slide.
3. Click Sli̲de Show, Animation S̲chemes (Alt+D, C) on the menu bar.
   PowerPoint displays the list of animation schemes in the task pane, as shown at the right.
   Schemes are divided into three categories: Subtle, Moderate, and Exciting.
4. Click *Appear and dim* in the Subtle category, and observe the effect.
   This scheme specifies an Entrance and Emphasis effect, with the Emphasis (dimming) as a separate action.
5. Click the Slide Show button 🖳 Slide Show on the task pane or the Slide Show button 🖳 at the lower left of the PowerPoint window.
   The slide appears with its transition, and then the title appears automatically.
6. Click the mouse button or press the Enter key to display the subtitle.
7. Repeat step 6 to cause the subtitle to dim (emphasis effect).
8. Click the mouse button or press the Enter key to display slide 2.
9. Press the Esc key to end the slide show.
10. Select slide 1 in the Outline/Slides pane.

🖥 Try It!

Try Other Animation Schemes for the Title Slide
1. Scroll to the Exciting category, and click *Pinwheel.*

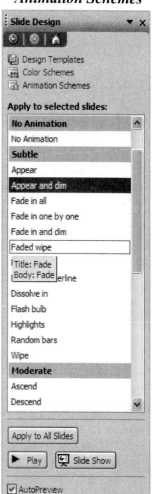

Animation Schemes

The title enters with the Pinwheel motion path, and the subtitle enters by scrolling up. No emphasis effect is specified.

2. Scroll up to locate the Moderate schemes.

3. Select *Compress.*

   The Compress scheme specifies an Entrance and a Motion Path for each slide element.

4. Apply at least two additional schemes.

5. End by applying the *Rise Up* scheme in the Moderate category.

6. Save the presentation.

7. Run the slide show and press the Esc key when slide 2 appears.

⌨ Try It!

Combine Animation Scheme and Custom Animation for Slide 2

1. Select slide 2.

2. In the Moderate animation schemes, select *Elegant.*

   The Elegant animation scheme specifies an Entrance and a Motion Path. Note that the third bullet and its sub-bullets are treated as a single element. To animate the sub-bullets, you need to use Custom Animation.

3. Click Slide Show, Custom Animation (Alt+D, M).

   PowerPoint displays the Custom Animation options in the task pane, and small numbers beside each text element on the slide, as shown in the following illustration.

Slide Ready for Custom Animation

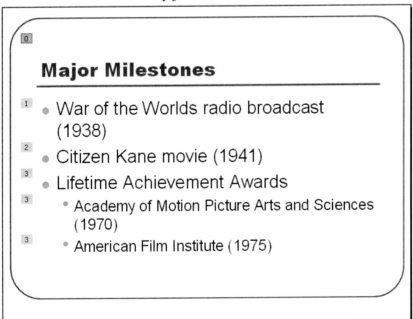

4. Click the ⬜0 to the left of the title.

   The title is selected in the task pane, as shown in the illustration at the right.

5. Click the ⬜1 to the left of the first bullet.

Moderate Rise Up Animation Scheme

Custom Animation

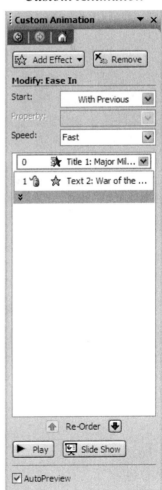

The first bullet is selected in the task pane and the other text in the text placeholder appears in the task pane, as shown in the following illustration.

First Bullet Selected

6. If a bullet or sub-bullet does not appear, click the expansion arrows ⧰ to reveal all the text.

7. Click *Academy of Motion...* to select it 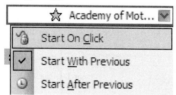.

8. Click the drop-down arrow and select Start On <u>C</u>lick as shown in the following illustration.

Specify Start on Click

This selection will cause the sub-bullet to be animated as a separate element rather than with its main bullet. The Elegant animation scheme controls the entrance and motion of the element.

9. Repeat steps 6 and 7 for *American Film Instit...*

10. Click the Play button ▶ Play at the bottom of the pane to review the animation.

11. Save the presentation.

🖥 Try It!

Animate Slides 3 and 4

1. Select slide 3.

2. Click the Back button 🔄 on the task pane to return to the Slide Design and Animation Schemes options.

3. For slide 3, apply the *Zoom* scheme (in the Moderate category).

4. Select slide 4, and apply the *Wipe* scheme (in the Subtle category.)

5. Save the presentation.

6. Select slide 1 and run the slide show.

7. Press Enter or click to move from element to element and slide to slide.

8. Press the Esc key to end the slide show at any time.

🖥 Try It!

Animate Slide 5 including its Content

1. Select slide 5.

2. If necessary, click the Back button 🔄 at the top of the task pane to return to the Slide Design and Animation Schemes options.

3. Apply the *Compress* scheme (in the Moderate category).

4. Switch to the Custom Animation options on the task pane.

5. Select the graphic on the slide.

6. Click the Add Effect button 🔲 Add Effect ▾ .

7. Point to <u>E</u>ntrance and click Split, which may be available only if you click <u>M</u>ore Effects.

8. In the task pane, under Direction, click the drop-down arrow and choose <u>V</u>ertical In.

9. For Speed, select Very Fast.

The task pane should look as shown at the right.

Task Pane for
Shanghai Graphic

🖥 Try It!

Change the Order of an Element

1. With Custom Animation options showing in the task pane, select *shangai* and let the mouse pointer rest on the selection.

shangai Selected

Note that when you linger on the entry, PowerPoint displays a ScreenTip that summarizes the animation for the element.

At the bottom of the task pane are the Re-Order buttons 🔼 Re-Order 🔽.

2. Click the Up button 🔼 three times to move the shangai entry so that it becomes the second entry, as shown on the left in the illustration on the next page.

3. Click the Down button 🔽 once to move the shangai entry so that it becomes the third entry, as shown on the right in the illustration on the next page.

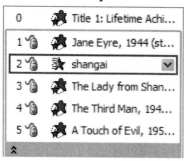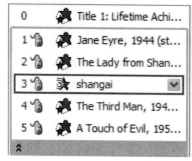

4. Click the Play button  to review the change.

5. Save the presentation.

🖳 Try It!

Animate Slide 6 including the Graphics

1. Select slide 6.

2. Apply the *Fade in all* scheme (in the Subtle category).

3. Click the Forward button 🔘 at the top of the task pane to display the Custom Animation options.

4. Select the director's chair image.

5. Click the Add Effect button ⬚ Add Effect ▾ near the top of the task pane.

6. Choose Entrance, Wedge from the menu, as shown in the following illustration. You may need to click More Effects to find Wedge.

Add Entrance Effect for Director's Chair

7. Save the presentation.

8. Click slide 1 and run the slide show.

9. Close the presentation. Exit PowerPoint unless you are continuing with the Exercise Directions.

Summary of Animation Procedures

- You can quickly animate text by applying an **Animation Scheme**. Keep in mind that not all animation schemes act on all text elements. Apply a scheme and watch its effect to determine if the scheme is right for the slide you are editing.

- To display animation schemes in the task pane:

    - At any time, click Slide Show, Animation Schemes (Alt+D, C) on the menu bar.

    OR

    - After applying an animation scheme and moving on to some other task, click the Back button at the top of the task pane.

- You can apply **Custom Animation** after applying an animation scheme, or you can skip using an animation scheme altogether. You must use custom animation to animate sub-bullets as separate elements or to animate content (graphics).

- To display the custom animation options in the task pane:

    - At any time, click Slide Show, Custom Animation (Alt+D, M) on the menu bar.

    OR

    - After applying custom animation and moving on to some other task, click the Back button at the top of the task pane.

- Custom Animation offers the following additional options:

    - Start method: On Click, With Previous, After Previous (number of seconds).

    - Speed of animation: Very Slow, Slow, Medium, Fast, Very Fast.

    - To remove animation, select the element and click the Remove button in the task pane.

In this exercise, you will add transition and animation to the fractals presentation.

EXERCISE DIRECTIONS

Open the Presentation

1. Open 🖳 **Fractals3**, or open 💿 **04Fractals3** from the data files.
2. Save the presentation as **Fractals4**.

Apply Slide Transitions

1. Switch to Slide Sorter view.
2. Select the title slide.
3. Click the Transition button on the toolbar.
4. Set the Speed: Medium option.
5. Be sure that On mouse click is selected for Advance slide.
6. Apply the transitions specified in the following table, using Medium for Speed in each case.
7. After applying the transitions, run the slide show.

Slide	Transition
1 Fractal Facts	Cover Down
2 Fractal Properties	Cover Up
3 Sierpinski Triangle	Cover Left
4 Koch Snowflake	Cover Right
5 Mandelbrot Set	Cover Left-Down
6 Sample Fractals	Cover Left-Up
7 Fractal Web Sites	Cover Right-Down

Specify Animation Effects

For each slide, specify the animation as outlined in the table at the right.

Remember that you can switch from Animation Scheme to Custom Animation using the Slide Show menu or by clicking the Back 🔵 and Forward 🔵 buttons on the task pane.

After you apply the animation schemes, the slide transitions may differ from those you specified in the first part of this exercise.

Note also that when you view an animation scheme, such as Grow and exit to a slide, the Custom Animation task pane shows the animations used to create the scheme.

Save the presentation after each slide. Play the slides and review the slide show as often as necessary.

Run the Slide Show

1. Display the title slide in Normal view.
2. Click the Slide Show button 🖵 and run the slide show.
3. After reviewing the slide show, make any necessary changes, and then run the show again.

4. Save and close the presentation, and exit PowerPoint.

Slide Animations

Slide	Name and Animation
Fractal Facts — Brief Introduction to the Beauty of Fractal Geometry	1 Fractal Facts Scheme: Grow and exit
Fractal Properties — • Geometric shapes generated from formula • Iteration: repeated application of a formula to all parts of the shape • Self-similarity: each small portion is a miniature of the whole • Fractional dimension: see http://math.rice.edu/~lanius/frac	2 Fractal Properties Scheme: Title arc
Sierpinski Triangle — • Create half-size triangle on each side of a triangle • Apply each iteration to all triangles – Top picture shows iteration 3 – Bottom shows iteration 5	3 Sierpinski Triangle Scheme: Float Custom: Sub-bullets Start On Click
Koch Snowflake — • Start with triangle • Make a kink on each side • Iterate – Top picture shows iterations 1-4 – Bottom shows flake with triangles in different colors	4 Koch Snowflake Scheme: Rise up Custom: Sub-bullets Start On Click
Mandelbrot Set	5 Mandelbrot Set Scheme: Boomerang and exit

Sample Fractal Images	6 Sample Fractal Images
	Scheme: Elegant
	Custom: Upper left – Box, In
	    Upper right – Diamond Out
	    Lower left – Wipe, From Top
	    Lower right – Blinds, Vertical
	Change the order of these elements so that they display in the following order:
	  1 Lower right
	  2 Upper left
	  3 Lower left
	  4 Upper right

Fractal Web Sites — • http://math.rice.edu/~lanius/frac • http://www.best.com/~ejad/java/fractals/intro.shtml • http://library.thinkquest.org/3703/?tqskip=1 • http://www.deepleaf.com/fractal/ • http://aleph0.clarku.edu/~djoyce/julia/julia.html • http://www.kcsd.k12.pa.us/~projects/fractal/	7 Fractal Web Sites Scheme: Show in reverse

Lesson 8: Microsoft Office Access 2003

Introduction to Access

- ♦ **What is Access?**
- ♦ **What is a Database?**
- ♦ **What is a Database Management System?**
- ♦ **How is Database Organized?**
- ♦ **The Database Window**
- ♦ **What are Database Objects?**
- ♦ **How is a Table Structured?**
- ♦ **Field Data Types**
- ♦ **How are Tables Related?**
- ♦ **Planning a New Database**

Exercise 1: Explore a Database

- ♦ **Start Access and Open a Database**
- ♦ **Explore a Database**
- ♦ **Print a Database Object**

Exercise 2: Get Started with Access

- ♦ **Copy the Data Files and Deselect the Read-only Attribute**
- ♦ **Open an Existing Database**
- ♦ **Enter Data**

Exercise 3: Work with Table Design

- ♦ **Modify a Table Design**
- ♦ **Change Column Widths**
- ♦ **Summary of Data Entry Aids**

Exercise 4: Create a Database and Table

- ♦ **Create a Database**
- ♦ **Set File Format Option**
- ♦ **Convert Database to Access 2002 – 2003 File Format**
- ♦ **Create a Table Using the Table Wizard**
- ♦ **Modify the Table Design**

Exercise 5: Create and Use a Form

- ♦ **Create a Form Using AutoForm**
- ♦ **Add a Record in Form View**
- ♦ **Modify a Form**

Exercise 6: Filter and Sort a Database

- ♦ **Filter By Selection**
- ♦ **Filter By Form**
- ♦ **Advanced Filter/Sort**

Exercise 7: Work with Queries

- ♦ **Add Records in Form View**
- ♦ **Create a Query**
- ♦ **Copy a Query**
- ♦ **Edit a Query**

Exercise 8: Work with Reports

- ♦ **Create a Report Using AutoReport**
- ♦ **Set Default Print Margins**
- ♦ **Create a Report Using the Report Wizard**
- ♦ **Change the Report Title**
- ♦ **Resize and Move Fields**

Introduction to Access

■ What is Access? ■ What is a Database?
■ What is a Database Management System? ■ How is Database Organized?
■ The Database Window ■ What are Database Objects? ■ How is a Table Structured?
■ Field Data Types ■ How are Tables Related? ■ Planning a New Database

NOTES

What is Access?

- Access is the **database management system** in Microsoft Office. To understand a database management system, study the information about database basics that follows.

What is a Database?

- A **database** is an organized collection of related data. A database stores data and provides repeated reference to information to aid in calculations and business decisions. An address book or a library's catalog is a database. Student records and inventory records are also databases.

- To maintain simple databases kept by hand requires time and labor. Suppose you need to update the telephone number and address of a friend who just moved to Boise. You must page through your address book, locate the entry, and make the change.

Examples of Manual Database Records

Address Book Entry	*Card Catalog Entry*
Name	Call Number
Address	Author
City St Zip	Title
Telephone	Subject

- An **Access database** is the electronic equivalent of a manual database. It lets you organize and maintain the data electronically. To update the telephone number of your friend in Boise, you select the friend's entry and make the change.

What is a Database Management System?

- An electronic database management system like Access provides ways to store, search, sort, query, and report on the data in the database. For example, suppose you wish to find all your address book entries of people who live in your hometown. To do this manually, you must read the address book entries and write down the name of each person. Such a search could be quite time-consuming. With an automated database management system like Access, however, you can locate and print the records of all the hometown addresses using its filter or query capabilities and a few simple keystrokes.

Uses of Databases

Businesses use their databases to answer such questions as:

Which products are performing profitably?

Which products are doing poorly?

Have we expanded our customer base within the last year?

Are we retaining customers or are they leaving us for other suppliers?

What is our cost per sale? (This question may involve analyzing database information using a spreadsheet.)

How is a Database Organized?

- The Access database management system uses the **Database window** to maintain **database objects** (see below) in one file. The Database window contains an Objects bar with a button for each type of object. You click a button to display a list of the objects of that type.

The Database Window

- Each time you open a database, the Database window displays information about the database and the objects it contains.

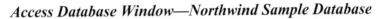

Access Database Window—Northwind Sample Database

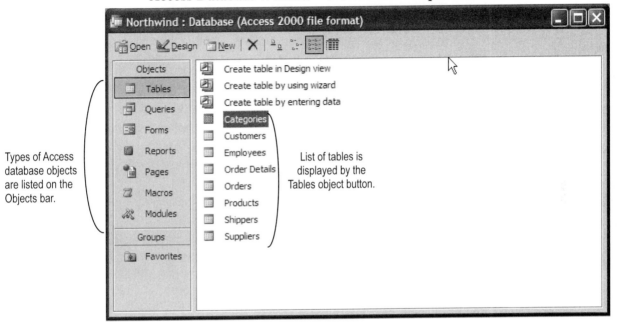

Types of Access database objects are listed on the Objects bar.

List of tables is displayed by the Tables object button.

Note that the title bar shows (Access 2000 file format). *Microsoft provides the sample database in this format. Access 2003 can open databases created in Access 2000 or Access 2002, but Access 2000 cannot open databases created in Access 2003.*

- The Database window includes an Objects bar that lists several types of objects. When you click on a button on the Objects bar (in the illustration, the Tables button has been selected), a list of the corresponding objects appears.

- In Access, you organize the data into separate electronic storage containers called **tables**. Each table contains a specific kind of data. Consider a company that sells computer hardware and software. The company database may contain one table that identifies customers, another that describes its hardware products, a third that tracks software, a fourth that maintains data about the sales force, and a fifth that tracks sales. These tables form the database.

What are Database Objects?

- To help you use your database efficiently, modern database management systems, like Access, provide database objects. Database objects are the tools you need to store, maintain, search, analyze, and report on the data in your database.

Object	Description
Table	Also called a **datasheet**. Data is formatted in a table. Each row in a table represents one record in a database. The **Tables** button [⊞ Tables] displays a list of all tables in the current database. It lets you open an existing table, modify its design, or create a new table.
Query	A structured way to tell Access to retrieve data that meets certain criteria from one or more database tables. A query lets you see relationships among the data that are not apparent in the table or form views. For example, a query may request that Access retrieve data on all printers sold within the last six months. The **Queries** button [⊡ Queries] displays a list of all queries in the current database. It lets you open an existing query, modify its design, or create a new query.
Form	A formatted data entry window that lets you enter, display, and edit data. A form generally displays one record at a time. The **Forms** button [⊞ Forms] displays a list of all forms in the current database. It lets you open an existing form, modify its design, or create a new form.
Report	A formatted way to display information retrieved from the database. A report formats and analyzes data you specify. Examples of reports include sales summaries, phone lists, and mailing labels. The **Reports** button [⊟ Reports] displays a list of all reports in the current database. It lets you preview the report, modify its design, or create a new report.

- Space and time limits do not permit coverage of data access pages, macros, and modules in this text, but you may see them referred to as you use Access.

How is a Table Structured?

- A table is a grid of rows and columns. Each row contains one **record**. A record is a set of details about a specific item. For example, one record in a company's hardware inventory table could contain details on one of its HP LaserJet® printers, including a product identifier, manufacturer, model number, cost, and purchase date. When database users mention the "HP LaserJet printer record," they are referring to the details in the table row that describes the printer. Similarly, a record in a personnel database will include the employee's name, address, and so on.

- Details of a record are broken down into small units, called **fields**, to make them easy to use and refer to. Each field contains one kind of data and is identified by a **field name**. In Access, each field name becomes a column heading in a table. Each row in the column contains specific data called the **field contents**. For example, the field *Manufacturer* in one of the hardware records would contain the entry HP (for Hewlett-Packard) to identify the printer's maker. When data processing people ask, "What's in the manufacturer field?" they are asking about the field contents of the field name *Manufacturer*.

- A sample address record is shown below:

Last Name	First Name	Address 1	Address 2	City	ST	ZIP
Jones	Bob	275 Madison	12th Floor	New York	NY	10016

ZIP field

Field names

Field contents (record)

- The way the address data is broken down into fields is important. By having last name and first name as two separate fields, users can easily sort or locate people by last name or first name. City, ST (State), and ZIP Code are separate fields to make it easy to locate addresses by any one of those criteria. It may not be obvious at first, but if the City and State were in the same field, it wouldn't be easy to produce a listing of all the addresses in the database of just the people who live Springfield, MO or Springfield, IL.

Field Data Types

- In Access, you must define the type of data that each field (column) can contain. For example, some fields can contain text; others can contain numbers or dates. Data types are described as you use them in this lesson.

How are Access Tables Related?

- Database tables that share common fields are **related**. For example, in a book collection database, the Books table may use the record identifier from the Authors table to connect authors and their works. A common field that connects the tables allows you to create a **query** that lists authors and titles in the query result (called a **recordset**).

Planning a New Database

- Before creating tables for a new database, take time to plan your tables and define your fields. You should know in detail what kind of information you plan to store, how you want to format it, and from what source the information will come.

- Here is a set of starter guidelines:
  - Gather all your sources of information: invoice forms, employee records, pay stubs, order forms, product information, and so on.
  - Determine what types of information you will need to locate or report: names, ID's, prices, shipment dates, and so on.
  - Decide how much flexibility you need in locating and reporting the data. This in turn will determine how specific you must be in defining the fields.
  - Write down everything you want to accomplish with your database.
  - Break down information into its smallest practical units. For example, rather than have a field called "Name," which contains a customer's first, middle, and last name, it may be more useful to have three fields: "First Name," "Middle Initial," and "Last Name."
  - A database is only as good as the accuracy of the data it contains. Try to do everything possible to ensure that all data is entered correctly.

Recordset

The term *recordset* refers to a group of records created by a query or a **filter**. (A filter is a function that extracts records from one table while a query may use more than one table.)

If the data in the recordset can be edited to change the data in the underlying table(s), the result is also called a **dynaset**. If the data cannot be edited, the results are called a **snapshot**.

Exercise 1

Explore a Database
■ Start Access and Open a Database
■ Explore a Database ■ Print a Database Object

NOTES

Start Access and Open a Database

■ You start Access 2003 like other Microsoft Office 2003 applications. Unlike the others, however, Access does not display a blank database document automatically. Instead, it displays the opening window with a task pane that lets you open an existing database or start a new one.

Access Opening Task Pane

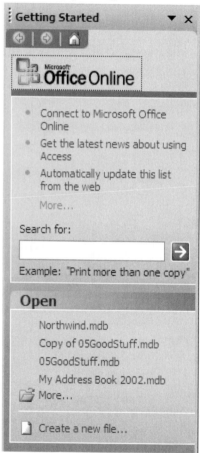

Explore a Database

■ In the Try It! activities in this exercise, you will explore the sample Northwind database provided by Microsoft. The quick tour of this database demonstrates the variety of objects and information a database contains. It also shows how quickly you can find information.

🖳 Try It!

1. Start Access.

2. Click <u>H</u>elp on the menu bar.

3. Point to Sample <u>D</u>atabases, and select Northwind Sample Database as shown in the illustration below.

Open Northwind Sample Database

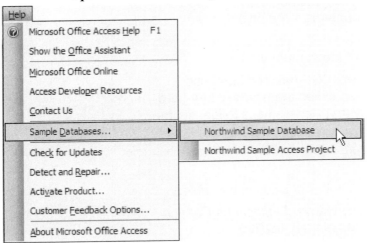

Northwind Traders Logo Screen

The Northwind Traders logo screen appears, giving you some information about the database. (See the illustration at the right.)

4. Click the OK button ⬚OK⬚, or press Enter.

The Main Switchboard appears, as shown below.

Northwind Database Main Switchboard

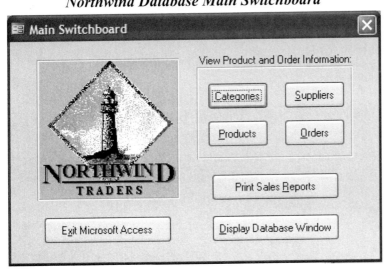

Objects Bar

5. Click the <u>D</u>isplay Database Window button ⬚Display Database Window⬚.

The Database window appears as illustrated in the introduction to this lesson. Its Objects bar is shown at the right.

6. Click the Tables button ⬚ Tables⬚ on the Objects bar, if it is not already selected.

A list of the tables in the database appears.

Try It!

Explore a Table

1. Double-click **Customers**.

   OR

   Select **Customers**, and click the Open button on the Database window.

   From now on, the instructions will say, "Open the (database object)." You will have to remember to double-click the object, or select it and click the Open button.

2. Scroll vertically to review some of the company names.

3. Note that the left column—CustomerID—has an alphabetic abbreviation. This is a special field called the **primary key field**; each record has a unique primary key that Access uses to identify the record.

   Later in this lesson, you will create a primary key field that is a single number.

4. Scroll horizontally to review the number of fields in the table.

5. Scroll down and find the Company Name: *Rattlesnake Canyon Grocery*. (The customers are listed alphabetically.)

6. Click the Close button ✖ on the **Customers** table.

Try It!

Locate an Order for Rattlesnake Canyon Grocery

1. Open the **Orders** table.

2. Click anywhere in the Customer field (second column of the table), and click the Sort Ascending button ⬇ on the toolbar.

3. Scroll down until you find the entries for Rattlesnake Canyon Grocery.

4. Find order number *11077*.

5. Click the Close button ✖ on the **Orders** table, and click the No button ⬜ No ⬜ on the message that appears as a warning box.

   To close any database object without saving changes, click the Close button on the object's window and answer No if Access prompts you to save changes.

Try It!

Locate the Details of Order 11077

1. Open the **Order Details** table.

2. Click in the first record of the Order ID field.

3. Click the Find button 🔍, or click Edit, Find (Alt+E, F).

4. Complete the Find dialog box as shown on the next page and click the Find Next button ⬜ Find Next ⬜.

Find Dialog Box for 11077

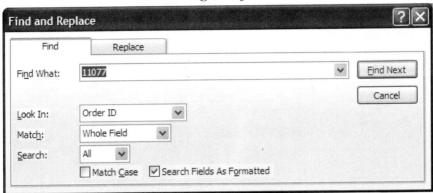

You should find that the first item in the order is for Chang.

5. Scroll down to see other items included in the order. (There are more than twenty.)

6. Click the Cancel button [Cancel] to close the Find dialog box.

7. Close the **Order Details** table without saving the changes.

Try It!

Look at the Order in More Detail

1. Click the Queries button [Queries] on the Objects bar.

2. Open the **Order Details Extended** query.

3. Repeat the Find command by doing one of the following:

   - Press Shift+F4.

   - Click the Find button and click the Find Next button [Find Next].

   - Click Edit, Find, and click the Find Next button [Find Next].

4. Maximize the Order Details Extended window.

5. Find the Chang item again. What is the cost (Extended Price) of the 24 units of Chang? $22.55, $364.80, or $14.00? _____

6. Click the lower Restore button to return Order Details Extended query window to its original size.

7. Click the Close button X to close the query; do not save any changes.

Try It!

Look at the Order Form

1. Click the Forms button [Forms] on the Objects bar.

2. Open the **Customer Orders** form.

3. Click the field name Company Name at the top of the form. *The field contents are selected.*

4. Click the Find button , or click Edit, Find (Alt+E, F).

5. Complete the Find dialog box as shown below, and click the Find Next button Find Next .

Find Rattlesnake Canyon Grocery

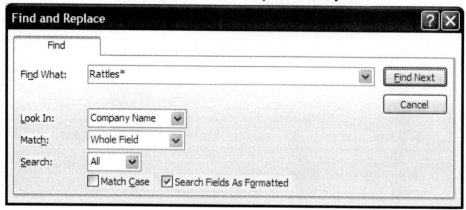

6. Click the Cancel button Cancel to close the Find dialog box.
7. In the top table of the form, scroll down until you find order *11077*.
8. Click the gray box to the left of the order number.
   The details of the order appear in the lower part of the form.
9. Scroll in the lower part of the form until you find *Chang*.
10. Close the Customer Orders form without saving any changes.

Try It!

Look at the Invoice

1. Click the Reports button Reports on the Objects bar.
2. Open the **Invoice** report.
3. The report opens in Print Preview.
4. Maximize the report window.
5. Find *Chang* on the invoice. (It is the first entry in the body of the report.)
6. Drag the mouse pointer onto the report display.
   The pointer turns into a magnifying glass.
7. Click anywhere on the report.
   The report display enlarges so you can read the text easily.
8. Click again anywhere on the report.
   The report display returns to its original size.
   The Invoice has two pages.
9. To see the second page, use the page buttons at the bottom of the window.
10. Close the **Invoice** report without saving any changes.

Page Buttons

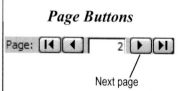

Next page

Print a Database Object

- Access lets you Print Preview and print database objects.

💻 Try It!

Print Preview a Database Object

1. Click the Tables button [▦ Tables].

2. Open the **Employees** table.

3. Click the Print Preview button [🔍].

   OR

   Click File, Print Preview (Alt+F, V).

4. Look at the first page.

5. Click the Next page button [▶] twice at the bottom of the Print Preview window.

   The table will print on multiple pages because it is too wide to print on one page in Portrait mode. Access prints as much of the table as fits on one page, then breaks the table to the next page.

   You can change the Page Setup so that the table prints on fewer pages.

💻 Try It!

Change Page Setup for a Database Object

1. Click File, Page Setup (Alt+F, U).

2. Click the Page tab, and select the Landscape option, as shown on the left in the following illustrations.

3. Click the Margins tab, and change the Left and Right margins to 0.5", as shown on the right in the following illustrations.

> ✓ **Page and Column Breaks in Print Preview**
>
> Because of differences in printer capabilities, your tables and reports may have different page and column breaks than those illustrated in this text. If yours are different, you haven't done anything wrong; your printing environment is different from the one used in creating this book.

Page Setup Dialog Box

Page Tab with Landscape Selected *Margins Tab with Landscape Selected*

4. Click the OK button [OK].
5. Review the Print Preview of the table.
   The table now fits on two pages, breaking after the Region column.

6. Click the Print button 🖨.
7. Review the printed copy of the **Employees** table.
8. Close Print Preview.
9. Click the Close button ⊠ on the Database window.
10. Exit Access unless you are continuing with the Exercise Directions.

In this exercise, you will explore an existing database to learn what it contains.

EXERCISE DIRECTIONS

Explore a Table

1. Start Access if it is not already running.
2. Open 💿 **01Classic** from the data files.
3. Click the Tables button on the Objects bar.
4. Open the **Discs** table.
5. Click the Disc Title column heading.
6. Click the Sort Ascending button $\frac{A}{Z}\downarrow$ to alphabetize the records by Disc Title.
   How many tracks on the Vivaldi/Marcello disc?

   _____

   What is the Disc Type of Symphony No. 1 with a Disc Label of Vox?

   _____

7. Sort the Disc Label column in ascending order.
   How many Vox discs are there?

   _____

   How many Deutsche Grammophon discs?

   _____

8. Click the Close button ⊠. Do not save any changes to the table.

Look at a Form

1. Click the Forms button on the Objects bar.
2. Open the **Soloists** form.
   Note the Record information at the bottom of the form.

Soloists Form

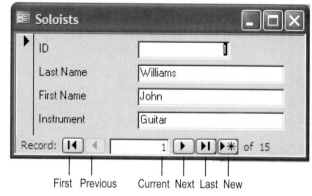

3. Click the Last Record button [▶|].
   What is the name of the soloist?

   _____

   What is the soloist's instrument?

   _____

4. Click in the Last Name field.
5. Click Edit, Find, or click the Find button 🔍.
6. Locate the record of the soloist whose last name is Mutter.
   What is the soloist's first name?

   _____

   What is the soloist's instrument?

   _____

7. Close the Find dialog box.
8. Click the Previous Record button [◀] to display record 6.
   What is the soloist's full name?

   _____

   What is the soloist's instrument?

   _____

9. Close the form without saving any changes.

Investigate a Query

1. Click the Queries button on the Objects bar.
2. Open the **Brahms Recordings** query.
3. Click the Musical Piece column heading.
4. Sort the column in ascending order.

   How many recordings of Symphony No. 2 are listed in the query?

   _____

   How many recordings of the Violin Concerto in D major are listed in the query?

   _____

5. Close the query without saving any changes.

Print a Table

1. Click the Tables button on the Objects bar.
2. Open the **Discs** table.
3. Click the Print button 🖨 to print a copy of the table in Portrait mode.
4. Close the **Discs** table.

Print Preview a Table

1. Open the **Musical Pieces** table.
2. Print Preview the table.

   Note that the Table breaks after the Composer column and again after the Conductor column, so that the table fits on three pages.

3. Click File, Page Setup.
4. Change all margins to 0.5".
5. Click the Page tab.
6. Change the Orientation to Landscape.
7. Click OK.
8. Review the Print Preview.

   Note that the table breaks after the Soloist column and the table fits on two pages.

9. Click File, Page Setup.

10. Change the Top and Bottom margins to 1".
11. Click OK.
12. Look at the effects of the changes in Print Preview.

    Note that the table breaks after the Soloist column as before. It also breaks after ID row 33 (Symphony No. 4 in E minor, op. 98 by Brahms). (Yours may break on a different row.) The table now covers four pages.

13. Close Print Preview.
14. Close the **Musical Pieces** table without saving any changes.

Review and Print a Report

1. Click the Reports button on the Objects bar.
2. Open the **Musical Pieces** report.

   How many pages does the report cover?

   _____

   What is the name of the Musical Piece of the last recording on page 2?

   _____

   What is the name of the Musical Piece of the last recording on page 1?

   _____

3. Click the Print button 🖨 to print a copy of the report.
4. Close the report.
5. Close the database, and exit Access.

Exercise 2

Get Started with Access
■ Copy the Data Files and Deselect the Read-only Attribute
■ Open an Existing Database ■ Enter Data

NOTES

Copy the Data Files and Deselect the Read-only Attribute

- **IMPORTANT NOTE:** Access does not let you perform a Save As on a database. Since files copied from the data CD are read-only, you must complete the following steps to make the data files usable:

  1. Copy the Access data files to a hard drive.
  2. Open Windows Explorer, and locate the drive and folder where you stored the copies.
  3. Select all the Access data files. (Click one file and then press Ctrl + A.)
  4. Right-click on the selected files.
  5. Select Properties from the shortcut menu.
  6. Deselect Read-only in the Attributes section as shown in the illustration below.

Deselect Read-only Attribute

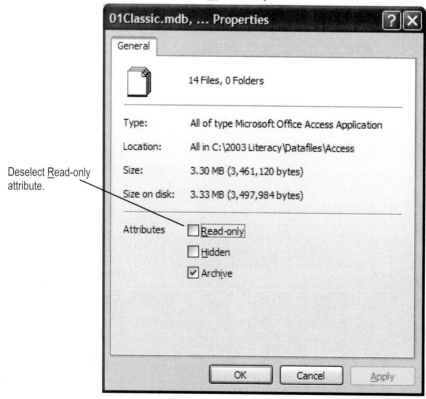

Deselect Read-only attribute.

Open an Existing Database

- You will create database objects later in this lesson. In this exercise, you will enter data to begin learning about elements of a database table.

- In the Try It! activities, you will use the database of Good Stuff Distributors, a small wholesale company that distributes restaurant products. This company's database lists the products it sells or distributes, their prices, their sources (suppliers), the quantity on hand, and the quantity on order.

⌨ Try It!

1. Start Access.
   The Access window appears with the task pane listing recently opened files.

2. Select More... 📂 More... to display the Open dialog box.

   OR

   Click File, Open (Alt + F, O).

3. Change to the location of the Access data files.

4. Open 💿 **02GoodStuff** from the data files.

   - Double-click the file name.

   OR

   a. Select the file name in the list.

   b. Click the Open button 📂 Open, or press Enter.

   The database opens as shown in the following illustration.

02GoodStuff Database

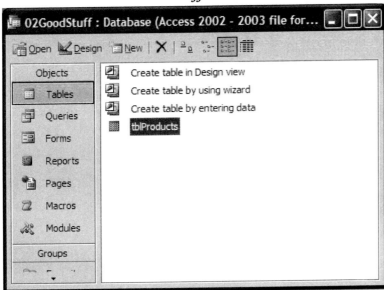

Enter Data

⌨ Try It!

1. Click the Tables button 📰 Tables on the Objects bar if it is not already selected.

2. Open the **tblProducts** table (double-click it, or select it and click the
   Open button ![Open]).

   *The tblProducts table opens in Datasheet (Table) view ready for data
   entry with the Product ID field selected, as shown below.*

   *If your datasheet does not have a row with (AutoNumber), see the
   first page of this exercise for instructions on copying the data files
   and deselecting the Read-only attribute.*

Datasheet View

In Datasheet view, the
records are displayed in
rows. Each column is a
field with the field names
at the top.

tblProducts Table in Datasheet (Table) View

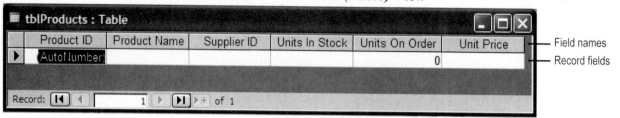

Field names — Record fields

*At the bottom of the Datasheet window in the status bar is an
indicator that tells you which record you are working with.*

3. Press the Tab key.
   The insertion point moves to the Product Name field.
4. In the Product Name field, type **Bread**.
   *The Product ID field changes to 1. ProductID is an AutoNumber field
   and is completed automatically by Access when you start typing in
   the next field.*
5. Press Tab to move to the Supplier ID field.
6. In the Supplier ID field, enter **11**.
7. Press Tab to move to the Units In Stock field.

   Note the message in the status bar: When stock drops below 100, reorder.

   *The database designer creates such a message to aid in data entry.
   If this field is less than 100, an order with the supplier must be
   placed, and an entry made in the next field (Units On Order).*
8. In the Units In Stock field, enter *200*.
9. Press Tab to move to the Units On Order field.
   *Note the 0 already entered in the field. This is a default value. Note
   the message in the status bar:* Valid entries are 0, 50, 100, and 200.
10. Press Tab to accept the default value and move to the Unit Price
    field.
11. In the Unit Price field, enter **.89** for 89 cents.
12. Press the Tab key to move to the Product ID field for the next record.
    *The first row of the table should look like the one shown in the
    illustration on the next page.*

    The record is saved when you press Tab after entering Unit Price.

Enter a Record

The term *enter* means to
type the data and press
Tab or Enter to move to
the next field.

Default Value

Value supplied by the
database designer to
speed data entry. If the
default value is correct,
you press the Tab key to
accept the default and
move to the next field.

370

tblProducts Table, First Row Completed

Product ID	Product Name	Supplier ID	Units In Stock	Units On Order	Unit Price
1	Bread	11	200	0	0.89
(AutoNumber)				0	

 Try It!

Invalid Values

To find out what happens when you enter invalid data (data that is not acceptable in a field), try the following:

1. Click in the Units On Order field of the Bread record you just entered. *Note the message in the status bar at the bottom of the window.*

   Valid entries are 0, 50, 100, and 200.

2. Enter **25**, and press Tab to move to the next field.

Invalid Entry Message

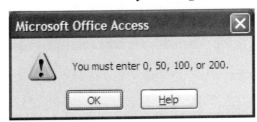

3. Click the OK button [OK].
4. Click in the Units On Order field, select the value in the field, and type **0** to replace *25* with *0*.
5. Press Tab to move to the Unit Price field.

 Try It!

Enter Another Product

1. Press Tab until you reach the Product Name field again.
2. Enter **Pickles**.
3. Press Tab, and enter **13** for Supplier ID.
4. Press Tab, and enter **250** for Units In Stock.
5. Press Tab twice to accept the default value for Units On Order.
6. In the Unit Price field, enter **.95**, and press the Tab key.
   The top two rows should look like the following.

tblProducts Table, Two Rows Completed

Product ID	Product Name	Supplier ID	Units In Stock	Units On Order	Unit Price
1	Bread	11	200	0	0.89
2	Pickles	13	250	0	0.95
(AutoNumber)				0	

Invalid Data

Invalid data is data that does not meet the restrictions set for the field. Database designers set the **validation rules** so that data that is not acceptable is rejected when entered.

Make a Mistake?

If you make a mistake when entering data, you can correct it by clicking in the field and editing the data.

If you put records in a different order, don't worry. The order of records is not important.

If gaps appear in the Product ID numbers because you start a record over, don't worry. The gaps do not harm the database.

🖳 Try It!

Enter More Products

1. Enter the six products listed in the table below.

   Let Access assign the Product ID automatically.

Product Name	Supplier ID	Units In Stock	Units On Order	Unit Price
Onions	13	150	0	.69
Hot Sauce	13	98	200	2.98
Hamburger	15	45	50	4.25
Ketchup	13	300	0	.79
Mustard	13	243	0	.39
Hot Dogs	15	75	50	2.28

When you finish the list, the Datasheet should look like the one shown in the following illustration.

tblProducts Table, Eight Products Entered

Product ID	Product Name	Supplier ID	Units In Stock	Units On Order	Unit Price
1	Bread	11	200	0	0.89
2	Pickles	13	250	0	0.95
3	Onions	13	150	0	0.69
4	Hot Sauce	13	98	200	2.98
5	Hamburger	15	45	50	4.25
6	Ketchup	13	300	0	0.79
7	Mustard	13	243	0	0.39
8	Hot Dogs	15	75	50	2.28
(AutoNumber)				0	

2. Click the Close button ❎ on the **tblProducts** table to close it.

   The data in the table is saved each time a record is entered.

3. Click the Close button ❎ on the Database window to close the database.

   The database is saved automatically when you close it.

4. Exit Access unless you are continuing with the Exercise Directions.

- **NOTE:** If you make a mistake and start a record over, the Product ID numbers may have gaps. Access does not reuse numbers in an AutoNumber field, so your numbers may differ from the illustrations in this lesson. The database is still correct.

In this exercise, you will enter data into a database that stores information for Arthur Treacher Middle School (a fictitious school) in Whitefish Bay, Wisconsin. As you enter data, you will use default values and learn about two other data entry aids—Input Mask and Lookup List.

EXERCISE DIRECTIONS

Open the Database and Open the Table

1. Start Access if it is not already running.
2. Open ⊙**02Arthur** from the data files.
3. Open the **tblStudents** table.

Add the First Record

1. Press Tab to move to the First Name field, and type **James**.
   Access assigns the ID # 1 automatically.
2. Press Tab to reach Middle Name, and type **Arthur**.
3. Press Tab to reach Last Name, and type **Holmes**.
4. Press Tab to reach Parent's Name, and type **Schwartz, Crystalen**.
5. Press Tab to reach Address, and type **34 Haddock Way**.
6. Press Tab twice to accept the default for City.
7. Press Tab again to accept the default value for State.
8. Press Tab again to accept the default for ZIP Code.
9. In the Phone Number field, type **5551111**.
   *The database designer has created a data entry aid called an **Input Mask**. The Input Mask for Phone Number speeds data entry by allowing you to type only the local telephone number. The area code and parentheses have already been entered as default values.*
   The hyphen that separates the prefix from the four-digit number also appears automatically.
10. Press Tab to reach the Notes field.
11. Press Tab to leave it blank.

Add Records 2 through 4

1. Press Tab to start the next record.
   Access assigns the ID # 2 automatically when you press Tab and start entering data in the First Name field.
2. Enter the data shown in Illustration A for records 2 – 4.
3. Accept the defaults for City, State, and ZIP Code.
4. Leave the Notes field blank.

Add Record 5 and Use Lookup List

1. For First Name, enter **Rosemarie**.
2. For Middle Name, enter **Judith**.
3. For Last Name, enter **Winderlin**.
4. For Parent's Name, enter **Winderlin, Robert**.
5. For Address, enter **1603 Robalo Ave**.
6. Accept the defaults for City and State.
7. In the ZIP Code field, click the drop-down arrow.
   A list of two ZIP Codes appears, 53217 and 53211, as shown below.

*The database designer has provided a data entry aid called a **Lookup List**. The Lookup List lets you to select the alternative ZIP Code 53217 when the default is not correct. (Whitefish Bay has two ZIP Codes; most Arthur Treacher students live in 53211, so it was used as the default.)*

8. Select *53217* from the list, and press Tab.
9. For Phone Number, enter **5554343**.

Illustration A. Records 2 – 4

First Name	Middle Name	Last Name	Parent's Name	Address	ZIP Code	Phone Number
Lawrence	Gilbert	Bommer	Bommer, Annette	1734 Sharkfin St	53211	(414) 555-1211
Miguel	Angel	Palacio	Palacio, Jose	846 Robalo Ave	53211	(414) 555-1345
Cassandra	Postman	Pierce	Pierce, Franklin	983 Snell Blvd	53211	(414) 555-6789

Add Records 6 through 16

1. Add the records shown in Illustration B.
   - Use the default values for City and State.
   - Use the Lookup List for ZIP Code when 53217 is needed.
   - Leave the Notes field blank for all records. *When you finish the last record, your Datasheet view should look like the one in Illustration C. (Your ID # fields may differ from the numbers shown.)*
   - To enter the data shown in the shaded cells, you can press Ctrl+' (single quotation mark). *Ctrl+' is a shortcut that copies the data from the same field in the previous record. (Note that the cells are shaded only to call attention to them; they will not be shaded in the Access table.)*

2. When you complete the records, review them for any typing errors.
   To correct an error, select the field, press the F2 key and position the insertion point to correct the error.

3. Close the table.

4. Close the database, and exit Access.

Illustration B. Records 6 – 16

First Name	Middle Name	Last Name	Parent's Name	Address	ZIP Code	Phone Number
Florence	Meisner	Wunderlich	Wunderlich, Fritz	1314 Trout St.	53211	(414) 555-5656
Maria	Elena	Agnelli	Agnelli, Louis	1532 Trout St.	53211	(414) 555-4646
Marya	Ukrania	Daniw	Daniw, Leo	1634 Robalo Ave.	53217	(414) 555-6767
Carlton	A.	Doermann	Morgenstern, Rhoda	1822 Haddock Way	53211	(414) 555-7373
Natasha	Nickolayevna	Borodin	Borodin, Nickolai	22 Alewife Lane	53211	(414) 555-9191
Raleigh		Durham	Durham, Leon	911 Garfish Ct.	53211	(414) 555-3232
Prudence	Nancy	VanAntwerp	VanAntwerp, Jay	36 Alewife Lane	53211	(414) 555-9988
Dill	Earl	VanAntwerp	VanAntwerp, Jay	36 Alewife Lane	53211	(414) 555-9988
Thomas	Charles	Purma	Purma, Susanna	986 Starfish Pl.	53217	(414) 555-2323
Sandra	Olivia	Newcomer	Newcomer, Ima	1234 Sharkfin St.	53211	(414) 555-2222
Sonya	French	Newcomer	Newcomer, Ima	1234 Sharkfin St.	53211	(414) 555-2222

Illustration C. Completed tblStudents Table

ID #	First Name	Middle Name	Last Name	Parent's Name	Address	City	State	ZIP Code	Phone Number	Notes
1	James	Arthur	Holmes	Schwartz, Crystalen	34 Haddock Way	Whitefish Bay	WI	53211	(414) 555-1111	
2	Lawrence	Gilbert	Bommer	Bommer, Annette	1734 Sharkfin St.	Whitefish Bay	WI	53211	(414) 555-1211	
3	Miguel	Angel	Palacio	Palacio, Jose	846 Robalo Ave.	Whitefish Bay	WI	53211	(414) 555-1345	
4	Cassandra	Postman	Pierce	Pierce, Franklin	983 Snell Blvd.	Whitefish Bay	WI	53211	(414) 555-6789	
5	Rosemarie	Judith	Winderlin	Winderlin, Robert	1603 Robalo Ave.	Whitefish Bay	WI	53217	(414) 555-4343	
6	Florence	Meisner	Wunderlich	Wunderlich, Fritz	1314 Trout St.	Whitefish Bay	WI	53211	(414) 555-5656	
7	Maria	Elena	Agnelli	Agnelli, Louis	1352 Trout St.	Whitefish Bay	WI	53211	(414) 555-4646	
8	Marya	Ukrania	Daniw	Daniw, Leo	1634 Robalo Ave	Whitefish Bay	WI	53217	(414) 555-6767	
9	Carlton	A.	Doermann	Morgenstern, Rhoda	1822 Haddock Way	Whitefish Bay	WI	53211	(414) 555-7373	
10	Natasha	Nickolayevna	Borodin	Borodin, Nickolai	22 Alewife Lane	Whitefish Bay	WI	53211	(414) 555-9191	
11	Raleigh		Durham	Durham, Leon	911 Garfish Ct.	Whitefish Bay	WI	53211	(414) 555-3232	
12	Prudence	Nancy	VanAntwerp	VanAntwerp, Jay	36 Alewife Lane	Whitefish Bay	WI	53211	(414) 555-9898	
13	Dill	Earl	VanAntwerp	VanAntwerp, Jay	36 Alewife Lane	Whitefish Bay	WI	53211	(414) 555-9898	
14	Thomas	Charles	Purma	Purma, Susanna	986 Starfish Pl.	Whitefish Bay	WI	53217	(414) 555-2323	
15	Sandra	Olivia	Newcomer	Newcomer, Ima	1234 Sharkfin St.	Whitefish Bay	WI	53211	(414) 555-2222	
16	Sonya	French	Newcomer	Newcomer, Ima	1234 Sharkfin St.	Whitefish Bay	WI	53211	(414) 555-2222	
						Whitefish Bay	WI	53211		

tblStudents : Table

Exercise 3

Work with Table Design
■ Modify a Table Design ■ Change Column Widths ■ Summary of Data Entry Aids

NOTES

Modify a Table Design

■ In Exercise 2, you added records in Datasheet view. In this exercise, you will learn about Design view, which lets you change the characteristics of a table's fields. In Design view, you control field names, the types of data the fields can contain, and the kinds of entries that are valid (acceptable) in the field.

▣Try It!

1. Start Access.
2. Open 🔘 **03GoodStuff** from the data files.
3. Select the **tblProducts** table, and click the <u>D</u>esign button on the database window.

   OR

   Open the **tblProducts** table, and click the Design View button on the toolbar.

   The tblProducts table opens in Design view as shown below.

tblProducts Table in Design View

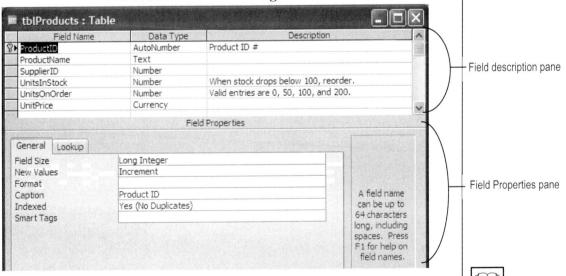

Field description pane

Field Properties pane

*Table Design view has two panes. The upper pane contains the field names, their data types, and their descriptions. The lower pane specifies the characteristics (called **Field Properties**) of the field currently selected.*

The following indicator appears on the status bar:

Design view. F6 = Switch panes. F1 = Help.

📖

Data Type
The data type limits the kind of data the field can store.

4. Click in the ProductID cell if it is not already selected.

ProductID is designated as the primary key, as indicated by the key symbol . *Its data type is set to AutoNumber. During data entry, it automatically increases by one each time a new record is added, providing a unique primary key for each record.*

5. Look in the Field Properties pane at the Field Size property.

It is set to Long Integer.

6. Click Long Integer in the Field Properties pane, and press the F1 key.

Access displays a Help window that describes the options available for the Field Size property. (Maximize the Help window if necessary to see the information about the Field Size property.) Note that Long Integer is a whole number (no fractions) between −2,147,483,648 and 2,147,483,647. Since AutoNumber is always a positive number, it can identify over two billion records in the same table.

7. Click the Close button ❌ on the Help window.

8. Look at the Caption property.

Caption defines the name of the field when you view the table in Datasheet view. If you leave it blank, the field name is used as the caption.

🖥️ Try It!

Make Required Fields

One way to help make sure that data is entered accurately is to require an entry in a field. When a field is **required**, Access does not allow the field to remain empty during data entry.

1. Click in the ProductName cell in the upper pane.

Its Data Type is Text. In the Field Properties pane, its Field Size specifies that the ProductName field can store up to 50 characters. The Caption is set to Product Name.

2. Click in the Required property in the Field Properties pane.

3. Click the drop-down list arrow ⌄ at the right of the box.

4. Select Yes from the list.

5. Click in the UnitsInStock field in the upper pane.

Note the phrase in the Description field. These are the words that appear in the status bar as a reminder during data entry.

6. Make UnitsInStock a required field by selecting Yes from the drop-down list in the Required property in the Field Properties pane.

🖥️ Try It!

Create a Lookup List

In the Exercise Directions of Exercise 2, you used a Lookup List for the ZIP Code. In this Try It!, you will create a Lookup List for the UnitsOnOrder field, which can contain only 0, 50, 100, or 200.

1. Click in the UnitsOnOrder field in the top pane.

Note that the default value in Field Properties is set to 0.

2. In the Data Type field, click the drop-down arrow and select Lookup Wizard.

Key field

A **key field** is a field by which a table file is sorted or searched. For example, if a file of names and addresses is to be sorted by ZIP Code, then ZIP Code is the key field.

A **primary key** is a field whose values uniquely identify each record in a database, just as a license plate number identifies a car, and which is used by one table to refer to specific records in another table.

Field Names and Captions

In Design view, the field names are *ProductName, SupplierID, UnitsInStock,* and so on. In Datasheet view, the Caption properties, *Product Name, Supplier ID, Units In Stock,* and so on, display as the field names.

Required Field

To help during data entry, you might put a notation such as REQUIRED as part of the field description in the top pane.

Select Lookup Wizard

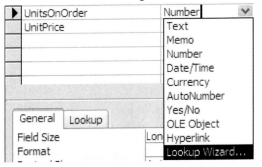

Access displays the first Lookup Wizard dialog box

Lookup Wizard, Choose Data Source

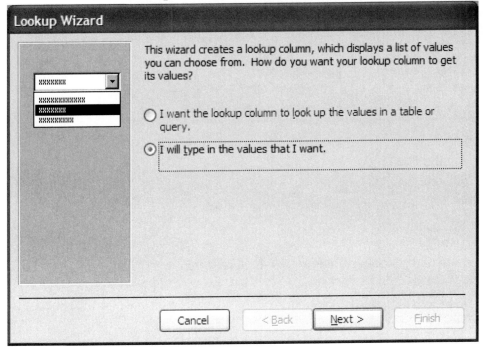

3. Select *I will type in the values that I want.*

4. Click the Next button [Next >].

   Access displays a dialog box that lets you specify the values you want for the lookup list.

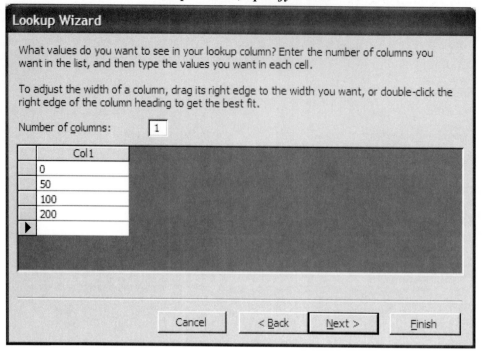

5. Leave the *Number of columns* as 1.
6. Press the Tab key to reach the field under Col1.
7. Type **0**, and press the Tab key.
8. Type **50**, press Tab, type **100**, press Tab, and type **200**, as shown in the preceding illustration.
9. Click the Next button [Next >].
10. Accept the suggested name for the lookup column UnitsOnOrder by clicking the Finish button [Finish].
11. Click the Lookup tab in the Field Properties pane.
   It should look as shown in the following illustration.

Lookup Tab

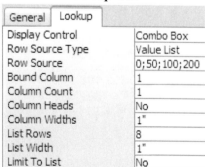

12. Click the Save button 💾 on the toolbar to save the table design.
   Access may display a message warning that the rules for data integrity have changed and may cause a loss of data, as shown in the illustration on the next page.

Data Integrity Message

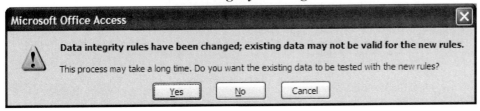

> **Microsoft Office Access**
>
> ⚠ Data integrity rules have been changed; existing data may not be valid for the new rules.
>
> This process may take a long time. Do you want the existing data to be tested with the new rules?
>
> [Yes] [No] [Cancel]

13. Answer Yes [Yes] to the question.

The changes you just made will not change existing data.

🖥 Try It!

Add a Record to Check the Design Changes

1. Click the Datasheet View button 🔲 ▾ on the toolbar.

   The tblProducts table appears in Datasheet view.

2. Enter the following record. (Click Product Name field in the last row of the table.) When you reach the Units On Order field, click the drop-down list arrow ▾ to display the Lookup List you just created, and select the number shown in the following illustration.

Product Name	Supplier ID	Units In Stock	Units On Order	Unit Price
Paper Plates	14	90	200	.20

3. Enter the following record. Try to leave the Units In Stock field blank as indicated in the table.

Product Name	Supplier ID	Units In Stock	Units On Order	Unit Price
Napkins	14		0	.59

When you press Tab after typing the Unit Price, Access displays a message indicating that the field cannot contain a Null value and that you must make an entry in the UnitsInStock field. This message appears because the field is now a Required field.

4. Click OK.

5. Enter **300** in the Units In Stock field.

6. Add the following record.

Product Name	Supplier ID	Units In Stock	Units On Order	Unit Price
Forks	14	325	0	.20

The tblProducts table in Datasheet view should look like the one shown on the next page.

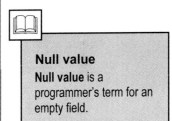

Null value
Null value is a programmer's term for an empty field.

tblProducts Table with Eleven Records Entered

tblProducts : Table

Product ID	Product Name	Supplier ID	Units In Stock	Units On Order	Unit Price
1	Bread	11	200	0	0.89
2	Pickles	13	250	0	0.95
3	Onions	13	150	0	0.69
4	Hot Sauce	13	98	200	2.98
5	Hamburger	15	45	50	4.25
6	Ketchup	13	300	0	0.79
7	Mustard	13	243	0	0.39
8	Hot Dogs	15	75	50	2.28
9	Paper Plates	14	90	200	0.20
10	Napkins	14	300	0	0.59
11	Forks	14	325	0	0.20
(AutoNumber)				0	

Change Column Widths

- To see all data in table displays, you may need to change the column widths. Changes in the width of columns in Datasheet view do not affect the field size.

💻 Try It!

1. With **tblProducts** open, point the mouse to the boundary between Product ID and Product Name.

2. Double-click the boundary line.

   Access adjusts the width to best fit the longest entry in the column.

   OR

   Drag the boundary to the left until the column is slightly larger than the field caption (Product ID), as shown below.

Drag Column Boundary

tblProducts : Table

Product ID	Product Name
1	Bread
2	Pickles
3	Onions
4	Hot Sauce

You have changed the column width of the first field. You can change other column widths using either of these techniques. The next few steps show you how to adjust all column widths to best fit the longest entry in each field.

3. Point to the field caption Product ID.

   The pointer changes to the Column Select arrow ↓ .

4. Click to select the column.

5. Hold the Shift key, and select all the other columns in the table.

6. Click Format, Column Width (Alt+O, C).

   Access displays the Column Width dialog box shown in the following illustration.

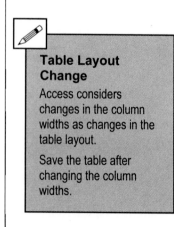

Table Layout Change

Access considers changes in the column widths as changes in the table layout.

Save the table after changing the column widths.

380

Column Width Dialog Box

7. Click the Best Fit button [Best Fit].
   Access changes the column widths to accommodate the longest entry in each field.

8. Click the Save button 🖫 to save the changes to the table layout.

9. Close the **tblProducts** table, and close the database. Exit Access unless you are continuing with the Exercise Directions after reviewing the Summary of Data Entry Aids that follows.

Summary of Data Entry Aids

- The following is a brief summary of the aids you can provide in Design view to help during data entry.

AutoNumber Data Type

Each record in a table needs a unique identifier. Using the AutoNumber data type for the first field ensures that each record will be identified by a unique number. This field is also usually designated as the primary key field of the record.

Status Bar Messages (Descriptions)

In the **Description** cell of each field, you can enter a message that appears in the status bar when the field is selected during data entry.

Formats

The Format property can aid in data entry by specifying the kind of display expected for numeric fields. For example, the UnitPrice field in the tblProducts table has a data type of Number and a Format of Currency using the Fixed format with two decimal places.

Input Mask

As you saw with the Phone Number in the Arthur Treacher School database, an Input Mask formats data so that fewer keystrokes are needed to complete a field.

Validation Rules and Validation Text

Validation rules set criteria for values that can be entered in a field. Validation text is displayed when entries in the field violate the validation rule.

Default Values

When you specify a **default value** for a field, that value is automatically entered when a new field is created. This is very useful if the majority of the entries are the same. In the tblProducts table, 0 is the default value for UnitsOnOrder because most of the entries do not require other values in that field. In the Arthur Treacher School database, the default City and State may never need changing.

Required Fields

If you require a field, data for the field *must* be entered before the record can be saved.

> *In this exercise, you will modify the design of the tblStudents table in the Arthur Treacher School database.*

EXERCISE DIRECTIONS

Open the Database and Open the tblStudents Table in Design View

1. Start Access if it is not already running.
2. Open 💿 **03Arthur** from the data files.
3. Open the **tblStudents** table in Design view.
   a. Select tblStudents.
   b. Click the <u>D</u>esign button 📝 <u>Design</u> on the database window.

   OR

   a. Double-click **tblStudents** to open it in Datasheet view.
   b. Click the Design View button 📝 ▾ on the toolbar.

   The tblStudents table opens in Design view.

Add Descriptions

1. Add and change the Description for the fields, as shown in Illustration A.

   Note that some entries may already exist.

2. Click the Save button 💾 to save the changes to the table design.

Set Required Fields and Rename Fields

1. Click in the FirstName field.
2. In the Field Properties pane, click in the Required property.
3. Click the drop-down arrow 🔽 and select Yes.
4. Click LastName in the top pane.
5. Set its Required property to Yes.
6. Make the following fields required as well:
   ParentsNames, Address, City, StateOrProvince, PostalCode
7. Click the Save button 💾 to save the changes to the table design. Click Yes, if prompted.
8. Click in the StateOrProvince field in the upper pane.
9. Press the F2 key to edit the field.
10. Change the field name to State.
11. Change the PostalCode field name to ZIPCode.
12. Click the Save button 💾 to save the changes to the table design. Click <u>Y</u>es, if prompted.
13. Close the table.
14. Close the database, and exit Access.

Illustration A. Descriptions for Fields in tblStudents Table

Field Name	Description
StudentID	Do not type anything in this field; it's automatic.
FirstName	REQUIRED
MiddleName	Middle name or initial.
LastName	REQUIRED
ParentsNames	REQUIRED: Last name, first name of one parent or guardian.
Address	REQUIRED: Student's street address and Apt. # (if any).
City	REQUIRED
StateOrProvince	REQUIRED
PostalCode	REQUIRED: Use drop-down list.
PhoneNumber	Local telephone number; no separators needed.
Notes	Additional information about student.

Exercise 4

Create a Database and Table
■ Create a Database ■ Set File Format Option
■ Convert Database to Access 2002 – 2003 File Format
■ Create a Table Using the Table Wizard ■ Modify the Table Design

NOTES

Create a Database

- When you start a new database, you name and create a database **file**. This file will contain the database's objects—tables, queries, forms, and reports. In this exercise, you will create a database, then a table.

- In the Try It! activities of this exercise, you will begin creating a database of addresses for your personal use.

🖥️Try It!

1. Start Access.
2. On the Getting Started task pane, click the Create a new file option.

   Access displays the New File task pane.

3. On the New File task pane, click Blank Database 📄 Blank database... to start a new database. (The other options on the task pane are outside the scope of this book.)

   The File New Database dialog box appears with the default file name db1.mdb (or dbn.mdb) highlighted.

4. Change to the folder where you want to store the database.
5. Type **My Address Book** in the File name box.

Getting Started Task Pane

Click to start a new blank database.

File New Database Dialog Box

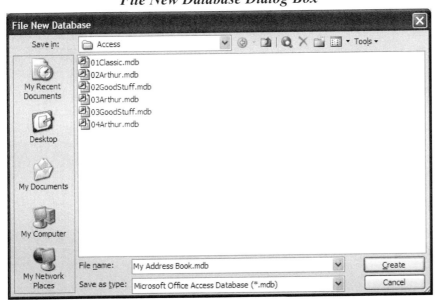

6. Click the Create button [Create], or press Enter.

*Access creates the new file in the folder shown in the Save in box and displays the Database window of the **My Address Book** database.*

My Address Book Database Window

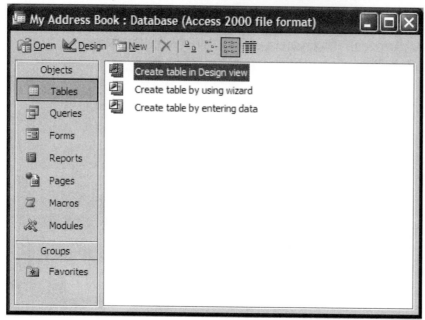

Set File Format Option

- As you can see in the preceding illustration, the default file format for new Access databases is set to Access 2000. Before you create other new databases with Access 2003, you should set the file format option to Access 2002 - 2003, especially if you want to take advantage of its features added since Microsoft Office 2000. If the title bar of your new database displays **(Access 2002 -2003 file format)**, your system is already set to create files in Access 2002 - 2003 format.

🖥 Try It!

1. Click Tools, Options (Alt+T, O).
2. Click the Advanced tab.
3. Click the drop-down arrow for the Default File Format field.
4. Select Access 2002 – 2003.
5. Click the OK button [OK].

Select Access 2002 - 2003 as Default File Format

Default File Format

Access 2000	⌄
Access 2000	
Access 2002 - 2003	

Convert Database to Access 2002 - 2003 File Format

- If your My Address Book database is in Access 2000 file format, you can convert it to the file format of Access 2002 - 2003.

💻**Try It!**

1. With the database open, click Tools, and point to Database Utilities

2. Point to Convert Database and select To Access 2002 -2003 File Format.

Convert to Access 2002 - 2003 File Format

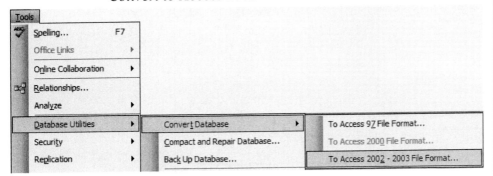

Access displays the Convert Database Into dialog box.

3. Give the converted database a new name (My Address Book 2003, for example).

4. Click the Save button [Save].

Access displays a message telling you that the converted file cannot be used by users of Access 2000 or Access 97. Access leaves the current database open; it does not automatically open the converted database.

5. Close the Access 2000 version of the database.

6. Open the converted database from the location where you saved it.

Create a Table Using the Table Wizard

- You are now ready to create a table. In this case, you will create a table that stores the names, addresses, and home telephone numbers of the people you want to put in your address book.

💻**Try It!**

Select Fields for the Table

1. Double-click the option *Create table by using wizard*
   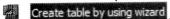.

   The first Table Wizard dialog box appears.

2. Click the Personal option to list sample databases for personal use.

Table Wizard Dialog Box 1

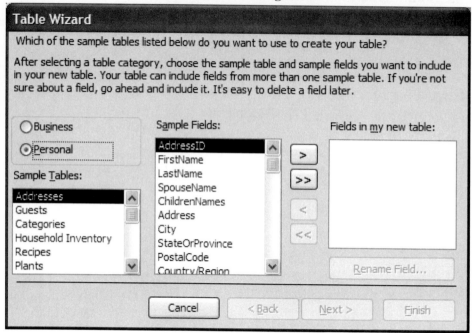

3. Select Addresses in the Sample Tables list if necessary.
   The Sample Fields box lists fields for an Addresses table.

4. Double-click AddressID in the Sample Fields box, or select
   AddressID and click the Add Field button [>].
   The predefined AddressID field appears in the Fields in my new table box.

5. Add the following fields, using the same method as in Step 4:
   FirstName, LastName, Address, City, StateOrProvince, PostalCode,
   Country/Region, EmailAddress, HomePhone

6. In the Fields in my new table box, select Address.

7. In the Sample Fields box, select Address.

8. Click the Add Field button [>].
   *Address1 appears under Address. This gives you two fields for the
   address—one for the street address and another for apartment or
   floor.*

Try It!

Rename Fields

You can rename fields as part of table design, but you can also rename
fields using the wizard during table creation.

1. In the Fields in my new table box, select Address1.

2. Click the Rename Field button [Rename Field...].
   *Access displays the Rename Field dialog box shown in the following
   illustration.*

Rename Field Dialog Box

3. Change the field name to **Address2** and click the OK button OK or press Enter.

4. In the Fields in my new table box, select Address.

5. Click the Rename Field button Rename Field....

6. Change the field name to **Address1** and click the OK button OK or press Enter.

7. Use the same procedure to change *StateOrProvince* to **State**, and *PostalCode* to **ZIPCode**.

Try It!

Name the Table and Set a Primary Key

1. Click the Next button Next > (Alt+N).

The next Table Wizard dialog box appears, with a suggested (default) name for the new table.

2. Change the default name to **tblNameAndAddress**.

3. Select *Yes, set a primary key for me.*

Table Wizard Dialog Box, Name and Primary Key Options

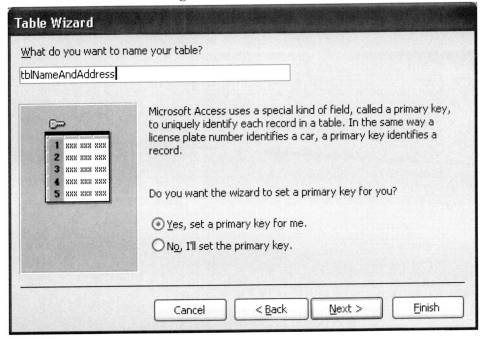

Object Names

The addition of the prefix *tbl* to a table name helps identify the object as a table. When you create other objects, you will use different prefixes to help identify the object type.

💻**Try It!**

Choose to Modify the Table Design

1. Click the <u>N</u>ext button | Next > | (Alt+N).

   The final dialog box of the Table Wizard appears.

2. Select <u>M</u>odify the table design.

3. Click the <u>F</u>inish button | Finish |, or press Enter.

   The tblNameAndAddress table appears in Design view, as shown below.

Table Wizard Dialog Box, Final Options

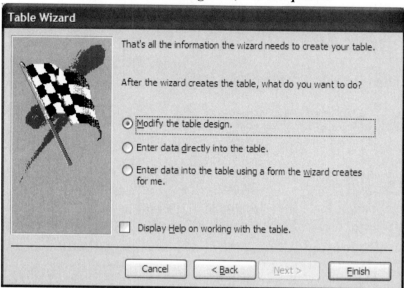

tblNameAndAddress Table in Design View

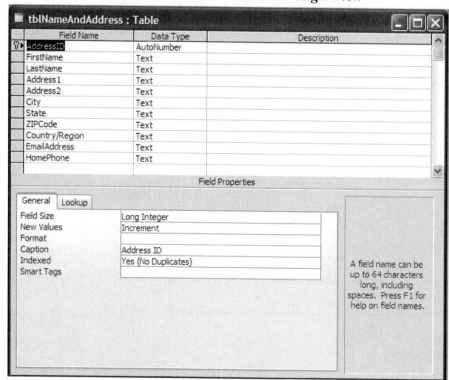

Modify the Table Design

- The table as created by the Table Wizard needs some changes to the design to make data entry easier.

Try It!

1. Change the Field Size property of Address1 to **50**, and change its Caption property to **Address 1**.

2. Change the Field Size property of Address2 to **50**, and change its Caption property to **Address 2**.

3. Change the Caption property of ZIPCode to **ZIP Code**.

4. Select the Country/Region field, and

   - Change its field name to Country by deleting /Region.

   - Change ts caption to Country by deleting /Region.

   - Change its default value property to **USA**.

5. Press the Tab key.

   Access places quotation marks around the entry. USA is now the default value for Country.

6. Click the Save button to save the changes to the design.

7. Click the Datasheet View button 〓 ▾ on the toolbar to switch to Datasheet view.

Try It!

Add Records

1. Add the following two records.

   Note that you must type the entire telephone number, including area code. Area code is not part of the input mask.

First Name	Last Name	Address 1	Address 2	City
Scott	Freeh	275 Madison Ave.		New York
Roger	Houston	275 Madison Ave.		New York

State	ZIP Code	Email Address	Phone Number
NY	10016	sfreeh@zzzyyy.net	(212) 555-5556
NY	10016	rhouston@zzzyyy.net	(212) 555-5567

   Note that your ZIP Code field may include a hyphen. See the side note to learn how to avoid this hyphen.

2. Add your own name and address.

3. Add a friend to the table.

   Note that the data files for this database in later exercises will not contain these additional records unless you use your own My Address Book database.

4. Close the table.

5. Close the database, and exit Access unless you are continuing with the Exercise Directions.

✓

Edit Input Mask

The default input mask for ZIP Codes causes a hyphen to display in the field even if you do not have the four-digit extension to the ZIP Code. You can prevent the hyphen from displaying by completing the following steps:

1. Click in the Input Mask property of PostalCode.

2. Replace the \- with a C (uppercase).

   If you want to include the four-digit extension to a ZIP Code, you must then type the hyphen.

   In the illustrations, data files, and solutions for this book, the hyphens are not displayed.

> *In this exercise, you will use the Table Wizard to build a table that stores information about teachers.*

EXERCISE DIRECTIONS

Open the Database

1. Start Access if it is not already running.
2. Open 🖭 **04Arthur** from the data files.

Create a Table

1. Click the Tables button ⊞ Tables on the Objects bar if it is not already selected.
2. Double-click the option *Create table by using wizard* 🖭 Create table by using wizard .
3. Select Bu<u>s</u>iness and in the list of Sample <u>T</u>ables, select Students, as shown in Illustration A.

Illustration A. Select Students Sample Table

4. Click the Add All Fields button >> to put all fields in the Fields in my new table box.
5. Select Major in the Fields in <u>m</u>y new table box, and click the Remove Field button < to remove it from the list.
6. Select StudentNumber and remove it from the list.
7. Select ParentsNames and rename it to **SpouseName**.
8. Select StateOrProvince and rename it to **State**.
9. Select PostalCode and rename it to **ZIPCode**.
10. Click the <u>N</u>ext button Next > .
    The Table Wizard dialog box for naming the table appears.
11. In the naming dialog box, change the suggested table name to **tblTeachers**.
12. Allow Access to set a primary key.
13. Click the <u>N</u>ext button Next > .
    The Table Wizard dialog box for relationships appears with the Students table selected.

Tell Access the Tables are Not Related

When a new table is created by the Table Wizard, Access lets you indicate whether the tables are related. You need to specify that the tables, in this instance, are not related.

1. Click the <u>R</u>elationships button Relationships... .
   Access displays the Relationships dialog box.

Relationships Dialog Box

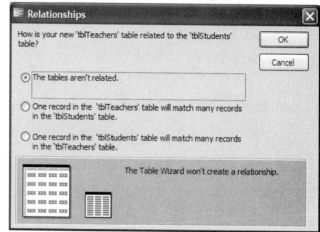

2. Select *The tables aren't related* option
   ⊙ The tables aren't related. .
3. Click the OK button OK .
4. Click the <u>N</u>ext button Next > .
5. Select <u>M</u>odify the table design.
6. Click the <u>F</u>inish button Finish .
   The tblTeachers table opens in Design view.

Modify the Table Design

1. Change the StudentID field name to **TeacherID**.
2. Add the following description to the TeacherID field: **Do not type anything in this field; it's automatic.**
3. Change its Caption property to **Teacher ID**.
4. Note that the captions for FirstName and Last Name are set to *First Name* and *Last Name*.
5. In the Description cell of SpouseName, type **First and last names of husband or wife or NONE.**
6. Change its Caption property to **Spouse's Name**.
7. In the Description cell of Address type **Street address and apartment number, if any.**
8. Change the Field Size property of Address to **75**.
9. Make the default value for State *"WI"*.
10. Change the Caption property of ZIPCode to **ZIP Code**.
11. In the Description cell of PhoneNumber, type **Home telephone number.**
12. Change the Field Name EmailName to **EmailAddress**.
13. Change its Caption to **Email Address.**
14. For the Notes field, add the following description: **Additional information about the teacher.**
15. Click the Save button .
16. Click the Datasheet View button .
17. Click the Close button to close the table.
18. Close the database, and exit Access.

Exercise 5

Create and Use a Form
■ Create a Form Using AutoForm ■ Add a Record in Form View ■ Modify a Form

NOTES

Create a Form Using AutoForm

- Another data entry aid that Access provides is the **form**. You can use it to enter, display, and edit data. As you enter data in a form, you are also adding it to the table(s) on which the form is based. A form provides another way of looking at the data in a table. The table shows all data at once; the form shows data one record at a time.

- In Access you can create forms using Design view, AutoForm, or the Form Wizard.

🖳Try It!

Create the Form

1. Open 💿 **05GoodStuff** from the data files.

2. Click the Tables button [🔲 Tables] on the Objects bar.

3. Select the **tblProducts** table, but do not open it.

4. Click the drop-down arrow on the New Object button [🔏 ▾] on the toolbar, and select the AutoForm option [🔏 AutoForm] from the drop-down list.

   Your New Object button may have a different appearance. It is located near the right end of the toolbar, just to the left of the Help button as shown on the right. The appearance of the New Object button depends on the last object created using the button.

   Access creates and displays the form using the Standard style.

5. Click the Save button [💾] on the toolbar.

   Access displays a Save As dialog box with the suggested name tblProducts.

6. Change the suggested name to **frmProducts**, and click the OK button [OK].

New Object Menu

New Object Table Button on Toolbar

New Object: Table

New Object AutoForm Button on Toolbar

New Object: AutoForm

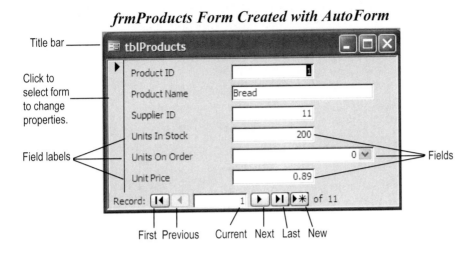

frmProducts Form Created with AutoForm

Title bar

Click to
select form
to change
properties.

Field labels

Fields

First Previous   Current Next Last New

Add a Record in Form View

- When you use a form to enter or edit data, the changes are automatically reflected in the table that was used as the record source for the form.

- To move from field to field within a form, press the Tab key. You can also select a specific field and change its contents by clicking and editing the field.

Try It!

1. Click the New record button ▶✱ at the bottom of the form, or click the Next record button ▶ until a blank form appears.

2. Press the Tab key to let Access complete the Product ID field.

3. Complete the remaining fields as shown below.

Spoons Record for Products

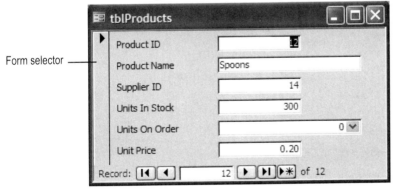

Form selector

4. Press the Tab key after completing Unit Price to display a new blank record.

5. Press the Previous record button ◀ to redisplay the Spoons record.

6. Click the Tables button [Tables] on the Objects bar.

7. Open the **tblProducts** table to verify that the Spoons record has been added.

8. Close the table.

Modify a Form

- A form can be modified in several ways. You can change its title bar by changing the form's Caption property. You can modify the form's background and text appearance by using one of several AutoFormats that Access provides. You can add and delete fields. You can also rearrange the position and size of fields on a form.

📺 Try It!

Modify the Form's Title Bar

Note that the title bar of the form retains the name *tblProducts* even though the object's name is *frmProducts*. When a form is created with AutoForm, Access uses the source of the records (*tblProducts*) as the window title. You can change this title bar display.

1. Click the Form selector at the left side of the form (see the previous illustration).

   Selecting the form permits you to change the properties of the form itself rather than a field within the form.

2. Click the Properties button on the toolbar.

   OR

   Right-click on the Form selector and click the <u>P</u>roperties option
   [🖳 <u>P</u>roperties] section.

   *Access displays the Form **properties** box, as shown below.*

📖

Properties
Objects and fields within objects are defined by their **properties**. During table design, you were specifying properties for each field in the table.

When you work with a form, you can define properties for the form itself and for each field within the form.

Form Properties

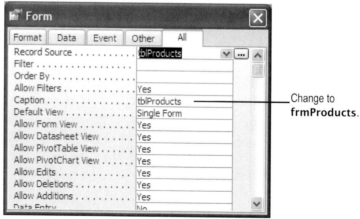

Change to **frmProducts**.

Right-Click Menu

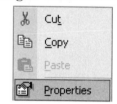

✂	Cu<u>t</u>
📋	<u>C</u>opy
📋	<u>P</u>aste
🖳	<u>P</u>roperties

3. Click the All tab if it is not already selected.
4. Locate the Caption property.
5. Change it to **frmProducts**.
6. Click the Close button ❌ on the Form properties box to close it.
   The form's title bar now displays frmProducts.

📺 Try It!

Modify the Form's Background

1. Click the Design View button on the toolbar.
   The form is displayed in Design view.

2. Click Format, AutoFormat on the menu.
Access displays the AutoFormat dialog box, shown in the following illustration.

AutoFormat Dialog Box

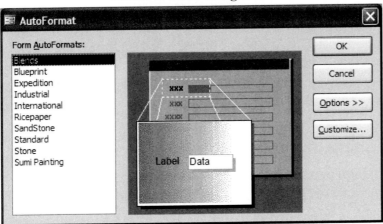

3. Select Blends from the list, and click OK [OK].
Access applies the AutoFormat.

4. Click the Form View button [▦ ▾] on the toolbar.
Access displays the form in Form view.

🖥 Try It!

Delete a Field from a Form

When you enter data into a form, the data is also automatically entered into the table used as a source for the form. If you have an AutoNumber field in each record, you can eliminate one keystroke during data entry by deleting the field from the form. It will be updated automatically as each record is completed.

1. Click the Design View button [◹ ▾] on the toolbar.
The form is displayed in Design view.

2. Click the ProductID field (not the field label) to select it.
Both the field name and the field are selected.

3. Press the Delete key.
The ProductID field label and field disappear from the form.

🖥 Try It!

Reposition Fields on a Form

You now have empty space at the top of the form. You can move the fields up to use this space.

1. Hold down the Shift key and click to select each remaining field (not the field label).
If you need to enlarge the Form window to see all the fields in Design view, point to its bottom edge and drag down.

2. Point to the middle of any field text box.
The mouse pointer turns into a hand 🖑 .

3. Click and drag the fields toward the top of the form, as shown in the following illustration.

Dragging Form Fields

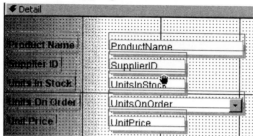

4. When ProductName is near the top of the form, release the mouse button.
5. Point to the bottom edge of the form grid.
   The pointer turns into a horizontal two-headed arrow ✛.
6. Drag the border up until it is within a couple of rows of dots of the last field.
7. Click the Save button 🖫 to save the changes to the form design.
8. Click the Form View button 🖾 ▾ on the toolbar.
   Access displays the form in Form view.
9. Click Window, Size to Fit Form, as shown below.
   The window size adjusts to fit the new size of the form.

Size to Fit Form

Window
Tile Horizontally
Tile Vertically
Cascade
Arrange Icons
Hide
Unhide...
Size to Fit Form
1 05GoodStuff : Database (Access 2002 - 2003 file format)
✓ 2 frmProducts

Your form should now resemble the one in the following illustration.

Completed Form After Modifications

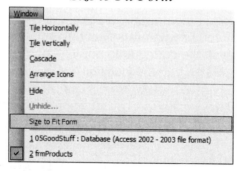

10. Click the Save button 🖫 to save the changes.
11. Close the form, close the database, and exit Access unless you are continuing with the Exercise Directions.

In this exercise, you will create a form using the AutoForm function. The form will let you add information to the Teachers table for Arthur Treacher Middle School.

EXERCISE DIRECTIONS

Create a Form using AutoForm

1. Start Access if it is not already running.
2. Open ✪ **05Arthur** from the data files.
3. Click the Tables button [🗔 Tables] on the Objects bar.
4. Select the **tblTeachers** table, but do not open it.
5. Click the drop-down arrow on the New Object button [📇 ▾] on the toolbar.
6. Select the AutoForm option [📇 AutoForm].
   Access creates and displays the form using the Standard style. This method ensures that all the field names are visible. With the wizard, some of the field names are partly obscured.
7. Click the Save button [🖫] on the toolbar.
   Access asks you to name the form.
8. Name the form **frmTeachers**, and click OK.

Change the Form's Background

1. Click the Design View button [📐 ▾] on the toolbar.
   The form is displayed in Design view.
2. Click Format, AutoFormat on the menu.
   Access displays the AutoFormat dialog box.

3. Select Industrial from the list, and click OK.
   Access applies the AutoFormat.
4. Click the Form View button [📇 ▾] on the toolbar.
   Access displays the form in Form view.

Change the Form's Caption

Note that the title bar of the form retains the name tblTeachers even though the object's name is frmTeachers. You can change this title bar display.

1. Click the form selector at the left side of the form.
2. Click the Properties button on the toolbar.
3. Click the All tab if it is not already selected.
4. Locate the Caption property.
5. Change it to **frmTeachers**.
6. Click the Close button on the Form properties box to close it.
   The form's title bar now displays frmTeachers.

Add Records

1. Use Form view to add the records shown in Illustration A.
2. To start, click the New Record button [▶✱] at the bottom of the form to display a blank record.

Illustration A. Teacher Information to Input using Form

First	Middle	Last	Spouse	Address
Bruce	F.	Sonoma	Anna Sonoma	89 Alewife Lane
Cheryl	Regina	Miller	Pablo Miller	1945 American Way, Apt. 612
Bertha		Fuhlhage		467 Robalo Ave.
Anne	Reilly	Wood	Merrill O. Wood	3722 Watson Ave.
Edmund	J.	Wilson	Nancy Wilson	484 Robalo Ave.
Larry	Dean	Thomas		7684 Millington Ave,

City	State	ZIP Code	Phone	Email	Notes
Whitefish Bay	WI	53211	(414) 555-4567	Bsonoma@atms.edu	
Glendale	WI	53211	(414) 555-3456	Gbball@atms.edu	
Whitefish Bay	WI	53217	(414) 555-2345	Bspanish@atms.edu	
Milwaukee	WI	53221	(414) 555-5432	Awood@atms.edu	
Whitefish Bay	WI	53217	(414) 555-6543	Musicman@atms.edu	
Milwaukee	WI	53263	(414) 555-7654	Chorale@atms.edu	

Print the Form

1. When you have added all the records, click the Print Preview button 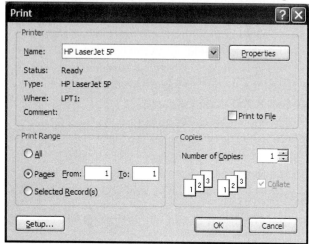.

   Access displays the forms on several pages in Portrait orientation, with three or so forms per page.

2. Close the Print Preview window.

3. Click File, Print and choose to print Pages From 1 to 1, as shown in Illustration B, to print the first page of the form.

4. Click OK to print.

Illustration B. Print Dialog Box to Print Page 1

Print the Table

1. Close the Form.

2. Click the Tables button Tables on the Objects bar and open the **tblTeachers** table.

3. Print one copy of the table in Landscape orientation with margins of 1". (See Exercise 1.)

   The table prints on two pages, breaking after ZIP Code.

4. Close the table.

5. Close the database, and exit Access.

Exercise 6

Filter and Sort a Database
■ Filter By Selection ■ Filter By Form ■ Advanced Filter/Sort

NOTES

Filter By Selection

- A **filter** lets you select records in a table or form based on criteria you specify. In the following Try It! activity, you will specify a filter by selecting a field in a form and requesting Access to display all matching records.

💻 Try It!

1. Start Access.
2. Open ⊚ **06My Address Book** from the data files.
3. Click the Forms button ⊞ Forms on the Objects bar.
4. Open the **frmNameAndAddress** form.
5. Click the Next Record button ▶ until you find the first person who lives in Illinois (IL).
6. Click in the State field.
7. Click the Filter By Selection button 🏷 on the toolbar, or click Records, Filter, Filter By Selection (Alt+R, F, S).

   Access displays the first record that matches the selected field. After a brief pause, it also displays the number of records that match, as shown below.

   *The records that display are called a **recordset** because they are a set of selected records, not the entire table.*

   Status Bar of Form Window with Filter By Selection

   Record: ◄◄ ◄ [1] ▶ ▶◄ ▶※ of 14 (Filtered) ─── Number of records that match the filter criteria

8. Click the Next Record button ▶ until you have reviewed several of the matching records.
9. Click the Remove Filter button 🏷 on the toolbar to remove the filter.

Filter By Form

- When you use the Filter By Form option, you enter the criteria you want to use to find matching records.

💻 Try It!

1. With **frmNameAndAddress** open, click the Filter By Form button 🗏 on the toolbar.

   Access displays a blank form with the filter criteria most recently used, as shown in the illustration on the next page.

Form for Filter By Form

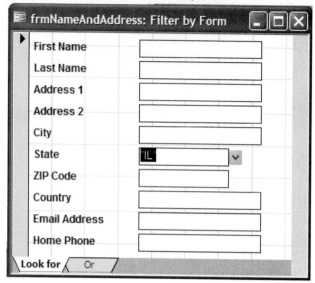

2. Delete the entry in the State field.

3. Click the City field, and click the drop-down list arrow and select *Scott City* from the list.

   The Records menu changes to become the Filter menu.

4. Click the Apply Filter button , or click Filter, Apply Filter/Sort (Alt+R, Y).

   Access displays the first record in the table that matches the filter, and changes the Filter menu back to the Records menu.

First Matching Record Displayed

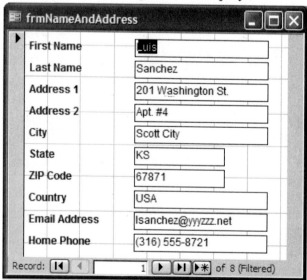

5. Click the Next Record button ▶ until you have looked at all the records that match the filter.

6. Click the Remove Filter button ▼, or click Records, Remove Filter/Sort (Alt+R, R).

7. Leave the **frmNameAndAddress** form open.

Filter by More than one Field

You can filter by more than one field by entering criteria in additional fields.

Advanced Filter/Sort

■ Another way to set criteria for a filter is to use the Advanced Filter/Sort feature.

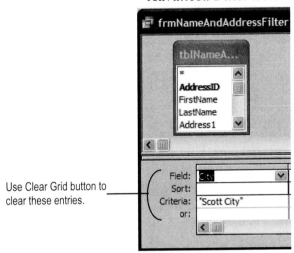💻Try It!

1. Click <u>R</u>ecords, <u>F</u>ilter, <u>A</u>dvanced Filter/Sort (Alt+R, F, A).

   Access displays a window that contains a list of the fields in the table and a grid.

Advanced Filter Sort

Use Clear Grid button to clear these entries.

2. Click the Clear Grid (delete) button ✖.

   The entries in the lower part of the grid are erased.

3. In the field list in the top pane, click on LastName and drag it to the Field cell in the first column of the grid in the lower part of the window.

   As you drag, the pointer turns into the Drag Field pointer 🔲.

4. Release the mouse button when the pointer is in the Field cell of the first column of the grid. (See the following illustration.)

Advanced Filter/Sort Grid with Drag Field Pointer in Field Cell

Field list

Drag LastName.

The Field cell displays LastName.

✏️

Filter a Table

You can also use Filter By Selection and Filter By Form on tables.

To Filter By Selection:

1. Open the table.

2. Click in the field that contains the entry you want to match.

3. Click the **Filter By Selection** button 🔳.

To Filter By Form:

1. Open the table.

2. Click the **Filter By Form** button 🔳.

3. Enter the criteria you want to match in the appropriate field(s).

4. Click the **Apply Filter** button 🔽.

5. Click in the Sort cell under LastName.

6. Click the drop-down arrow and select *Ascending*.

7. Scroll down the field list to locate ZIPCode.

8. Drag ZIPCode to the Field cell of the second column.

9. Click in the Criteria cell of ZIPCode.

10. Type **606*** and press Enter.

    The asterisk is a wildcard that tells Access to choose all records with a ZIP code beginning with 606. When completed, the grid should look like the one below.

Wildcard
You can use the asterisk wildcard in a Filter By Form as well as in the advanced filter grid.

Filter Grid Completed

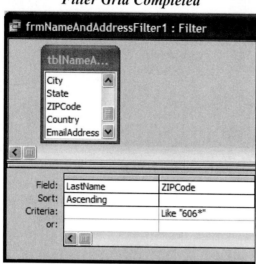

11. Click the Apply Filter button ▽.

    In the form, Access displays the first record that matches 606*.

12. Use the Next record button ▶ to view three or four records.

    Note that the records are sorted alphabetically by last name.

13. Close the Form, and then open it again.

14. Use the Next record button ▶ to view three or four records.

    Closing the form removes the filter. When you reopen the form, the records are no longer filtered.

15. Click the Apply Filter button ▽, or click <u>R</u>ecords, App<u>l</u>y Filter/Sort (Alt+R, Y).

16. Review three or four records. The filter has been saved with the form.

    The filter is still available for the form.

17. Click the Remove Filter button ▽, or click <u>R</u>ecords, <u>R</u>emove Filter/Sort (Alt+R, R).

18. Close the **frmNameAndAddress** form.

💻 Try It!

You can also filter the records in a table using the Advanced Filter/Sort feature.

1. Open the **tblNameAndAddress** table.

2. Click <u>R</u>ecords, <u>F</u>ilter, <u>A</u>dvanced Filter/Sort (Alt+R, F, A).
   Access displays the list of the fields and the grid.

3. Delete any entries that appear in the filter grid.

4. Drag the LastName field from the list to the Field cell in the first column of the grid.

5. Drag ZIPCode to the Field cell in the second column.

6. Click in the Sort cell of LastName and select Ascending.

7. Click in the Criteria cell under ZIPCode and type **678***, and press the Enter key.
   Access changes the entry in the Criteria cell to Like "678". The asterisk (*) is a wildcard that takes the place of any characters that follow 678.*

8. Click the Apply Filter button ☒.
   The resulting table is also called a **recordset** *because it is a set of selected records, not the entire table.*

9. Click the Close button ☒ to close the recordset.
   Access displays a message asking if you want to save the changes to the design of the Name and Address table.

10. Answer <u>Y</u>es.
    The filter is saved with the table.

11. Open the **tblNameAndAddress** table.

12. Click the Apply Filter button ☒.
    The filter you just created is reapplied.

13. Click the Remove Filter button ☒, or click <u>R</u>ecords, <u>R</u>emove Filter/Sort (Alt+R, R).

14. Select the AddressID column.

15. Click the Sort Ascending button ☒ to sort the records by AddressID.

16. Close the **tblNameAndAddress** table, saving the changes when prompted.

17. Close the database, and exit Access unless you are continuing with the Exercise Directions.

Double-click a Field Name
Rather than drag a field to the grid, you can double-click a field name to add it to the next open column on the grid.

Add two records using the frmStudents form and use Advanced Filter/Sort to look at records in the database.

EXERCISE DIRECTIONS

Open a Table and Adjust Column Widths

1. Start Access if it is not already running.

2. Open 💿 **06Arthur** from the data files.

3. Open the **frmStudents** form.

4. Use Form view to add the records shown in Illustration A on the next page.

Hint: *Click the New Record button* ▶✱ *to display a blank form.*

5. Press Tab when finished with the last field.

6. Leave the form open.

Illustration A. Students to Add

First Name	Middle Name	Last Name	Parent's Name	Address
Denise	M.	LeBihan	LeBihan, Pierre	365 Fisherman Way
William	Cook	Sonoma	Sonoma, Bruce	89 Alewife Lane

City	State	ZIP Code	Phone Number	Notes
Whitefish Bay	WI	53217	(414) 555-0909	Speaks French
Whitefish Bay	WI	53211	(414) 555-4567	Teacher's child

Use Advanced Filter/Sort for frmStudents

1. With the **frmStudents** form open, click <u>R</u>ecords, <u>F</u>ilter, <u>A</u>dvanced Filter/Sort.

   Access displays the field list and grid for filtering the form.

2. Drag LastName from the field list to the Field cell in the first column of the grid.

3. Drag Address from the field list to the Field cell of the second column of the grid.

4. In the Sort cell under LastName, select Ascending.

5. In the Criteria cell under Address, type *****Alewife*****.

6. Press Enter.

   *Access changes the entry to Like "*Alewife*".*
   *Use of the * wildcards lets you filter the records using only a portion of the data in the field.*

7. Click the Apply Filter button .

8. Use the Next Record button ▶ to review the records.

9. Click the Print Preview button 🔍 to view the filtered forms.

10. Print the filtered forms in Portrait mode. (They should require two pages.)

11. Close the form.

Use Advanced Filter/Sort for tblTeachers

1. Open the **tblTeachers** table.

2. Click <u>R</u>ecords, <u>F</u>ilter, <u>A</u>dvanced Filter/Sort.

   Access displays the field list and grid for filtering the form.

3. Drag LastName from the field list to the Field cell in the first column of the grid.

4. In the Sort cell under LastName, select Ascending.

5. Drag City from the field list to the Field cell in the second column.

6. In the Criteria cell under City, type **Mil***.

7. Press Enter.

   Access changes the entry to Like "Mil".*

8. Drag ZIPCode from the field list to the Field cell of the third column of the grid.

9. In the Criteria cell under ZIPCode, type **Like 532***.

   These two entries let you filter the records using criteria for two different fields.

10. Click the Apply Filter button .

11. Review the recordset.

12. Click the Remove Filter button ▽.

    The table displays all records.

Change Criteria for tblTeachers

1. Click <u>R</u>ecords, <u>F</u>ilter, <u>A</u>dvanced Filter/Sort.

   Access displays the field list and grid for filtering the form. The grid displays the fields and criteria used for the previous filter.

2. In the Criteria cell under City, replace the existing entry with **Like B* OR G***.

3. Press Enter.

   Access changes the entry to Like "B" Or Like "G*".*
   This entry lets you filter for cities beginning with B or G.

4. Click the Apply Filter button ▽.

5. Review the records.

6. Click the Remove Filter button ▽.

   The table displays all records.

Challenge Filter/Sort for tblTeachers

1. Use Advanced Filter/Sort to find out how many teachers live in ZIP Code 53263.

2. Use Advanced Filter/Sort to find out how many teachers live on American Way.

3. Use Advanced Filter/Sort to find out how many teachers live on Robalo Ave. or Alewife Lane.

4. Close the Teacher's table; save the changes if prompted.

5. Close the database, and exit Access.

Exercise 7

Work with Queries
■ Add Records in Form View ■ Create a Query ■ Copy a Query ■ Edit a Query

NOTES

Add Records in Form View

■ Before you start completing the activities in this exercise, you need to be introduced to the new information added to the **My Address Book**. This database now contains the **tblBirthdays** table and the **frmBirthdays** form. The tblBirthdays table stores the information about the birthdays of the people in the tblNameAndAddress table.

■ You will add birthday information for two people using the frmBirthdays form.

🖥 Try It!

Add Two Records in Form View

1. Start Access.

2. Open ◉ **07My Address Book** from the data files.

3. Open the **frmBirthdays** form, and add the two records shown in the following illustrations. (Be sure to click the New Record button ▶✳ to display a blank form for the first record.)

   ◆ **Name**: Click the drop-down arrow and locate the Name in the Lookup list. The names are listed alphabetically by last name.

   ◆ **Birthdate**: Type both digits for the month and day or type one digit and a slash (when the entry is one digit). You must type the last two digits for the year; the format changes when you move to the next field.

   ◆ **Gift**: This field has a data type of Yes/No. A checkmark means Yes. A blank means No.

   ◆ **Notes**: This is a Memo data type field. Simply type the appropriate entry (if any) and press the Tab key.

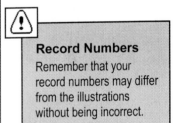

Record Numbers
Remember that your record numbers may differ from the illustrations without being incorrect.

Records to be Added in Form View

Create a Query

- A **query** lets you retrieve data from one or more tables and display it in a new table. Queries are built on a grid similar to the one used for filtering records (Exercise 6).

- In the Try It! practices in this exercise, you will create a query that shows you the birthdays and names and addresses for people who receive gifts.

🖳Try It!

Start a New Query

1. Close the **frmBirthdays** form if it is open.

2. Click the Queries button ⊟ Queries on the Objects bar.

3. Double-click *Create query in Design view* option
   Create query in Design view.

   A Query grid appears similar to the one used for advanced filtering, and the Show Table dialog box appears.

🖳Try It!

Select Tables for the Query

Show Table Dialog Box (Top Portion)

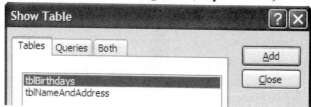

1. Select the **tblBirthdays** table, and click the Add button ⎓ Add ⎓.
   The Birthdays table field list appears in the upper part of the grid.

2. Select the **tblNameAndAddress** table, and click the Add button
   ⎓ Add ⎓.

   The Name and Address table field list appears in the upper part of the grid.

3. Click the Close button ⎓ Close ⎓ on the Show Table dialog box.

   The Query1 Select Query window should look as shown in the following illustration.

Query1: Select Query Window

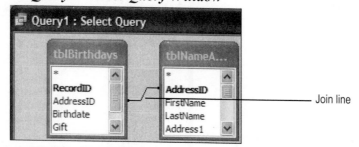

🖥 Try It!

Note the Join Line to Show the Connection Between Tables

When the tblBirthdays table was created, it was related to the tblNameAndAddress table by use of the AddressID field. The join line between the two tables shows that the tables are related by the AddressID field, which is common to each table.

🖥 Try It!

Drag the Fields to be Displayed in the Recordset

The result of a query is a recordset displayed as a new table. You are ready to specify which fields to include in the recordset.

1. From the tblNameAndAddress field list, drag the following fields:
   - FirstName to the Field cell of the first column
   - LastName to the Field cell of the second column
2. From the tblBirthdays field list, drag the following fields:
   - Birthdate to the Field cell of the third column.
   - Gift to the Field cell of the fourth column.
   - Notes to the Field cell of the fifth column. Scroll to the column if necessary.
3. From the tblNameAndAddress field list, drag the following fields:
   - Address1 to the Field cell of the sixth column.
   - Address2 to the Field cell of the seventh column.
   - City to the Field cell of the eighth column.
   - State to the Field cell of the ninth column.
   - ZIPCode to the Field cell of the tenth column.
4. In the Sort cell under LastName (second column), click the drop-down arrow and select Ascending to sort the records by last name.
5. In the Criteria cell under Gift (fourth column), type **Yes**.

   Your grid should resemble the one in the following illustration. (Note that the cells have been narrowed for the illustration, your cells may be wider.)

> **Why AddressID?**
> Although the Birthdays table displays the joined first and last names of the person, it is actually storing the AddressID number.

Completed Query Grid

Field:	FirstName	LastName	Birthdate	Gift	Notes	Address1	Address2	City	State	ZIPCode
Table:	tblNameAni	tblNameAr	tblBirthdays	tblBirthda	tblBirthda	tblNameAndAddre	tblNameAndAddr	tblNameAndAddr	tblNameAndAddre	tblNameAndAddres
Sort:		Ascending								
Show:	✓	✓	✓	✓	✓	✓	✓	✓	✓	✓
Criteria:										

6. Click the Run button 🔴.

   The resulting recordset should look as shown in the following illustration on the following page. (Column widths were adjusted to make the illustration easier to read. Your columns may be wider.)

Query Results

qryGift : Select Query

First Name	Last Name	Birthdate	Gift	Notes	Address 1	Address 2	City	State	ZIP Code
Jane	Austen	3/25/1947	☑	Flowers	1 Persuasion Ave.		Chicago	IL	60606
Gleaner	Baldwin	3/15/1986	☑	Money	1804 Reaper Road		Davenport	IA	52805
Creighton	Barrel	4/22/1932	☑	Candy	2727 Knife and Fork Road		Chicago	IL	60639
Jatinder	Boxx	7/18/1988	☑	Money	1925 Cordwood St.		Woodbury	NY	11797
Daniel	Fetty	5/16/1976	☑	Candy	Box 0003		Leoti	KS	67871
Tabitha	Fetty	12/15/1973	☑	Flowers	Box 0003		Leoti	KS	67871
Scott	Freeh	9/22/1945	☑	Money	275 Madison Ave.		New York	NY	10016
LaTrice	Johnson	7/16/1983	☑	Money	1322 N. Damen Ave.		Chicago	IL	60622
Miguel	Palacio	4/13/1945	☑	Candy	846 Robalo Ave.		Whitefish Bay	WI	53217
Lou	Tennant	4/16/1982	☑	Candy	2 Army Trail Rd.		Hartsdale	NY	10530
Justin	Thyme	6/18/1992	☑	Money	2138 Expeditious Towers	Apt. 3218	Prompton	PA	18456
Emma	Woodhouse	5/22/1985	☑	Flowers	99 Hartfield Lane		Scott City	KS	67871
Karen	Worthington	5/27/1981	☑	Money	1234 Saucer Place		Roswell	NM	82201
Bradley	Worthington	2/5/1984	☑	Money	1234 Saucer Place		Roswell	NM	82201
Geoffrey	Worthington	12/15/1976	☑	Candy	1234 Saucer Place		Roswell	NM	82201
*			☐						

Record: ⏮ ◀ 1 ▶ ⏭ ▶* of 15

7. Click the Save button 💾.

   Access displays the Save As dialog box.

8. Type **qryGift**.

9. Click OK.

10. Click the Close button ❎ to close the query's recordset.

11. Run the query again by double-clicking its name in the Queries list.

12. Close the query's recordset.

Copy a Query

- You can copy a query and paste it into the same database or open a different database and paste it into the one you open. In this Try It!, you'll copy a query into the same database so you can edit it.

   1. Select the **qryGift** query.

   2. Click the Copy button 📋.

   3. Click the Paste button 📋.

   4. In the Paste As dialog box, type the Query Name **qryBirthdaysByMonth**.

   5. Click the OK button ⬜ OK .

Paste As Dialog Box

408

Edit a Query

- You can edit the query you just copied so that it displays birthdays by month. In the following Try It! activity, you will create a query that prompts the user for a month when the query runs. The query recordset will display all birthdays in the specified month.

💻 Try It!

1. Select the **qryBirthdaysByMonth** query.

2. Click the Design button on the database window toolbar.
   The query design window opens.

3. Select the *Yes* under Gift and delete it.

4. Scroll horizontally to the first empty Field cell. (It appears after ZIPCode.)

5. In the Field cell, type **[Which month?]**.
   Be sure to type the square brackets. This text will appear as a prompt when you run the query.

6. Press Enter.
   Access displays Expr1: [Which month?].

7. Deselect the check box in the Show cell for the expression so that the expression does not display in the recordset.

8. In the Criteria cell under the Which month? prompt, type the following: **DatePart("m",[Birthdate])**
   Be sure to type the parentheses, quotation marks, comma, and brackets exactly as shown.
   The last two columns should look like the ones shown below.

Last Two Columns of Grid

ZIPCode	[Which month?]
tblNameAndAddres:	
☑	☐
	DatePart("m",[Birthdate])

The text in the Criteria cell is a built-in function of Access that lets you retrieve information by specifying only a part of the date. The "m" stands in place of the month.

9. Click the Save button to save the query design.

10. Click the Run button ⚡.
    Access displays the Enter Parameter Value dialog box shown below.

Enter Parameter Value Dialog Box

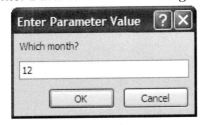

✓ **Run a Query**
If you double-click a query name, the query runs and the resulting recordset displays. You can then switch to Design view if you want to edit the query.

✓ **Error?**
If Access displays an error, check your typing. You may have omitted the comma, bracket, or parenthesis.

Dates in Access are stored in a form that requires entry of the number of the month rather than the letters.

11. Type **12**, and click OK.

    The resulting recordset is shown in the illustration that follows.

December Birthdays

First Name	Last Name	Birthdate	Gift	Notes	Address 1	Address 2	City	State	ZIP Code
Robert	Benwick	12/25/1984	☐	Send card	6735 S. Cottage Grove Ave		Chicago	IL	60653
Tabitha	Fetty	12/15/1973	☑	Flowers	Box 0003		Leoti	KS	67871
Geoffrey	Worthington	12/15/1976	☑	Candy	1234 Saucer Place		Roswell	NM	82201

12. Press Shift+F9 to rerun the query.

13. Type **3** in the Enter Parameter Value dialog box, and click OK.

14. Repeat steps 12 and 13 using **4**, **7**, and **9** as parameter values to check the results.

15. Close the query recordset when you have viewed the results of September (9).

 Try It!

Specify An Additional Criterion

You can specify more than one selection criterion in the same query.

1. Copy the **qryBirthdaysByMonth** query.

2. Paste it as **qryBirthdaysByCity&Month**.

3. Select the pasted query.

4. Click the Design button on the Database Window toolbar.
   The query design window opens.

5. In the Criteria cell under City, type **[Which city?]**.

6. Click the Save button 💾 to save the changes to the query.

7. Click the Run button ❗.

8. For the Which city? parameter, type **Scott City**.

9. Click OK.

10. For the Which month? parameter, type **6**, and click OK.

    How many people in Scott City have June birthdays?

11. Check some other months, if you wish, then close the database, and exit Access unless you are continuing with the Exercise Directions.

⚠️ **Order of Prompts**

If the "Which month?" prompt displays before "Which city?", your query is still correct and will generate the desired recordset.

In this exercise, you will create queries to determine who is participating in Arthur Treacher school activities.

EXERCISE DIRECTIONS

Review the Contents of New Tables

1. Start Access if it is not already running.
2. Open ☉ **07Arthur** from the data files.

   *Note that two new tables—**tblActivities** and **tblActivityParticipation**—have been added. They list activities offered by the school and the students who participate in them.*

3. Open the **tblActivities** table.

   The table lists each activity, its faculty sponsor, its location, and the days and the time it is held.

   *The Sponsor field is a lookup list that draws its information from the **tblTeachers** table. The Caption property is Sponsor; the field name is TeacherID to link it to the source table.*

4. Review the **tblActivities** table in Design view if you wish.
5. Close the **tblActivities** table.
6. Open the **tblActivityParticipation** table.

   *Besides the Record ID, this table contains two lookup lists. One uses the **tblStudents** table as its source; the other uses the **tblActivities** table.*

   If you review the table in Design view, you will note that the StudentID field has a Caption property of Student, and the ActivityID field has a Caption property of Activity. These fields are linked to their source tables.

7. Close the **tblActivityParticipation** table.

Review an Existing Query

1. Click the Queries button 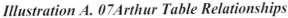 on the Objects bar.

   A query has already been created in this database. You will copy and edit this query to create three additional queries.

   The first query has been created so that the students' and teachers' names have been combined (official term concatenated). The names read in first name, last name order.

2. Open the **qryBoysBasketball**.

   The query lists those signed up for boys' basketball.

3. Click the Design View button ✎▾ on the toolbar to review the query's definition.

   The query uses all four tables. Note the join lines, as shown in Illustration A.

Illustration A. 07Arthur Table Relationships

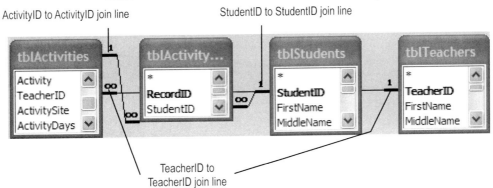

ActivityID to ActivityID join line

StudentID to StudentID join line

TeacherID to TeacherID join line

4. Double-click the right column boundary of the first field (Student), as shown in Illustration B.

Illustration B: Expand Student Field

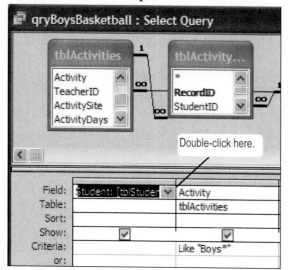

The expression used to concatenate (combine) the student's first and last names becomes completely visible as shown in Illustration C.

Illustration C. Student's Name Concatenated

Field:	Student: [tblStudents.FirstName] & " " & [tblStudents.LastName]
Table:	
Sort:	
Show:	☑
Criteria:	
or:	

5. Note the entry *Student:*.

   The word followed by a colon tells Access to display Student *as the name for the field in the recordset.*

6. Note also the *[tblStudents.FirstName]*.

   The use of tblStudents *is necessary to distinguish the student's first name from the FirstName field from the* tblTeachers *table.*

7. Note the Criteria cell – *Like "Boys*"* – under Activity.

Create qryGirlsBasketball

1. Close the query design grid.
2. Select the **qryBoysBasketball** query, and copy it.
3. Paste it as **qryGirlsBasketball**.
4. Select the **qryGirlsBasketball** query.
5. Click the Design button 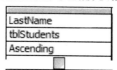 on the Database Window toolbar.

   The pasted query displays in Design view.

6. Change the entry *Like "Boys*"* to **Like "Girls*"**.
7. Click the Save button to save the changes to the query design.

8. Click the Run button.

   The resulting recordset lists the participants in girls' basketball.

9. Print a copy of the resulting recordset in Portrait orientation.
10. Close the query recordset.

Create qryActivity

1. Copy the **qryGirlsBasketball** query.
2. Paste it as **qryActivity**.
3. Change the Criteria cell for Activity to read as follows:

   Like [First Letters of Activity Name]+"*"

   This entry creates a prompt to which a user responds with the first few letters of an activity name to find out which students participate in the activity.

   To see the entire command, widen the grid column for Activity.

4. Save the query design.
5. Run the query, and enter **Ten** when prompted.

   The recordset shows the students participating in tennis.

6. Press Shift+F9 to run the query again.
7. Enter **Ch** at the prompt.

   The recordset shows the students participating in Cheerleading, Chess Club, and Chorale.

8. Print a copy of the recordset in Landscape orientation.

   Hint: Use *File, Page Setup* to switch to Landscape orientation.

9. Close the query.

Create qryStudent

1. Copy the **qryActivity** query.
2. Paste it as **qryStudent**.
3. Open the **qryStudent** query in Design view.
4. Delete the entry in the Criteria cell under Activity.
5. Scroll to the right to locate the last entry in the query grid, as shown in Illustration C.

Illustration C. Sort Field for Student's Last Name

| LastName |
| tblStudents |
| Ascending |

This field is used to sort the query recordset by the student's last name. If you were to specify a sort in the first field (concatenated student's name) the records would be sorted by the student's first name. This entry tells Access to sort using the student's last name, but not to display the field.

6. In the Criteria cell under this field, enter the following:
   Like [First Letters of Student's Last Name]+"*"

   This entry creates a prompt to which the user responds with the first few letters of a last name. The resulting recordset will show activities for each student whose last name begins with the letters entered.

7. Save the query design.

8. Run the query, and enter **P** at the prompt.

   The recordset shows the activities for Miguel Palacio, Cassandra Pierce, and Thomas Purma.

9. Press Shift+F9 to rerun the query, and enter **Pa** at the prompt.

   The recordset shows the activities for Miguel Palacio.

10. Rerun the query, and enter **New** at the prompt.

11. Print the resulting recordset in Landscape orientation.

12. Close the query, close the database, and exit Access.

Exercise 8

Work with Reports

- Create a Report Using AutoReport ■ Set Default Print Margins
- Create a Report Using the Report Wizard
- Change the Report Title ■ Resize and Move Fields

NOTES

Create a Report Using AutoReport

- Access **reports** offer a way to use the information in tables and queries and format it for printing. In this exercise, you will create reports based on queries using built-in report creation features. You will also make minor edits to the reports.

🖥️**Try It!**

Open the Database

1. Start Access.

2. Open 💿**08My Address Book** from the data files.

3. Click the Tables button [⊞ Tables] on the Objects bar.

🖥️**Try It!**

Create a New Report using AutoReport: Tabular

1. Open the **tblNameAndAddress** table.

2. Click in the Last Name field of any record.

3. Click the Sort Ascending button ⬛ to sort the records by Last Name.

4. Click the Save button ⬛ to save the changes to the table layout.

5. Close the table.

6. With the table selected, click the drop-down arrow beside the New object button ⬛ ▾ on the toolbar.

   Your New object button may have a different appearance. The symbol displayed indicates the kind of object last created using the New object drop-down list.

7. Click the Report option [⬛ Report].

   Access displays the New Report dialog box shown in the illustration on the next page.

New Report Dialog Box

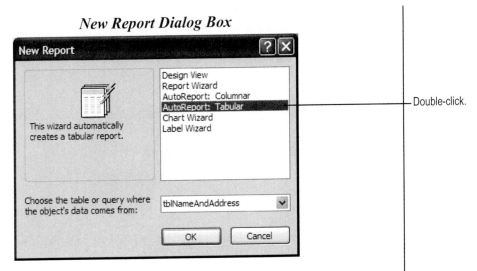

Double-click.

8. Double-click AutoReport: Tabular.

Access creates and displays the report in Preview mode with the mouse pointer as a magnifying glass ⌕. The top portion of a sample report is shown in the following illustration. The style of your report may differ. The style used depends on the report style used most recently. The style illustrated is called Corporate.

Tabular Report from tblNameAndAddress

tblNameAndAddress

dress ID	First Name	Last Name	Address 1	Address 2	City	State	ZIP Cod	Country	Email Addre	Home Phone
32	Jane	Austen	1 Persuasion Av		Chicago	IL	60606	USA	jausten@mwnn	(312) 555-9090
3	Gleaner	Baldwin	1804 Reaper R		Davenport	IA	52805	USA	gbaldwin@aaab	(319) 555-1234
4	Creighton	Barrel	2727 Knife and		Chicago	IL	60639	USA	cbarrel@aaabb	(312) 555-8888
33	Elizabeth	Bennett	10 Pemberly Pla		Scott City	KS	67871	USA	ebennett@yyyz	(316) 555-0404
42	Robert	Berwick	6735 S. Cottage		Chicago	IL	60653	USA	rberwick@mwn	(312) 555-6363

🖥 Try It!

Review the Report

1. Click anywhere within the report.

   The view changes to show the entire page.

   Note that some field labels are cut off and some data is not completely visible. Although you can edit the report to solve most of these problems, it may be easier to base the report on a query.

2. Click the Close button ✖ on the report display.

   Access asks if you want to save the changes.

3. Answer <u>Y</u>es and name the report **rptNameAndAddressTabular**.

Set Default Print Margins

- The default margins for Access printing are 1" for top, bottom, left, and right. For some objects, such as reports, smaller left and right margins make more data visible, requiring less editing after the report is created.

- To set new default margins, you use the Tools, Options command.

🖥️ Try It!

Set Default Margins

1. Click <u>T</u>ools, <u>O</u>ptions on the menu (Alt+T, O).

2. Click the General tab.

   Access displays the Options dialog box shown in the illustration that follows.

3. Change the left margin to 0.5" and the right margin to 0.5", as shown in the illustration.

4. Click the OK button [OK] .

Set Default Margins

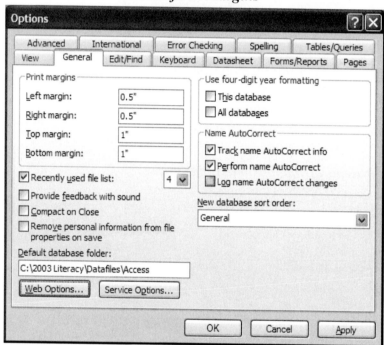

Create a Report Using the Report Wizard

- The Report wizard guides you step-by-step in creating a report based on tables, queries, or a combination of the two.

🖥️ Try It!

1. Click the Reports button [🗐 Reports] on the Objects bar.

2. Double-click [🔲] [Create report by using wizard] .

   The first Report Wizard dialog box appears Like a form, a report can be based on a table or a query.

3. From the <u>T</u>ables/Queries drop-down list, select Query: **qryMyAddressBook**, as shown in the illustration on the following page.

4. Click the Add All Fields button [>>] to move all the <u>A</u>vailable Fields to the <u>S</u>elected Fields list.

Report Wizard Dialog Box, Select Query and Fields

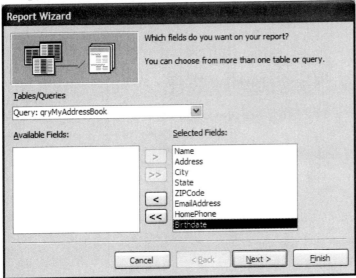

5. Click the Next button Next > .
   A dialog box appears asking if you want to group data in the report.

6. Click the Next button Next > . You do not want any grouping levels.
   A dialog box appears asking if you want to sort by any fields. The query has a built-in sort.

7. Click the Next button Next > . The query has a built-in sort.
   The layout dialog box appears.

Try It!

Specify a Layout and Style

1. Select Tabular layout and Landscape orientation.

2. Be sure to select the option *Adjust the field width so all fields fit on a page*.

Report Wizard Dialog Box, Choose Layout

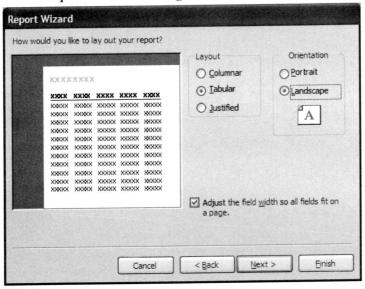

3. Click the Next button [Next >].

   The style dialog box appears, as shown in the following illustration.

4. Select the Casual style, as shown in the illustration.

Report Wizard Dialog Box, Select a Report Style

Try It!

Name the Report and Display It

1. Click the Next button [Next >].

   The final Report Wizard dialog box appears, as shown in the following illustration.

2. Change the title to **rptMyAddressBook**, as shown in the illustration. Be sure *Preview the report* is selected.

Report Wizard, Name the Report

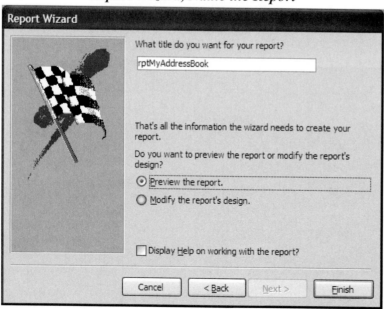

3. Click the Finish button ⟨ Finish ⟩.

   Access creates and displays the report. The top portion of the report is shown in the following illustration.

4. If necessary, point to the body of the report to change the pointer to a magnifying glass and click to reduce or enlarge the report display.

5. Page through the report using the Page buttons at the bottom of the report display ⟨ Page: |◄ ◄ 1 ► ►| ⟩.

   As you page through the report, note which fields seem to be wider than necessary (Name, for example) and which seem to be too narrow (Email Address, for example). You will want to edit the report to improve the appearance of these fields.

rptMyAddressBook Report when Wizard is Finished

rptMyAddressBook

Name	Address	City	State	ZIP Code	Email Address	Home Phone	Birthdate
Jane Austen	1 Persuasion Ave.	Chicago	IL	60606	jausten@mwnnn.net	(312) 555-9090	3/25/1947
Gleaner Baldwin	1804 Reaper Road	Davenport	IA	52805	gbaldwin@aaabbb.ne	(319) 555-1234	3/15/1986
Creighton Barrel	2727 Knife and Fork	Chicago	IL	60639	cbarrel@aaabbb.net	(312) 555-8888	4/22/1932
Elizabeth Bennett	10 Pemberly Place	Scott City	KS	67871	ebennett@yyyzzz.net	(316) 555-0404	3/18/1985
Julia Benwick	6735 S. Cottage Grov	Chicago	IL	60653	jbenwick@mwnnn.ne	(312) 555-6363	9/17/1986
Robert Benwick	6735 S. Cottage Grov	Chicago	IL	60653	rbenwick@mwnnn.ne	(312) 555-6363	12/25/1984

Address is too wide for column.

Email Address is too wide for column.

Change the Report Title

- Access places the title of a report in a text box—called a **control**—at the top. You can click the text box and edit the report title. (Note that this changes the report title in the display; it does not change the name of the report object itself.)

Control

Any element on a report or form, such as a field label or field contents. A control can be resized, moved, and edited.

Try It!

Change the Report Title

1. Click the Design View button on the toolbar.

   The report displays in Design view.

rptMyAddressBook in Design View

2. Click the title text box in the Report Header area.

3. Change the title to **My Address Book**.

Change Report Title

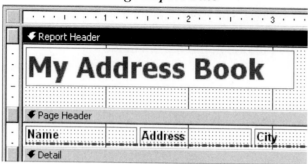

4. Click the Print Preview button on the toolbar or the report View button ▣ ▾ in the upper left of the toolbar.
   The report displays the new title.

5. Click the Save button 💾 to save the changes.

Resize and Move Fields

- Access provides tools for editing a report so that you can adjust field widths and move them so that all data is visible. You can resize and move the field (column) label and the field contents box by selecting both controls and editing them together.

- In the Try It! activities in this section, you will do the following:

  - Narrow the State and ZIPCode controls.

  - Widen the Email Address controls.

  - Move the City and State controls.

  - Widen the Address controls.

🖥️ Try It!

Narrow the State and ZIPCode Controls

1. Click the Design View button ☑ ▾ on the toolbar.
   The report displays in Design view.

2. Select both State controls.

   a. Click *State* in the Page Header area.

   b. Hold down the Shift key.

   c. Click *State* in the Detail area.
      The mouse pointer turns into a small hand 🖐️.

3. Point to the right side of either control until the pointer turns into a two-headed arrow ↔.

4. Click and drag the edge of the control to the left until it nearly touches the right side of the word State.

   The illustration on the following page shows the steps in this procedure.

🖉

Problem Editing?

If you have trouble selecting controls, click anywhere outside the report design grid to deselect all controls and start over.

It takes practice to become proficient in the use of these editing techniques.

If you shrink, enlarge, or move a control more than you want, use **Undo** (Ctrl+Z) to remove the changes.

Narrowing the State Controls

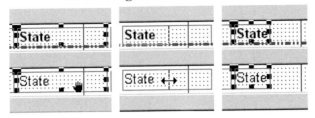

ZIPCode Controls with Width Reduced

5. Select the two ZIPCode controls.

6. Shrink them to the right side of the text to achieve the result shown in the illustration at the right. Leave at least one column of dots after the *e* in the label so that the word *Code* displays completely.

7. Click the Save button 💾 to save the changes to the report design.

🖥 Try It!

Widen the Email Address Controls

1. Select the two Email Address controls.

2. Click and drag the left side of the controls until they reach the gridline to their left.

3. Click the Save button 💾 to save the changes to the report design.

Email Address Controls Widened

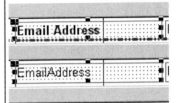

🖥 Try It!

Move the City and State Controls

1. Select the City controls and the State controls.

2. Click and drag them to the right until the State controls almost touch the ZIPCode controls.

3. Click the Save button 💾 to save the changes to the report design.

City and State Controls Moved

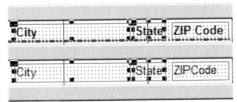

🖥 Try It!

Widen the Address Controls

1. Select the two Address controls.

2. Click and drag the right side of the controls until they nearly touch the City controls.

3. Click the Save button 💾 to save the changes to the report design.

City and State Controls Moved

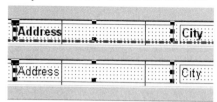

4. Click the Print Preview button to review the results.

   The top portion of the report should resemble the following illustration.

5. Close the database, and exit Access unless you are continuing with the Exercise Directions.

Completed My Address Book Report

My Address Book

Name	Address	City	State	ZIP Code	Email Address	Home Phone	Birthdate
Jane Austen	1 Persuasion Ave.	Chicago	IL	60606	jausten@mwnnn.net	(312) 555-9090	3/25/1947
Gleaner Baldwin	1804 Reaper Road	Davenport	IA	52805	gbaldwin@aaabbb.net	(319) 555-1234	3/15/1986
Creighton Barrel	2727 Knife and Fork Road	Chicago	IL	60639	cbarrel@aaabbb.net	(312) 555-8888	4/22/1932
Elizabeth Bennett	10 Pemberly Place	Scott City	KS	67871	ebennett@yyyzzz.net	(316) 555-0404	3/18/1985
Julia Benwick	6735 S. Cottage Grove Ave.	Chicago	IL	60653	jbenwick@mwnnn.net	(312) 555-6363	9/17/1986
Robert Benwick	6735 S. Cottage Grove Ave.	Chicago	IL	60653	rbenwick@mwnnn.net	(312) 555-6363	12/25/1984

In this exercise, you will create and edit a report for the Arthur Treacher Middle School.

EXERCISE DIRECTIONS

Create a Report with the Report Wizard

1. Start Access if it is not already running.

2. Open 💿 **08Arthur** from the data files.

3. Click the Reports button [📄 Reports] on the Objects bar.

4. Double-click 📄 [Create report by using wizard].

   The first Report Wizard dialog box appears.

5. From the Tables/Queries drop-down list, select the query: **qryStudentsByActivity**.

6. Click the Add All Fields button [>>] to move all the Available Fields to the Selected Fields list.

Specify View and Grouping Options

1. Click the Next button [Next >].

   A dialog box appears asking how you want to view the data, as shown in Illustration A.

2. Ensure that **tblActivities** is selected.

*As shown in the right pane of the dialog box, the information from the **tblActivities** table will appear first in the report.*

Illustration A. View by tblActivities

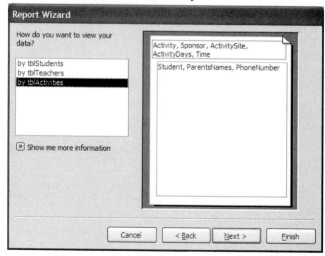

3. Click the Next button 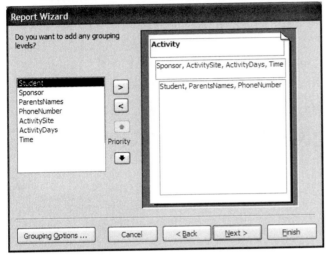.

A dialog box appears asking if you want any grouping levels, as shown in Illustration B.

4. In the left pane, double-click the Activity field.

The Activity field appears in blue at the top of the right pane.

Illustration B. Group by Activity Field

Specify Sort, Layout, and Style Options

1. Click the Next button 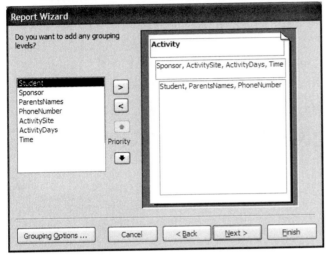.

A dialog box appears that asks for a sort order for the details.

2. Click the Next button. You do not want to sort any detail fields.

The layout dialog box appears.

3. Select Align Left 2 and Portrait orientation, as shown in Illustration C.

Illustration C. Layout Dialog Box

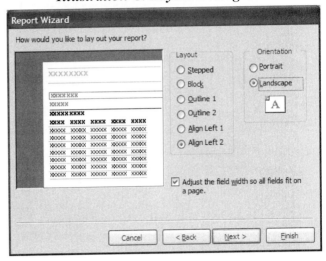

4. Click the Next button.

The style dialog box appears.

5. Select the Bold style.

6. Click the Next button.

7. In the final dialog box, name the report **rptStudentsByActivity**.

8. Click the Finish button to display the report in Preview mode, as shown in Illustration D.

9. Scroll through the report page by page. Note that the list of sponsors and students sometimes get separated. They need to be grouped so that they do not break across pages.

Illustration D. Top Portion of rptStudentsByActivity in Preview Mode

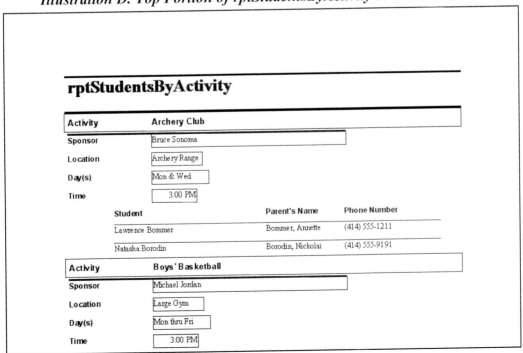

Edit the Report Design

1. Click the Design View button 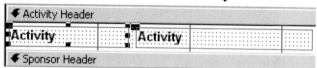.
2. Change the report title to **Students by Activity**.
3. In the Activity Header area, select the Activity label as shown below.

Illustration E. Select Activity Label

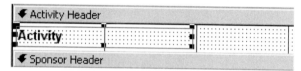

4. Press the Delete key to delete the Activity label. If you accidentally delete both controls, click Undo to restore them, and then try again to delete just the label.
5. Drag the Activity field to the left until it almost touches the left edge of the design grid, as shown in Illustration F.

Illustration F. Activity Field Moved

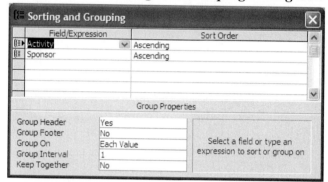

6. Click the Save button 🖫 to save the report design.

Use the Sorting and Grouping Dialog Box

1. Click the Sorting and Grouping button 🖫 on the toolbar.

   The Sorting and Grouping dialog box appears.
2. Be sure that *Activity* is selected in the upper pane.
3. In the Keep Together field, click the drop-down list, and choose *Whole Group*, as shown in Illustration G.

   This option ensures that all students who participate in an activity appear on the same page as the Activity field.

Illustration G. Sorting and Grouping Dialog Box

4. Close the Sorting and Grouping dialog box.
5. Click the Save button 🖫 to save the report design.
6. Click the Report View button 🔍 to display the redesigned report.

   If you use slightly smaller margins, some of the pages will look better because they'll contain more records.
7. Click File, Page Setup.
8. Change the top and bottom margins to 0.75", and click OK.
9. Scroll through the report.
10. Print the report.
11. Close the report.
12. Close the database, and exit Access.

Lesson 9: Computer Communications

Exercise 1: Learn about File Server Local Area Networks

- ◆ Introduction to Computer Communications
- ◆ File Server Local Area Networks (LANs)
- ◆ File Server Network Components
- ◆ How Network Components are Organized
- ◆ Network Use
- ◆ Explore a File Server Network (Novell)

Exercise 2: Learn about Peer-to-Peer Networks

- ◆ Introduction to Peer-to-Peer Networks
- ◆ Learn the Name and Workgroup of a Computer
- ◆ Explore a Peer-to-Peer Network
- ◆ Share Workstation Resources

Exercise 3: Learn about the Internet

- ◆ The Internet
- ◆ Internet Addresses—URLs (Uniform Resource Locators)
- ◆ Internet Use
- ◆ Introduction to Internet Explorer
- ◆ The World Wide Web
- ◆ Online Services
- ◆ Electronic Mail (E-mail)
- ◆ File Transfer Protocol (FTP)

Exercise 4: Learn about Other Communications Methods

- ◆ Wide Area Networks (WANs)
- ◆ Intranets
- ◆ Telecommuting
- ◆ PC-to-Mainframe Communications

Exercise 1

Learn about File Server Local Area Networks

■ Introduction to Computer Communications ■ File Server Local Area Networks (LANs)
■ File Server Network Components ■ How Network Components are Organized
■ Network Use ■ Explore a File Server Network (Novell)

NOTES

Introduction to Computer Communications

- All computers communicate. The CPU talks to the hard drive controller; the video card communicates with the monitor and the CPU. The printer and the CPU talk to each other. Each element uses a **communications protocol**—a set of send and receive signals following rules that have been agreed upon by computer manufacturers or established by governmental or professional organizations.

- For example, when you print a document, the program in the computer that handles printing sends a signal to the printer that asks whether it is ready to receive data. The printer normally signals that it is ready. When its print **buffer** is full, the printer signals the computer that it cannot receive more data. The computer waits, periodically asking if the printer is ready for more, until the printer signals its readiness.

- But when people talk of computer communications, they usually mean the ability of one computer to talk with other computers. When personal computers became common in businesses, managers and users began to look for ways to make it possible for personal computers to share data and programs with one another.

- The first solution was **sneaker net**. Users copied files from one computer and carried them to another. That method, however useful, had limits. If the receiving computer was across town, it took a while for the communication to be completed. In addition, businesses have large amounts of data residing under the control of their mainframe computers, but the personal computers on desktops at first couldn't make use of that data. Communication was a problem that needed to be solved.

- Today, PC users can share data and programs over networks; they can use the facilities of the company's mainframe computers using terminal emulation software and hardware. They can communicate with colleagues in remote locations through networks, electronic mail, and the Internet and World Wide Web—all because the communications problem was solved by connecting personal and other computer types into networks.

- There are two common types of network:
  - **File server** local area networks (described in this exercise).
  - **Peer-to-peer** local area networks (described in the next exercise).

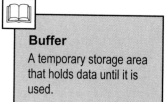

Buffer
A temporary storage area that holds data until it is used.

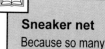

Sneaker net
Because so many computer users dress casually, wearing sneakers rather than dress shoes, the method of walking with diskettes from one computer to another became known as *sneaker net*.

File Server Local Area Networks (LANs)

- If you use a personal computer in a reasonably large organization—school, university, or company—you probably work on a Local Area Network or LAN. Your computer can work **locally**, using the programs and drives that are installed on it. Your computer, however, can work as a **workstation**, a machine that can use the drives, folders, files, and programs on the network.

- On **file server** networks, one or more computers act as the central storage and file management system for the **clients** on the network. Data and programs that are to be shared reside on the disk drives controlled by the servers. Smaller organizations may have only one server; larger organizations may have dozens. (The number of workstations a server can support depends on the server's capacity.)

- File server LANs usually involve workstations in the same building or group of neighboring buildings that can be connected directly by cables. The following illustration gives a generalized picture of a file server network. The network has two servers and is connected to the **Internet** through a **firewall**.

- Not shown are patch panels, hubs, and switches used to connect the computers and printers to the servers.

Generalized File Server Local Area Network

Client

A client is a workstation that is actively using the network's facilities.

Firewall

A software program or hardware/software combination that prevents users of the Internet from gaining unauthorized access to a network or computer.

Internet

The collection of inter-connected computers that includes the World Wide Web, e-mail servers, and other publicly available computer systems.

File Server Network Components

- File server networks include the following elements:

  - The **server** is a computer that provides files or services to another computer. The server has programs that let it communicate with other computers and provide services to them. A server usually controls a group of hard drives called a drive **array** where its programs and data files for clients are stored.

- **Client workstations** are computers that request files or services from servers. Most modern networks can mix computers of different types and capabilities, including Apple machines running MacOS, PCs running Windows or DOS, and computers running the UNIX operating system.

- **Printers** are shared across the network. Each printer is identified by a name or number. When users want to print, they choose a printer through the application they are using. Other peripherals such as scanners can be managed in the same way as printers.

- **Network cards** convert binary data from the computer into signals that can be transmitted over cables to and from other computers. Each workstation requires a network card in one of its bus slots.

- **Cables** connect computers to one another and to the server.

  - **Coaxial** cable is similar to the cable used for most cable television systems. It consists of two conductors—a central wire and an outer woven wire—wrapped in outer insulation and separated by an inner layer of insulation. For some years, coaxial cable was the most common type of network cabling. Coaxial cables connect to computers and network outlets in the same way that a television connects to a VCR. The end of the cable has a cap that screws on to the outlet and secures the conductor in the center of the outlet.

  - **Twin twisted pair or Category 5 or 6** consists of pairs of wires twisted together. The twisting improves resistance to interference. In the past few years, this method of cabling has overtaken coaxial cable as the most common for new network installations. Connections are made with snap-in connectors that are similar to, but larger than, normal telephone connections to prevent confusing the two. (Telephone connections usually have two pairs of twisted wire, while network cables have four pairs.)

  - **Fiber optic cable**, which uses light to communicate, consists of a glass filament encased in a plastic coating. The light travels along the filament and reflects off the coating material.

- When network wiring stretches over long distances, a series of **hubs** or other signal repeating devices may be used to increase the signals that are transmitted across the cables. The distance from one hub to another depends on the cable type, with fiber optic cables allowing the longest runs without a hub to boost the signal.

- A network may connect to the Internet using one or more of the following pieces of software and hardware:

  - A **proxy server** is a computer program running on a server that acts as an intermediary between a Web browser (for example, Microsoft Internet Explorer) and the World Wide Web. Proxy servers give users rapid access to popular Web destinations by storing frequently requested pages. Storing pages in this way reduces the number of times the browser must link to the Web and permits more control over the Web sites that users can visit.

  - A **firewall**, which can be a software program or programmable hardware, prevents unauthorized intrusions into the local network.

More on Networks
The Web site of the networking equipment manufacturer Cisco has excellent, technical information about the components and architecture of file server and other networks.

http://www.cisco.com/ univercd/cc/td/doc/cisintwk /idg4/index.htm

Category 5 or Category 6
For more information on Category 5 and Category 6 cable specifications, see, http://www.tiaonline.org/sta ndards/category6/.

◆ A **router** is a device that connects the network to another network, helping to manage traffic between the networks. For example, a router can be used to connect two LANs or a LAN and the Internet.

How Network Components are Organized

■ To make management and use of the network as easy as possible, the components of a file server network are organized into **physical** and **logical** units. Physical units are servers and the actual hard drives that are connected together to form the network. Logical units are **volumes**, **drives**, and folders (or directories) that allow users to locate and manage the data they need.

■ **Server**. Servers are computers especially designed for running networks. Each server is identified by a name, and each has one or more hard drives attached. Like a workstation computer, the server has a CD-ROM drive for use in updating its software. A server usually also has a tape drive or removable disk drive for creating backups.

■ The server has an operating system such as Novell NetWare or Windows Server 2003. The operating system and its management functions provide network administrators with the tools they need to keep the network running.

■ **Hard Drives**. The hard drives are usually linked together into a group called an **array**. For example, a small server named Net_Svr may have eight hard drives in its array. Each hard drive has a capacity of 18.2 Gigabytes (GB), giving the server a storage capacity of close to 145 GB. (The actual number is less because of the way drive arrays operate.)

■ **Volume**. A volume is a name assigned to organize a portion of the hard drive array attached to a server. The volume name does not correspond to a specific physical area of the array. It is an organizing principle for managing storage space. For example, the array of eight hard drives attached to Schs_admin3 is organized into four volumes: SYS, VOL1, VOL2, and VOL3. SYS is used by the network's administrators; the other three volumes contain data used by SCHS's business units.

■ **Drive**. A drive is a letter assigned to organize a portion of a volume. Like the volume name, the drive letter is an organizing principle that lets users store their data and network administrators manage storage space. Drive letters are said to be **mapped** to a particular unit of storage. A drive letter can be mapped to a volume, a folder, or a sub-folder.

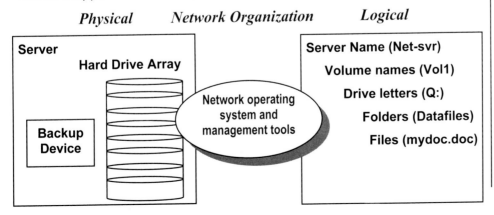

Physical   *Network Organization*   *Logical*

Network Use

- When you turn on a computer attached to a network, it boots up, but before you actually start using it, you are requested for a **login name** or **user name** and **password**. The login name identifies you to the network and the password ensures that you are the person who is identified. If you do not have a valid login name or you don't remember your password, you are not allowed to use the network.

Login Screen for Novell intraNetWare™ Network

- The login or user name is a string of characters assigned by network administration that identifies you as a network user. Your rights to use network folders and files are defined to the login name.

- You **log in** to the network for two complementary purposes:
  - Access data and programs that you have rights to use
  - Ensure that unauthorized users do not gain access

- On LANs your access is usually restricted to certain drives, folders, and files. On a file server network, maintaining access rights is the job of the **network administrator**. The network administrator assigns login IDs, defines and maintains access rights, ensures that backups are performed regularly, and works to keep the network operating smoothly.

- It is convenient to speak of workstations when describing network communications, but a network also includes hard drives for data storage and printers.

Explore a File Server Network (Novell)

- Windows provides several ways to see how your computer fits into the network environment. If you are connected to a network, the desktop contains an icon for the Network Neighborhood or My Network Places as shown at the right.

- When you double-click on the network icon, the Network Neighborhood window appears, as shown in the illustration on the next page. In this window, you double-click the network object about which you want information.

  ✓ *All the illustrations in this section are drawn from a Novell file server network. The objects on your network will have different names.*

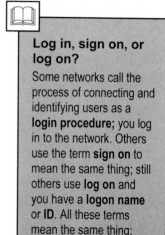

Log in, sign on, or log on?

Some networks call the process of connecting and identifying users as a **login procedure;** you log in to the network. Others use the term **sign on** to mean the same thing; still others use **log on** and you have a **logon name** or **ID**. All these terms mean the same thing: Identify yourself and provide the password to determine what drives, folders, files, and programs you can use.

Guest login

Many networks maintain a login ID, usually *guest*, that does not require a password but has limited rights to network's drives and folders. Guest IDs are maintained for the convenience of visitors who may need to use a computer temporarily.

Windows XP

Network Neighborhood Window

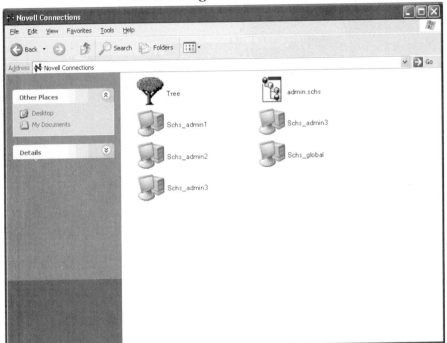

- While you may wish to explore the network using the windows that can be opened from the Network Neighborhood, you can get the same information through Windows Explorer. The drives and other objects for exploring a network are listed in the left pane, as shown in the illustration that follows.

Sample View of User's Workstation Logged In to Network

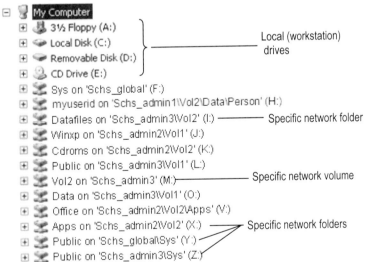

- In the preceding illustration, drives F:, H: through M:, and O:, V:, X:, Y, and Z: are network drives. The drive identifier includes the name of the volume (and folder if any) to which the drive is mapped. Drives are often mapped to the same volume although they are mapped to different folders, for example K:, V:, and X: in the previous illustration.

- Windows Explorer also contains an entry for the My Network Places (Network Neighborhood). When you expand My Network Places, a list appears similar to the one shown in the illustration on the next page.

Drive Mappings

A drive is a logical division of a volume. In the illustration on the left, for example, **Vol2 on 'Schs_Admin3' (M:)** indicates that drive M: is mapped to an entire volume.

Datafiles on 'Schs_admin3\ Vol2' (I:) indicates that drive I: is mapped to a specific folder (Datafiles) on the volume (Vol2) on the Schs_admin3. The Datafiles folder is on the same volume (Vol2) to which drives L:,M:, and O: are mapped.

These mappings are useful because some network users need access to the entire logical unit Vol2 while some need access only to the Datafiles folder. Network administrators can set up the login routines to create these mappings for the users who require them.

- Note that the user's workstation illustrated on the previous page does not have drives mapped to all the available servers; the user's access is limited by network administration.

My Network Places

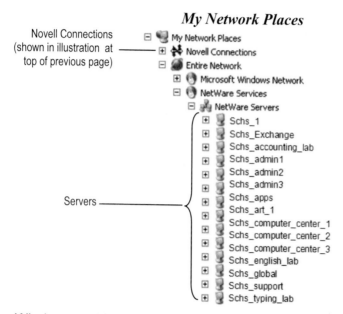

Novell Connections (shown in illustration at top of previous page)

Servers

- Windows and Novell provide several ways to look at the organization of the network.

  ✓ *The descriptions that follow use Windows Explorer rather than the Network Neighborhood window. If you use the window, you double-click the icon and open a window for the object rather than expand its list.*

  - **Entire Network**. When you expand the Entire Network, you display a list of the objects on the network, as shown in the illustration above. In the illustration, servers appear under Novell Connections, which shows servers currently connected to the local computer. The servers also appear under NetWare Servers, which lists all the servers to which the user can connect.

  - The Microsoft Windows Network in the previous illustration is available because the SCHS organization also has a server that operates a Windows NT network.

  - **Servers** (the computers that provide network facilities to workstations). Another way to view network facilities is to double-click one of the servers. The network used for illustration in this book has fifteen servers. When you expand the servers, a list of volumes (indicated by folders) appears. When you open a server, a list of the volumes and other objects belonging to the server appears in the right pane. The expanded server in the left pane and the opened server in the right pane are shown in the following illustration.

    The server Schs_admin3 server lists five volumes (_ADMIN, SYS, VOL1, VOL2, and VOL3) indicated by folder icons. The _ADMIN server is used by the Novell Netware system. SYS is a volume used primarily by network administration. The other volumes (VOL1, VOL2, VOL3) are accessible by network users. The server also has some printers, some of which are listed in the right pane when the server is opened in Windows Explorer.

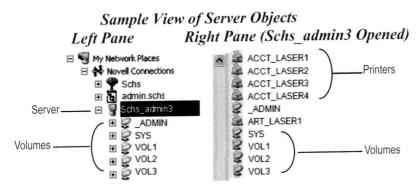

Sample View of Server Objects
Left Pane   *Right Pane (Schs_admin3 Opened)*

- **Tree** views show Organizations and Organization Units. Trees are identified by name, and each tree includes portions of the network. In the illustration that follows, SCHS is an Organization, and admin.schs is an Organization Unit within the Schs Tree.

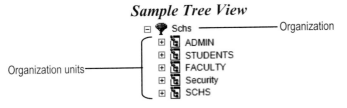

Sample Tree View

- The last item shown is the **Organization Unit**. When you expand an Organization Unit in the left pane and open it in the right pane, the system lists all the elements of the network belonging to that unit. This display is the same as that produced by expanding and opening the same organization unit in Tree view.

Object Properties and Other Information

When you right-click on a network object, a shortcut menu appears to let you choose the kind of information you wish to review. The illustration that follows shows the options available when you right-click on a server. Different menus appear for different network objects.

Right-Click Menu for a Server

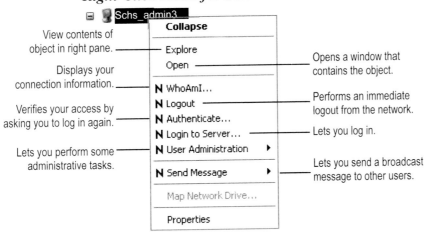

WhoAmI

You can check your login ID by clicking <u>W</u>hoAmI on the shortcut menu to display a message box similar to the one shown below.

Connection Information (Login ID)

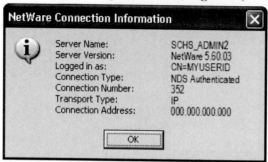

Rights

- The Network Administrator establishes rights to particular volumes, drives, and folders. To review your rights, right-click the volume or drive and click P<u>r</u>operties, then click the Rights tab. The illustration that follows shows the user's rights to the Vol2 on the Schs_admin3 server.

Sample User Rights

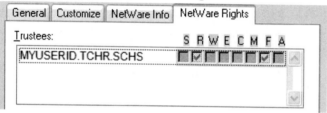

- The rights shown in this dialog box are described below. The active rights are those with check marks.

  Rights to a folder do not necessarily extend to folders within that folder.

Abbreviation	Description
S(upervisor)	User has all rights to the folder.
R(ead)	User can read (retrieve) files from the folder.
W(rite)	User can save files (write) to the folder.
E(rase)	User can delete files from the folder.
C(reate)	User can create files and folders within the folder.
M(odify)	User can change folder and file names. Does not grant right to change folder or file contents.
F(ile scan)	User can view the folder contents in Windows Explorer or Network Neighborhood.
A(ccess Control)	User can control who has rights to the folder.

Volume Usage

Another property that you may wish to review is the amount of storage remaining on a volume. To do so, complete the following two steps.

1. Right-click a drive (such as N:) mapped to the volume. (The visual representation of storage is not available when you do not select a drive.)

2. Click Properties, and select the General tab to display a dialog box like the one shown in the illustration below.

General Tab of Properties Dialog Box for Drive

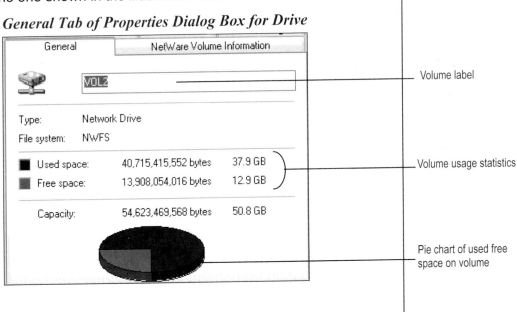

Volume label

Volume usage statistics

Pie chart of used free space on volume

In this exercise, you will use Windows Explorer to view the elements of your file server network. You can follow the directions only if you are connected to a file server network, such as a Novell network. The directions are tailored to a Novell network, but they can be followed for other file server networks as well.

EXERCISE DIRECTIONS

Explore a Novell File Server Network

1. Start Windows Explorer.
2. Find a server identifier and right-click it. A sample icon appears below.

3. Click WhoAmI to review your login ID.
   A message box displays your login name and other information.
4. Click OK to close the message box.
5. Right-click the server again.
6. Click Properties.
   Note the entry near the bottom of the dialog box. CN= gives the server name. OU= is the Organization Unit. O= is the Organization.
7. Write down the names of the Server, Organization Unit, and Organization displayed.
8. Close the Properties dialog box.
9. Close down all applications so that only Windows Explorer remains active.

10. Right-click on a server.
11. Click Logout.
    After a few moments, the drives associated with that server disappear from the left pane of Windows Explorer.
12. Log in again.
    a. Right-click on Network Neighborhood.
    b. Click IntranetWare Login.
    c. Complete the log in screen.
    OR
    a. Click the Start button .
    b. Point to All Programs.
    c. Point to your network login program (for example, Novell) and click on Netware Login.
    d. Complete the log in screen.
13. Return to Windows Explorer to verify that you have access to the network in the way that you expect.

Exercise 2

Learn about Peer-to-Peer Networks

■ Introduction to Peer-to-Peer Networks ■ Learn the Name and Workgroup of a Computer
■ Explore a Peer-to-Peer Network ■ Share Workstation Resources

NOTES

Introduction to Peer-to-Peer Networks

■ On **peer-to-peer** networks, each workstation can have disk areas that are accessible to other users. In such a network, no machine acts solely as a server. If you want a file from another workstation, you act as a client and the other machine is the server; if someone retrieves files from your machine, your workstation is the server and the other is the client.

■ Peer-to-peer networks usually work best when only a few users are involved, as in a home or small office.

■ Combinations of file server and peer-to-peer networks often exist within a single company. Several users who are working on the same project may work on a peer-to-peer network. They may need, for example, to retain close working-group control of specific files. But when members of the group need to communicate with or use files that belong to the organization as a whole, they may access the file server network that everyone in the company uses.

Peer-to-Peer Network Components

- **Workstations** are independent computers that can share data and resources with each other directly rather than through a server. Users can control access to the resources on their machines even if, in practice, much of the administration of the network is handled by one user.

- **Printers** are shared across the network. Each printer is identified by a name. When users want to print, they choose a printer through the application they are using. Other peripherals are managed in the same way as printers.

- **Network cards** are specific to the type of peer-to-peer network being used. They convert binary data from the computer into signals that can be transmitted over cables to and from other computers.

- **Cables** connect computers to a router or hub or directly to one another.

■ The illustration on the next page shows a four-station peer-to-peer network and its connection through a router or hub to the Internet.

Hybrid File-Server and Peer-to-Peer Networks

Many local area networks offer both file-server and peer-to-peer networking. Users connect to a server for most applications, but they can also connect directly to other users' computers in peer-to-peer communications.

Four-Station Peer-to-Peer Network

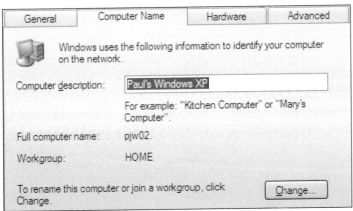

Ink Jet Printer — Windows 98 — Windows XP — Windows Me — Router or Hub — Windows 2000 — Laser Printer

Cable or DSL or Telephone Modem

Internet

Learn the Name and Workgroup of a Computer

- To use a peer-to-peer network, you need to know the name of the computer you are using and the workgroup to which it belongs. In most peer-to-peer networks, all computers belong to the same workgroup, which is just a name that organizes groups of computers. The computer name and workgroup are either assigned during installation of the operating system or when it is configured with the network identification software.

Try It!

1. On the desktop, right-click the My Computer icon.
2. Click Properties.
3. Click the Computer Name tab.

   Windows displays the name and workgroup of the computer. The illustration on the next page shows portions of the displays.

Windows XP Computer Name

General	Computer Name	Hardware	Advanced

Windows uses the following information to identify your computer on the network.

Computer description: Paul's Windows XP

For example: "Kitchen Computer" or "Mary's Computer".

Full computer name: pjw02.

Workgroup: HOME

To rename this computer or join a workgroup, click Change. [Change...]

Explore a Peer-to-Peer Network

- You can explore a Windows peer-to-peer network through Windows Explorer. The following illustration shows portions of a four-workstation, peer-to-peer network displayed in Windows Explorer.

Windows Explorer View of Peer-to-Peer Network

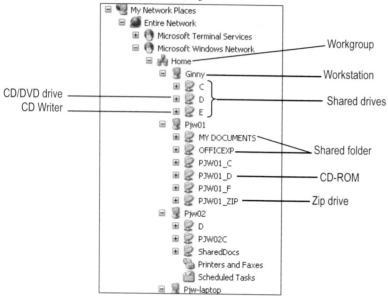

- Any drive on a machine can be shared. Note, for example, the Ginny workstation shares its CD-ROM and CD Writer as well as its C: drive, and PJW01 shares an Iomega® Zip drive to provide additional storage on 100 MB removable disks.

- When you right-click on one of the drives, a shortcut menu appears, as shown in the illustration at the right. (For the Sharing and Security options, see later in this exercise on page 439.)

Try It!

View Workstation's Properties

1. Open My Network Places.

2. Under Network Tasks, click View workgroup computers
   View workgroup computers.

3. Right-click the name of a workstation Pjw-laptop.

4. Click Properties to display a dialog box similar to the one in the following illustration.

Peer-to-Peer Workstation Properties, General Tab

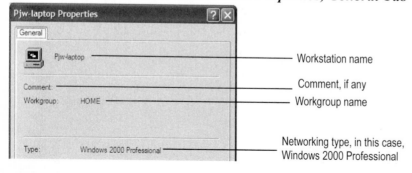

Peer-to-Peer Workstation Shortcut Menu

Expand

Explore
Open
Search...

Sharing and Security...
Scan with Norton AntiVirus
Add to Zip

Format...

Copy

Rename

Properties

- The information displayed in the Type field depends on the operating systems of the two workstations. For example, the following illustration shows several workstations and how other versions of Windows display the Type field.

*Windows XP
Viewing Windows 2000*

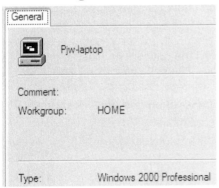

*Windows XP
Viewing Windows XP*

Share Workstation Resources

- Workstation **resources** include drives, folders, files, printers, scanners, and other peripherals. Access to these resources is managed through the Sharing option on the shortcut menu.

- To share a resource, you right-click on the resource (drive C:, for example) to be shared, and choose Sharing and Security. The Properties dialog box Sharing tab appears, as shown in the illustrations on the next page.

  ✓ *Note that the Sharing tab appears on the Properties dialog box only when you activate the Sharing and Security option.*

- You click the options *Share this folder on the network* and you can type a *Share name*. The option *Allow network users to change my files* give users full access to the resource. If the option is not selected, users have read-only access.

- When a resource is shared, a small hand appears as part of its icon when the resource is viewed through Windows Explorer.

Peer-to-Peer Workstation Properties, Sharing Tab

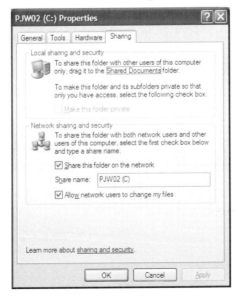

> *In this exercise, you will explore portions of a peer-to-peer network.*

EXERCISE DIRECTIONS

1. Start Windows Explorer.
2. Expand (click the + symbol to the left of) My Network Places.
3. Expand Entire Network.
4. Expand Microsoft Windows Network.
5. Expand the workgroup.

   The left pane of Windows Explorer should look similar to Illustration A.

6. Select any of the workstations but the one you are using.

   The left pane shows shared drives and folders; the right pane lists all shared resources.

7. In the right pane, review the resources that are shared across the network. In Illustration B, for example, four drives, three folders, and three printers are shared.
8. In the right pane, open one of the resources.
9. Review its contents.
10. Close Windows Explorer.

Illustration A. Expanded Network Neighborhood or My Network Places

Illustration B. Shared Resources

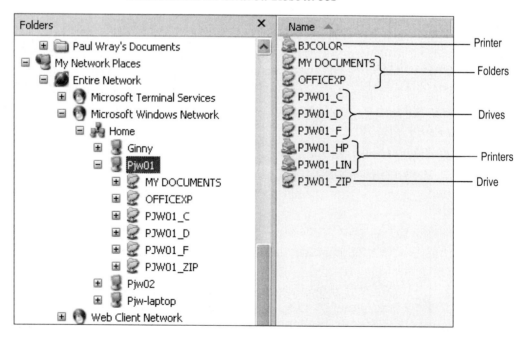

Exercise 3

Learn about the Internet

■ The Internet ■ Internet Addresses—URLs (Uniform Resource Locators) ■ Internet Use
■ Introduction to Internet Explorer ■ The World Wide Web ■ Online Services
■ Electronic Mail (E-mail) ■ File Transfer Protocol (FTP)

NOTES

The Internet

- The Internet is a network of computers. It combines client-server and peer-to-peer networking to make it possible for computer users all over the globe to share the network's facilities and to communicate with other users.

- The Internet resulted from the desire to have computers talk to one another so that users could share information, data, and ideas. It originated as a way for researchers, especially in defense industries and universities, to share information. With the introduction of the World Wide Web in 1989, businesses, schools, governments, and nonprofit organizations realized that it would be a valuable tool to communicate with customers and clients and to provide information and services.

- Now nearly every television and radio commercial and newspaper and magazine ad gives an address where the company or organization can be contacted on the Internet.

- The Internet is a large number of computers linked by a variety of connections—cables, telephone lines, satellite. They pass information back and forth using the communications protocol called **TCP/IP** (Transmission Control Protocol/Internet Protocol). TCP/IP is actually a suite of protocols that make the Internet work. It performs the following communications functions:
  - Permits login from remote computers.
  - Routes data between Internet servers.
  - Makes sure that data packets are error-free and assembled in the right sequence.
  - Converts text-based domain names into numerical IP addresses.

- The computers that form the Internet can be divided into the following groups:
  - **Clients** are computers that connect to the Internet to do research and send e-mail. Most personal computers that access the Internet are in this category. Client computers access the Internet in one of three ways:
    - Internet Service Provider (see following page).
    - Online service, such as America Online (AOL) or Prodigy (see following page).
    - Direct access through a dedicated communications line (telephone or cable television) that is continuously connected to the Internet.

IP Address
Four-part number that identifies a computer linked to the Internet. Each part of the number is a number from 0 and 255, and some numbers are reserved. For example, the IP address 192.168.0.1 identifies a computer on a home network that connects to the Internet through a modem and router or hub.

The modem for such a network has an IP address assigned by the Internet Service Provider.

IP addresses may be **static** (associated with a specific device) or **dynamic**. If an address is dynamic, the device (modem or computer) is assigned a different IP address each time it connects to the Internet.

- **Online services** provide a variety of shopping, research, and e-mail services and also provide access to the Internet. America Online (AOL) and Prodigy are the most well-known of these services. Such services are not actually part of the Internet, but to most users the distinction between AOL and the Internet is a distinction without a difference.

- **Internet Service Providers (ISPs)** are computers that provide other computers with access to the Internet. Networks such as Earthlink, NetCom, and AT&T Worldnet are ISPs.

- **Internet servers** (sometimes called *hosts*) are computers that provide access to information. When an Internet user contacts an Internet site, the computer that contains the site is a server. Internet servers may also act as clients when they request a link to another site. Some servers offer specialized services, such as e-mail and file transfer.

  - **Search engines or sites** are Internet computers dedicated to providing information about other Internet sites. Yahoo!, Google, HotBot, Lycos, and AltaVista are examples of search sites although most of these provide many services in addition to search capabilities.

  - **E-mail servers** are computers that provide electronic mail boxes and service.

  - **File transfer protocol (FTP) servers** are computers dedicated to allowing the transfer of files from one computer to another.

Internet Addresses—URLs (Uniform Resource Locators)

- Because the Internet is not a single network but a collection of networks, a naming system called the **domain** name system is used to identify the exact location of Internet servers and their primary Internet activity. It's something like the telephone numbering system that includes country codes, area codes, and individual phone numbers.

- An Internet address (IP address) is made up of a four-part series of numbers. The domain-name system translates the numbers into a user-friendly system of text-based names. So instead of typing in http://4.18.84.83/ to order a pizza over the Internet, you can type in "www.pizzahut.com." Text is easier to remember.

- To locate an Internet site, you enter an address, called a **URL (uniform resource locator)**. Usually this address is a group of characters that looks like the following:

  http://www.phschool.com

  - **http** stands for HyperText Transfer Protocol, the communications protocol used by sites on the World Wide Web.

  - **www** stands for World Wide Web, the largest part of the Internet, but not the only part (see next page).

  - **phschool** is the name used to identify the organization responsible for the content of the site. It is usually some form of the name of the company or organization, for example, phschool is the identifier for Pearson Prentice Hall, the publisher of this book.

  - **com** is the **domain** identifier. Different types of organizations have different domain names.

442

■ Internet domains include the ones listed below. Others such as **.biz**, **.info**, **.name**, and **.pro** may also be available.

Domain:	Used By:
.com	Commercial/business
.gov	Government
.edu	Educational
.org	Various organizations, usually non-profit
.mil	Military
.net	Network resources

■ The Internet includes:

- The World Wide Web
- E-mail servers
- File Transfer Protocol sites

■ The Internet also includes Gopher, Usenet, and Telnet, which are defined at the right but not otherwise described in this book.

Internet Use

■ To use the Internet you need:

- **Internet browser**, such as Microsoft Internet Explorer or Netscape Navigator. A browser is an application that:
  - ◆ Lets you connect to the Internet either directly or through a modem and a telephone line using an ISP or online service.
  - ◆ Lets you enter URLs.
  - ◆ Displays information provided by an Internet site.
  - ◆ Lets you save or print displayed information so it can be reviewed later.
  - ◆ Recognizes and lets you activate connections (called **hyperlinks**) to other addresses.
  - ◆ Lets you save addresses that you'd like to visit again using **favorites** (Internet Explorer) or **bookmarks** (Netscape Navigator).
- **Internet connection**. The link to the Internet may be a cable modem and cable TV line using the same connection as your cable TV. It may be a DSL (Digital Subscriber Line) modem and regular telephone line treated in a special way. Or, it may be a traditional modem and voice telephone line.
- Cable and DSL connections are generally significantly faster than traditional modems. Traditional modems are usually rated at 56K BPS **bits per second (BPS)**. A traditional 56K modem sends and receives a maximum of 56,000 bits every second. Cable and DSL modems usually transfer data at more than triple that speed.
- Even higher data transfer speeds are achieved with such direct connections as T1 and T3 lines.
- **ISP** or **online service** (or direct Internet connection) that gives you access to the Internet.

Gopher

A browsing system for Internet resources that predates the World Wide Web. Gopher works much like a directory, listing Internet sites in a menu.

Usenet

A global system of discussion groups called *newsgroups*. Many Internet browsers include a newsreader program to access the newsgroups.

Telnet

A program that lets one computer log on to a remote computer. Telnet is often used to search libraries and databases.

Introduction to Internet Explorer

- This book does not go into detail about how to use Internet Explorer, one of the most popular Internet browser applications available. This section provides a brief look at the Internet Explorer window and what it contains.

Internet Explorer Window

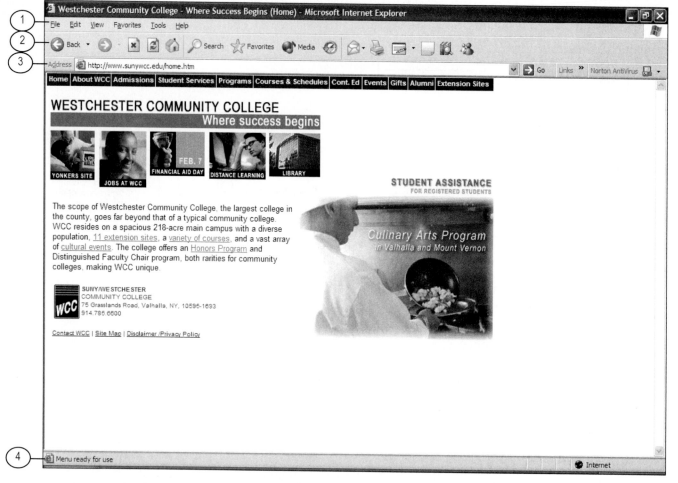

1. The **menu bar** gives access to functions that let you open HTML documents saved on your machine, save and print Web pages, perform some edits (copy and paste, for example), change your view of Internet displays, move from one Internet site to another, save favorite sites so you can revisit them, and get help.

2. **Toolbar buttons** are described below.

3. In the **Address box**, you enter the URL of the site you want to visit.

4. The **status bar** provides information about your use of Internet Explorer.

- Internet Explorer's toolbar has several buttons that help you find your way around the Internet. Your toolbar may not include all the buttons and may include buttons not described below.

 Back lets you return to the previous page.

 Forward lets you move to a page you previously viewed. This button is active only if you have previously used the Back button.

Stop interrupts the attempt to display the current page. If a page is taking a long time to display completely, you can click this button to stop the display.

 Refresh redisplays the current page, updating any elements that have changed.

 Home returns you immediately to your home page, the page that first appears when you start the browser.

 Search lets you search the Internet for information.

 Favorites lets you save site addresses so you can revisit them later.

 History lets you review and return to sites that you have visited.

 Mail lets you send e-mail.

 Print lets you print the currently displayed page.

 Edit opens the current Web page in a word processor or text editor.

 Discuss lets you link to a discussion server. The first time you click this button, Internet Explorer starts a wizard that guides you in adding a discussion server.

 Messenger is a Microsoft service that lets you send instant messages to other users. You must be signed up to use the service.

 Status icon. The status icon is the Windows flag icon or the Internet Explorer *e* icon. When Internet Explorer is connecting to a page, the icon is animated until the page is fully displayed.

The World Wide Web

- The World Wide Web portion of the Internet contains **Web sites**. Web sites are addresses on the Internet maintained by various organizations and individuals to provide information and services to Internet users.

- A Web site is built from **Web pages**, which are specially designed and formatted to display text and graphics. Most Web pages are built using the programming language called **HTML** (HyperText MarkUp Language). Many Web pages also include objects that are presented using Java, another programming language.

- When you enter the URL of a Web site, you are usually taken to a site's **home page**, the starting point for exploring the site. If you know or have saved the URL of a different page within the site, you can go directly to that page by entering its full address. A portion of the home page of the Smithsonian Institution (*www.si.edu*) is shown on the following page.

    Web sites change frequently. As companies and organizations stress new services and new information, they change their Web sites.

HTML (HyperText MarkUp Language)
HTML is the most common of the programming languages used in building Web pages.

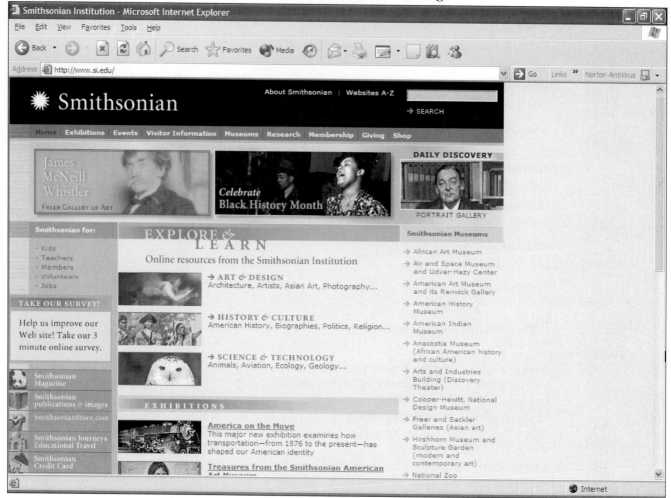

- When a Web page is displayed, you can point your mouse to graphics or underlined text. When the mouse pointer turns to a hand 🖑, you can click to activate a link to another page or another Web site.

- You can return to a previous Web page by clicking the Back button on the browser's toolbar.

Online Services

- America Online (AOL), Microsoft Network, and Prodigy are online services that provide more than just a connection to the Internet and e-mail. They offer a large number of services that may connect you to Web sites, but just as often keep you within the services hosted by the company itself. For example, when you sign on to AOL, the opening window offers a variety of options, only some of which take you immediately to the Internet. The other services, including Channels, Mail Center, and People Connection, are all part of the services offered by AOL. The opening AOL Window (version 9.0) is shown in the following illustration.

AOL 9.0 Opening Window

Electronic Mail (E-mail)

■ Very early on, networks provided a way to pass messages from one user to another. As mentioned in Exercise 1 of this lesson, Novell networks offer a way to broadcast messages to one or more users. (Send Message was an option on the right-click menu.) These messages are sent and then disappear. They are not saved on the network and cannot be reviewed after they are first viewed.

■ Software companies developed electronic mail (e-mail) applications to provide a way to save messages, make sure that messages were received by the addressee, and provide more privacy in their transmission.

■ At first, these e-mail systems were internal. Internal e-mail systems have been in use for some time in most companies. If you need to send an agenda for a meeting to several coworkers, you can address an e-mail message to them.

■ With the explosion in growth of the Internet, companies recognized the value of e-mail from one organization to another. Thus, they began to provide e-mail capabilities that used the Internet to send messages anywhere.

- E-mail finds its destination because it has been properly addressed. The e-mail address has three components, as shown in the example that follows:

  username@earthlink.net

  - **username** is the **e-mail ID**. It is an identifier that tells who is sending or receiving the message. Most often, this part of the address identifies a specific person, but sometimes you can send a message to a company or organization without a specific person's name. An entry is required, however, before the @.

  - **@ (at)** is the symbol that separates the ID from the name of the e-mail domain name.

  - **earthlink.net** is the domain name of the e-mail server. Quite often, this domain is the same as the recipient's ISP, but it may be a different domain entirely, such as *yahoo.com* or *hotmail.com*.

E-mail Use

To use e-mail, you need:

- An **e-mail address**. Many ISPs and all online services provide e-mail addresses. In addition, there are a number of e-mail servers devoted to e-mail traffic.

- An **e-mail application**. Most Internet browsers offer e-mail as one of their programs. Online services also have e-mail built-in. A popular e-mail option for those who do not have a browser or online service is Eudora, an e-mail application created at the University of Illinois.

- The illustration below and on the next page shows two sample e-mail messages. One message was created in Outlook Express, the other in AOL. While other e-mail applications have slightly different looks, the basic information necessary to send a message is the same.

Outlook Express E-mail Message

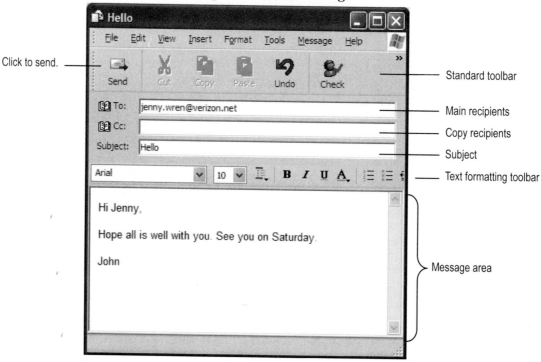

America Online E-mail Message

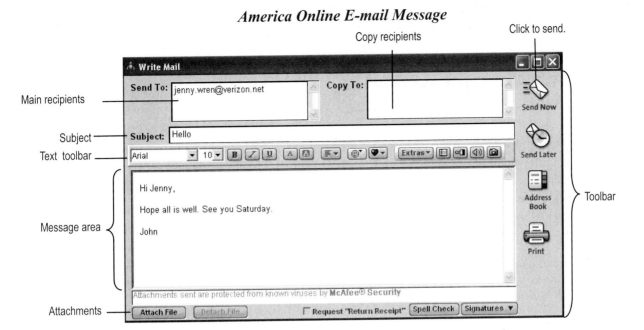

File Attachments

- Besides sending messages to coworkers and friends, e-mail users often attach files to their messages.

- For example, if you want to share a story you have written with a friend, you can attach the story to an e-mail message and send it along. When the friend receives the message, the e-mail application notifies him or her that a file is attached, and the friend can download the file to the local computer.

- Many files are transferred this way every day, but FTP (see below) is a faster alternative that is often used, especially for large files.

File Transfer Protocol (FTP)

- **File Transfer Protocol (FTP)** is another area of the Internet. FTP sites let users **download** (retrieve files from a server) and **upload** (send files to a server). The Internet includes a number of FTP sites and users can take advantage of FTP capabilities, especially when they have large files that they need to download or upload.

- FTP sites are specially designed to shorten the time it takes to transfer files. Most sites require a password and authorized access to their files and folders. Most also maintain an **anonymous logon**, which gives access to limited areas of the site.

In this exercise, you will explore some of the World Wide Web. You will need Internet access in order to complete the exercise.

EXERCISE DIRECTIONS

Internet Access
1. Start your browser and connect to the Internet.
2. Open the page that has the following URL:
   http://www.si.edu
3. Continue with *Activate Some Links* below.

Activate Some Links

The Smithsonian Institution Web home page appears. The Smithsonian home page may differ from the one illustrated. If the links listed below are no longer available, explore other areas of the Web site. (The illustration at the right shows only a portion of the page.)

1. Click the <u>Science & Technology</u> link or the photograph of the owl. *You know the text or picture can be clicked because the mouse pointer turns into a hand.*

   The Smithsonian Science and Technology page opens.

Smithsonian Institution Home Page

Smithsonian Science and Technology Page

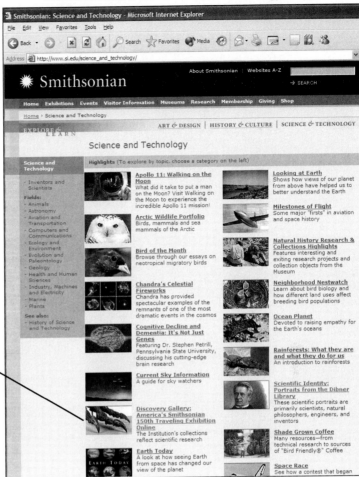

2. Click the following link:
   <u>Discovery Gallery: America's Smithsonian 150th Traveling Exhibition Online</u> or click the picture of the bird's talons.

The Smithsonian Discovery Gallery appears as shown at the right.

Smithsonian Discovery Gallery Page

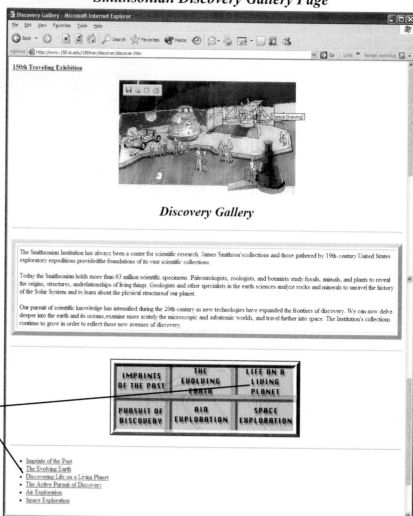

3. Click the Life on a Living Planet button or the link <u>Discovering Life on a Living Planet</u>.

The Discovering Life on a Living Planet page opens as shown at the right.

Discovering Life on a Living Planet Page

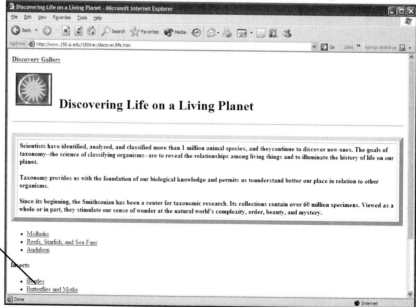

4. Click on the following link: <u>Beetles</u>.

The Beetles page appears as shown on the following page.

Smithsonian Beetles Page

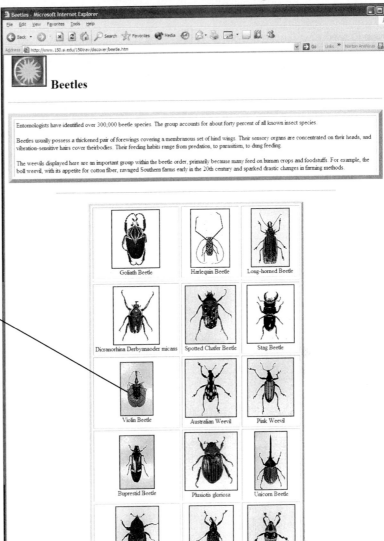

5. Scroll down until you locate the Violin Beetle.
6. Click the picture of the Violin Beetle to display the Violin Beetle page.

Review Violin Beetle Page

1. Scroll down to read material that is not visible at first.
2. Click the Back button to return to the Beetles page.
3. Click the Back button again to return to the Discovery Gallery page.
4. Click the Forward button to return to the Beetles page.

   Browsers have Back and Forward buttons to help you move among pages you have opened.

5. Close your browser and disconnect from your service provider.

Violin Beetle Page

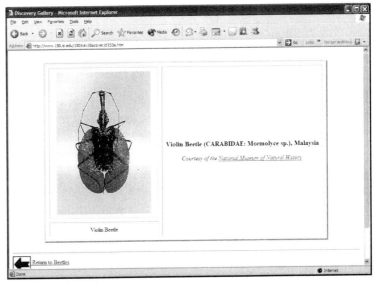

Exercise 4

Learn about Other Communications Methods
■ Wide Area Networks (WANs) ■ Intranets
■ Telecommuting ■ PC-to-Mainframe Communications

NOTES

Wide Area Networks (WANs)

- Another kind of network is called a Wide Area Network (WAN). In some companies, a WAN is used to connect workers in different geographic locations. In the central location, the network operates like a LAN. Workers outside the central location communicate with the network via modem, satellite, or leased telephone lines through hardware and software facilities called *gateways*. The gateways give distant users access to the services of the central location.

- Most people reserve the term WAN for networks that serve only members of the same company or organization. Others consider AOL, Prodigy, and the World Wide Web as WANs.

Intranets

- Many users within an organization may have access to the Internet, using their Internet browsers to find information, send e-mail, and exchange files with coworkers. But when they leave the Internet, many of them have to use other applications to review information and exchange files.

- Increasingly, therefore, companies are creating internal Webs to allow employees to access company information using the same application they use to access the Internet. These internal Webs are known as **intranets**.

- Intranets are created and managed within an organization. Users outside the organization generally cannot gain access to them. This means that information that is inappropriate for an Internet site, such as personnel policies or intra-company news, can be provided on an intranet. Using their Internet browsers, workers can use the intranet in the same way they use the Internet.

- Some companies also provide access to their intranets to authorized outside users. For example, a company may wish a supplier to be able to review specifications for a purchase that is about to be made. The supplier then uses an Internet browser, contacts the intranet (often through the Internet) and gains access to the intranet through an ID and password. The companies that provide such access call this an **extranet**.

- An intranet may have connections to the Internet, but these connections are constructed to prevent unauthorized access. The term *firewall* is used to describe protecting a network or computer from unauthorized access.

Telecommuting

- More and more workers are working away from the office. Some of them simply use their PCs as local machines and communicate with the office only when they have files they want to send or receive. Such users may use the Internet or e-mail service as their way to communicate with the office and never actually log in to the office's computers.

- Other workers, however, connect via telephone lines and work directly on the office network. Telecommuting of this type requires hardware and software on both the workstation and the server. Usually the telecommuter starts the communications software on the workstation, dials up the office computer, and logs in as a network user. The full facilities of the company's network are then available to the workstation.

- For example, employees may use a popular telecommunications program called Symantec® pcAnywhere™, a product of the same company that offers Norton AntiVirus™ software.

- As part of the Windows XP Professional operating system, Microsoft provides called Remote Desktop Connection, which offers functions similar to those of pcAnywhere.

- Another common way for users to connect to an organization's computers is through a **virtual private network** (VPN). VPN connections use public facilities – DSL, cable, dial-up – to connect to another computer. The communication is conducted in code (coding and decoding are part of the VPN software) to prevent unauthorized interception.

PC-to-Mainframe Communications

- To use a company's mainframe computing capacity, workers require a **terminal**. Terminals are pieces of hardware that have no software of their own. They are connected to the mainframe computer via cables and their communication is managed by a **controller**, another piece of hardware that provides the link between terminals (one controller can handle many terminals) and the mainframe. Terminals are single-use devices; they cannot function apart from the mainframe. If they get disconnected from the computer or the mainframe stops working, their users are no longer computing.

- In the first days of the personal computer, users thought it would be good to use them just like terminals. But terminals operate differently from PCs. PCs do not require controllers and ordinarily do not speak the same language as controllers. Often workers who needed both a personal computer and access to the company's mainframe had both a PC and a terminal on their desks. Soon after the introduction of IBM's PC in the early 1980s, however, both hardware and software solutions were created.

- **Terminal emulation software**, programs that mimicked mainframe terminals, was created as early as 1981 for computers built by Digital Equipment Corporation. DEC mainframes used ASCII (American Standard Code for Information Interchange) for encoding characters. Since PCs also used ASCII, it was possible to create software that let a PC work with a DEC mainframe.

- IBM mainframes, however, were a different matter. Rather than use ASCII codes, they use a coding system called EBCDIC (sometimes pronounced EB-sid-ick, short for <u>E</u>xtended <u>B</u>inary <u>C</u>oded <u>D</u>ecimal <u>I</u>nterchange <u>C</u>ode). Differences between the ASCII and EBCDIC coding systems made it necessary to create **terminal emulation hardware** so the PC and the IBM mainframe could communicate.

- In most installations where PCs and mainframes communicate today, a combination of hardware and software does the job. In many companies, users are connected to a local area network and log on (or sign on) to the organization's mainframe without disconnecting from the network. The personal computer then operates not only as an independent machine but also as a network workstation and as a mainframe terminal.

Lesson 10: Computer Care

Exercise 1: Manage Your Disks
- ♦ Check a Disk for Problems
- ♦ Defragment the Hard Drive
- ♦ Format a Diskette

Exercise 2: Use Backup
- ♦ Back Up Files
- ♦ Restore Backed Up Files

Exercise 3: Learn about Virus Protection
- ♦ Protect against Viruses
- ♦ Set Windows for Automatic Updates
- ♦ Run a Virus Scan
- ♦ Review Scan Results

Exercise 4: Add Software to Your Computer
- ♦ Install Software
- ♦ Install a Printer

Exercise 5: Keep Your Computer System Clean
- ♦ General Care Instructions
- ♦ Clean the Monitor
- ♦ Are Screen Savers Necessary?
- ♦ Clean the Keyboard
- ♦ Clean the Mouse
- ♦ Clean the Cases
- ♦ Maintain Computers and Peripherals

Exercise 1

Manage Your Disks
■ Check a Disk for Problems
■ Defragment the Hard Drive ■ Format a Diskette

NOTES

Check a Disk for Problems

■ If you have ever turned off Windows before its shutdown was complete or had to reboot because the system failed, you may have seen Windows run ScanDisk or a disk checking routine when you next started your computer. Windows uses these disk-checking programs to determine if a disk is damaged or contains data that seems not to be part of a file.

💻Try It!

1. Open the My Computer window.
2. Select the drive containing the disk you want to check.
3. Click File, Properties to display the Properties dialog box.
4. Click the Tools tab to display the dialog box shown in the illustration that follows.

Drive C: Properties Dialog Box, Tools Tab

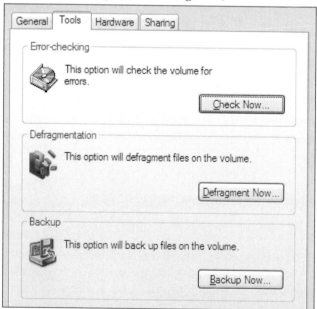

Check Now Unavailable

If you have a program such as Norton Utilities installed on your machine, some of the options described in this section may be unavailable.

5. Click the Check Now button [Check Now...] to display the Check Disk dialog box, as shown in the illustrations on the next page.
6. Complete the dialog box as outlined in the table that follows the illustration:

Check Disk Dialog Box

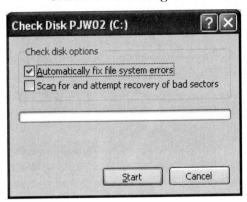

7. Select *Automatically fix file system errors* to scan the system and solve problems with the file system.

8. Select *Scan for and attempt recovery of bad sectors* if you believe some portions of your hard drive are not storing data correctly.

   Select this option if you are scanning a diskette. If Windows detects surface errors, copy data you want to save to another disk. Then try reformatting the diskette. If the reformat results show errors, discard the diskette. Damaged diskettes can cause you to lose data.

9. Click the Start button [Start].

   If you have selected drive C:\ (the drive where Windows itself is installed), the system displays the message shown in the following illustration, indicating that the procedure can run only when you restart the machine.

Windows XP Checking Disk Dialog Box

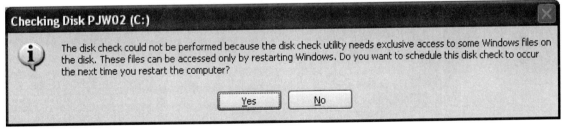

10. Click the Yes button [Yes].

    The next time you start Windows, the check disk procedure will run

Defragment the Hard Drive

- Occasionally, you may need to let Windows **defragment** the hard drive. If you find that files are taking a long time to open, you should run the defragmenting procedure to improve system performance. This procedure can take a long time. Run it only when you have time to let it complete unless you are willing to interrupt it before it finishes.

💻 Try It!

1. Click the Start button [start].

2. Point to All Programs, Accessories, System Tools, and click Disk Defragmenter .

The Disk Defragmenter dialog box appears.

Windows XP Disk Defragmenter Dialog Box

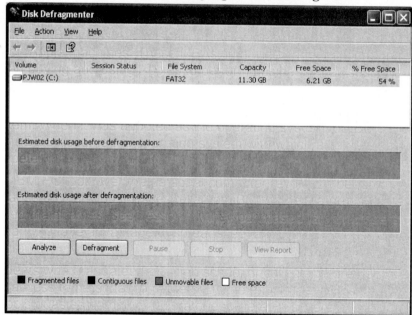

3. Select the drive to be defragmented.

4. Click the Analyze button ▭ Analyze ▭ .

   Windows checks to see how much fragmentation exists on the disk.

   When analysis is complete Windows displays a message box. The message recommends defragmentation if it will help improve your system's performance.

5. If Windows recommends defragmentation, click the Defragment button ▭ Defragment ▭ on the message box to start the procedure.

   When defragmentation is complete, Windows displays the results in the lower portion of the Disk Defragmenter dialog box.

Disk Defragmentation Complete

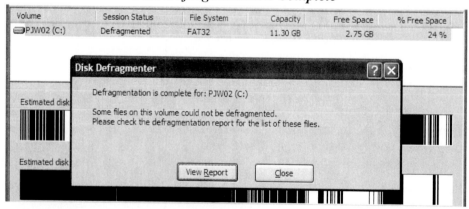

6. Click the Close button ▭ Close ▭ .

7. Click the Close button ✖ on the Disk Defragmenter dialog box.

Defragment

When you save a file, the operating systems are written (saved) in allocation-unit-sized chunks. These chunks are not necessarily saved to consecutive allocation units on your hard disk. After a while, data in files gets scattered, and the operating system takes longer to retrieve the pieces of the file. Defragmenting improves performance by rearranging the data so that the chunks of a file are stored in allocation units that are next to each other.

🖥 Try It!

Use My Computer to Start Defragmentation

You can also start the defragmentation procedure through My Computer, as described below.

1. Open My Computer, and select the drive to be defragmented.

2. Click File, Properties to display the Properties dialog box.

3. Click Tools to display the Tools tab, and look at the Defragmentation status, as shown in the illustrations that follow.

   Note that Windows indicates either that it cannot determine when the drive was last defragmented or the date of the most recent defragmentation.

Properties Dialog Box, Tools Tab, Defragmentation

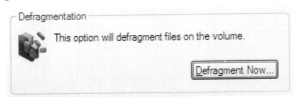

4. Click the Defragment Now button [Defragment Now...].

   Windows starts defragmentation and displays the Defragmenting Drive progress box shown on page 460.

Format a Diskette

- Most diskettes come preformatted to be compatible with your computer. When you buy them, be sure to get diskettes that are formatted for use with Windows machines (sometimes these are still called MS-DOS or PC-DOS or even IBM PC compatible).

- When you have used a diskette for a while and you no longer need the data stored on it, you may get better performance if you reformat it. Formatting erases all existing data and resets the recording medium to receive new data.

   ✓ *Use the procedure below only for 3½" diskettes. Do not use this procedure for drives that contain other removable media. Iomega and SyQuest drives have utility programs that allow you to format their disks.*

🖥 Try It!

1. Place the diskette in the diskette drive.

2. Open My Computer and select the drive (usually drive A:).

3. Click File, Format to display the Format dialog box, as shown in the illustration on the next page.

4. Choose the options you want for the format.

   ◆ *Quick* (erase) or *Quick Format* simply erases the files. Use it if you are sure the diskette has already been formatted and is not damaged.

   ◆ *File System* and *Allocation unit size* cannot be changed for 3½" diskettes.

♦ *Label* or *Volume label* lets you specify a label for the diskette. Labels can be helpful in identifying the owner or content of a diskette.

♦ *Create an MS-DOS startup disk* copies the system files to the diskette. You can use a diskette created in this way to start your computer when you cannot locate your Windows XP installation CD.

5. If you are formatting a diskette, click the Start button [Start].

   Windows 2000 and XP: *Windows displays a warning similar to the one shown in the illustration below.*

   If you are not formatting a diskette, click the Close button [Close].

Format Dialog Box

Format Warning

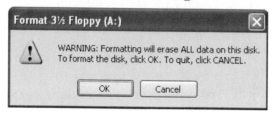

6. To proceed with the formatting, click the OK button [OK].

   To cancel the formatting, click the Cancel button [Cancel].

   The Format procedure begins and a progress bar at the bottom of the dialog box shows how much of the job is complete.

7. When the job is complete, the message box shown below appears.

8. Click the OK button [OK].

9. Close the main Format dialog box.

Format Complete Message Box

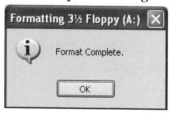

Exercise 2

Use Backup
■ Back Up Files ■ Restore Backed Up Files

NOTES

Back Up Files

- **Backup** is the process of copying files from your hard drive to a medium that can be stored elsewhere and retrieved when you need to restore the data because the hard drive is damaged, the file becomes corrupted, or the file is accidentally erased. Backup can save you time because you can recover earlier versions of files rather than have to create them all over again.

- If you work on a computer that is not connected to a network, you need to be certain that you back up your files frequently.

- If you work on a network, your system administration probably handles backup for your network files. You still need to back up any local files that you do not want to lose.

- **Frequency of backup** depends on the data you have and how much you use your machine. At least once a week you should ensure that all new and changed files are backed up. You should run backup every day if you use your hard drive to create files that you do not want to lose.

- If your computer has a CD writer included, you may wish to back up your data onto CDs. To do so, you use the same application program that you use to create any CD. You simply tell the program which files you want to back up onto the CD.

- Windows also provides a backup program that you can use to perform periodic backups. The Try It! activities below outline the steps for Windows XP. The Backup and Restore wizards for Windows 98, Me, and 2000 have more dialog boxes than those shown here, but their essential features are similar.

💻 Try It!

Prepare for Backup

1. Collect enough clean, formatted diskettes to contain the data you intend to back up. If you have an Iomega Zip or Jaz drive or a SyQuest system attached to your machine, you can back up to those removable media.

2. Open the My Computer window, and select a drive.

3. Click File, Properties, and click the Tools tab. (This dialog box is illustrated in Exercise 1 in this lesson.)

4. Click the Backup Now button to start the backup process with the Welcome to the Backup or Restore Wizard dialog box, as shown on the next page.

Moving Files
Moving files from the hard disk to a diskette when you no longer need them is a good idea, but it is not backup. Moving does not ensure the integrity of the files that remain on the hard drive; backup does.

Removable Media
Many companies provide special drives with removable media that can be used for backup. These include tape drives, which usually come with their own backup software, and other removable disks such as Iomega Zip and Jaz and SyQuest.

5. Select *Always start in wizard mode* unless you are knowledgeable about using the backup system.

6. Click the Next button [Next >].

   The Backup Wizard asks you to select backup or restore, as shown in the following illustration.

7. For this Try It!, select *Back up files and settings*.

Backup or Restore Wizard, Backup or Restore

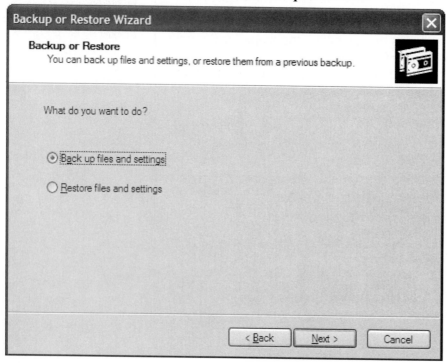

Select Objects for Backup

The Backup Wizard lets you choose to back up entire drives, specific folders, or specific files. You display objects in the window in the same way that you do in Windows Explorer except that each object is preceded by a check box.

Try It!

1. Click the <u>N</u>ext button 【 <u>N</u>ext > 】.

Backup or Restore Wizard, What to Back Up

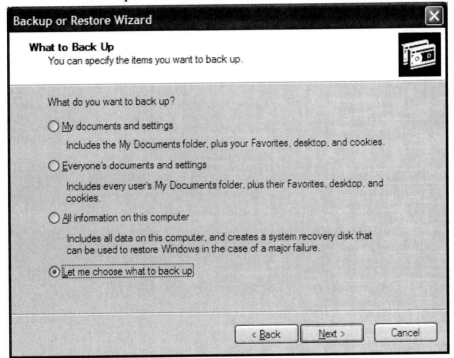

> **Backup or Restore Wizard**   ⊠
>
> **What to Back Up**
> You can specify the items you want to back up.
>
> What do you want to back up?
>
> ○ <u>M</u>y documents and settings
>
>   Includes the My Documents folder, plus your Favorites, desktop, and cookies.
>
> ○ <u>E</u>veryone's documents and settings
>
>   Includes every user's My Documents folder, plus their Favorites, desktop, and cookies.
>
> ○ <u>A</u>ll information on this computer
>
>   Includes all data on this computer, and creates a system recovery disk that can be used to restore Windows in the case of a major failure.
>
> ⦿ <u>L</u>et me choose what to back up
>
>   【 < <u>B</u>ack 】 【 <u>N</u>ext > 】 【 Cancel 】

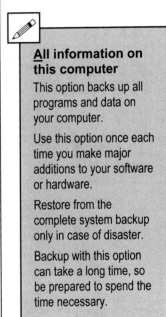

All information on this computer

This option backs up all programs and data on your computer.

Use this option once each time you make major additions to your software or hardware.

Restore from the complete system backup only in case of disaster.

Backup with this option can take a long time, so be prepared to spend the time necessary.

2. For this Try It! activity, select *Let me choose what to back up*.

3. Click the <u>N</u>ext button 【 <u>N</u>ext > 】.

    Windows displays a dialog box similar to Windows Explorer with two panes, so you can select specific items to be included in the backup, as shown in the illustration on the next page.

4. In the left pane, select the drives and folders you want to include. In the right pane, you can select specific files as well as drives and folders.

    For this Try It! activity, select any three items that are small enough to fit on a diskette (less that 1.44 MB total).

    Selected items have a blue check mark (black in the illustration).

    Note the gray check mark in the box next to the 2003 Literacy folder. The gray check box indicates that only some objects in that folder are included in the backup.

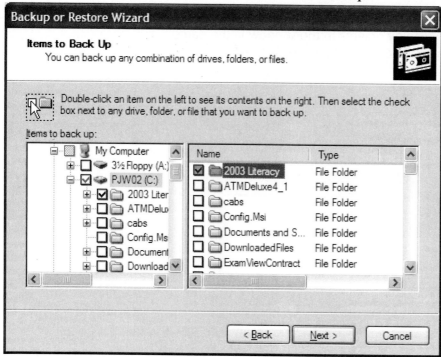

5. After selecting the objects to be included, click the Next button [Next >].

   Backup displays a dialog box in which you select a location to save the backup and give the backup a name. In the following illustration, the backup will be saved to the PJW01 Zip drive. (The default drive is diskette drive A:.)

Backup or Restore Wizard, Backup Type, Destination, and Name

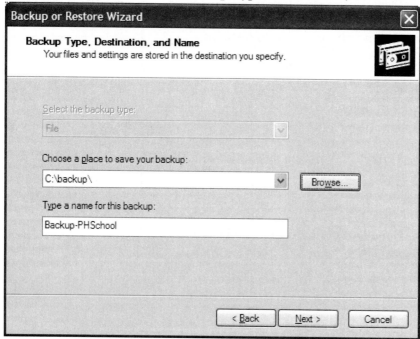

💻**Try It!**

Select Backup Destination

1. Click the <u>N</u>ext button [Next >].

   Backup displays a dialog box that summarizes the backup job, as shown in the following illustration.

Backup or Restore Wizard, Completing

2. Click the Finish button [Finish] to start backup and display a progress box.

Backup Progress

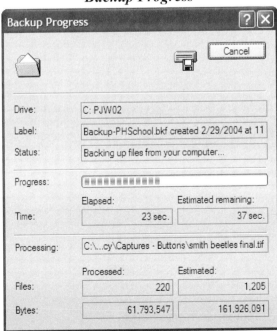

🖥 Try It!

Review the Report

When backup is complete, the progress box indicates that the job was successful.

Successful Backup

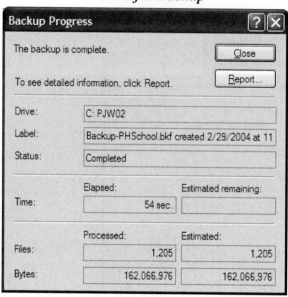

1. Click the <u>R</u>eport button [<u>Report...</u>] to see a printable version of the results in a text editor called Notepad.

2. Click the Close button ✕ on the report display.

3. Click the <u>C</u>lose button [<u>C</u>lose] on the progress box.

4. Close the property sheet from which you started backup.

Restore Backed Up Files

- Restoring files from backup follows a pattern similar to the backup procedure. You use this procedure when you need to retrieve a backup file that is damaged or otherwise not usable.

🖥 Try It!

1. Locate the diskette (or tape) that contains the backup of the files you want to restore.

2. Open the My Computer window, and select the drive to which files are to be restored.

3. Click <u>F</u>ile, <u>P</u>roperties, and click the Tools tab. (This dialog box is illustrated in Exercise 1 in this lesson.)

4. Click the <u>B</u>ackup Now button [Backup Now...] to start the backup process.

   The Backup or Restore wizard starts with the Welcome message.

5. Click the <u>N</u>ext button [<u>N</u>ext >].

6. On the Backup or Restore dialog box, select *<u>R</u>estore files and settings* ⊙ Restore files and settings .

⌨ **Try It!**

Select What to Restore

1. Click the Next button [Next >].

   The Backup or Restore wizard starts and asks you to select the backup file and the items you wish to restore.

2. In the right pane, select the backup from which you want to restore.

   ### *Backup or Restore Wizard, What to Restore*

Backup Identification Label	Me
Backup-XPLiteracy..bkf created 1/26/2...	\\Pj
Backup-XPLiteracy..bkf created 1/26/2...	\\Pj
Backup-XPLiteracy..bkf created 1/26/2...	Y:\E
Backup.bkf created 1/26/2002 at 8:08 ...	\\Pj

3. In the left pane, begin selecting the items you want to restore. Double-click to expand items, and select as you did in backup. Select the items you backed up in the previous Try It! activity.

   ### *Backup or Restore Wizard, What to Restore*

   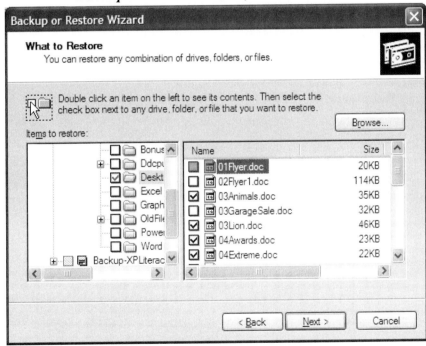

4. Click the Next button [Next >].

5. Review the Restore options you've specified, and click the Finish button [Finish].

   The Restore Progress box appears and displays a message when the restoration is complete.

6. Close the Restore Progress dialog box, and close the property sheet from which you started the Restore procedure.

Exercise 3

Learn about Virus Protection

■ Protect against Viruses ■ Set Windows for Automatic Updates
■ Run a Virus Scan ■ Review Scan Results

NOTES

Protect against Viruses

- Computer viruses range from the simply irritating to the completely devastating. The Have a Nice Day virus, for example, simply turns every Word document (.DOC) into a template (.DOT) file when it is saved. Once the virus is eliminated, the data in the .DOT file can be copied back into a .DOC. Many users may not know that such a virus has infected their files.

- Other viruses can cripple your machine or make it completely unusable. Some of these viruses attack the integrity of the hard drive and destroy the system's ability to save and retrieve files. Others reformat the hard drive, or infect the boot information on the disk so that you cannot start your machine.

- Viruses are the products of malice. Those who create them and those who knowingly pass them on to others are the same as thieves, stealing time and data from victims and disrupting normal work.

- You can help protect your computer against viruses by being watchful and cautious and taking simple steps.

  - Always install the *critical updates* recommended by Microsoft. At http://v4.windowsupdate.microsoft.com/en/default.asp, you can check your system to be sure that you are up to date. It is wise to set your system to check the Web site and download the updates when they become available.

  - Install and regularly use virus-checking software such as McAfee VirusScan or Norton AntiVirus. These programs check files as they are opened on your computer to ensure that no known virus can infect your machine.

  - If you have a virus-checking program, be sure to get the periodic updates to the virus recognition files from the manufacturer. The files are available via downloads from Web sites. It is especially important to keep your virus scanner up to date if you use the Web frequently.

  - Run the virus scan on your disks regularly, especially after you have transferred files from the Web or another computer.

  - Download files from Web sites with caution. Be sure you can trust the source of the files you are taking from the Web to your local machine. When in doubt, don't download.

  - Do not open e-mail from any source you do not recognize. E-mail is a frequent carrier of viruses, and some virus creators piggy-back disk-destroying viruses on **spam** (junk e-mail), luring unsuspecting users into infecting their local computers.

- Borrow diskettes only from people you trust. Scan the disk for viruses as the first step in transferring files from it to your machine.

- **Heed warnings.** Pay attention to messages from Microsoft applications. For example, if you save a file from the Web as HTML, you can open the file in Internet Explorer from the folder where you saved it. When you start to open it, Internet Explorer may display a message warning that downloaded files can contain viruses. Do not open a file if you have any doubts about it. Click Cancel or Do Not Open unless you are sure it is safe to do so.

- Similarly, Microsoft Office applications warn you if they encounter a **macro** in a file. For example, if the Excel file has a macro , Word displays the message shown in the illustration that follows when you open the template.

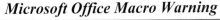
Microsoft Office Macro Warning

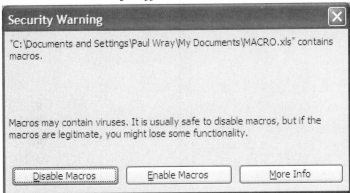

Macro
A series of commands and keystrokes, often recorded as they are performed by a user; they are saved and then executed at later times to quickly perform the same actions in a document.

Set Windows for Automatic Updates

- You can set Windows to download critical updates automatically. Windows will download the updates and notify you when an update is ready to install by displaying a message in the notification area at the right end of the taskbar.

🖥 Try It!

1. Click the Start button ![start].

2. Right-click My Computer, and click Properties.

3. Select the Automatic Updates tab.

   Windows displays the dialog box shown in the following illustration.

4. If you have a DSL, cable modem, or other constant high-speed connection to the Internet, select Download the updates automatically and notify me when they are ready to be installed.

5. Choose either of the other options if you prefer more control over the update process, but be sure that you update your Windows operating system regularly.

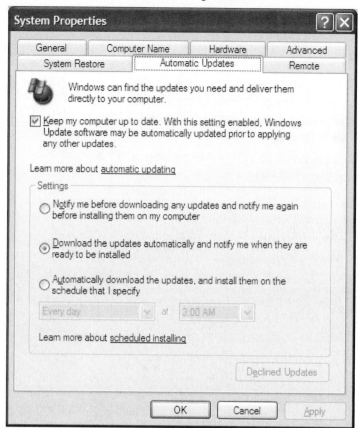

Automatic Updates

Run a Virus Scan

- When you install virus protection software, it automatically places itself as a watchdog over the activity on your system. When files are opened or downloaded or when you look at the contents of diskettes, the virus scanner checks each action to be sure that no file or disk houses a recognizable virus.

- To check whether the virus protection is active, point to the icon for the automatic virus scanner that appears in your Windows taskbar. The illustration that follows shows the position of the Norton AntiVirus Auto-Protect icon. Linger on the icon to display a ScreenTip that tells you whether automatic protection is enabled.

Automatic Virus Protection

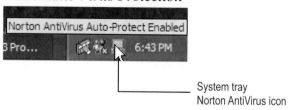

System tray
Norton AntiVirus icon

- Besides this automatic protection, virus scanners let you scan your system or a disk for viruses at any time. The following Try It! activity uses Norton AntiVirus as an example. Steps to run scans in other anti-virus programs are different, but the concepts are the same.

🖥️**Try It!**

1. Double-click the Norton AntiVirus icon on the desktop, or use the Start button and start the program from the menu.

   The Norton AntiVirus program starts and displays a window similar to the following, which displays the status of Norton AntiVirus. Note the options that are enabled.

   *The **Security Scanning Features** indicate that the Auto-Protect, Email Scanning, and Script Blocking features are on.*

   ***Virus Definition Service** options indicate that automatic updates to the virus definitions are active and they will end on March 15, 2005.*

Norton AntiVirus
Desktop Icon

Norton AntiVirus 2002 System Status Window

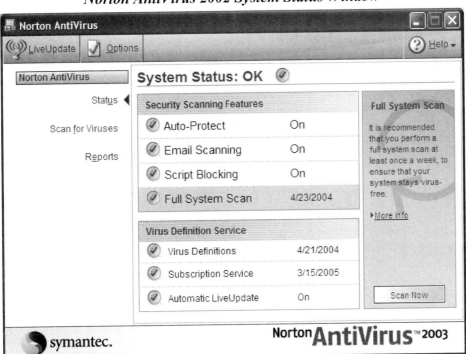

2. To scan drives, folders, or other resources, click Scan for Viruses.

   Norton AntiVirus displays the Scan for Viruses options so you can choose the resource to scan.

   - *Scan my computer* scans the entire local computer.
   - *Scan all removable drives* scans floppy, CD/DVD, and Zip, Jaz, and other removable disks.
   - *Select all floppy disks* scans diskettes only.
   - *Scan drives* lets you choose the drives to be scanned.
   - *Scan folders* lets you choose the folders to be scanned.
   - *Scan files* lets you choose the files to be scanned.

Norton AntiVirus Scan for Viruses

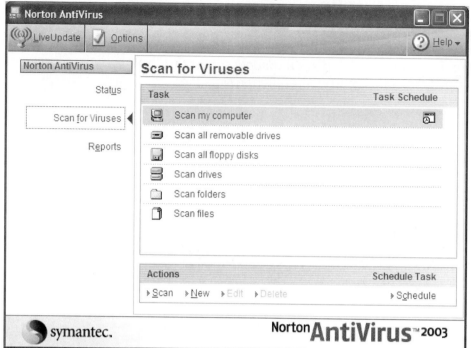

3. Click Scan drives.

   Norton AntiVirus displays the Scan Drives dialog box that lists the drives on your computer.

Norton AntiVirus Scan Drives Dialog Box

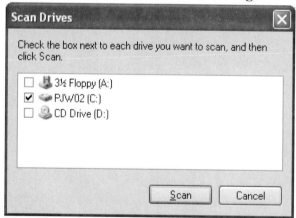

4. Select drive C:.

   Note that running a scan can take several minutes depending on the size of your hard drive and the speed of your computer.

5. Click the Scan button Scan .

6. To stop the scan at any time, click the Stop Scan button Stop Scan .

   Norton AntiVirus displays a message asking if you are sure you want to stop the scan.

7. Click the Yes button Yes .

Review Scan Results

- By default, Norton AntiVirus is set to repair an infected file when it detects a virus. If it cannot repair the file, Norton AntiVirus may ask what you want to do to the file:

  - Quarantine the file, that is, put it in a location where it can do no harm until Norton AntiVirus can repair it, or you decide to delete it. At some later time, you can review the quarantined items and decide what action to take.

  - Deny access to the file, which leaves the file in the current location but does not let any program open the file.

- When a virus scan ends, Norton AntiVirus displays a summary of the actions taken.

Norton AntiVirus Summary

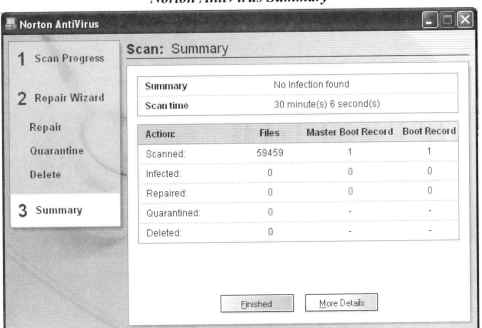

Exercise 4

Add Software to Your Computer
■ Install Software ■ Install a Printer

NOTES

Install Software

■ When you purchase a new software package or need to reinstall an application, read through the installation instructions before attempting to add it to your system. Generally, the following advice is helpful:

- Shut down all active applications, including Windows Explorer. No other application should be running when you install software.

- If requested by the installation instructions, disable the automatic virus scanner. Virus scanners are set to prevent changes to certain operating system components that some software needs to alter as part of installation. Be sure to enable the virus scanner after installing the new software.

- Most software nowadays comes on a CD-ROM. It is helpful to know the drive letter of your CD-ROM drive.

- Learn whether your software uses Install or Setup as the command to start installation.

To Start Installation

1. Place the installation source in the appropriate drive. If you are installing from downloaded files, be prepared to tell Windows in which folder the files reside.

   If your software comes on a CD-ROM, it may display installation options automatically using a feature called Autorun. If so, start installation from the screen that appears.

2. If your new software does not display installation options automatically, click the Start button and click <u>R</u>un to display the Run dialog box, as shown below.

Run Dialog Box

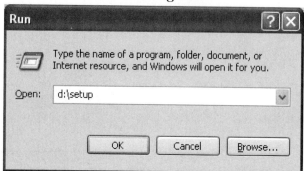

Scan First

If you download software from the Web or acquire free software from any source, make sure your automatic virus scan has checked the installation files for viruses.

Freeware and Shareware

Many useful programs are available free (**freeware**) or at a nominal cost (**shareware**).

If you acquire shareware and find the program useful, you are expected to send the program's author the small fee to help ensure that the program gets continued support.

Before downloading any freeware or shareware, be sure your virus protection software is up to date and enabled.

3. In the <u>O</u>pen text box, type the path of the installation program, or use the <u>B</u>rowse button  to locate the installation program.

4. Click the OK button 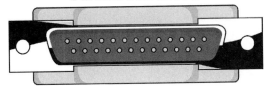.

The installation program starts. You must then carefully follow the instructions that appear on the screen and in the documentation that accompanies the software.

Install a Printer

- When you acquire a printer, you must connect its cable to the computer and add it to Windows' list of printers before you can use it.

- To connect your printer, shut down your computer and connect the printer cable to the correct computer **port** (see below) and plug the electric cord into an outlet.

- Some printers are connected to your computer through the **printer port LPT1:**. This is called a **parallel port** because communications go both ways along the cable. Often manufacturers label this and other ports on the back of your computer case.

- Your main printer is usually connected through LPT1:. You can recognize LPT1: because it has 25 pinholes to receive the end of the cable—13 in the top row and 12 on the bottom, as shown below.

Parallel Port Socket

- Some printers and other peripherals, using a different cable, can be connected through a **communications** or **serial port** with a name like COM1: or COM2:. Some computers also connect the mouse to one of the COM (serial) ports. (Other mouse devices connect through a USB (<u>U</u>niversal <u>S</u>erial <u>B</u>us) port or a bus connection and are called **bus mouse devices.**)

- Other printers, particularly new ink jet printers, connect through USB ports. These connections have flat rectangular ends and connect to special ports on your computer.

Sample USB Cables

- Once you have connected your printer and plugged it in, you are ready to add your **printer driver** (software that lets the printer work) to Windows. To do so, complete the procedure outlined in the steps that follow.

Connecting Cables

Computer cables and connectors are built so that you cannot connect a parallel printer cable to a serial port. Match the cable end to the correct socket and you will find that plugging in a cable is easy.

Never force a connector; all connections slide easily into place when they are properly positioned.

Automatic Recognition

Windows may recognize the new device automatically and display a dialog box that gives you the option to install the device.

🖥 Try It!

1. Have your Windows installation CD-ROM or disks handy. You may need them to install the printer.

2. Turn on your computer and get Windows started.

3. Turn on your printer.

4. Click the Start button **start**, and then click Control Panel **Control Panel**,

5. Either:

   a: If you are in Category view, click the Printers and Other Hardware

   option **Printers and Other Hardware**

   b: Click the option View installed printers and or fax printers
   View installed printers or fax printers.

   OR

   • If you are in Windows Classic view, click the Printers and Faxes

   icon Printers and Faxes.

   The Printers or Printers and Faxes folder opens as shown in the following illustration.

Printers Folder Opened
(Windows XP using Windows classic folders, Icons view)

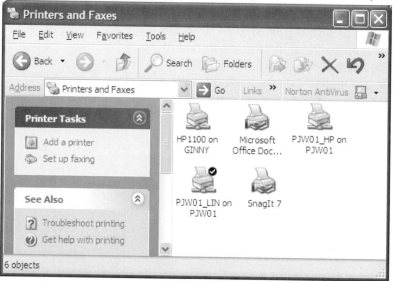

🖥 Try It!

Start the Procedure and Select a Printer

1. To start the Add Printer Wizard, click the Add a printer option
   Add a printer in the Printer task pane in the left side of the window of the icon.)

The Add Printer Wizard starts and displays a dialog box to get you started.

2. Click the Next button ⟨ Next > ⟩ to display the dialog box shown in the illustration that follows.

Add Printer Wizard: Choose Local or Network

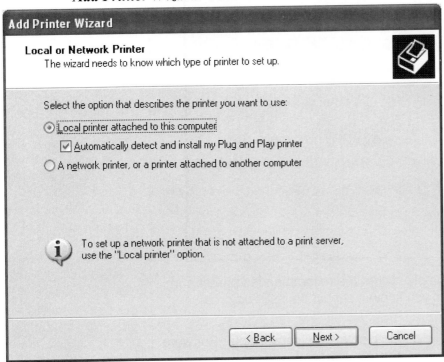

3. Select Local printer attached to this computer to install the printer driver on your computer.

   If you are on a network and know the network address of the printer, you can choose A network printer, or a printer attached to another computer.

4. Click the Next button ⟨ Next > ⟩ to display the New Printer Detection dialog box, indicating that Windows is looking for a plug-and-play printer.

Add Printer Wizard: New Printer Detection

Windows is searching for new Plug and Play printers to install.

Searching...

If Windows does not find a printer, it displays the following message.

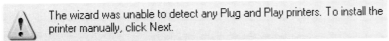

5. Click the Next button ⟨ Next > ⟩ to display the port selection dialog box as shown in the following illustration.

Add Printer Wizard: Select a Printer Port

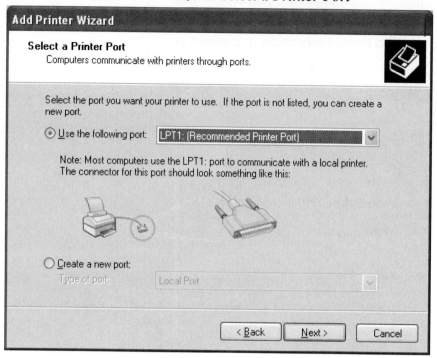

6. In most cases, you can simply accept the recommended printer port of LPT1:. Change it only if you know it should be installed on a different port.

7. Click the Next button [Next >] to display the Install Printer Software dialog box as shown in the following illustration.

Add Printer Wizard: Install Printer Software

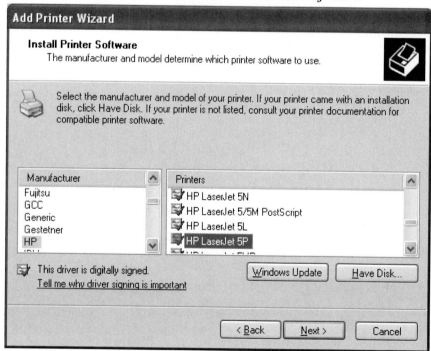

8. In the left pane, select the manufacturer of the printer.

    If your manufacturer provides a driver file on disk, place the disk in the appropriate drive and click the Have Disk button | Have Disk... |.

    The Add Printer Wizard displays a dialog box that allows you to specify the location of the printer driver file. (The box offers a Browse button to help you locate the file.)

    If you are uncertain about whether to click the Have Disk button, do not use it. Windows contains drivers for all the printers with check marks listed in the right pane.

9. In the right pane, select the specific printer you are installing.

10. When you have selected the manufacturer and the printer, click the Next button | Next > | to display the Name Your Printer dialog box.

🖳 Try It!

Name the Printer and Print a Test Page

1. Accept the name Windows suggests or type the name you prefer as shown in the following illustration.

2. If this is the printer you want to user for most of your printing, select Yes to make it the default; otherwise, click No.

Add Printer Wizard: Name Your Printer

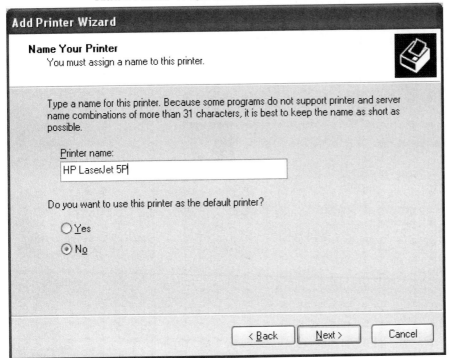

3. When you have named the printer, click the Next button | Next > | to display the Printer Sharing dialog box.

    This dialog box does not appear if you are not on a network with sharing enabled.

Add Printer Wizard: Printer Sharing

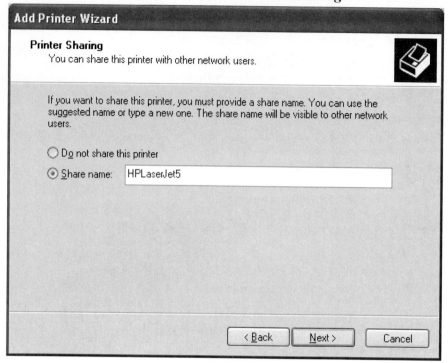

4. Select the option you wish. If you select Share name, accept the suggested name or give it a new one.

5. Click the Next button [Next >] to display the Location and Comment dialog box.

Add Printer Wizard: Location and Comment

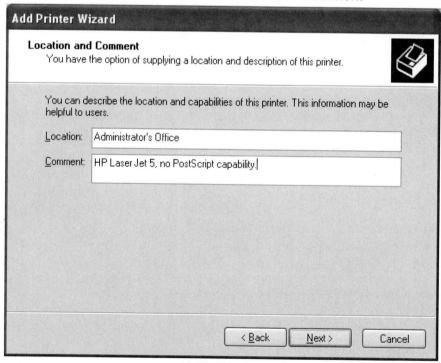

6. Click the Next button [Next >] to display the Print Test Page.

7. Select Yes to print a test page.

8. Click the <u>N</u>ext button [<u>N</u>ext >] to display the Completing the Add Printer Wizard dialog box.

Add Printer Wizard: Completing

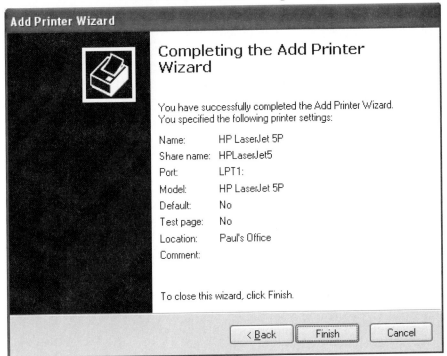

9. Click the Finish button [Finish].

The test page prints, and your printer appears in the Printers folder as shown in the illustration below.

Printers Folder with New Printer

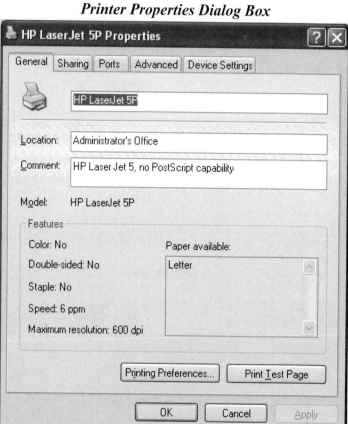

🖥 Try It!

Check the Printer Properties

You can review the printer's settings and change them, if necessary, through the Properties dialog box.

1. Right-click the icon of the printer you added to display a shortcut menu and select Properties, or select the printer and click File, Properties (Alt+F, R).

   The Properties dialog box appears, as shown in the following illustration.

Printer Properties Dialog Box

2. Click the other tabs on the dialog box to review the options and settings. Your tabs and options may differ from those illustrated.

3. Close the dialog box when you complete your review.

Printing

You can check printing as it is running by double-clicking the printer icon in the Printers folder or double-clicking the printer icon that appears at the far right of the task bar. A dialog box appears that lets you monitor printing progress. All files sent to the printer are listed in the dialog box.

Exercise 5

Keep Your Computer System Clean
■ General Care Instructions ■ Clean the Monitor ■ Are Screen Savers Necessary?
■ Clean the Keyboard ■ Clean the Mouse ■ Clean the Cases
■ Maintain Computers and Peripherals

NOTES

IMPORTANT NOTE

- **Before cleaning any computer component, shut the computer down and disconnect from electricity sources.**

- The recommendations in this exercise are based on the instructions from several computer manufacturers. Read the manufacturer's instructions and rely on them whenever possible. The recommendations here can help when the manufacturer's instructions are missing.

General Care Instructions

- Keep food and drink far away from computer components. A spill of coffee, water, soda pop, or tea can ruin a keyboard or a printer, even though manufacturers try to protect sensitive electronic components.

Clean the Monitor

- Monitor screens get smudged from fingers that point to important displays. They get dirty from the dust motes that float in the air. You need to clean the monitor screen from time to time.

- Manufacturers recommend wiping the screen with a soft cloth that has been sprayed with a small amount of mild glass cleaner. Do not spray the monitor screen directly.

- Gently wipe the screen with the cloth and let it dry before restarting your computer. Specially prepared and individually packaged screen cleaning cloths are available from computer stores.

Are Screen Savers Necessary?

- Screen savers were invented to prevent displays from leaving ghostly patterns on the monitor screen because of a process called "burn-in." Most recent PCs, however, can automatically turn the monitor dark when no processing has taken place for a while. Therefore, screen savers, while sometimes artful and attractive, may not really be necessary.

- In addition, screen saver programs take up valuable room in memory and on the hard disk, and they sometimes interfere with other applications.

- You can determine whether your monitor can automatically turn off through the Control Panel.

Try It!

1. Open the Control Panel (see Lesson 2, if you have forgotten how).

2. Click Appearance and Themes.

3. Double-click the Display icon 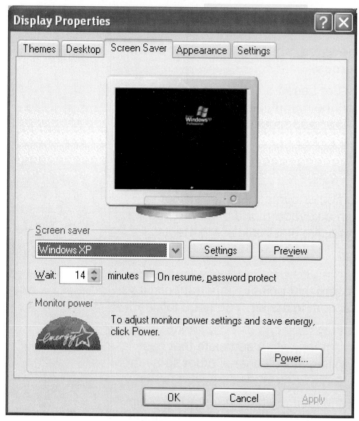 in the lower part of the window.

4. Click the Screen Saver tab.

    The Display Properties dialog box appears, as shown below.

    Display Properties Dialog Box, Screen Saver Tab

5. Click the Power button [Power...] in the lower section of the dialog box.

    Windows displays The Power Options Properties dialog box shown in the following illustration.

Power Options Properties Dialog Box

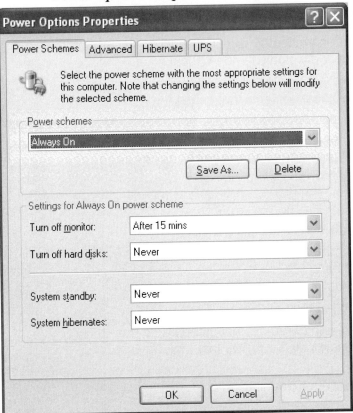

6. Select Turn off monitor, and specify the number of minutes or hours before the monitor automatically turns dark.

7. Select Turn off hard disks, and specify the number of minutes or hours before the hard disk turns off.

8. Generally, you should leave the other settings as the defaults.

9. Click the OK button [OK].

10. Click the OK button [OK] again to close the Display Properties dialog box.

Clean the Keyboard

- Use a can of compressed air that has a long, small-diameter straw inserted in the nozzle. Spray between the keys to remove any dust and other particles.

- If you do spill liquid on your keyboard, immediately turn your keyboard upside down to drain out the liquid and shut down your system. After letting the keyboard drain, hold the keyboard upside down and use the compressed air can to remove the remaining moisture. You may be able to salvage the keyboard by quick action.

- To clean the keyboard case and keys, spray a soft, lint-free cloth with a small amount of cleaner and gently wipe the keys and the case. Do not spray the keyboard directly. After wiping with the cloth, use compressed air to remove any cloth particles that may remain between the keys.

Clean the Mouse

- The mouse consists of a case with two or more buttons and perhaps a wheel (the IntelliMouse). If you have an optical mouse, it works because of the differences in the amount of light transmitted as you slide it across a surface. The remainder of this section applies only to non-optical mice.

- If you have a non-optical mouse, it works because, as you slide it across the surface, a rolling ball activates electrical contacts that cause the mouse pointer to move.

- If you turn your mouse over, you will see that the ball is held in place by a circular holder that can be turned to allow removal of the ball from the inside of the mouse.

🖥️Try It!

1. Turn the mouse upside down and remove the circular cover.
2. Cup your hand over the ball and turn the mouse right side up to allow the ball to drop into your cupped hand.
3. Once the ball is free, use the sticky side of adhesive tape to remove any lint or other particles that cling to the ball.
4. Use rubbing alcohol on a cotton swab to remove any debris from the inside of the mouse. Lint accumulates on the rollers that make contact with the ball.
5. Allow the mouse to dry completely after cleaning.
6. Replace the mouse ball and cover after the mouse is dry.

- To clean the outside of the mouse, use a soft cloth that has been sprayed with a small amount of cleaner and gently wipe the outside of the mouse. Let the mouse dry completely after cleaning.

Clean the Cases

- To clean the cases of your monitor, computer, printer, speakers, and other peripherals, spray a soft, lint-free cloth with a small amount of cleaner. Gently wipe away any smudges and dust.

- Allow the surfaces to dry completely before using your computer again.

Maintain Computers and Peripherals

- Keep all manufacturer's instructions on the maintenance and care of your computer, printer, and other peripherals. Follow the manufacturer's instructions carefully when performing any maintenance.

- Pay attention to announcements of new printer drivers and other maintenance software. Acquire new maintenance software as soon as possible to keep your system up to date.

- When changing ink or toner cartridges in printers, read the installation instructions completely through before starting the procedure. Be careful to follow manufacturer's instructions for cleaning the printer when you change the ink or toner cartridge.

- Make sure that the paper and ink or toner you use meet manufacturer's standards.

Appendix

Appendix A: A Brief History of Computers

Appendix A

A Brief History of Computers

■ History of Computers ■ Early Computing Machines ■ Vacuum Tube Computers
■ Semiconductors and Portable Programs ■ The Personal Computer

NOTES

History of Computers

- The electronic digital computer, the kind you are using with this book, is an invention of the 20th century. Computer-like functions, however, have been around for years. Some people date the invention of the computer to the invention of the *abacus*, a device on which beads are manipulated to perform calculations. The abacus is still used in many Asian nations.

- Other computer historians point to Frenchman Joseph Marie Jacquard. Jacquard automated a loom that operated by dropping needles through holes punched in cards. Every time a needle passed through a hole, it lifted a weaving thread. Needles that did not drop through caused their weaving threads to lower. The weaving shuttle then passed through the threads and a pattern developed. Because the needles were either up or down (on or off, like binary numbers), the Jacquard loom is considered a true digital computer. (http://www.computer.org/history/development/1801.htm)

Early Computing Machines

- Two computing machines were the forefathers of modern electronic computers. In the mid-1800s, Charles Babbage constructed a mechanical device that he called the Difference Engine. It could perform complicated calculations by working with the differences in positions of various levers and gears.

- Because it was mechanical and used metal, as the arrangement of gears and levers became increasingly complex, the performance of the Difference Engine was hurt by the expansion and contraction of its metal components. Changes in temperature and humidity seriously impaired its efficiency. Imprecision in the manufacture of its components and the quality of the materials also caused problems. The metal-working technology of the day wasn't up to the demands of Babbage's design. (http://www.cbi.umn.edu/exhibits/cb.html).

- In 1890, the US Census was projected to take more than 10 years. But Herman Hollerith built a punched card machine to process census data and sped things up considerably. Later, he founded Hollerith Tabulating Company, which eventually became IBM.

Computer History

For a more detailed look at the history of computers, see the Web sites listed in the text and the following site, maintained by the IEEE Computing organization.

http://www.computer.org/50/history/

A good pictorial history with significant dates in the history of computing can be found at the following URL.

http://www.computer.org/computer/timeline

Vacuum Tube Computers

- In the 1940s, at the University of Pennsylvania, a group of electronics experts developed the computer ENIAC, which is often credited as the first modern computer. ENIAC bears little resemblance to today's computers. It could be programmed only by rewiring. Its vacuum tubes heated its environment so much that tubes were constantly burning out. Since ENIAC was being used to help the military calculate weapons' trajectories for Word War II, a team of people worked inside the computer to replace vacuum tubes as they burned out.

- Other computers were also being developed in the 1940s. An interesting term for resolving computer problems came into use at that time. Grace Hopper was a programmer hired to work on the computers Mark I and Mark II at Harvard University. In 1945, she found a moth dead in the jaws of a mechanical relay, causing the machine to malfunction. She glued the bug into the operator's logbook; after that, resolving programming and other computer problems was known as **debugging**.

Debug
While the first "debugging" involved a real insect, the term today is used for investigating and solving any hardware or software problem.

Semiconductors and Portable Programs

- The spread of the electronic computer was made possible by the invention of the transistor by John Bardeen, William Shockley and Walter Brattain at Bell Laboratories in the late 1940s. The transistor (TRANsfer reSISTOR) replaced vacuum tubes in radios and televisions and created a new industry—semiconductors. Semiconductors, naturally occurring substances such as silicon and germanium, make it possible to place the functions of a computer on a thin wafer, the microchip.

- In the 1950s, transistors began replacing vacuum tubes in computers. Tens of transistors could be placed in the same amount of space as one vacuum tube, so computers became smaller. In addition, transistors didn't burn out or overheat like vacuum tubes, so computers became more reliable.

- One other development hastened the spread of computers. The 1940s and 1950s saw a critical change in the way computers are programmed. To program ENIAC, a host of wires had to be moved and reconnected. The programming was tedious, time-consuming, and couldn't be transferred from one computer to another.

- The invention of programming languages and the ability of computers to accept instructions through holes punched in cards allowed computers to work on a variety of scientific, mathematical, and business problems. These uses of the computer came to be called **applications** because they *applied* the computer to solving problems. The term application is still used today to refer to the use of computer programs to perform specific tasks.

- By the 1970s, IBM, Sperry-Rand (now UniSys), Digital Equipment Corporation (DEC), Data General and other computer manufacturers had their machines in most companies and universities. But the early 1980s saw the computer change from a large tool used by experts and specially trained personnel into a consumer electronics product.

Semiconductor
Semiconductors, such as silicon and germanium, allow control of the flow of electricity; some areas can be designated as current conductors and adjacent areas as insulators. Since the areas of conductivity can be defined selectively, these substances are called **semiconductors**.

Metals, such as copper, are **conductors**. They conduct electricity non-selectively; areas of copper cannot be designated for conduction and insulation. All parts of copper conduct current.

The Personal Computer

- Apple Corporation was founded in the mid-1970s. Initially, the founders, Steve Jobs and Steve Wozniak, thought the Apple® computer would be a machine for electronics hobbyists to compete with the popular Commodore and Atari computers.

- One application, the VisiCalc spreadsheet, changed that. Graduates with Masters in Business Administration (MBAs) learned that VisiCalc could run on Apple machines. These MBAs, in a wide variety of companies, began buying and using Apples to perform business analyses. The personal computer revolution was on.

- Microsoft's Bill Gates and others developed DOS, the Disk Operating System. When it was adopted as the operating system for IBM's PC in 1981, DOS became the operating system with which all others had to compete.

- The IBM PC took over the personal computer revolution begun by Apple. Because so many businesses relied on IBM for their large computers (called mainframes, see Lesson 1), they purchased large numbers of PCs, primarily to take advantage of spreadsheet and word processing programs.

- Students who graduated from high school or college before 1985 seldom had access to personal computers. By the end of the 1980s, many schools boasted computer laboratories where PCs were available.

- The table below illustrates how far computing has come since the 1940s. It compares ENIAC with the 150 MHz Pentium processor, a CPU microchip from the Intel Corporation. Newer chips run at eight or nine times the speed of the 150 MHz Pentium.

Personal computer revolution

A lively and opinionated review of the beginnings of the PC revolution is provided by:

Cringely, Robert X. *Accidental Empires: How the Boys of Silicon Valley Make Their Millions, Battle Foreign Competition, and Still Can't Get a Date.* Reading, MA: Addison Wesley, 1992.

ENIAC Versus 150 MHz Pentium

It is quite probable that your computer is anywhere from seven to thirteen times as fast as a 150 MHz Pentium, so the differences between it an ENIAC are even more pronounced.

Measurement	ENIAC	150MHz Pentium
Speed	5,000 additions per second	300,000,000 additions/second
Memory	200 digits	16,000,000 digits
Elements	18,000 vacuum tubes	
	6,000 switches	
	70,000 resistors	4,000,000 transistors (CPU)
	10,000 capacitors	
	1,500 relays	
Size	10 feet tall x 1,800 square feet	9" x 12" x 2" (laptop)
Weight	30 tons	6 pounds

(http://mbhs.bergtraum.k12.ny.us/cybereng/nyt/databox.htm)

Index

Index

Index

501

SINGLE PC LICENSE AGREEMENT AND LIMITED WARRANTY

READ THIS LICENSE CAREFULLY BEFORE OPENING THIS PACKAGE. BY OPENING THIS PACKAGE, YOU ARE AGREEING TO THE TERMS AND CONDITIONS OF THIS LICENSE. IF YOU DO NOT AGREE, DO NOT OPEN THE PACKAGE. PROMPTLY RETURN THE UNOPENED PACKAGE AND ALL ACCOMPANYING ITEMS TO THE PLACE YOU OBTAINED THEM. THESE TERMS APPLY TO ALL LICENSED SOFTWARE ON THE DISK EXCEPT THAT THE TERMS FOR USE OF ANY SHAREWARE OR FREEWARE ON THE DISKETTES ARE AS SET FORTH IN THE ELECTRONIC LICENSE LOCATED ON THE DISK:

1. GRANT OF LICENSE and OWNERSHIP: The enclosed computer programs and data ("Software") are licensed, not sold, to you by Pearson Education, Inc. ("We" or the "Company") and in consideration of your purchase or adoption of the accompanying Company textbooks and/or other materials, and your agreement to these terms. We reserve any rights not granted to you. You own only the disk(s) but we and/or our licensors own the Software itself. This license allows you to use and display your copy of the Software on a single computer (i.e., with a single CPU) at a single location for academic use only, so long as you comply with the terms of this Agreement.

2. RESTRICTIONS: You may not transfer or distribute the Software or documentation to anyone else. Except for backup, you may not copy the documentation or the Software. You may not network the Software or otherwise use it on more than one computer or computer terminal at the same time. You may not reverse engineer, disassemble, decompile, modify, adapt, translate, or create derivative works based on the Software or the Documentation. You may be held legally responsible for any copying or copyright infringement which is caused by your failure to abide by the terms of these restrictions.

3. TERMINATION: This license is effective until terminated. This license will terminate automatically without notice from the Company if you fail to comply with any provisions or limitations of this license. Upon termination, you shall destroy the Documentation and all copies of the Software. All provisions of this Agreement as to limitation and disclaimer of warranties, limitation of liability, remedies or damages, and our ownership rights shall survive termination.

4. LIMITED WARRANTY AND DISCLAIMER OF WARRANTY: Company warrants that for a period of 60 days from the date you purchase this SOFTWARE (or purchase or adopt the accompanying textbook), the Software, when properly installed and used in accordance with the Documentation, will operate in substantial conformity with the description of the Software set forth in the Documentation, and that for a period of 30 days the disk(s) on which the Software is delivered shall be free from defects in materials and workmanship under normal use. The Company does not warrant that the Software will meet your requirements or that the operation of the Software will be uninterrupted or error-free. Your only remedy and the Company's only obligation under these limited warranties is, at the Company's option, return of the disk for a refund of any amounts paid for it by you or replacement of the disk. THIS LIMITED WARRANTY IS THE ONLY WARRANTY PROVIDED BY THE COMPANY AND ITS LICENSORS, AND THE COMPANY AND ITS LICENSORS DISCLAIM ALL OTHER WARRANTIES, EXPRESS OR IMPLIED, INCLUDING WITHOUT LIMITATION, THE IMPLIED WARRANTIES OF MERCHANTABILITY AND FITNESS FOR A PARTICULAR PURPOSE. THE COMPANY DOES NOT WARRANT, GUARANTEE OR MAKE ANY REPRESENTATION REGARDING THE ACCURACY, RELIABILITY, CURRENTNESS, USE, OR RESULTS OF USE, OF THE SOFTWARE.

5. LIMITATION OF REMEDIES AND DAMAGES: IN NO EVENT, SHALL THE COMPANY OR ITS EMPLOYEES, AGENTS, LICENSORS, OR CONTRACTORS BE LIABLE FOR ANY INCIDENTAL, INDIRECT, SPECIAL, OR CONSEQUENTIAL DAMAGES ARISING OUT OF OR IN CONNECTION WITH THIS LICENSE OR THE SOFTWARE, INCLUDING FOR LOSS OF USE, LOSS OF DATA, LOSS OF INCOME OR PROFIT, OR OTHER LOSSES, SUSTAINED AS A RESULT OF INJURY TO ANY PERSON, OR LOSS OF OR DAMAGE TO PROPERTY, OR CLAIMS OF THIRD PARTIES, EVEN IF THE COMPANY OR AN AUTHORIZED REPRESENTATIVE OF THE COMPANY HAS BEEN ADVISED OF THE POSSIBILITY OF SUCH DAMAGES. IN NO EVENT SHALL THE LIABILITY OF THE COMPANY FOR DAMAGES WITH RESPECT TO THE SOFTWARE EXCEED THE AMOUNTS ACTUALLY PAID BY YOU, IF ANY, FOR THE SOFTWARE OR THE ACCOMPANYING TEXTBOOK. BECAUSE SOME JURISDICTIONS DO NOT ALLOW THE LIMITATION OF LIABILITY IN CERTAIN CIRCUMSTANCES, THE ABOVE LIMITATIONS MAY NOT ALWAYS APPLY TO YOU.

6. GENERAL: THIS AGREEMENT SHALL BE CONSTRUED IN ACCORDANCE WITH THE LAWS OF THE UNITED STATES OF AMERICA AND THE STATE OF NEW YORK, APPLICABLE TO CONTRACTS MADE IN NEW YORK, AND SHALL BENEFIT THE COMPANY, ITS AFFILIATES AND ASSIGNEES. HIS AGREEMENT IS THE COMPLETE AND EXCLUSIVE STATEMENT OF THE AGREEMENT BETWEEN YOU AND THE COMPANY AND SUPERSEDES ALL PROPOSALS OR PRIOR AGREEMENTS, ORAL, OR WRITTEN, AND ANY OTHER COMMUNICATIONS BETWEEN YOU AND THE COMPANY OR ANY REPRESENTATIVE OF THE COMPANY RELATING TO THE SUBJECT MATTER OF THIS AGREEMENT. If you are a U.S. Government user, this Software is licensed with "restricted rights" as set forth in subparagraphs (a)-(d) of the Commercial Computer-Restricted Rights clause at FAR 52.227-19 or in subparagraphs (c)(1)(ii) of the Rights in Technical Data and Computer Software clause at DFARS 252.227-7013, and similar clauses, as applicable.